Nebraska
Symposium on
Motivation
1990

Volume 38

University of Nebraska Press
Lincoln and London 1991

Nebraska Symposium on Motivation 1990

Perspectives on Motivation

Richard Dienstbier

Series Editor and Volume Editor

Presenters

Mortimer H. Appley

President Emeritus, Clark University

Albert Bandura

David Starr Jordan Professor of Social Science in Psychology, Stanford University

Bernard Weiner

Professor of Psychology, University of California, Los Angeles

Carol S. Dweck

Professor of Psychology, Columbia University

Edward L. Deci

Professor of Psychology and Director of the Human Motivation Program, University of Rochester

Richard M. Ryan

Associate Professor of Psychology and Director of Clinical Training, University of Rochester

Douglas Derryberry

Assistant Professor of Psychology, University of Oregon

Don M. Tucker

Professor of Psychology and Director of Clinical Training, University of Oregon

*Nebraska Symposium on
Motivation, 1990*, is Volume 38
in the series on
CURRENT THEORY AND
RESEARCH IN MOTIVATION

International Standard Book Number
0-8032-1693-9 (Clothbound)
International Standard Book Number
0-8032-6590-5 (Paperbound)

The paper in this book meets the minimum
requirements of American National Standard for
Information Sciences—Permanence of Paper for
Printed Library Materials, ANSI Z39.48–1984.

"The Library of Congress has cataloged
this serial publication as follows:"
Nebraska Symposium on Motivation.
Nebraska Symposium on Motivation.
[Papers] v. [1]–1953–
Lincoln, University of Nebraska Press.
v. illus., diagrs. 22cm. annual.
Vol. 1 issued by the symposium under
its earlier name: Current Theory and
Research in Motivation.
Symposia sponsored by the Dept. of
Psychology of the University of Nebraska.
1. Motivation (Psychology)
BF683.N4   159.4082   53-11655
Library of Congress

Preface

This volume of the Nebraska Symposium on Motivation heralds a return to the topic of motivation.

This year the roles of volume editor and series editor are combined. With no volume editor to thank, I shall use this occasion instead to extend thanks on behalf of the Symposium Committee and the Department of Psychology to our friends at the University of Nebraska Press. They have been patient with us and with occasionally tardy contributors and have, through their professionalism, helped us maintain the quality of this series.

The Symposium series is supported largely by funds donated in memory of Professor Harry K. Wolfe to the University of Nebraska Foundation by the late Professor Cora L. Friedline. This Symposium volume, like those of the recent past, is dedicated to the memory of Professor Wolfe, who brought psychology to the University of Nebraska. After studying with Professor Wilhelm Wundt, Professor Wolfe returned to this, his native state, to establish the first undergraduate laboratory of psychology in the nation. As a student at Nebraska, Professor Friedline studied psychology under Professor Wolfe. The editors are grateful to the late Professor Friedline for her bequest and to the officers of the University of Nebraska Foundation for their continued interest in and support of the series.

RICHARD A. DIENSTBIER
Series Editor

Contents

Introduction

Richard A. Dienstbier
University of Nebraska–Lincoln

This 38th session of the Nebraska Symposium on Motivation coincided with the 100th anniversary of the teaching of psychology at the University of Nebraska (1889) and with the 50th anniversary of the founding of the Department of Psychology (1939). The originator of early psychological instruction here, and the person to whom all recent volumes of this Symposium have been dedicated, is Harry K. Wolfe, one of Wilhelm Wundt's first two American students. In part because of the significance of these anniversaries, and because of the identification of this Symposium with psychology at the University of Nebraska, the Symposium Committee and I decided to devote this volume entirely to the topic of motivation. As this Symposium developed, however, we became convinced that we should undertake a more permanent change in focus toward motivation.

Beginning with the second Nebraska Symposium in 1953 and continuing for a decade, these volumes were singularly devoted to the topic of motivation. However, reflecting a concern within the field of psychology that the concept of motivation was no longer particularly useful, the Symposia and resulting annual volumes focused on diverse topics, with a tradition begun in the early 1970s that each volume would be devoted to a single topic. Each year we noted that ours was a series on "current theory and research in motivation," but the change to topics other than motivation was reflected in the use of appropriate subtitles, beginning with the 1975 volume's *Conceptual Foundations of Psychology*. (See Benjamin and Jones, 1979, for a description of the first 25 years of the Symposium.)

With this 1990 Symposium and continuing in the volumes from 1992 onward, we shall confront motivation directly. This effort to "return to our roots" reflects more than a historical concern or an effort to be more true to our title. Instead, along with the contributors to this volume, the Symposium Committee and I see a resurgence in the use of motivational concepts in diverse areas within psychology.

The reliance of psychology graduate programs in the 1950s on volumes of this series for information on motivation was replaced in the 1960s by reliance on *Motivation: Theory and Research* by Charles Cofer and Mortimer H. Appley (Benjamin & Jones, 1979). As the founding editor (in 1977) of the journal *Motivation and Emotion*, Mortimer Appley played a role in the recent resurgence of interest in motivation and was the obvious choice for a scholar to reflect upon the history and possible future of this topic.

For Appley, the fundamental motivational process is equilibration—seeking for equilibrium or homeostasis. But the term and the approach are often misunderstood, with the assumption made that such approaches cannot account for creativity, growth, or the seeking of stimulation and high arousal levels. Appley's equilibration process functions both to maintain balance and to allow responsiveness to the environment. These processes are arranged in complex hierarchies, so that the outcome of one homeostatic process may be the input for the next. Appley's description of hierarchical integration of homeostatic processes at various levels fits well with the "onionlike" character of neocortical layers discussed by Derryberry and Tucker in this volume. Appley sees cognitive processes as subsystems of the "larger motivational dynamic," with motivation often stimulated by discrepancies between the current situation and some comparison memory or standard. For example, discrepancies between entities such as the self schema and an idealized self-image are directly motivating. Appley concludes that human motivation cannot be understood without reference to the self-concept. His concerns with how the self-concept influences motivational patterns could serve as an introduction to Carol S. Dweck's chapter, which begins with a similar orientation.

Like Appley, Douglas Derryberry and Don M. Tucker present a broad and fundamental model of motivation. They approach motivation through the evolution and neural architecture of the human brain. For readers with minimal physiological knowledge, this is a challenging chapter, for it is thorough and rich in descriptions of brain structure. However, the chapter evolves toward motivational issues considered at levels and in terms similar to those in the other chapters. Derryberry and Tucker emphasize the vertical dimension of neocortical organization, noting that from more ancient and basic brain structures through the many layers of the neocortex, neural networks describe a bottom-up, fan out pattern of organization, particularly relevant to effector function, while a top-down, fan in pattern is associated with sensory and perceptual organization. They suggest that psychological approaches to motivation should be consistent with those underlying neurological patterns, particularly the bottom-up networks from brainstem and limbic areas, noting that the lower centers exert the most general motivational control; articulation of goals and means may be achieved at higher levels. Derryberry and Tucker note that the different neural "modulators" (emphasizing noradrenaline and dopamine) influence attention and personality by biasing the sensitivity of different neural systems. Noradrenaline pathways show responsivity to novelty, fast time courses, phasic alertness in the context of novel or stressful events, and right hemispheric cognitive activity; dopaminergic paths are associated with motor pattern perseveration, a slower time course, tonic arousal, anxiety, and left hemispheric function. These functional relationships provide a neurological basis for such diverse features as Osgood's basic dimensions of meaning, Watson's two-factor mood dimensions, and Thayer's dual systems of arousal. Relevant to Dweck's concerns with how goals and implicit personality theories modulate the impact of failure experiences, the work of Derryberry and Tucker provides a possible neurological basis for understanding how successes and failures bias subsequent perceptual and cognitive processes.

In her chapter, Carol S. Dweck approaches personality development through motivational concepts—especially goals that are relevant to self-concept. The initial sections of the chapter depend upon her work with school-age children identified as "mastery oriented" or as "helpless" based on their response to failure. Helpless children attribute failure to a lack of ability and tend to remember more failures than successes in all circumstances, whereas mastery children are likely to try harder and to organize their efforts more systematically, seeing failures as minor setbacks on the way to continued development. Dweck conceptualized these two types of children as having different goals and even different theories of skills and of intelligence (as fixed entities versus as being incremental with practice and learning). Noting that younger children are usually characterized as resilient in failure contexts, Dweck and her colleagues undertook studies of preschoolers and found that young children could be characterized according to their persistence in the face of failure. Those who persisted in accepting new challenges after setbacks saw their performance in more positive ways and resisted labeling themselves "bad" after minor failures in their real or fantasy performances. Those who did not persist saw even minor imperfections in their performance as diminishing their self-worth. Dweck discusses how developmental processes affect these attributional tendencies and the implications of these dispositions for other aspects of behavior and personality.

Bernard Weiner's attribution-based understanding of motivation (internal vs. external locus of causality, stability, and controllability of causes) has been broadly influential. In his chapter, Weiner discusses the importance of the perceived controllability of the causes of one's situation and of solutions to one's problems. He focuses on affective reactions and the actions motivated by affective responses. Responsibility judgments are a fundamental category of attribution, activated in a variety of contexts and unifying the areas of helping, reactions to stigmas, appraisals of achievement, and excuse giving. For example, when negative states obtain, the perceived controllability of the causes determines whether pity or anger is directed toward the victim. Stigmatized states for which personal responsibility is not attributed to the actor lead to pity, helping, and liking, whereas the attribution of personal responsibility (blame) for negative states leads to anger, disliking, and less helping. Therefore, in offering excuses for bad outcomes, one minimizes one's own level of responsibility to dispose potential helpers toward pity, liking, and helping rather than toward anger. For a variety of afflictions Weiner discusses the reactions of individuals and funding agencies to different attributions of responsibility for causes and "cures."

Albert Bandura approaches motivation through the concept of self-efficacy. He suggests that both attributional approaches to motivation and traditional expectancy-value theories can be subsumed by self-efficacy. Thus, where motivation seems affected by attributions, those impacts are due to the effects of the attributions on one's feeling of self-efficacy (not one's actually ability). Feelings of self-efficacy in turn affect attributions. Similarly, expectancy-value based predictions of motivation account for a minor component of variance beyond that accounted for by self-efficacy, since feelings of self-efficacy largely subsume expectations that one will be able to achieve the desired goal. Bandura offers a goal-oriented approach to motivation through theory and research on long- or short-term goals and on the relation of goal attainment to intrinsic interest and one's sense of self-efficacy. Concerning the issue central to Dweck's chapter, of skills perceived to be fixed entities (rather than acquirable), Bandura examines the effect of those orientations on managerial efficiency. Interrelations of mood and emotional states on goal attainment and self-efficacy are discussed, as is the relation of self-efficacy and behavioral and cognitive control to anxiety. Anxiety and avoidant behavior are seen as coeffects of low self-efficacy rather than as effects of each other. Reminiscent of Dweck's concern with children's experience of themselves as good or bad after failure, Bandura sees parallels between areas of achievement and social motivation on the one hand and morality on the other, with both dependent upon internalized standards that are relatively consistent within the individual. The latter part of his chapter explicates that moral connection.

Growth and continued development are central motivational forces in the system presented by Edward L. Deci and Richard M. Ryan. Also emphasized are the three primary psychological needs for competence, autonomy or self-determination, and relatedness to others. Deci and Ryan explicate the dimension of internal versus external motivation. This is not the often-cited "locus of control" concept, but rather constitutes a focus on the perceived source of the motivation for action. Behaviors are described as self-determined (internal), controlled (experienced as coerced by internalized rules or standards or by external forces, but not experienced as freely chosen), or amotivated. Thus, in controlled behavior one may have a sense of being able to control the outcome and a sense that one has initiated the behavior, but not a sense of being able to freely chose whether to perform the behavior. Such a behavior would be seen as internal through the perspective of locus of control theory, but it is not internal in Deci and Ryan's system. The concept relates somewhat to Weiner's concern with responsibility for cause versus responsibility for outcome or solution and to Bandura's self-efficacy. But whereas Bandura might focus on an enhanced sense of self-efficacy after the successful completion of behavior, Deci and Ryan note that one may still experience oneself as being a pawn, without freedom of choice. In Deci and Ryan's system, intrinsic motivation is experienced as truly self-determined (what one wants to do, with a sense of freedom of choice, not controlled even by internalized rules that one experiences as coercive). The authors relate this dimension to issues of emotion, ego involvement (antithetical to intrinsic motivation, as are all forces experienced as controlling), and their view of self-concept. The processes of self are seen as motivational rather than cognitive, with the core concept being growth motivation. In their descriptions of individuals motivated to seek challenge and growth, in contrast to feeling defensive in response to a sense that controlling forces are motivating them (antithetical to self-determination), one easily sees similarities to the persistent challenge-seeking children of Dweck's research.

The authors of these chapters do not uniformly confront motivational issues at the same levels of analysis, nor, when they do, are they in agreement on all points. They were invited because each had a powerful and unique approach to motivation, and they have uniformly fulfilled that promise in these chapters. I give them my heartfelt thanks for their conscientiousness at all points in this process and for these excellent chapters. Reviewing them in preparation for this brief introduction has strengthened my belief that the time has indeed come to focus this Symposium more consistently on the topic of motivation.

REFERENCES

Benjamin, L. T., Jr., & Jones, M. R. (1979). From motivational theory to social cognitive development: Twenty-five years of the Nebraska Symposium. In R. A. Dienstbier & H. E. Howe, Jr. (Eds.), *Nebraska Symposium on Motivation, 1978: Human emotion.* Lincoln: University of Nebraska Press.

Motivation, Equilibration, and Stress

Mortimer H. Appley
Clark University

Background

Some 25 years ago, Charles Cofer and I published an extensive review and evaluation of the status of then extant theory and research in motivation (Cofer & Appley, 1964). We chronicled what we saw as the end of an era (of drive and drive reduction theories), recognized the growing interest in anticipatory/cognitive concepts, and proposed a dual mechanism equilibration theory of motivation as a foreseeable best fit to the broad range of conceptions and data available. In this chapter I assess some of the changes since that time.

Our review suggested that, despite many subtle and some not so subtle differences among them, "motivation theories could be divided into two camps: those which posit essentially conservative

Neither Charles Cofer nor Richard Trumbull can be held responsible for the contents of this paper, but I am indebted to both for their friendship and for their enormous contributions, both motivational and stressful, to my continuing education over the many years of our several collaborations. I also express appreciation to Mr. and Mrs. Henry J. Leir of Luxembourg and New York for the support they provided me, through a series of grants from the Ridgefield Foundation, during my final year as president of Clark University and the subsequent four years as visiting scholar/visiting professor in the Harvard University Psychology Department.

Mortimer H. Appley is president emeritus, Clark University. (Correspondence should be addressed to the author at 221 Mt. Auburn Street, #606, Cambridge, MA 02138.)

principles and those which hold that growth is the overriding behavioral orientiation. [Underlying both, we concluded, was] some form of equilibrium concept . . . of fundamental import to the former, and . . . in fact assumed as a part of many growth theories as well" (Cofer & Appley, 1964, p. 302). Although our book sold exceedingly well for an advanced text and we had a number of highly favorable reviews, it seems clear that—though not why—we did not lead a parade in the direction we thought we had set out so carefully in 1964.

Here I intend to examine the strength of our conclusion of that time in light of at least a sampling of the literature on motivation theory that has appeared since it was drawn[1] and to consider how such a principle may help provide a unifying base for understanding motivational and stress phenomena.

In our 1964 analysis, we traced the underlying assumption of equilibrium seeking or maintenance through early motivation theories, ethological instinct theories, theories relating bodily conditions to behavior, theories of emotion as motivation, conflict and stress theories, drive concepts in learning theory and in psychoanalytic theory, and a range of theories of acquired or socially derived motivation. I shall not attempt to review or summarize the literature we examined, but I can assure you that it was sizable and that our study of it, which took us some seven years, was reasonably exhaustive.[2]

EQUILIBRATORY CONCEPTS

Cofer and I responded to the challenge of the late R. C. Davis (1958) to carefully evaluate the increasingly popular concept of homeostasis before it was any more widely adopted "in rivalry with the time-honored formula of stimulus-response" (p. 8). We reviewed the various treatments of homeostasis and related equilibration concepts to see how well equilibration might be able to serve as "an all-around model for behavior" (Cofer & Appley, 1964, 302; see also Appley, 1962a). Our review ranged from Cannon's *homeostasis* in physiology (cf. Cannon, 1932, 1939, 1941, 1945; Bernard, 1859; Child, 1924) and its extension into behavior (cf. Richter, 1937, 1942–1943) to Fletcher's *psychological homeostasis* (cf. Fletcher, 1938, 1942, with supporting evidence from psychophysics, studies of work and efficiency, studies of "level of aspiration," and clinical studies). Stagner's *dynamic homeostasis* (cf. Stagner 1951, 1954, 1961; Emerson, 1954; see also Stagner, 1977; Stagner & Solley, 1970) and theories of *social perceptual constancies* (Stagner & Karwoski, 1952) to Lecky's *self-consistency* (Lecky, 1945); *personality/ego/self as highest level of integration* (cf. Allport, 1937, 1953; Menninger, 1954; Teitelbaum, 1956) and *psychopathology as breakdown of equilibratory processes* (cf. Lindner, 1945; Van Vorst, 1947; Rosenzweig, 1955; and see Tallman, 1967) and extended to *values* (cf. Mace, 1953) and *social/cultural homeostasis* (cf. Henry, 1955).

EQUILIBRATORY MODELS

We next examined, in some detail, four quite different homeostatic/equilibratory models: (1) G. L. Freeman's *"neuromuscular homeostasis"* (1948), with principles dealing with energy mobilization, backlash, habitual energy baselines, optimal reaction range, residual load, and tension discharge types; (2) Harry Helson's *"adaptation-level" (AL) theory* (1953, 1959; [and see Helson, 1964, 1967, 1971]), with its emphasis on the bipolarity of responses, change in AL in adjustment to changing background stimulus level, the phenomena of decentering and of anchoring stimuli, and its extension to personality dynamics and social phenomena (cf. Blake, 1958; and see various authors in the Helson festschrift [Appley, 1971]); (3) Wiener and Ashby's *cybernetics and feedback models* (cf. Wiener, 1948, 1954; Ashby, 1956, 1960; and see Vickers, 1973; Carver & Scheier, 1981), with their emphasis on self-regulation, system organization, adaptiveness, goal seeking, stable equilibria, critical states, step-functions, multistable systems, and so on; and (4) Kurt Lewin's *psychological field theory* (1936, 1938, 1948, 1951; Cartwright, 1959; and see Atkinson, 1964), with its notions of life space, regions and boundaries, valences, tension, force, and equilibration.

The fact of an equilibratory principle underlying such disparate theories—in psychophysiology, psychophysics, cybernetics, and psychological field theory—was encouraging to us as we sought general laws of behavior motivation, and we hoped it would form a basis for integrating the different theoretical approaches.

EQUILIBRATION THEORY ASSUMPTIONS

Common assumptions of equilibration theories were/are that

> [1. the organism (or system)] tends to resist changes in its environment that are of a magnitude large enough to upset its equilibrium or threaten its survival as a stable system . . . [2.] biological [and social] systems are *open,* having continuous energy exchange with the environment . . . [3.] equilibrium can be achieved even though there is a continuous supplanting of specific materials in both [individual and environment] . . . [4. *disturbed systems need not return to their status quo ante,* but have] a variety of means and states through which and at which stability can be reached.
>
> [5.] Adaptation—acquiring stability in the face of disturbance—is achieved automatically. [6.] There is no fixed and immutable system, either under cortical dominance or otherwise, but a continuing set of systems maintaining a balance of relationships within the environment created by all the other systems and part-systems and the environment at large. [See especially our discussion of Ashby's (1956) use of step-functions as a means of extending homeostatic concepts to allow for reequilibration at different loci and levels.] [7.] Genetically determined optima set the limits within which variability may be consistent with survival, but ample evidence is available to show that adaptation can take place to drastic disturbances of system integrity. (Cofer & Appley, 1964, pp. 264–265)

CRITICISMS OF HOMEOSTATIC/EQUILIBRATORY THEORIES

In our 1964 analysis, Cofer and I identified three major categories of criticism that were being made of homeostatic theory: that it was essentially negative in nature—conceiving of systems only in terms of response (to disturbance) and not allowing for spontaneous behavior; that it was unable to account for altruistic and creative behaviors; and conversely, that it could not explain behaviors that are seemingly self/system destructive. These objections, it seemed to us, "all revolve around the thesis that the richness of experience and the complex structure of particularly human strivings cannot be so simply explained as avoidance of disequilibrating stimulation" (p. 366).

But the criticisms were of a more simplistic concept than was being described. A complex, multilevel equilibratory system concept, such as Cofer and I detailed and like some that have been proposed subsequently by others (cf. Stagner, 1977, discussed below; Stagner & Solley, 1970; Carver & Scheier, 1981), *could* satisfactorily handle the issues that have been raised (see below).

I must regrettably note, however, that the same kinds of objections identified in 1964 are still being registered more than twenty years later, with no apparent attention to the careful explanations that have been provided in the meantime. Weiner (1986), for example, acknowledges that "an array of clinical and empirical evidence supports this intuitively appealing homeostatic principle . . . [but summarily dismisses it with the unsupported objection that] the greater part of human behavior cannot be subsumed within the concept" (p. 282).

He cites the frequently observed induction of disequilibrium (as in thrill seeking, giving up comfort for discomfort or challenge) and "the prominent psychogenic motivations"—desires for success, for power, to be with others, to help others—as apparently "beyond the range of homeostatic explanations" (p. 282). Awareness as well as deprivation is needed, Weiner avers, to account for behavioral instigation in some circumstances (he uses anoxic deprivation as an example of its absence), setting the stage for elaboration of a cognitive motivation theory not as an extension of but as an alternative to equilibratory motivation theory (Weiner, 1972, 1980, 1986).

Whereas in his earlier book (1972) Weiner described Heider's (1946, 1958) postulation of "cognitive balance . . . as a principle of motivation because imbalance corresponds to a state of disequilibrium, is unpleasant, and produces behaviors instrumental to the attainment of a balanced state" (p. 293), his more recent writing (1986) makes no mention of such an equilibration principle. He seems to reject it, along with hedonism, as less than adequate in the absence of what he calls "cognitive functionalism." Regrettably, as I have noted, his references reveal little awareness of—or seeming willingness to deal with—the literature that answers the kinds of objections he has raised. This unfortunately has been true for many other cognitive theorists as well (cf. author index in Sorrentino & Higgins's *Handbook of Motivation and Cognition* [1986b]).

EQUILIBRATION AS A UNIFYING PRINCIPLE OF MOTIVATION

In our final chapter, titled "Toward a Unified Theory of Motivation," Cofer and I suggested that "an equilibration model is sufficiently descriptive of motivated behavior sequences generally as to assume the status of a fundamental principle" (1964, p. 810).

We tried to show how such a model could explain effects previously described in terms of the then dominant but more limited drive and need-reduction models; to point to the wide acceptance, even by advocates of self-actualization, of underlying equilibratory mechanisms; and to suggest that seemingly nonequilibratory acts could be explained within an equilibratory framework (see "assumptions," above)—for example, by showing how disequilibration at one level of functioning would be a necessary step in establishing equilibrium at a superordinate level (see discussion of Carver & Scheier's control ideas, below) and by invoking the notion of acquired norms (adaptation levels—ALs) to show how new equilibratory bases and disequilibratory criteria and thresholds could be established.

Recognizing that "apparent exceptions to a universal equilibratory principle may require additional or supplementary explanation, [we immodestly suggested that] they no more restrict or invalidate the principle of equilibration than does the fact that objects heavier-than-air rise from the ground destroy the principle of gravity" (p. 812).

We looked to the outcome of further research in four areas that were developing at that time to throw light on the issues raised and on possible mechanisms by which the equilibratory principle is made operative in relation to exogenous processes, and on the role of learning in relation to equilibratory norms: "(1) studies of sensory deprivation and sensory overloading, (2) effects of early (including prenatal) experiences on later behavior, (3) neurohumoral activation mechanisms, and (4) social influences on normative behaviors." Data from the first three areas were already suggesting, even at the time we were writing (1964), what we described as "the remarkable resilience of living systems under extreme and unusual circumstances, as well as the persistence of latent sensitizing factors which combine with later stimulus effects to either facilitate or disrupt ongoing behaviors . . . [and] the capability of living systems to organize and reorganize themselves in many alternative ways" (p. 813). (See Young, 1971; Trumbull & Appley, 1967; Appley, 1962b, 1967, 1984.) We particularly looked to the fourth area "to reveal more clearly the nature of the mechanisms of social influence and . . . the ways in which organisms incorporate change and yet appear to retain integrity. Starting from the assumption of a dynamic, equilibratory series of systems as a model for the behaving organism [would, we thought] provide a fruitful point of departure" (p. 813).

Finally, we proposed two "invigoration" mechanisms that we felt would be useful explanatory constructs to replace prevalent notions of drive and arousal and that could, within the framework of an equilibratory theme, provide the basis for a comprehensive theory of motivation. The first was an *anticipation-invigoration mechanism* (AIM), "dependent on [internal or external] stimuli which have regularly antedated or accompanied consummatory behavior . . . [and which, we stressed] may come through learning to evoke anticipations (and thus arousal) and . . . serve (after learning) as cues to responses" (p. 822). (Anticipations, we believed, could occur in the absence of deprivation, in response to cues associated with satisfactions or pleasures; see Jones, 1977.) The second was a *sensitization-invigoration mechanism* (SIM), modeled after the late Frank Beach's (1956) sexual arousal mechanism (SAM), in which hormonal/physiological readiness appears to sensitize the organism selectively with respect to ranges or bands of stimuli, which we invoked to account for motivated behavior in the absence of prior learning. (We chose the term invigoration, admittedly similar to arousal, to describe what our mechanisms *did* in order to avoid the necessity of implying an intermediate arousal state.)

The Equilibration Concept

Allport (1953) offered these insightful comments: "[The] integrative action of the nervous system is basically a wholesome mechanism that keeps motivation up to date. It tends to bring about both an internal consistency and a reality testing among the elements entering into motivational patterning. . . . Insight, a clear self-image, and the little understood factor of homeostasis may be mentioned among the balancing factors"(p. 116). It seems amazing to me how far we have strayed from this succinct summary of what motivation may be all about. But Allport did not intend to give all such processes equal weight. Despite his seeming acceptance of what he called "the little understood factor of homeostasis," he rejected "striving for equilibrium" along with "tension reduction" and "death wish" as "seemingly trivial and erroneous representations of normal adult motivation" (p. 118). Instead, drawing on Grinker and Spiegel's (1945) descriptions of wartime breakdown and recovery, he opted for the notion of an "active ego" consisting of "psychogenic interests . . . sustaining and directing tension rather than avoiding it. . . . Whether . . . called desires, interests, values, traits or sentiments . . . what a person is trying to do persistently, recurrently, as a function of his own internal nature, is often surprisingly well focused and well patterned" (p. 118).

It is this more dynamic concept that we will next explore, to see the degree to which it may be compatible with a general equilibration theory.

A PERVADING TOPIC

The theme of maintenance or restoration of equilibrium, balance, stability, or consistency after disequilibration pervades the literature of motivation, development, personality, social psychology, and psychology generally. It describes "self-regulatory processes functioning through negative feedback mechanisms to reduce the differences between some preferred internal state and the organism's current state" (Pittman & Heller, 1987, p. 467).

The biologically based homeostatic motives, deriving from clear tissue deficits and resulting in deficit reduction or balance restoration, clearly fit such a definition, as I have already shown. (It is not limited to such cases, however, as many of its critics fail to recognize.) The model next was extended to non-tissue-deficit situations, which, influenced by the historical dominance of deprivation theory of the period, initially posited forms of tension that needed to be relieved (cf. Cofer & Appley, 1964, chap. 7; Pittman & Heller, 1987, pp. 467 ff.). But later it was modified to remove deficit reduction as a necessary condition and to allow that even stimulus seeking could be part of a discrepancy resolution (or equilibrating) mechanism (as between "new input and the organism's earlier experience"; Ulvund, 1980, p. 18; and see Ashby, 1956; Stagner, 1977).

In Piaget's (1952) theory, for example, motivation is seen in terms of cognitive adaptation as regulated by an equilibration process "bringing assimilation and accommodation into balanced coordination"(Flavell, 1963, p. 239; Ulvund, 1980, p. 22).

Before proceeding further, I should probably make clear what I mean by the term *cognitive*, which will be coming up more and more. For our purposes here we can adopt Oatley and Johnson-Laird's (1987) use of the concept to refer to "psychological explanations in terms of the representation and transformation of knowledge which may or may not be conscious" (p. 30). This, for them, includes what they call "tacit knowledge." Two further elements of cognitive processes for them are *goals* ("symbolic representations of possible states of the environment that a system will try to achieve") and *plans* ("sequences of transformations between representations, that link a current state of the environment to a goal"). To make a plan "is to assemble such a sequence." Of importance, from my perspective, is that these authors see such terms as "neutral as to whether they are conscious" (p. 30).

A cognitive change or "perturbing event" (Kessen, 1971, p. 301) leads to disequilibrium and the initiation of the equilibration process. Motivation dissipates when "there is little or no discrepancy between the individual's schemas and the problem which the individual is struggling to attack" (Ulvund, 1980, p. 21). Ulvund points to the similarity between Piaget's, White's (1959, 1960), and Hunt's (1965) views in attempting integration of frankly cognitive theories with an equilibratory motivational principle, and he espouses a similar view, especially as regards early infancy, when the two types of processes are clearly indistinguishable.

White (1959, 1960) rejected homeostatic drives or anxiety-reduction explanations of such activities as play, curiosity, exploration, and an "urge toward mastery," competence, or effectance (i.e., to produce an effect on the environment). However, his conception was not all that different from an equilibratory position. He assumed uncertainty or incompetence as a starting point, in allowing that having an effect on the environment confirms one's sense of competence and that effectance motivation subsides when a situation holds no more mystery for the individual exploring it. In addition, he allowed, as did Maslow (1954), that the so-called homeostatic drives could gain ascendancy under conditions of deprivation. Further, failure to confirm one's competence may lead to a sense of helplessness, the converse of effectance (see Lamont, 1983).

Though widely accepted, White's concept of competence has not been without its critics. Harter (1978), for example, considers it to have little explanatory value, and Nygard (1977) suggests that it is "a concept which assumes all that it was intended to predict" (p. 53).

Hunt's (1965) theory of intrinsic motivation was likewise based on an "incongruity principle," or a discrepancy from standard hypothesis (as in Miller, Gallanter, & Pribram's 1960 TOTE model). Although he posited a sensory deficit basis for curiosity, Hunt allowed explicitly for adjustment in the standard, via Helson's (1964) adaptation levels (ALs) or expectations based on the individual's previous experience (Hunt, 1965, p. 202).

Notwithstanding the considerable influence of his theory, Hunt (1981) was himself to conclude that it was too broad and undifferentiated and that "no single generic construct such as 'incongruity' could serve adequately for discrepancies between the organizations of action and the perceptual and conceptual constructions established from past experience, on the one hand, and for the demands upon coping or upon recognition and understanding, on the other" (pp. 174–175; see Cofer & Appley, 1984, pp. 426–427).

McCall and McGhee (1977) review a series of studies of attention in infants in a contribution to a festschrift for Hunt. They propose "subjective uncertainty" as a more appropriate descriptor of the process of evaluating an unfamiliar stimulus than the concept of incongruity or (stimulus) discrepancy. Subjective uncertainty, which arises when a stimulus is examined for familiarity by comparison with stored memory, "increases linearly with the amount of 'information potential' [new but processable stimulus information] inherent in the . . . stimulus" (pp. 190–191). Stimuli judged unfamiliar do not produce comparison; on the other hand, extreme levels of subjective uncertainty can lead to "relative perceptual avoidance . . .

'motivated inattention,' physiological agitation, and even mild negative affect" (p. 198).

DeCharms (1968, 1980), like White and Hunt, proposed an overarching *"primary motivational propensity . . . to be effective in producing changes in the environment . . .* to strive to be a causal agent . . . to be master of one's fate" (1968, p. 269). Obviously akin to mastery, personal causation forms a basis on which specific motives (for food, success, friendship, etc.) can operate. They in turn feed into growth of responsibility and development of the self-concept (see below).

Other examples of nonbiologically based motives, presented in more clearly cognitive terms, are the perception of threats to freedom leading to reactance (Brehm, 1966) and dissonance or inconsistency leading to an effort to restore "cognitive homeostasis" or balance (Festinger, 1957; Heider, 1958; see below).

Yarrow and Pederson (1976), while not disagreeing with such views, insist that cognition is not enough. For them "the need to reconcile discrepancies, to master the environment, and to repeat activities that produce interesting results all involve more than cognition. They require the coordination of intellect with motivation" (p. 396).

Evaluating the attribution literature, Pittman and Heller (1987) show how perceived or actual lack or loss of control leads to attributions that then "render the social world predictable and controllable" (p. 468; Pittman & Pittman, 1980; McCaul, 1983), a theme common to motivation theory. They cite a series of studies supporting their contention that control deprivation (or threat of control deprivation)—as in instances where unexpected information is provided (Pyszczynski & Greenberg, 1981), where unusually negative events occur (Diener & Dweck, 1978), or where there is personal involvement with outcome (Jones & Davis, 1965)—intensifies effortfulness, accuracy, and the data-driven nature of information-processing attributional analyses and explanations (cf. D'Agostino & Pittman, 1982; Pittman & D'Agostino, 1985).

Pittman and Heller (1987) suggest that this "concern for control [links] . . . motivational . . . and information-processing perspectives" (p. 470). Using hypothesis-testing as a case study, "because it has been viewed primarily as a cognitive process relatively devoid of motivational features . . . , [they make the point that] both motivation and hypothesis-testing . . . are negative feedback mechanisms that aid an individual to act on the environment so as to cause a match between some internal standard and the external world" (p. 474). The often unexpected persistence of such expectancies (cf. Darley & Fazio, 1980) suggests to Pittman and Heller (1987) that they are filling a motivational function of "guiding behavior rather than simply being subjected to scrutiny" (p. 474). (There is a similarity here, it seems to me, to the role ascribed to the AIM mechanism that Cofer and I [1964, pp. 821 ff.] described earlier.)

COLD COGNITION

Although they acknowledge similarities between cognitive and motivational explanations (as of hypothesis testing, for example), Pittman and Heller (1987) decry the absence, in the cognitive approach, of "any appropriate mechanism that would account for variability in the intensity or urgency of an individual's actions, the very characteristics that make motivation 'hot' . . . [such as] connection with the visceral drive mechanisms . . . [and] affect" (p. 474; see further discussion below).

They cite Buck's (1985) prime theory (see below) in accepting the notion of a hierarchical arrangement of motivations and affects, beginning with biologically necessary homeostatic motives, acquired drives, and primary affects, all helping "to guide the organism in manipulating its internal states and external environment in order to maximize control" (p. 476).

In sum, it seems to me that the equilibration concept has stood the test of time as a universal motivational principle. The issue seems to be not so much whether it is valid but whether it stretches far enough to cover the full range of motivational phenomena. I will return to this question after we have looked at what has been called "the cognitive revolution" and its influence on motivation theory.

The "Cognitive Revolution"

Although my review of the "derived motives" literature in 1969 (Appley, 1970) uncovered no significant trend toward cognitive concepts, D'Amato (1974), writing on the same topic only four years later, found what he called a "cognitive revolution . . . an extraordinary proliferation and development of cognitive concepts in psychology" (p. 100). He suggested that the ghost of early cognitive learning theorist E. C. Tolman would "revel in the fury of the cognitive assault that threatens to capture almost the full range of nonreflexive behavior in both humans and animals" (p. 100). Observing the rich variety of cognitive concepts employed, however, D'Amato wondered aloud "whether much more is being accomplished than relabelling[!]" (p. 100).

Equally direct, and more accepting, was Dember's announcement, in the same year, that "psychology has gone cognitive, and so has motivation" (1974, p. 161), reflecting the addition of active stimulus *seeking* to the traditional stimulus reduction model of motivation, but rejecting extension of the "need reduction" concept to cover such activities (though see above, and Cofer & Appley, 1964, chaps. 7, 10, and 11).

There were some indications of a shift even earlier. Helson (1967), in his *Nebraska Symposium* paper, though ignoring the issue of mechanism, had suggested that "cognitive processes per se [drive to find a solution (intellectual drive—predominant ideas)] . . . may generate as strong and even stronger drives than . . . hunger or sex" (p. 176). "It is time [he concluded] that the driving power of *conscious perceiving and thinking* be recognized as much as the driving power of tissue needs" (p. 179).

And Tallman (1967), a sociologist, writing on the applicability of Merton's (1949) social theories to illegal behavior, cited Festinger (1957) and others as authority to use "the notion of balance among relevant cognitive elements as a basic principle governing behavioral choices" (p. 341) and, further, to describe "psychological discomfort" as brought about by "dissonant cognitions" and behavior as motivated by "attempts to bring these cognitions into balance." Of interest and relevance here are his observations that deviant individuals whose desired goals are blocked appear to seek a balance of values in such alternative choices as devaluing an unattainable goal, denying or downplaying their use of illegitimate means of attaining a desired goal, and finding a reference group that approves the chosen (illegal) behavior.

Berlyne (1975), writing at the same time as D'Amato and Dember, described the paradigm shift in psychology away from behaviorism to what he called "the preferable paradigm"—variously identified with "cognitive theory" or "humanistic psychology" (p. 69).

Even my good friend and collaborator Charles Cofer allowed in 1978 that a revolution had occurred in the field of psychology since our 1964 book, "a revolution that has replaced or is replacing the S-R associationistic paradigm with a new [one], that of cognitive psychology." He warned, however, that this might be "in some hands . . . more a new bottle for old wine than . . . a new wine" (p. 1).

Using Weiner's (1972) minimum criterion of inclusion of an expectancy concept, both Cofer and I (Cofer & Appley, 1964, 1984; Appley, 1962a, 1962b, 1967, 1984; Cofer, 1972, 1978) would qualify as cognitive psychologists. I hasten to add that I would reject the either/or connotation of being cognitive versus dynamic as applied to motivation. So far as I am concerned, the two concepts cannot be mutually exclusive. I rather see them as complementary parts of a comprehensive equilibratory motivational process, a theme I have dealt with and will develop further.

In field after field, like the borders of nations throughout Europe at the onset of World War II, defenses collapsed under the blitzkrieg attacks of, in this case, the cognitive big guns.

Harter (1978), for example, admitting that developmental psychology "has been relatively one-sided . . . [of late] . . . giving short shrift to the study of motivational variables," agreed with the earlier observations, writing: "Within the realm of academic psychology in recent years it would seem that all things bright and beautiful bear the label 'cognitive.' Cognitive development, cognitive dissonance, cognitive style, cognitive information processing models, and the list goes on. . . . the *Zeitgeist* is . . . widespread: social, clinical, experimental psychologists, even learning theorists, are now talking cognitive" (p. 61). A much-cited early statement of the cognitive position among developmental psychologists is that of Kagan (1972), who defined a motive as "a cognitive representation of a [desired] future goal state," which can then be anticipated. Any uncertainty about the realization of such a desired experience activates/motivates the individual "to resolve the uncertainty" (p. 53). "When an event . . . is discrepant from an established schema . . . [it] recruits the individual's attention . . . [creates] a state of uncertainty and [primes a resolution] . . . by assimilating, removing, or escaping from the discrepant event [cf. Janis, 1959]. If the person cannot realize any of these goals, uncertainty mounts, and affective distress [anxiety, shame, or guilt] is likely to occur" (p. 55).

Kagan does not view the desire to resolve uncertainty as "a deprivation or tension-reduction process [because] . . . the person is not in a state of arousal. [Rather] the physiological state of 'alerting' [which accompanies uncertainty and] has an inherent lability . . . is usually followed by processes which produce a different organization of cognitive structures and, typically, dissolution of the state of alertness" (p. 58).[3] Sources of uncertainty, for Kagan, include the usual array of incompatibilities, incongruities, contradictions, and so on, between cognitive structures, experience, and behavior (see Campion & Lord, 1982). (Although uncertainty, which has broad meaning, is the primary motivator in Kagan's conceptualization, his intention is more restrictive in that he defines it as "a particular organization of cognitive structures" and uses such synonyms for it as *cognitive conflict, cognitive dissonance,* and *cognitive disequilibrium.*)

Kagan considers White's (1959) effectance motive to be very much like his own motive to control uncertainty but lacking in preceding alertness. He sees it as resulting from a desire to match behavior, to predict events, or to define the self (by gaining information to resolve uncertainty about the conceptualization of the self). He cautions that the tasks chosen for mastery must be those that "generate some uncertainty and for which [there is] some initial set of appropriate responses. Uncertain challenges that do not engage any behavioral implementation are shunned" (p. 61).

The interaction of development and uncertainty is made explicit by Kagan in his observation that successive stages of development [and experience] create recurrent needs to reexamine earlier belief systems. Especially in Western culture, he points out, "beliefs are a central part of an individual's identity . . . [and maintaining] . . . integrity of belief systems is . . . central to the conceptualization of the self" (p. 64).

Many other examples of cognitive motivation theories can be offered. Higgins, Klein, and Strauman (1985), described by Honess and Yardley (1987, p. 151) as "clearly within the cognitive tradition," see the person as a "'consistency seeker' . . . motivated by perceived discrepancies in cognitions." Moreover, they accept that affect follows the (cognitive) recognition and interpretation of such discrepancies, "which is also consistent with cognitive assumptions." This last is challenged by Honess and Yardley, on the basis that it may reflect *how* we have learned to organize our emotions rather than being cause and effect. They also criticize Markus and Nurius (1987), who as a result of their "broad cognitive perspective" ignore any input from "unconscious desire" in their description of "possible selves" and their functions (see discussion of "The Self Concept," below).

Sorrentino and Higgins (1986a), in the introductory chapter to their *Handbook of Motivation and Cognition* (1986b), acknowledge that in social psychology too, "a major shift in emphasis began occurring [in the 1970s]; cognition emerged as the dominant force, and motivation declined to a secondary, mostly implicit element [p. 5]. [And further] . . . in the area of social behavior . . . cognitive theories have become the *Weltanschauung*, whereas motivation may be best described as 'flat on its back'" (p. 8). They attribute the emergence of cognitive psychology (which they also call "information-processing approach") to human factors research in World War II and to interest in artificial intelligence and psycholinguistics, in all of which motivation had little place. "Cognition can account for many behaviors [they write] that others claim to be motivated" (p. 5). Individual differences can be attributed to "faulty computer" cold cognition factors (such as information-processing errors, cognitive limitations) rather than to motivational ones (cf. Nisbett & Ross, 1980).

After reviewing the varied contributions to their edited volume, Sorrentino and Higgins (1986a) conclude that "motivation and cognition are, in fact, inseparable . . . are *synergetic* in . . . operating together to produce combined effects . . . [and they recommend a] blending of 'cold' cognition and 'hot' motivational processes" (p. 8).

My own view is that, despite their somewhat contrary emphasis, this would not be an equal partnership, since cognitive processes are merely—and clearly—a subsystem of the larger motivational dynamic. But more of this later.

Observations and conclusions about the need for an integration of motivation and cognition appear again and again. Magnusson (1976), for example, in a paper distinguishing between consistency and coherence in personality, urged "development of information processing models integrating cognitive . . . motivation and physiological processes [though, he notes] most information processing models are limited by their deficient interest in motivation" (p. 19).

Bindra (1979), from the perspective of his "interaction model," likewise suggested a mutual dependency of motivation and perception and predicted integration of motivational ideas into the field of perception and thinking. In his view (one that Sorrentino & Higgins echo some seven years later), such a motivation-cognition connection has been long overdue. "Since motivational arousal depends on the perception of incentive objects, and perceptions are determined partly by current thinking sets, the cognitive factor must influence motivation, and because motivational priming influences perception and perception influences thinking, motivation must also influence cognition" (Bindra, 1979, pp. 32–33). Pervin's (1983) "theory of goals" emphasizes not only the purposive, goal-directed nature of human behavior but also "the inter-dependent nature of affective, cognitive, and behavioral functioning" (p. 45) in relation to goals and suggests how differential contribution of each can affect the nature, duration, and strength of goals.

And Tetlock and Levi (1982) scold advocates of *both* cognitive and motivational explanations (of attributional bias) for seeking crucial experiments to give advantage to their particular orientation rather than clarifying ambiguities in their own positions. They conclude that "current cognitive and motivational explanations are not distinguishable on the basis of attributional data" (p. 68).

One of the more ambitious recent efforts to integrate motivational concepts has been Buck's (1985) *prime theory,* which posits the development of a system of biologically based, hierarchically organized, primary motivational/emotional systems (primes) as *special-purpose systems* at various levels of organization. These begin with *tropisms, taxes,* and *reflexes,* go to instinctual *fixed action patterns, primary drives,* and *primary affects* and on to *effectance motivation,* interacting to an increasing extent as one moves up the ladder "with *general-purpose systems* of conditioning, learning, and cognition" (p. 392).

Buck's proposed hierarchical structure thus begins with systems directly responsible for bodily adaptations and the maintenance of biological homeostasis, moves through emotion as a communication or "readout" system, and goes on to "a direct [syncretic] internal cognitive readout system" (p. 397). Although some adaptive-homeostatic responses, expressive behavior, and direct subjective experience are conceived as functioning independently, they are "affected by analytic cognition." In fact, Buck sees this highest level as encouraging "cognitive participation in adaptive functions . . . [thus] increasing the . . . capacity for self-regulation." Cognitive information, he proposes, "may be necessary for the kind of adaptive anticipatory behavior and incentive motivation . . . that precedes homeostatic deficits . . . [and allows cognitive control of outward display of emotion] to fit the requirements of the situation" (p. 398).

Earlier I described Ulvund's (1980) similar emphasis on cognitive processes and their critical role in interaction with lower-level motivational mechanisms in infant development. Like Cofer and Appley (1964) and Stagner (1977), Ulvund's (1980) discrepancy model has no difficulty drawing stimulus seeking into an equilibration framework. Notwithstanding this, however, Ulvund concludes, as do Sorrentino and Higgins (1986a) in the preface to their later book, in describing the Möbius strip, that "there seems to be a continuous interaction between cognition and motivation . . . the two processes cannot be clearly distinguished from each other" (p. 17).

In the area of attitudes and attitude change, Chaiken and Stangor (1987) note the earlier prediction of Cooper and Croyle (1984) "that the dominance of cognitive approaches in the attitudes area would begin to recede as motivational issues returned to the forefront" (p. 615). They report what they call "healthy signs" of the raising of such concerns once again, though not at the expense of continued interest in cognition. Revising the previous emphasis on the dominance of cognition, even when it is intimately associated with motivation, they conclude that "the theme . . . emerging in the literature is that cognition cannot be studied in isolation from motivation and that a firm and explicit knowledge of the latter is a prerequisite for fully understanding the cognitive processes underlying attitude organization, formation, and change" (p. 615).

Yet Singer and Kolligian (1987), reviewing the personality area at the same time, repeat the theme that "the major paradigm shift in psychology that has characterized the period since the 1960s has reflected a move . . . toward a recognition that human beings bring meaning and organization into almost every new encounter in the physical or social environment" (p. 554). They allow, however, that plans and anticipations may become automatic and can thus function without cognitive awareness.

And even as currently as a review published last year (Carson, 1989) we still read: "The cognitive revolution throughout psychology continues to reverberate in the personality domain" (p. 229). However, noting Neisser's (1980) warning "against over-extending of information-processing models," the reviewer acknowledges that "the situation has improved appreciably—for example, by increased incorporation of motivational and other dynamic variables into the conception and design of cognitively oriented studies" (p. 229).

So how are we to read Harter's (1978) tongue-in-cheek observation that "all things bright and beautiful bear the label cognitive"? Increasingly skeptically, it seems. The attack on this position is becoming more virulent. Kuhl (1986), for example, argues that "cognitive psychologists use the term 'cognitive' in an overinclusive way . . . [to apply to] any process that is going on in the human mind" (p. 405), a meaning broadened beyond the original sense of "knowing" or conscious knowledge (p. 406).

Convinced that dynamic processes (such as perseverance or cross-situational cumulation of action tendencies) "may affect motivational states independent of any cognitive mediation," Kuhl concludes, "An information-processing approach to the study of motivation is defined by a certain level of analysis, rather than by a reduction of all mental states to cognitive processes. The fact that research into human information processing has almost exclusively focused on cognitive processes is a historic coincidence, rather than a logical or psychological necessity" (p. 429; see also Zajonc, 1980).

And Reeve and Cole (1987), looking at intrinsic motivation, weigh the relative arguments for an exclusively cognitive ("information processing and choice") interpretation (such as that of Deci & Ryan, 1985) and one based on affective/motivational instigation (such as that of Izard, 1977), where "motivation is a consequence of excitement . . . via curiosity and exploration, irrespective of cognition" (p. 442). They conclude that both contribute independently to the prediction of intrinsic motivation.

COGNITIVE HOMEOSTASIS

Finally, we may note an increase in efforts at "melding" the two positions. Pittman and Heller (1987), for example, treat control theory as a "cognitive model of homeostatic processes" (as in part do Carver and Scheier), with its key negative feedback and discrepancy-reducing components and hierarchical structure. They are encouraged by what they consider to be "new motivational formulations" in Carver and Scheier's (1981) suggestion that "feedback units are hierarchically arranged . . . the standard that guides behavior at one hierarchical level is the output of a higher level feedback unit. . . . [Providing] greater flexibility and some insight into how the mechanisms controlling moment-to-moment actions of individuals are related to higher level goals and aspirations" (p. 477; see Cofer & Appley, 1964, chap. 7, for discussion of similar treatments). Pittman and Heller (1987) finally consider it to be "entirely reasonable to assume that some fundamental conception of self . . . lies at the highest level of such a hierarchy . . . [and that] . . . the notion of self might explicitly link a wide range of lower level cognitive processes" (p. 478; see "The Self-Concept," below).

The emphasis on "cold cognition" (Jones, 1985; Pittman & Heller, 1987) often has obscured the necessary underlying linkage between cognition and motivation (and cognition and affect), and it is only of late that the common themes have begun to be acknowledged by cognitive theorists. (Even so, when I queried Allen Newell, at a reception following one of his series of invited Lowell Lectures at Harvard in 1987, about the absence of mention of motivation in his presentation, he allowed that the cognitive theorists at Carnegie-Mellon had yet to come to terms with motivational phenomena.)

In summary, I would venture to suggest that "the cognitive revolution" may have now reached the same stage as the major political revolutions of this century—where *perestroika* may reveal its shortcomings and herald its retreat from a preemptive position to a more modest one as *part* of a larger explanatory schema.

Is Homeostasis/Equilibration a Viable Conceptual Base for Motivation Theory in Psychology?

Clearly, Cofer and I thought so in 1964. We saw motivation as instigation to action, though we did not start with an inert individual. Kelly (1955), by contrast, emphasized his assumption of an intrinsically active organism, born "alive and kicking" and always doing something. In Kelly's clinically based *personal constructs theory* individuals live in a perceived or constructed psychological environment or life space in which they anticipate alternative outcomes ("by constructing their replications") (p. 50), discover similarities and differences among them, and choose among the alternatives in terms of expectancies, subjective probabilities, values, preferences, and goals, based on their personal constructs.

I suggest that our views and Kelly's were not so disparate as they may seem on the surface. Both gave emphasis to *anticipation*, to confirming or disconfirming expectations, and to the role of threat and anxiety in impelling corrective action. The more explicit reliance on *cognizing* or knowing in Kelly's theory is perhaps the one significant difference between us. (DuPreez, 1977, provides a useful discussion of Kelly's constructs.)

Allport (1953), writing in the heyday of drive theory, was critical both of it and of equilibration. While accepting that "basic drives seem to seek reduction of tension," he insisted that this was not enough. "These drives are not a trustworthy model for all normal adult motivation. . . . Normal people . . . are dominated by their 'preferred patterns' of self-actualization. Their psychogenic interests are modes of sustaining and directing tension rather than escaping it (Goldstein, 1940) . . . [they] complicate and strain our lives indefinitely" (pp. 117–118). (And see later.) Maslow (1954) proposed self-actualization as a higher-order, nonhomeostatic need able to be developed only after deprivation-based (homeostatic) needs lower in a hierarchy were able to be routinely satisfied. However, very few individuals could achieve self-actualization.

Two key issues recur in such criticisms—the blurring of the distinction between drive reduction and equilibration, and the related notion of an inactive organism needing to be aroused and then returning to an earlier quiescent state. This latter, indeed, may have been the model of some early theorists, such as Rignano (1923),[4] but it does *not* reflect the more dynamic views of equilibration described by Cofer and Appley (1964), by Stagner (1977), or by Carver and Scheier (1981), among others.

If one does not restrict the idea of *equilibration* to the particular contexts used by Rignano (1923) or by Cannon (1932, 1939), or other Cannon predecessors, such as Bernard (1859) or Child (1924), and if one rejects the unnecessary notion of an initially inert being, it is not at all evident that the concept is too limited to serve as an explanatory principle of motivation. Let us take a look at some of the recent (post-1964) arguments and developments, beginning with the concept of homeostasis from a biological perspective, from which generalizable, extractable elements may become evident.

Overmire (1974), in his *Encyclopaedia Britannica* treatment of the subject, includes "all processes of integration and coordination of function . . . [as] examples of homeostatic regulation . . . [that] tend to maintain stability while adjusting to conditions that are optimal for survival." He sees such self-regulating processes as applying not only to biological systems, "but also all levels of life" (p. 1014). Young (1971, p. 8) likewise sees "this capacity for maintenance of continuity [as] the central, characteristic, feature of life."

The three key elements of homeostasis, according to Overmire, are that it is *self-regulatory,* refers to *process* rather than status or state, and involves *simultaneous effort to maintain stability and to adjust.* He captures the essence of the process by comparing it to a pool below a waterfall, which maintains "a dynamic equilibrium, in which continuous change occurs yet relatively uniform conditions prevail" (p. 1014). Elements of the process include

> [1.] The homeostatic plateau . . . the "normal" range between high and low levels that sustains life . . . ; [2.] corrective action (through negative feedback) [which occurs when either extreme is reached] . . . ; [3.] oscillations inherent in the system [which] represent the compensatory adjustments to any deviation from the normal . . . ; [4.] response lag [that may lead to] overshoots of increasing magnitude [and, if uncorrected, to] collapse of the system . . . ; and [5.] [possible shifts in the homeostatic plateau itself, within which new oscillating patterns must be developed] if the system is to survive. (p. 1015; see Helson, 1964; Ashby, 1956, 1960)

Finally, and of importance to our theme, Overmire observes that "homeostasis is attained in the organism as a whole through several ordered levels of control and subsystems" (p. 1017). I shall return to these key points later.

HOMEOSTASIS VERSUS EQUILIBRIUM

The choice between the terms *homeostasis* and *equilibrium* continues to be a matter of personal preference, it seems. Cannon (1932), for example, explicitly rejected the term *equilibria* as having too exact a meaning

> as applied to relatively simple physicochemical states, in closed systems, where forces are balanced. [He considered] the coordinated physiological processes which maintain most of the steady states in the organism . . . so complex, and so peculiar to living beings [as to require a special descriptor, for which he coined the term *homeostasis*]. . . . The word does not imply something set and immobile, a stagnation. It means a condition . . . which may vary, but which is relatively constant. (p. 24; cf. Rignano 1923, cited above)

Horrocks and Jackson (1972), by contrast, used virtually the same definition as Cannon (1932) did for homeostasis but preferred instead (in their words) "the more dynamic term equilibrium, applying it to open as well as to closed systems, [and specifically extending it] to the neurological and perceptual processes composing cognition" (p. 16). They agree with Raup (1925) that equilibrium is "the most fundamental principle of all life processes as well as of . . . behavioral adjustment . . . [and that] . . . Maladjustment . . . [is] a disturbance of balance between an organism and its environment . . . [which] activates the drive to restore equilibrium [or what Raup called complacency]" (cited by Horrocks & Jackson, 1972, p. 16, n.).

Needless to say, despite Cannon's justification of his unique term, I likewise prefer *equilibrium* as a more dynamic concept. In any case, Cannon's use of the term homeostasis has so effectively tied its meaning primarily to the physiological systems he described as to make it unsuitable for the more generic use he himself envisioned.

Stagner (1977), an early and important advocate of the broad applicability of homeostatic theory to and in psychology (cf. Stagner, 1951, 1954), has continued to hold strongly to that view (and term). He argues that "homeostasis provides a framework and a mechanism which can integrate such views of motivation as are associated with terms like *dissonance, need achievement, competence,* and *self-actualization* into a biologically based theoretical structure" (p. 104). He objects to what he calls the "free-wheeling tendency to invent new motives to meet any observed requirement of an energizing component," holding instead that *"energy mobilization is a single process which varies in degrees, and which may be integrated into varied goal-directed action patterns"* (p. 106). Festinger's (1957) dissonance theory, for example, as well as social comparison and equity theory concepts, is basically homeostatic, according to Stagner.

To help clarify nomenclature, Stagner proposes that the term *motivation* be reserved for the general (energy mobilization) process and that *motive* "be used to identify specific deprivations, discrepancies, or expectancies which trigger energy mobilization" (p. 106). The *motive* (like an individual homeostat) has the dual function of eliciting energy mobilization and directing effort toward elimination of the discrepancy that instigated it.[5] As Stagner sees it, *"The organism manifests an increase in energy level when it encounters a discrepancy between current input and the established or preferred steady state with respect to that input. The increased level of effort tends to persist until the discrepancy has been removed [via contact with or anticipation of incentives or goal objects] . . . the degree of increase of effort is [ordinarily] proportionate to the magnitude of the discrepancy"* (p. 107). He claims that "the basic [motivational] mechanism . . . is a discrepancy-detecting and discrepancy-minimizing system" (p. 110). He notes, however, that "level of behavior effort may be modulated by a number of factors . . . [and that] some discrepancies necessarily . . . override others [in determining use of a] *final common path"* (pp. 112–113).

It has been suggested elsewhere (cf. Trumbull & Appley, 1986; Dienstbier, 1989) that condition of the organism—momentary as well as derivative of genetic and developmental factors, and changeable via training and over time (e.g., as in early development and in aging)—can have major modulating effects on level of effort and choice of response (or final common path?).

Sources of steady states include heredity, prenatal adaptation level (e.g., of temperature), imprinting, postnatal adaptation level, conformity (via peer group pressure, and both developing and ideal self-images, which may establish new preferred steady states), and what Stagner calls *"instrumentality* (objects, persons, and activities which have led to tension reduction in the past may be perceived as continuing to have that effect)" (p. 116).

In agreement with Miller, Galanter, and Pribram's (1960) TOTE unit concept, Stagner allows for "bias" (a genetically preset value for a given modality [e.g., osmotic pressure], which "sets up a criterion for ending the period of arousal by a 'feedforward' loop [e.g., satiety]" (p. 118). He concludes, as did Cofer and Appley (1964), and as I have several times already noted in this chapter, that

> contrary to some critics, homeostatic theory does not predict that the organism always reinstates a prior state. The bias value can be changed [e.g., via adaptation level or *acquired expectation of disequilibrium* after repeated, intense, or persistent disturbances], so that on a later occasion the input is tested against a corrected value. Similarly, a higher order homeostat may be imposed . . . facilitating or blocking . . . according to internal or external constraints. [And most important, as in acquired expectation of disequilibrium], this higher order steady state may be an anticipatory function, the organism mobiliz[ing] energy when a signal portends the onset of disturbance of equilibrium. ([pp. 118–119]; see Cofer & Appley's 1964 discussions of step-function changes [pp. 349–351] and their anticipation-invigoration mechanism [pp. 822–823])

For Stagner, most adult behavior falls into this category, being a function of acquired expectation of disequilibrium rather than discrepancy (what Pribram, 1971, called "biasing the homeostats"). Thus, for example, "self-definitions of situations and social comparison processes . . . may operate through arousal or inhibition of homeostatic mechanisms to bring out effortful behavior" (p. 120).

An important aspect of Stagner's (1977) model is his designation of a single final common path as "the sole and unique energy arousal mechanism. . . . If [the final common path] is preempted by one [discrepancy], that motive will dominate behavior and others will be blocked" (p. 121).

Agreeing with Lacey's (1967) careful arguments for recognizing differentiated (e.g., cortical, autonomic nervous system, glandular, and visceral) arousal pattern changes in stress situations, Stagner sees individual patterns as determining "the relative weighting of recorded [steady states] and input, as these might affect coping" (p. 125). He thus envisions developmental individuation in varieties of ways (cf. also Goldstein, 1940; Lewin, 1935; Murphy, 1947), including the coopting of the discrepancy mechanism, or final common path, to produce arousal and action "for dealing with the protection of [steady states] such as property or ego-status" (p. 127).

Stagner also agrees with Freud that "a defense against an unwelcome internal process will be modelled upon a defense adopted against an external stimulus . . . the ego wards off internal and external dangers alike along identical lines" (Freud, 1954, 20:22–23).

It is then not too far a step for him to propose (in an attempt to deal with hedonism and not destroy the generality of the homeostasis-discrepancy position) that "the affective system may become integrated into S-R units not involving any discrepancy. The fractionation of the pleasure system out of the total motivation system [he suggests] may thus be conceived as another example of Lacey's 'differential fractionation'" (p. 127). He concludes: "The basic commandment of homeostasis is: Control your environment or die. . . . *Uncertainty means danger* . . . expectancy of threat becomes a major arousal factor. . . . The individual develops a need to perceive, a need to sense changes in his world so he can either control them or take protective action against them" (pp. 134–135).

Stagner's updated (1977) homeostatic motivational system, then, is a proactive one, built around such concepts as "preferred steady state" and *anticipation* of (as well as contact with) incentives or goal objects; further, it utilizes a series of mechanisms (e.g., steady state, discrepancy, acquired expectation of disequilibrium, final common path) especially conceived to support it and make it more flexible.

This new iteration expands the notion of homeostasis (which term Stagner sentimentally and stubbornly retains) even further beyond its early, more limited (physiological) origins and use. In its more elaborated form, it also answers better concerns such as those expressed by Allport (1953), who, as I noted earlier, blurred the distinction between "striving for equilibrium" and "tension reduction" and then dismissed both as inadequate and incorrect explanations of the sustaining and directing power of "psychogenic interests" (p. 118).

Further, as one examines Stagner's new concepts, one finds little discrepancy from the language of discrepancy-reduction as found in the control system literature (cf. Carver & Scheier, 1981), to which we turn now.

DISCREPANCY MONITORING AND SELF-REGULATION

"Goalsetting and discrepancy reduction are normal consequences of the way in which the human being is organized as a self-regulating system," wrote Carver and Scheier (1981, p. 341). Campion and Lord (1982) provide a generic description of discrepancy-reducing control systems:

> Essentially, all control system models [cf. Van Sommers, 1974] contain the notion of a relevant environment being monitored via some sensor function [that] yields a signal which is then compared to a referent, standard, or desired state. *Any discrepancy or error between the sensor and referent signals creates a self-correcting motivation.* Depending on the characteristics of the individual and the situation [appraisal], a decision is . . . made as to whether an attempt will be made to modify the environment . . . or the referent itself. . . . Either way, the result is to maintain congruence between the environment and the desired state of affairs. (pp. 266–267, italics added)

Underlying this process is a basic structure built upon the negative feedback loop. Like Campion and Lord (1982), Carver and Scheier (1981) see the control system operation as including three functions: "The sensing of some condition external to itself, the comparison of this sensed state against some reference value or standard, and the exertion of some influence (direct or indirect) on the condition that is being sensed . . . to keep the discrepancy between the sensed value and the comparison value to a minimum" (p. 25). The negative feedback loops that compose the control system are linked to other such loops and are organized hierarchically. Such networking provides considerable flexibility in the conduct of self-regulation. It enables coordination across and among levels and systems and allows for the necessary differential timing of decisions/actions across levels. Standards salient in behavioral contexts are the comparison or reference values set (and resettable) at superordinate control levels. Higher-order systems, operating at a greater level of abstraction, require more time to make corrections than the more direct and immediate lower-order behavioral systems (Carver & Scheier, 1981, pp. 15–25). Thus, for example, in a school testing situation, behavioral responses (such as increasing effort), and strategic responses (such as increasing test goals), would occur faster than such cognitive changes as lowering course goals (which would be more common after multiple failures; Sibly & McFarland, 1974).

> The decision mechanism . . . may be characterized by relatively simple, sequential testing of alternative responses to failure [cf. Simon, 1955]. Subjects may merely "try out" well-known responses . . . [since doing so] requires less processing of information before decisions are made . . . if one selects more familiar responses first, a search for new responses or strategies would only be required after repeated failures . . . under conditions of uncertainty [March & Simon, 1958], trying a familiar response may be a means of gathering information about the environment as well as a means of altering outcome. (Campion & Lord, 1982, p. 284)[6]

In a quite recent appraisal, Ilgen and Klein (1989, p. 343) note the criticisms of control theory as being "too mechanical and rigid, due to the overreliance of early theorists on . . . mechanical analogies (Powers, 1973b)." Nevertheless, they see a significant advantage in the ability of the control-theory perspective "to parsimoniously integrate other theories, its range of applicability across numerous concepts, and the fact that it is a fluid model, allowing the conceptualization and investigation of dynamic processes (Campion & Lord, 1982; Lord & Hanges, 1987)" (p. 343). Cofer and I made a similar case, you may recall, for the scope of equilibratory theories (Cofer & Appley, 1964, chaps. 7, 16). Homeostasis, a concept with which we (and Stagner and others) were then concerned, is considered by Carver and Scheier (1981) to be "the most obvious application of control theory to living systems" (p. 26). They also cite Norbert Wiener's (1948) pioneering work in cybernetic theory, upon which control theory is based, and (in relation to perception, at least) note Helson's adaptation-level theory as a good example of a control theory approach.

(Regrettably, they do not cite Ashby 1956, 1960), whose work would have been a natural bridge from Wiener to them.)

As I noted earlier, Cofer and I built our case for the breadth and value of an equilibratory theory of motivation on examples of the various forms of homeostatic, cybernetic and adaptation-level theory concepts, along with Lewin's field theory and others we described. We provided what we thought were very good reasons for their inclusion and further elaboration (see Cofer & Appley, 1964, chaps. 7, 16; and see Helson, 1967, for application of AL theory to motivation). Carver and Scheier (1981), who otherwise provide an excellent systematic analysis of what they call "a control-theory approach to human behavior," unfortunately make no reference to our earlier extensive treatment of many of the same subjects in the realm of motivation, nor do they list Cofer and Appley (1964) in their bibliography, though they cite secondary sources that do. They thus missed the opportunity to connect more directly the equilibratory theme we and others (like Stagner, 1977) espoused and the control concepts they describe. Although I am not pleased with their omission, it does allow me to claim their thinking as *independent* affirmation of ours!

Of further interest to me is that, at the other end of the hierarchy from physiological feedback loops, Carver and Scheier (1981) "assume that self-esteem protection and enhancement *do* occur . . . [and] see such phenomena as being thoroughly consistent with a control-theory analysis of self-regulation" (p. 256). Citing Powers's (1973a) notions of superordinate control levels of "principle" and "system concepts," they suggest that "one such system concept . . . is the sense of coherence and adequacy associated with the self. This is a superordinate standard, to which one's present state can be matched by the specification of principles, which lead to the specification of programs of action, and so on. Perhaps the process of keeping discrepancies small with regard to this particular superordinate standard is what we have been calling self-esteem or egotism" (p. 257). Once again, these authors seem to come to conclusions similar to those Cofer and I reached. Citing work of Stagner (1961a), Davis (1958), Lecky (1945), Mace (1953), and others, we concluded: "The maintenance of a constant self-percept appears . . . to be a pivotal factor in the argument for psychological homeostasis. . . . [The] integrity of the self-picture is defended against threat (cf. Lecky,

1945). . . . [And because] the self participates in all of life's experiences, the strength (consistency) of the pervading self-percept is seen as the most important (generalized) source of motivation for social behavior" (Cofer & Appley, 1964, pp. 320–321). Reviewing some of the recent extensive considerations of the subject of "self" in its many variations convinces me not only that *the notion of self as superordinate, integrating equilibratory fulcrum continues to be a viable one*, but that a focus at this level may have value in unifying the outlook of a larger part of the psychological community than might have been recruitable to concepts describing lower levels of organization. Let us turn to some of the recent discussion of the self-concept and its scope.

The Self-Concept

We note first, with Markus and Wurf (1987) and Singer and Kolligian (1987), the marked recent increase ("almost an explosion") of interest in, research on, and attempted clarification of the concepts of *self* and of self-awareness, self-consistency, self-confirmation, self-assessment, self-enhancement, and so on (cf. Lynch, Norem-Hebeisen, & Gergen, 1981; Suls, 1982; Suls & Greenwald, 1983, 1986; Schlenker, 1985; Leahy, 1985; Yardley & Honess, 1987; Cheshire & Thomae, 1987; and see below). Nor is there any indication that the resurgence in such activity is abating. I personally find this new-found focus encouraging, especially to the extent that it allows the integration of a wide range of earlier work (cf. Cofer & Appley, 1964, on self). According to Markus and Wurf (1987):

> The unifying premise of the last decade's research on the self is that the self-concept does not just reflect ongoing behavior but instead mediates and regulates this behavior . . . ; is active, forceful, and capable of change . . . ; interprets and organizes self-relevant actions and experiences . . . ; has motivational consequences, providing incentives, standards, plans, rules, and scripts for behavior; and . . . adjusts in response to challenges from the social environment. (p. 299)

Singer and Kolligian (1987) likewise consider the self to be "a very rich structure," complexly linked to other affective and cognitive nodes in the personality, and even capable of functioning automatically or unconsciously. Anticipation is the key function of self-schemas, they suggest.

> A self-schema is a hierarchically organized body of knowledge or beliefs about one's intentions and capacities stored in long-term memory. . . . it provides selective criteria for regulating attention, to identify stimuli quickly, and to lend focus to the encoding, storage and retrieval of information . . . as well as plans for interpreting and gathering schema-relevant information about the self. (pp. 555, 557)

These two sets of observations appear to reverse Wylie's earlier conclusion, following her reviews of the literature, that the self-concept "could not be powerfully implicated in directing behavior" (1979, p. 300), and to encourage further inquiry into the functioning of the self-concept.

Magnusson (1976) had also earlier emphasized a mediating role for the self-concept ("the individual's self-perception and self-preoccupation") in selecting and interpreting situational information. (See Epstein, 1973, and Sarason, 1975, for other earlier emphases on self.)

Singer and Kolligian (1987) see roots for the concept of schemas, which they consider the most generic of all cognitive structures, in the work of Piaget, Lewin, Tolman, and Kelly, as well as in the psychoanalytic concept of the unconscious. (See also Cofer & Appley, 1964, on the development and function of Sullivan's [1947] self-dynamism.)

In their excellent review, Markus and Wurf (1987) likewise trace the development of the concept of self. They see it as having changed from what they call "an apparently singular, static, lump-like entity . . . [to a] multidimensional, multifaceted dynamic interpretive structure" mediating such significant *intra*personal processes as information processing, affect and motivation, and such *inter*personal processes as social perception and interaction strategies and reactions to feedback. They conclude that these processes are all in the service of such self-serving motives as self-enhancement, self-consistency maintenance, and self-actualization and are subject to influence by the contexts of particular social settings. "Whether . . . defined . . . in terms of hierarchies, prototypes, networks, spaces, or schemas, the self-concept is implicated in all aspects of social information processing" (p. 301).

Citing Cantor and Kihlstrom's (1986) proposal of a "life task" conception to tie motivation (self-regulation) to self-knowledge (structuring/organizing) strategies for accomplishing life tasks, Markus and Wurf (1987) see the role of self extended longitudinally. Singer and Kolligian (1987) similarly see a long-term mechanism provided by what they call "life-span schemas [including] powerful, emotion-laden scripts originating in childhood [and] magnified throughout adult life" (p. 560; also see Buhler, 1968).

Consistent with these positions is Brehm and Self's (1989) observation, in reviewing recent studies on the intensity of emotion, that the self percept mediates the mobilization of effort for tasks of differing difficulty. They report that "anticipatory motivational arousal" increases proportionate to task difficulty and drops off when effort is not warranted or when requisite skill is surpassed (p. 114). Further, "subjects with high self-perceived ability or esteem mobilize more energy for a difficult than for an easy task . . . those with low self-perceived ability . . . mobilize energy for the easy task, which they see as difficult, and not for the difficult task, which they see as impossible" (p. 121).

In another context, Markus (Markus & Nurius, 1987) defines her position as being a "cognitive approach to the self," because of its focus on the self-knowledge associated with one's "goals, fears and threats." Markus and Nurius (1987) write:

> In this approach the self-concept is not a unitary or monolithic entity but rather a system of salient identities or self-schemas . . . that lend structure and meaning to one's self-relevant experiences. These . . . generalizations about the self derive from past experience [and] help one to integrate and explain one's own behavior. . . . Self-schemas are our unique and fundamental self-defining elements. They reflect personal concerns of enduring salience and investment, and . . . have a systematic and pervasive influence on how information about the self is processed. (pp. 158–159)

They suggest a conceptual linkage between the self-concept and motivation by proposing that individuals generate "possible selves"—aspects of the self-schema that represent what they could or would like to become or what they fear they may become—and then strive to attain or avoid desired or feared outcomes. It is only through such future representations that self-schemas can guide or direct behavior, though they alternatively may constrain individuals or make them vulnerable, as when a desired self is not attainable. Markus and Wurf (1987) suggest that possible selves "function to individualize global motives (and thus can be viewed as the cognitive component of motivation). . . . [They] have been shown to regulate effort and task persistence (Ruvolo & Markus, 1986), and to be related to coping outcomes (Porter, Markus, & Nurius, 1984)" (p. 321; but see Honess & Yardley, 1987, comments below).

Similar to this notion of possible selves is Schlenker's (1985) concept of desired self-images. Wicklund and Gollwitzer's (1982) symbolic self-completion theory serves similar functions, if only indirectly or symbolically.

Singer and Kolligian (1987) assign this individualization function to "individuals' conscious beliefs and expectations" (p. 538), from which predictions of behavior in specific settings can be made (cf. Fishbein & Ajzen, 1975; Kreitler & Kreitler, 1982; McGuire, 1984). They further cite Carver, Antonini, and Scheier (1985) to suggest a moderator role for private self-consciousness in determining "people's tendencies to filter out and to avoid [negative, self-threatening] information," and Franzoi (1983), who showed a defensive inverse relationship between private self-consciousness and strength of self-concept.

We may note, even in this small sampling of a large literature, a fairly strong identification of the self in terms of cognitive variables. Unfortunately, in my view, giving such primacy to cognitive components leads to ignoring a whole range of other factors that may be of equal or greater significance (cf. Appley, 1962b; Cofer & Appley, 1964; Scheuch, 1986).

My concern for the arbitrary limitations on structure of mental processes that is thus self-imposed by those who choose explicitly to identify their approaches as "cognitive" apparently is shared by Honess and Yardley (1987), who, as editors of the volume containing Markus and Nurius's 1987 paper, comment that Markus and Nurius's "broad cognitive perspective" leads them to be "only concerned with information about self that is available to consciousness or working memory" (p. 151). Honess and Yardley suggest (and I emphatically agree) that this will prove too limiting, since it gives no attention to such phenomena as unconscious desires, self-deception, or the kind of "self-knowledge" that derives from doing, even without willful control (cf. Hamlyn, 1977; also Korchin, 1967; Laux, 1986).

Sherman, Judd, and Park (1989), reviewing even more recent work (under the title "social cognition"), agree with Markus and Wurf (1987) that "the self is best conceived as having a hierarchical and multifaceted structure." Citing Kihlstrom and Cantor (1984), Kihlstrom et al. (1988), Lecky (1945), and Markus and Sentis (1982), they observe that "despite the stability and consistency of the various aspects of the self, their relative accessibility may be variable (Natale & Hantas, 1982; Jones, Rhodewalt, Berglas, & Skelton, 1981)." In consequence, they conclude: "An individual's self-evaluation may depend [in part, at least] upon which self-aspect one is accessing at the time of judgment" (p. 309).

They further note that the content, structure, and focus of the self-concept develop, as does cognition generally, over the life span "from behavioral characteristics, to trait-like constructs, to more abstract, psychological constructs . . . [Harter, 1986; Rosenberg, 1986]" (p. 310). (And see earlier discussion of Singer and Kolligian's and Magnusson's views on life-span development, as well as Buhler, 1966, 1968, and Kreitler & Kreitler, 1987, below.)

Once again it strikes me that the cognitive brush paints a broader stroke than is warranted. *Including* cognition in the "hierarchical and multifaceted structure" would be more reasonable, it seems to me, than preempting the entire structure in the name of cognition.

McReynolds (1987), writing on the nature of self, draws a distinction between the executive self and the perceived self, noting: "The perceived self—which includes the notion of what one is and what one is capable of—is subject to ongoing, relatively constant examination and evaluation by the executive self. . . . [Self-esteem is] not merely a cognitive variable; rather, it is primarily a motivational variable, in the sense that persons constantly strive to maintain and increase their positive self evaluation" (p. 199). It is the decision making *executive* self (the "I") that, in evaluating the *perceived* self (the "me") as adequate or not, is capable of experiencing anxiety, guilt, or stress, according to McReynolds. He points out that much of the research and theory on the self "has traditionally concentrated on the perceived self (Kelly, 1955; Lecky, 1945; Mead, 1934; Rogers, 1959; Sullivan, 1953) . . . focused on the theme of consistency or disparities among different elements, or aspects of the self . . . and how it develops and changes (Allport, 1961; Kagan, Hans, Markowitz, Lopez, & Sigal, 1982; Feshbach & Weiner, 1982)" (p. 200).

In contrast, McReynolds (1987) points to the work of Miller et al. (1960), Rotter (1966), Levenson (1981), DeCharms (1968), Perlmuter and Monty (1979), Christensen (1981), and Burger (1985), among others, on planning and various aspects of control, as related to the executive self and its efforts to maintain internal consistency and positive self-esteem. But, he argues, the usual assumption that such incompatibilities are cognitive in nature "is actually unduly restrictive, since many of the mental disparities that people experience in everyday life turn out . . . not to be strictly cognitive" (p. 202).

McReynolds sees "achievement motivation, depression, [and] learned helplessness" as possibly derivative of efforts to maintain positive self-esteem (which he considers a fundamental, irreducible human motive) and to reduce dissonance, incongruity, incompatibilities, and internal inconsistencies in personality functioning, "including cognitive, affective and conative elements" (p. 202).

Here again we see an attempt to set priorities for variables. Cognitive elements are one among equals, so to speak; planning and control (not necessarily conscious) are equilibratory functions assigned to one aspect of self (the "I") that struggles to maintain internal consistency and positive self-esteem (in the "me"). Such positive as well as aversive (anxiety, guilt, stress) variables play roles in the search for balance in the face of change.

In contrast to McReynolds and to our own views, Kreitler and Kreitler (1987) narrow the focus in describing the "psychosemantic aspects of the self." They agree that the self is a complex, multi-dimensional structure (of many selves) (cf. Anderson, 1981; Epstein, 1973; McGuire & McGuire, 1981; Lewis & Brooks-Gunn, 1981; Harter, 1985; Glick & Zigler, 1985; Markus & Wurf, 1987), but they also believe that the consensus of investigators would be that the self is a "cognitive construct" or set of "cognitive generalizations" that guide processing and assimilation of beliefs, attitudes, and information about the self (cf. Markus, 1977; Cantor, Mischel, & Schwartz, 1982; Rosenberg, 1965; Fiske & Taylor, 1984; Epstein, 1983), and further, that it is "deeply enmeshed in the social sphere (Harré, 1983; Shane & Shane, 1980; Markus & Smith, 1981)" (p. 338).

Observing that practically all (95%) of self research has dealt with self-esteem, Kreitler and Kreitler (1987) examine differences in reported self-concepts across age groups. They find a number of rich and varied meanings applied to the self, which increase and vary with age. Thus, teenagers define self in terms of "actions the self does, emotions, size, weight and physical characteristics. . . . [For 20s to 60s:] actions the self does and actions done to or with the self . . . concern with style . . . emotions, possessions and . . . interpersonal relations. . . . [For ages 60+:] actions done to or with the person . . . health . . . group identity, development, and judgments and evaluations" (p. 351). Kreitler and Kreitler (1987) conclude that "the self may function as a basic matrix from which different samples may be drawn in line with specific contextual requirements. . . . Thus, the self can be assumed to be a unitary entity, though its particular manifestations may differ in different situations or roles, and a stable entity, though it may undergo developmental change" (p. 353). And finally, they believe that "content of the self [should be defined in terms of a] meaning system . . . rooted in cognitive theory . . . stable, independent of content . . . broad and reliable" (p. 354).

I would note here that Kreitler and Kreitler's use of the phrase "rooted in cognitive theory" does not follow from the analysis they provide in their paper. Nor would I leave unchallenged their arbitrary limitation on the self as "a cognitive construct or set of cognitive generalizations," although self certainly has been used that way. The restriction thus seems to me to be both superfluous and unwarranted, as I have perhaps already made clear.

Leventhal and Tomarken (1986), reviewing recent work on emotion, trace the development of sensorimotor, schematic, and conceptual mechanisms in emotional development. They show that the binding of the first two levels begins in the first days of life, *before* the development of complex verbal skills, leading them to question the reasonableness of representing "both schematic and verbal cognitive processes in a common conceptual network." The nonverbal schematic level, they also argue, "is crucial to the differentiation of self from other" (p. 600); and see Ulvund, 1980, discussed earlier).

Turner (1987), writing on "a sociological theory of motivation," notes, as have others already discussed, that "self-conceptions circumscribe . . . the construction of general orientations to situations. . . . one's self-conception sets into motion a derivative set of needs to maintain esteem of, and consistency among, the components of self-conception (Rosenberg, 1979)" (p. 19). He cites Anthony Giddens (1984), whose structural theory draws on the neo-Freudian psychoanalytic views of Erickson (1963) and Sullivan (1953). Giddens suggests that behavior is monitored at two levels of consciousness: *discursive*—"the capacity to give reasons for and to talk about what one does"—and *practical*—"the unarticulated stocks of implicit understandings about varying types of social situations," behind which are two unconscious drives: "to achieve a sense of trust with others . . . [and] for a kind of ultimate ontological security, where one feels that 'matters in the social world are as they appear to be'" (p. 20). Mediating such motive forces, according to Giddens, is anxiety, a result of unpredictability or failure of confirmation of expectations in social relations.

> Needs for symbolic and material gratification . . . revolve primarily around affirmations of self . . . and the potential anxiety associated with failure to achieve a sense of group inclusion. . . . That is, people seek to receive symbols and material props in their exchanges which confirm their self-conception and their membership in group activity. . . . Needs for the maintenance of self are the only motive state equally connected to all three unconscious needs for security, trust, and inclusion. (p. 24)

Here too there is a fundamental (equilibratory) motive of self-affirmation (in the context of social membership, as one might expect of a "sociological theory of motivation"), allowing for but not dominated by cognitive processes and having both positive (gratification) and negative (anxiety) components.

We see, then, in these recent treatments, a reasonable consensus on the nature of self as dynamic and active, developing out of the interactions with the environment and yet becoming an organizing "force" in itself. The consensus does *not* extend, as we have seen, to defining the self as cognitive.

SOME EFFECTS OF THREAT TO SELF: TASK PERFORMANCE

Kukla (1972) and Brehm, Wright, Solomon, Silka, and Greenberg (1983) have held that people reduce effort devoted to task accomplishment, regardless of the potential value of the outcome, if the task is perceived as very difficult or impossible. Pyszczynski and Greenberg (1983) interpret such a reduction in intended effort as an ego-defensive strategy to circumvent the perceived threat to self-esteem that might result from failure. They argue that "when the ego-threat implied by anticipated failure outweighs the value of the desired goal, reduction in intended effort, along with anticipatory defense strategies, become increasingly more likely to occur. However [they add] when the goal is very high in value, the comfort to self-esteem that such maneuvers provide may be foregone so as to enhance one's chances of attaining the goal" (p. 420). And, they conclude, "ego-defensive concerns" may play a larger role in motivation than previously thought. (See also Brehm & Self, 1989, discussed above.) I agree to the importance of such factors, a theme that I have emphasized before (cf. Appley, 1962a, 1962b, 1967) and will discuss again below in relation to psychological stress.

SOME EFFECTS OF THREAT TO SELF: RESPONSE TO OTHERS

Miller and Turnbull (1986), accepting that the self-concept is an important determinant of a person's behavior (Bem, 1972; Felson, 1984), report further that individuals' confidence in themselves (their self-concepts) influences their reactions to others' beliefs about them. Those who are relatively certain about their self-concepts accept congruent but resist incongruent conceptions of themselves from perceivers who are uncertain. However, according to Miller and Turnbull (1986): "Perceivers only induced [individuals] . . . to accept incongruent conceptions of themselves when the perceivers were certain of their conceptions and . . . [the individuals] were uncertain of theirs" (p. 242).

Pointing out that one's own actions are important to self-concept formation (Bem, 1972), Miller and Turnbull further cite Darley and

Fazio's (1980) findings that an individual may not only "behave consistently with [an erroneous] expectancy, but . . . conclude on the basis of this behavior that he or she is actually that type of person" (p. 249). Oatley and Johnson-Laird (1987) draw a similar conclusion, namely that "the content of the model of self includes an abstraction of what we have experienced in others' reactions to us" (p. 42).

Glaser (1982), emphasizing cognitive factors in a "symbolic interactionist social model of man," calls for consideration of the "meaning of the presence of others," proposing that the self "is created out of the 'reflected appraisals' of others." Thus, if the inferred information about the self is perceived as "subjectively negatively incongruent with the self," it will be a threat to the self and produce anxiety that will in turn "affect behavior and performance in two ways—directly, through the Yerkes-Dodson inverted-U relationship between anxiety and performance, and indirectly, through behaviors and cognitive processes . . . intended to enable the anxiety to be avoided, reduced, or escaped" (p. 276).

For Glaser, who emphasizes subjective meanings of others, tasks, and situations, cognition has mediating effects that extend and clarify the role of motivation. By contrast, Sanders (1981) argues that "the mere presence of others . . . creates a response conflict between ongoing task requirements and a tendency to attend to others" (p. 233), which "enhances dominant responses . . . independent of any informational or interactional influences the other may exert" (p. 227).

The issue of certainty of beliefs about self appears to be an important one, as we have already seen (cf. discussions of Kagan and of Miller & Turnbull, above). Conolley, Gerard, and Kline (1978) suggest that, in social comparison situations, a person may seek both self-appraisal information and (selectively) that which yields or supports positive self-appraisal. Under conditions of high uncertainty, however, they point out, there is an increase in motivation for self-protection against "ego-threat" over self-appraisal.

Stress

Twice so far I have commented on "explosions" of literature—concerning the "cognitive revolution" and the rekindled interest in the self-concept. But neither area has come close to producing the extraordinary (and seemingly continuing) outpouring of books, papers, and symposia, both scientific and popular, that followed Hans Selye's introduction of and extensive writing on systemic stress (1936 to 1983), and its extension into psychology, in part as a consequence of Selye's invited address to the American Psychological Association in Chicago in 1955 (cf. Selye, 1956; Appley & Moeller, 1957; Appley, 1962b; Cofer & Appley, 1964; Appley & Trumbull, 1967a, 1967b, 1986a, 1986b).

Stress obviously is too broad and important a topic[7] to be dealt with here in anything approaching a comprehensive manner. Nor would it be appropriate to do so. However, there are several aspects of the concept of stress—and more specifically of psychological stress—that I should like to address briefly. The first is the notion of stress as an extension of the homeostasis/equilibration concept; second, the relation among self, equilibration, and stress; and third, the relation between motivation and psychological stress. But let us first look briefly at some background.

SYSTEMIC STRESS

Selye,[8] who discovered the systemic stress syndrome in the mid-1930s, was very much in the equilibration tradition. He frequently and proudly identified his work as in a direct line of descent from that of Claude Bernard (1859) on the constancy of the *milieu intérieur* and of Walter Cannon (1932) on homeostasis.[9]

Selye observed that, in addition to the unique and specific responses of the body's various adaptive equilibratory systems to changes in particular kinds of stimulation (e.g., vasodilation to heat, vasoconstriction to cold), there was also, under excessive or continuing stimulation, a common *non*specific reaction to *any* demand placed upon the organism. This nonspecific, stereotyped response syndrome was what he called stress (cf. Selye, 1950, 1956, 1974).

Like Cannon before him, Selye saw low-level, modest, or short-term stressors as able to be resisted, whereas prolonged, repeated, or severe challenges from the environment would overwhelm the individual's defenses (cf. Cofer & Appley, 1964, chap. 9; Hobfoll, 1989). He described the stereotypic systemic stress response as a general adaptation syndrome, consisting of orchestrated organ and system responses in a sequence involving alarm, resistance, and exhaustion phases. Adaptive responding could foreshorten the sequence; failure to adapt would lead to exhaustion and death (Selye, 1974; and see Cofer & Appley, 1964; Appley & Trumbull, 1967a, for more complete definitions, descriptions and discussions of nuances and limitations of Selye's and others' stress concepts).

Also like Cannon (in his epilogue to *The Wisdom of the Body,* 1932), with similar enthusiasm but similarly limited justification in the way of direct observations or data, Selye extended his concept beyond the physiological systems he studied carefully to generalize about behavior. Much of the criticism directed at both investigators derives from this attempt to extend their work beyond the level at which their observations were made. This should not obscure the value to us of their basic ideas, however, even if it is left to others to spell out the differences necessary when applications are made to psychological and psychosocial levels (cf. Cofer & Appley, 1964, chap. 7; Lazarus, 1966; Appley & Trumbull, 1967a; McGrath, 1970; Selye, 1980, 1983; Lazarus & Folkman, 1984; Burchfield, 1985)

Hobfoll (1989) writes of the "Cannon-Selye tradition," in which both researchers emphasized *"stress as response,"* and notes widespread criticism of Selye's insistence on the uniformity of reactions in stress and of his circular use of outcome measures to define stress situations (cf. Appley & Trumbull, 1967a, 1986a; Lazarus & Folkman, 1984). Although conceivably appropriate at the physiological level, it is suggested that such a limited view ignores the varieties of behavioral responses possible in stress situations and further "precludes the possibility of prospectively identifying the cause[s] of stress" (Hobfoll, 1989, p. 514).

PSYCHOLOGICAL STRESS AND EQUILIBRATION

Like the systemic stress concept from which it derives, psychological stress is most often defined in terms of some form of equilibration model. I have elsewhere (Appley, 1962b; Cofer & Appley, 1964; Appley & Trumbull, 1967a) discussed stimulus, response, and interactive definitions of stress and their limitations (see also Hobfoll, 1989) and will not review such alternatives here. One element of my own and others'

definitions needs mention, however, and that is the mediating role assigned to perception (or cognition) in determining (or appraising) both
what is or is not threatening or stressful and what resources are needed
and available to cope with the perceived threat (cf. Cofer & Appley,
1964; Lazarus, 1966, 1967; Appley, 1967; Appley & Trumbull, 1967a;
McGrath, 1970; Trumbull & Appley, 1986; Hobfoll, 1989).

As Hobfoll (1989) has correctly pointed out, this dual assign-
ment provides no independent anchoring point and thus leads to a
circularity of reasoning. He writes that "an understanding of how
people who possess varying coping resources respond to a known
threat, including the degree to which they find the stimulus threatening, could help anchor the perceptive component, because the
stimulus is a known entity. However, if both the demand *and* the resources mobilized to combat that demand exist *only in the perceptual
world*, no such anchor point exists" (p. 515, italics added). Trumbull
and I (Trumbull & Appley, 1986) have proposed that the balance between demand and coping capacity can be upset when *either* real or
perceived demands outstrip the real or perceived carrying capacity
available (p. 34). By contrast, Lazarus and Folkman's (1984) "cognitive, relational conceptualization of stress" (p. 64) *requires* the kind of
perceptual mediation that Hobfoll has argued leads to circular reasoning. While neither position fully clears this hurdle, according to
Hobfoll (1989, p. 516), I believe the one that Trumbull and I have
taken begins to address the dynamics of the stress process more
fully by taking into account real as well as perceived demands and
capacities. Our proposed model also emphasizes the interactions of
physiological, psychological, and social processes and the changes
to be expected in these processes and in their interrelation *over time*.
(Hobfoll, 1989, addresses the same problems in terms of a resource
conservation model, which I believe is not dissimilar to the one
Trumbull and I proposed.)

In a symposium commentary on a paper by Lazarus (1967), I
proposed (Appley, 1967) that the appraisal presumably invoked in
potentially stressful situations is, in fact, ongoing—part of what
Arnold (1967) has called "a continuous unconscious appraisal" process (not unlike the TOTE processes of Miller et al. (1960) or equivalent evaluational procedures detailed by Carver and Scheier 1981; cf.
"Discrepancy Monitoring and Self-Regulation," above). The key
point I made then and would emphasize again is that the appraisal

process—which Lazarus at that time, as well as Arnold, conceded need not be conscious—needs to be *multidimensional*, to permit simultaneous (and continuous) appraisal of both task requirements (demands) and carrying capacity, in relation not only to the task at hand but to other aspects of the (internal and external) environment, to the anticipated and actual consequences of alternative coping responses, and to the kinds of environmental constraints or sanctions that are present or likely to be invoked by particular responses on the part of the individual. What I was trying to convey was the *complexity* of the dilemma induced by stressful situations, where responses may be required that exceed available (or potentially available) capacities or resources (cf. Appley, 1967; Appley & Trumbull, 1967a; Trumbull & Appley, 1967, 1986; Hobfoll, 1989).

I have spoken to the interaction of task difficulty and capacity earlier (see "Task Performance," above), and here I would merely reiterate the importance of capacity, as it varies over time and with context, as a critical determiner of the stressfulness of particular events. A number of individuals have attempted to address aspects of this issue in slightly differing ways. Among these, Dienstbier (1989) has described a "toughness" factor and Kobasa (1979) a personality "hardiness" factor; Hobfoll (1989) has written of resources, and Trumbull and Appley (1986) of latent factors and their interactions over time affecting carrying capacity.

Despite Hobfoll's reluctance to accept such a balance model, which he claims is "tautological, overly complex, and not given to rejection" (1989, p. 515), he nevertheless cites a number of recent studies (Cohen, Kamarck, & Mermelstein, 1983; Gentry & Kobasa, 1984; Kendall, 1983; Wilcox & Vernberg, 1985) to affirm that "the most commonly adopted model of stress employed by stress investigators today is a homeostatic model . . . [with stress] defined . . . as a 'substantial *imbalance* between environmental demand and . . . response capability' (McGrath, 1970, p. 17)" (Hobfoll, 1989, p. 515).

It must by now be evident that I share Hobfoll's conclusion but not his reservations. My reading of the stress literature—and my rejection of dependence on perceptual mediation—allows me to continue strongly to support this "most commonly adopted [equilibratory] model of stress."

Self, Equilibration, and Stress

I spoke earlier of the resurgent interest in the self-concept and its many ramifications. Yet Raynor and McFarlin (1986) have recently cautioned that "in spite of [a] large research literature and variety of theories, understanding of the self and its motivational implications for behavior is far from complete. On the other hand [they add], many theories of motivation have failed to systematically consider the role of self-system functioning as a determinant of action (Raynor, 1982)" (p. 315). A major problem with much of the research, they point out (and I agree), is its one-sided (cognitive *or* affective) orientation, and they urge serious attention to *both* as well as to "both personal and situational determinants of value in trying to understand functioning in the behavioral [and self] system[s]" (p. 344). The more limited perspectives, they correctly feel, "stand in the way of building an integrative theory of personality, motivation, and self-system functioning that is empirically based and subject to continuing refinement in light of subsequent research" (p. 344).

Cantor, Markus, Niedenthal, and Nurius (1986), going one step further along the lines I have been urging, suggest that "motivation cannot be fully understood without reference to the self-concept. . . . Self-knowledge . . . provides a sense of individual identity and continuity . . . [but] also [is] a significant *regulator* of ongoing behavior . . . [providing] a set of interpretive frameworks for making sense of past behavior [and] also . . . the means-end patterns for new behavior" (p. 97). These authors, writing from a cognitive viewpoint, place what I would consider undue emphasis on conscious planning and the use of strategies (see criticism by Raynor and McFarlin, above). Nevertheless, their reiteration of the importance of the link between motivation and self, and their emphasis on the regulating role of self, is part of a trend that is becoming increasingly popular (again).

Cantril (1967), in an earlier article emphasizing feelings as "the great activating force" ("sentio ergo sum"), rejected what appears to be a static and limited model of homeostasis as "clearly . . . inadequate . . . to account for the essential restlessness characteristic of human behavior" (p. 106). He preferred instead to see motivation as deriving from concepts of *self* and *self-consistency*, a position I find entirely compatible with an equilibratory model—more so when, at the same time, Cantril posits a vertically organized nervous system containing "the same basic built-in neurophysiological appetitive system the baby uses . . . [but evolving] in the human endeavor of becoming." "In the normal course of development [he explains], the Self is expanded as we become 'ego-involved' with more and more situations, individuals, groups, or ideologies which both broaden and solidify our sense of self and self-consistency and thereby enhance our basic feeling of satisfaction" (p. 103).

He concludes (in concept if not language surprisingly similar to Ashby's [1960] description of the *homeostat*), by positing "a Self striving to maintain its identity by changing itself in the ceaseless effort to enhance the quality, the adequacy, the range, and the validity of its own world" (p. 106). And Loevinger (1976), in her conceptualization of ego development, similarly characterizes it as an evolving process of integration of experience into a comprehensive self.

It will be evident from my earlier discussions that these uses of self are consistent with the more dynamic concepts of equilibratory (homeostatic) theory I have described and, in fact, would be a description of what has been referred to as "the notion of self as superordinate, integrating equilibratory fulcrum" (see above).

Such a view is not new but goes back a number of years. Epstein (1982) notes, for example, that Jung (1953) "introduced the concept of *self* [to] represent a high level of integration of differentiated personality structures . . . [and that] Adler (1954), following a different path, arrived at a similar conclusion" (p. 50). He further also identifies Lecky's (1945) theory of self-consistency (as I have noted; and see Cofer & Appley, 1964, p. 321) as the first of several self theories to assume that maintenance of "a coherent conceptual system is the most important motive in human behavior" (p. 63). Epstein writes: "Lecky believed that two major sources of stress producing incompatibilities are inconsistencies within the self-system and inconsistencies between the self-system and reality" (pp. 50–51). And supporting his concordance with Lecky's views, Epstein (1982) cites Pavlov's (1927) creation of experimental neuroses in dogs (by presenting them with increasingly difficult discrimination tasks—circle vs. ellipse) and similar studies in sheep (Gantt, 1944) and rats (Maier, 1949), to show that individuals (animals in these cases) that are unable to maintain unified conceptual systems cannot anticipate or cope with events (p. 62).

Decisions or response choices are usually made at levels below the "superordinate level of self." But in many difficult choice or conflict situations or in the case of sustained stimulation, lower-level adaptive responding is either not possible or not successful, and as has been suggested, the ego or self then becomes involved. Let us examine this concept briefly.

EGO INVOLVEMENT

There are many senses in which the term ego involvement can be used. Breckler and Greenwald (1986) offer three categories of ego or self concern: about one's public impression or evaluation by others (evaluation apprehension [Rosenberg, 1969] or approval motivation [Crowne & Marlow, 1964]); about one's private self-image, self-evaluation, self-esteem maintenance, or achievement motivation (comparing task performance with a personal standard of achievement [Atkinson, 1964]); and about one's role with respect to others (reference groups, both real and aspired [Sherif & Cantril, 1947, p. 96]).

In each of these areas of concern, according to Breckler and Greenwald, appropriate "ego tasks" can be performed to attain or restore one's "self-worth." But in addition to differentiating types of activity in relation to source or nature of threat (see "Motivation, Vulnerability, and Stress," below), it is important to distinguish between the mere invoking of more effortful task-related responses—as is done with "ego-involving instructions" such as identifying a task to be performed as an IQ test—and those situations that are truly *ego threatening*, that is, potentially destructive of life, identity, or integrity. It is only the latter category that is truly "ego involving," in my view, and we should probably use a new term, such as "ego or self-concept threatening" (which may have less surplus meaning) to designate threats of this magnitude.

My reason for insisting on this distinction (though it likely is a continuum) is to suggest that stress is invoked only in the latter situation (or the latter end of the continuum) and ordinarily not in the former. Thus, only when disequilibration or threatened disequilibration is at—or escalates to—the level of the self system and where there is difficulty, or anticipated difficulty, in restoring balance (at the self level) could we foresee the development of full-blown stress responses.

This differentiation of degree of involvement is the one I previously made between task and ego orientations (Appley, 1962a, 1962b, 1967; Cofer & Appley, 1964, chap. 9). What I proposed is actually a series of thresholds invoked sequentially by the failure or anticipated failure of coping responses at lower levels. Initially, a need, a desire, or an aversive condition would invoke use of available (innate or acquired) coping responses. Should these fail to satisfy the desire or remove the aversive condition, an *instigation threshold* would be reached, and new (or less used) responses engaged or acquired. (This is the stage of exploration, in which new learning is established or new habits formed.) If, in turn, such new responses are interfered with, are successively unsuccessful (or anticipated to be so), or induce a motive conflict, disequilibrium will persist or increase, and a higher *frustration threshold* will be reached, accompanied by such consequences as *threat perception, anxiety,* and the intrusion of *anxiety-related responses.*

> These in turn may lead to further intensification of response, introduction of competing responses, or to escape responses, or all three, depending on the nature of the situation and of the responses innately or previously attached to anxiety. . . . it is at this threshold that a shift in pattern of response occurs, from exclusively task-oriented, problem-solving behavior to the inclusion of ego-oriented, self- or integrity-sustaining behavior.
>
> It is . . . only *if and when* both [task- and ego-oriented] behaviors have persisted for a while without any effective change in the situation that a third, or *stress threshold,* is reached. At this point we may observe the dropping out of all task-oriented behaviors and the exclusive preoccupation . . . with ego protection. (Cofer & Appley, 1964, p. 452)

Failing restabilization at the self level, a final *exhaustion threshold* is reached, in which ego-defensive behaviors give way to either inactivity or disordered behavior (depending on predilection).

Laux (1986) sees a parallel to this "stress ladder" conceptualization in the ordered use of self-protecting strategies described by Schlenker and Leary (1982), in which individuals faced with damage or potential damage to their self-esteem will employ self-serving explanations (rationalizations) "to maintain images that are central to their self-esteem" (Laux, 1986, p. 239). When these are not viable in the face of a continuing threat to identity, and "when attractive alternative [self-serving] explanations are not available," self-handicapping strategies may be employed. Whereas such defenses are adaptive in "milder forms," Laux makes it clear that, like our stress threshold level responses, "the more extreme forms of self-handicapping must be regarded as ineffective and even pathological coping strategies (Snyder & Smith, 1982)" (Laux, 1986, p. 238).

Support of another kind can be drawn from studies in which shifts are reported from task- to ego-oriented behaviors. Thus Compas, Malcarne, and Fondacaro (1988), differentiating problem- and emotion-focused coping in the face of major stressful events, found that emotional disturbance (in young adolescents) was related negatively to problem-focused coping and positively to emotion-focused coping, with the match between perceived controllability of events and coping strategies adopted being an important factor. Galassi, Frierson, and Sharer (1981), consistent with Lazarus and Folkman's (1984) view that problem-focused coping is more related to task demands than to person factors, found test anxiety related to off-task thoughts (and see Sarason, 1975, below). Mandler (1982) has likewise observed that "the tendency to engage in task-irrelevant behavior [in stressful situations] is well known" (p. 97).

A related finding is that of Pyszczynski and Greenberg (1983), noted earlier, who showed how level of ego involvement determined the amount of effort devoted to task performance as a self-protecting strategy. When the probability of success is low, they found, effort is reduced to protect self-esteem from the consequences of failure; this is not so when ego involvement is low or the chance of self-enhancement (through goal attainment) is very high.

And Janis (1982), describing decision making under stress conditions, draws similar conclusions. Thus, "A high-level of stress reduces the decisionmaker's problem-solving capabilities . . . attention and perceptions are somewhat impaired . . . narrowing the range of perceived alternatives, overlooking long-term consequences, inefficient searching for information, erroneous assessing of expected outcomes, and using oversimplified decision rules that fail to take account of the full range of values implicated by the choice" (p. 70). Further support for the "stress ladder" concept is given by Janis in his description of responses to extreme emergencies (Schultz, 1964), where the individual, in a panic or near panic, "searches frantically for a way out of the dilemma, rapidly shifts back and forth between alternatives and seizes upon a hastily contrived solution that seems to promise immediate relief" (p. 72). Such re-sponses are most likely to occur under time pressure (Janis & Mann, 1977), when "people are exposed to serious threats of physical injury or death . . . or expect to be helpless to avoid being victimized unless they act quickly" (p. 80). And again we can cite Sarason (1975), who found that "under appropriate [ego-involving] conditions the performance of highly test-anxious subjects deteriorates . . . [and they] become self-preoccupied, attending to internal events rather than the task at hand" (p. 32).

Finally, lest the case for *"self* as fulcrum" be accepted too easily, I note with interest Sarason's observation that *not all persons* in the circumstances he describes become self-preoccupied, and that some continue to remain task-oriented regardless of pressures on them. Sorrentino and Short (1986) make a similar point even more forcefully, distinguishing between certainty- and uncertainty-oriented individuals. *Only the latter,* they suggest, "seek clarity about the self and the environment . . . [The 'need to know' types, for whom] . . . self-assessment, social (and physical) comparison, dissonance reduction, causal searches and attributions, possible selves, self-concept discrepancy reduction, self-confrontation, balance, cognitive dissonance, social justice, and equity are . . . characteristic. . . . It may be [they conclude] that certainty-oriented people do not use the self to direct motivational functioning" (p. 398; see also earlier discussion of uncertainty as motive). I accept that such exceptions to a normal self-protecting response pattern under stress may exist, but I expect that if they do, then, like Asch's (1956) nonconformers and Maslow's (1955) self-actualizers, they would be extremely rare. In any case, the matter clearly warrants further careful study.

Motivation, Vulnerability, and Psychological Stress

We have noted elsewhere that "any analysis of a stress situation must begin with what the individual *brings to* the situation and not the demand characteristics of the situation alone. [We refer here to] *predisposition* . . . the state or degree of susceptibility (to a potential stressor) that exists in the individual at any given time as a function of prior determinants" (Appley & Trumbull, 1986b, p. 311; and see Trumbull & Appley, 1967, 1986). Such *carrying capacity* in the individual's physiological, psychological, and social systems will change over time and with experience to create different states of vulnerability or susceptibility to stressful situations at different times. Magnusson (1982) writes, for example:

> On the person side [excepting environmental extremes that overwhelm], the occurrence of stress is determined by the individual's *vulnerability*, defined in terms of physiological predispositions, and coping competence. . . . An individual's current vulnerability is the result of a process of maturation and learning within the limits of inherited potentialities. Vulnerability may be specific, i.e., restricted to certain kinds of stressful conditions (e.g., phobic situations) or general, i.e., referring to most environmental stressors. (p. 235)

And Dohrenwend and Dohrenwend (1981) proposed a "vulnerability hypothesis" with regard to illness consequent to stress induction; such illness, in their view, occurs only when vulnerability already exists. According to Rabkin (1982), such vulnerability may result from childhood experiences, family relations, or genetic predisposition and may be mediated by resource availability (e.g., "social support, fiscal backing, or personal coping skills") (p. 567).

Rabkin also describes an "interactive model," similar to the Dohrenwends' vulnerability hypothesis, in which individuals "because of pre-existing deficiencies in coping or interpersonal skills [may be] unable to forestall the occurrence of undesirable life events, or by their behavior, actively provoke them while at the same time [lacking] the ability to make good things happen" (p. 568).

These hypotheses, derived from the perspective of psychiatric illness and thus dealing only with negative outcomes, are nevertheless similar to the positions taken by Magnusson and to the description of stress in terms of discrepancy between demand and carrying capacity offered by Trumbull and Appley (1986).

Finally, I note as supportive of my position Magnusson's (1982) finding, in his study of activating conditions (in adolescents), that situations involving "self" develop greater importance than those involving any other activating variable.

MOTIVATION AND STRESS: STRESS AND MOTIVATION

Let me conclude with one final observation, about the reciprocal nature of the relationship between motivation and stress. Disequilibration serves as instigation to action—or as motivator of behavior, as I have tried to spell out. At the same time, the conditions that give rise to disequilibration are not independent of the pattern of the individual's motivational propensities at physiological, psychological, and social levels. These form an integral part of the carrying capacity of the individual; they contribute to—if not actually form—the self-concept, help define priorities, and determine the areas of individual vulnerability. Rather than there being such a thing as general stress tolerance, I believe that resistance or vulnerability to stress is highly individual and that a *vulnerability profile* could be drawn for each person, based jointly on the nature of the individual's motivational pattern and the relevance of the available resources [or carrying capacity] to the gratification of the person's motivational priorities. Such a profile would then provide a means to identify the *kinds* of threats that would be effective for that individual and, along with their thresholds, would determine response persistence and intensity (see above, and Appley & Trumbull, 1967, pp. 10–11; see also Appley & Moeller, 1957; Cofer & Appley, 1964).

I said earlier that movement "up the stress ladder"—from task orientation to ego-defensive orientation—occurs as threat increases and the self (status, identity, integrity, life) becomes vulnerable. This translates, for me, into an increasing engagement of more central or meaningful parts of the individual's motive structure. It then seems reasonable to suggest that an examination of the makeup of the self-concept might provide a logical place to start the search for motive patterns and ways resources are able to be identified as *matching*—and thus vulnerability reducing—or *not matching*—and thus endangering to the self. I believe that equilibratory control theory would be helpful in such an analysis.

NOTES

1. My literature survey is undoubtedly incomplete, biased, and to a large extent inconclusive. Nevertheless, it may force some questions that

have needed to be asked about the motivation field and its purported lack of unity, a claim that may not survive a careful look beneath the rhetoric.

2. Our nearly one-thousand page hardcover book, selling for the then large sum of $12.50 (on publication), was complimented by its *Contemporary Psychology* reviewer as "expensive, but worth every penny!" (Siegel, 1965).

3. This distinction between arousal and alertness appears to be very much like the one Cofer and I earlier sought to draw between arousal and invigoration, and seemingly for much the same reason—not to have to carry excess baggage along with a more precise concept (cf. Cofer & Appley, 1964, pp. 837–838).

4. In an analysis preceding the first edition of Cannon's *Wisdom of the Body* (1932), Rignano (1923) saw every organism as "a physiological system in a stationary condition [that] tends to preserve that condition or to restore it as soon as it is disturbed by any variation occurring within or outside the organism. This property [he wrote] constitutes the foundation and essence of all 'needs,' of all 'desires,' of all the most important appetites. All movements of approach or withdrawal, of attack or flight, of seizing or rejecting . . . are only so many direct or indirect consequences of this very general tendency of every stationary physiological condition to remain constant" (Rignano, cited by Horrocks & Jackson, 1972, p. 15).

5. Horrocks and Jackson (1972) likewise consider there to be a "confusing tendency to assign fundamental drive status to needs and ignore the fact that they are the products of structural function and of specific experiences and socialization" (p. 21; and see Rignano citation, note 3). In another context, Appley and Moeller (1957) earlier tried to address this issue by proposing a distinction between *motives* as energizing and *modes* (Stagner's *motives*?) as particular directional components of motivated behavior. The distinction was/is important, we felt, because a single mode of behavior (e.g., achieving) could serve more than one motive, and a particular motive can be served by more than one behavior mode. Cofer and Appley (1964) proposed limiting motivation to energization, with direction being assigned to nonmotivational factors. Failure to keep such distinctions in mind, it seems to me, continues to befuddle communication in the field.

6. Though the language here suggests cognitive processing, a restriction to forethoughtful responding need not be inferred. Thus, for example, "mindless" yet systematic movement of one's hand in search of a snack dish outside one's line of vision while one is watching television would follow a similar pattern.

7. In 1980 the library and documentation service at Selye's International Institute of Stress in Montreal reportedly held over 150,000 different stress-related items!

8. It was my privilege to spend six months of a National Science Foundation Science Faculty Fellowship at Selye's institute at the University of Montreal in 1959, and I can attest to his being both extraordinarily gifted and a driven man. He worked himself and his colleagues extremely hard in an attempt to explicate the nature of the stress syndrome, which he considered

one of the most important discoveries in medicine in this century.

9. During Selye's tenure as director of the Institut de Médecine et de Chirurgie expérimentales, Université de Montréal, the Institut's prestigious invited lecture series was named in honor of Claude Bernard.

REFERENCES

Adler, A. (1954). *Understanding human nature.* New York: Fawcett.
Allport, G. W. (1937). *Personality: A psychological interpretation.* New York: Holt.
Allport, G. W. (1953). The trend in motivation theory. *American Journal of Orthopsychiatry, 23,* 107–119.
Allport, G. W. (1961). *Pattern and growth in personality.* New York: Holt, Rinehart and Winston.
Anderson, L. W. (1981). An examination of the nature of change in academic self-concept. In M. D. Lynch, A. A. Norem-Hebeisen, & K. Gergen (Eds.), *Self-concept: Advances in theory and research* (pp. 273–282). Cambridge, MA: Ballinger.
Appley, M. H. (1962a). Motivation, threat perception, and the induction of psychological stress. *Proceedings of the Sixteenth International Congress Psychology, Bonn 1960* (pp. 880–881). Amsterdam: North-Holland.
Appley, M. H. (1962b, November). *Psychological stress.* Paper presented to Psychology Colloquium, University of Toronto.
Appley, M. H. (1967). Invited comment. In M. H. Appley & R. Trumbull (Eds.), *Psychological stress: Issues in research* (pp. 169–172). New York: Appleton-Century-Crofts.
Appley, M. H. (1970). Derived motives. *Annual Review of Psychology, 21,* 485–518.
Appley, M. H. (Ed.). (1971). *Adaptation-level theory: A symposium.* New York: Academic Press.
Appley, M. H. (1984). Motivation theory: Recent developments. In B. Wolman (Ed.), *International encyclopedia of psychiatry, psychology, psychoanalysis and neurology: Progress Volume* (Vol. 1, pp. 279–283). New York: Aesculapius.
Appley, M. H., & Moeller, G. (1957, January). *The role of motivation in psychological stress.* (Technical Report No. 3, Project NR 172–228, Contract Nonr. 996[02]). New London: Connecticut College.
Appley, M. H., & Trumbull, R. (1967a). On the concept of psychological stress. In M. H. Appley & R. Trumbull (Eds.), *Psychological stress: Issues in research* (pp. 1–13). New York: Appleton-Century-Crofts.
Appley, M. H., & Trumbull, R. (Eds.). (1967b). *Psychological stress: Issues in research.* New York: Appleton-Century-Crofts.
Appley, M. H., & Trumbull, R. (Eds.). (1986a). *Dynamics of stress: Physiological, psychological, and social perspectives.* New York: Plenum Press.

Appley, M. H., & Trumbull, R. (1986b). Dynamics of stress and its control. In M. H. Appley & R. Trumbull (Eds.), *Dynamics of stress: Physiological, psychological, and social perspectives* (pp. 309–327). New York: Plenum.

Arnold, M. B. (1967). Stress and emotion. In M. H. Appley & R. Trumbull (Eds.), *Psychological stress: Issues in research* (pp. 123–140). New York: Appleton-Century-Crofts.

Asch, S. E. (1956). Studies of independence and conformity: I. A minority of one against a unanimous majority. *Psychological Monographs 70* (Whole No. 416).

Ashby, W. R. (1956). Design for an intelligence-amplifier. In C. E. Shannon & J. McCarthy (Eds.), *Automata studies* (pp. 215–234). Princeton: Princeton University Press.

Ashby, W. R. (1960). *Design for a brain* (rev. ed.). New York: Wiley.

Atkinson, J. W. (1964). *Introduction to motivation*. New York: Van Nostrand.

Beach, F. A. (1956). Characteristics of masculine sex drive. In M. R. Jones (Ed.), *Nebraska symposium on motivation, 1956* (pp. 1–32). Lincoln: University of Nebraska Press.

Bem, D. J. (1972). Self-perception theory. In L. Berkowitz (Ed.), *Advances in experimental social psychology* (Vol. 6, pp. 1–62). New York: Academic Press.

Berlyne, D. E. (1975). Behaviourism? Cognitive theory? Humanistic psychology?—To Hull with them all. *Canadian Psychological Review, 16,* 69–80.

Bernard, C. (1859). Lecons sur les propriétés physiologiques et les alterations pathologiques des liquides de l'organisme (Vols. 1 and 2). Paris: Ballière.

Bindra, D. (1979). *Motivation, the brain, and psychological theory*. Unpublished manuscript, Psychology Department, McGill University, Montreal.

Blake, R. R. (1958). The other person in the situation. In R. Tagiuri & L. Petrullo (Eds.), *Person perception and interpersonal behavior* (pp. 229–242). Stanford: Stanford University Press.

Breckler, S. J., & Greenwald, A. G. (1986). Motivational facets of the self. In R. M. Sorrentino & E. T. Higgins (Eds.), *Handbook of motivation and cognition: Foundations of social behavior* (pp. 145–164). New York: Guilford Press.

Brehm, J. W. (1966). *A theory of psychological reactance*. New York: Academic Press.

Brehm, J. W., & Self, E. A. (1989). The intensity of motivation. *Annual Review of Psychology, 40,* 109–131.

Brehm, J. W., Wright, R. A., Solomon, S., Silka, L., & Greenberg, J. (1983). Perceived difficulty, energization, and the magnitude of goal valence. *Journal of Experimental Social Psychology, 19,* 21–48.

Buck, R. (1985). Prime theory: An integrated view of motivation and emotion. *Psychological Review, 92,* 389–413.

Buhler, C. (1966). The life cycle: Structural determinants of goal-setting. *Journal of Humanistic Psychology, 6,* 37–52.

Buhler, C. (1968). The course of human life as a psychological problem. *Human Development, 11,* 184–200.

Burchfield, S. R. (1985). *Stress: Psychological and physiological interactions.* New York: McGraw-Hill.

Burger, J. M. (1985). Desire for control and achievement-related behaviors. *Journal of Personality and Social Psychology, 48,* 1520–1533.

Campion, M. A., & Lord, R. G. (1982). A control systems conceptualization of the goal-setting and changing process. *Organizational Behavior and Human Performance, 30,* 265–287.

Cannon, W. B. (1932). *The wisdom of the body.* New York: W. W. Norton.

Cannon, W. B. (1939). *The wisdom of the body* (2nd ed.). New York: W. W. Norton.

Cannon, W. B. (1941). The body physiologic and the body politic. *Science, 93,* 1–10.

Cannon, W. B. (1945). *The ways of an investigator.* New York: W. W. Norton.

Cantor, N., & Kihlstrom, J. F. (1986). *Personality and social intelligence.* Englewood Cliffs, NJ.: Prentice-Hall.

Cantor, N., Markus, H., Niedenthal, P., & Nurius, P. (1986). On motivation and the self-concept. In R. M. Sorrentino & E. T. Higgins (Eds.), *Handbook of motivation and cognition: Foundations of social behavior* (pp. 96–121). New York: Guilford.

Cantor, N., Mischel, W., & Schwartz, J. C. (1982). A prototype analysis of psychological situations. *Cognitive Psychology, 14,* 45–77.

Cantril, H. (1967). Sentio ergo sum: "Motivation" reconsidered. *Journal of Psychology, 65,* 91 107.

Carson, R. C. (1989). Personality. *Annual Review of Psychology, 40,* 227–248.

Cartwright, D. (1959). Lewinian theory as a contemporary systematic framework. In S. Koch (Ed.), *Psychology: A study of a science* (Vol. 2, pp. 7–91). New York: McGraw-Hill.

Carver, C. S., Antonini, M., & Scheier, M. F. (1985). Self-consciousness and self-assessment. *Journal of Personality and Social Psychology, 48,* 117–124.

Carver, C. S., & Scheier, M. F. (1981). *Attention and self-regulation: A control-theory approach to human behavior.* New York: Springer-Verlag.

Chaiken, S., & Stangor, C. (1987). Attitudes and attitude change. *Annual Review of Psychology, 38,* 575–630.

Cheshire, N., & Thomae, H. (Eds.). (1987.) *Self, symptoms and psychotherapy.* New York: Wiley.

Child, C. M. (1924). *Physiological foundations of behavior.* New York: Holt.

Christensen, J. (1981). Assessment of stress: Environmental, intrapersonal, and outcome issues. In P. McReynolds (Ed.), *Advances in psychological assessment* (Vol. 5, pp. 62–123). San Francisco: Jossey-Bass.

Cofer, C. N. (1972). *Motivation and emotion.* Glenview, IL: Scott, Foresman.

Cofer, C. N. (1978, August). *Cognitive psychology and the problem of motivation: Implications for I/O psychology.* Invited address, Division of Industrial and Organizational Psychology, American Psychological Association, Toronto.

Cofer, C. N., & Appley, M. H. (1964). *Motivation: Theory and research.* New York: Wiley.

Cofer, C. N., & Appley, M. H. (1984). Motivation and personality. In N. Endler & J. McV. Hunt (Eds.), *Personality and the behavior disorders* (2d ed.) (pp. 413–438). New York: Wiley.

Cohen, S., Kamarck, T., & Mermelstein, R. (1983). A global measure of perceived stress. *Journal of Health and Social Behavior, 24*, 385–396.

Compas, B. E., Malcarne, V. L., & Fondacaro, K. M. (1988). Coping and stressful events in older children and young adolescents. *Journal of Consulting and Clinical Psychology, 56*, 405–411.

Conolley, E. S., Gerard, H. B., & Kline, T. (1978). Competitive behavior: A manifestation of motivation for ability comparisons. *Journal of Experimental Social Psychology, 14*, 123–131.

Cooper, J., & Croyle, R. T. (1984). Attitudes and attitude change. *Annual Review of Psychology, 35*, 395–426.

Crowne, D., & Marlowe, D. (1964). *The approval motive*. New York: Wiley.

D'Agostino, P. R., & Pittman, T. S. (1982). Effort expenditure following control deprivation. *Bulletin of the Psychonomic Society, 19*, 282–283.

D'Amato, M. R. (1974). Derived motives. *Annual Review of Psychology, 25*, 83–106.

Darley, J. M., & Fazio, R. H. (1980). Expectancy confirmation processes arising in the social interaction sequence. *American Psychologist, 35*, 867–881.

Davis, R. C. (1958). The domain of homeostasis. *Psychological Review, 65*, 8–13.

DeCharms, R. (1968). *Personal causation*. New York: Academic Press.

DeCharms, R. (1980). The origins of competence and achievement motivation in personal causation. In L. J. Fyans, Jr. (Ed.), *Achievement motivation: Recent trends in theory and research* (pp. 22–33). New York: Plenum.

Deci, E. L., & Ryan, R. M. (1985). *Intrinsic motivation and self-determination in human beings*. New York: Plenum.

Dember, W. N. (1974). Motivation and the cognitive revolution. *American Psychologist, 29*, 161–168.

Diener, C. I., & Dweck, C. S. (1978). An analysis of learned helplessness: Continuous changes in performance, strategy, and achievement cognitions following failure. *Journal of Personality and Social Psychology, 36*, 451–462.

Dienstbier, R. A. (1989). Arousal and physiological toughness: Implications for mental and physical health. *Psychological Review, 96*, 84–100.

Dohrenwend, B. S., & Dohrenwend, B. P. (1981). Life stress and illness: Formulation of the issues. In B. S. Dohrenwend & B. P. Dohrenwend (Eds.), *Stressful life events and their contexts* (pp. 1–27). New York: Prodist (Watson).

duPreez, P. (1977). Action and anticipation in Kelly's theory of personal constructs. *Journal of Behavioral Science, 2*, 211–216.

Emerson, A. E. (1954). Dynamic homeostasis: A unifying principle in organic, social and ethical evolution. *Scientific Monthly, 77*, 67–85.

Epstein, S. (1973). The self-concept revisited: Or, A theory of a theory. *American Psychologist, 28*, 404–416.

Epstein, S. (1982). Conflict and stress. In L. Goldberger & S. Breznitz (Eds.), *Handbook of stress: Theoretical and clinical aspects* (pp. 49–68). New York: Free Press.

Epstein, S. (1983). A research paradigm for the study of personality and emotions. In R. A. Dienstbier & M. M. Page (Eds.), *Nebraska symposium on motivation, 1982* (pp. 91–154). Lincoln: University of Nebraska Press.

Erickson, E. H. (1963). *Childhood and society* (rev. ed.). New York: W. W. Norton.

Felson, R. B. (1984). The effect of self-appraisals of ability on academic performance. *Journal of Personality and Social Psychology, 47*, 944–952.

Feshbach, S., & Weiner, B. (1982). *Personality*. Lexington, MA: D. C. Heath.

Festinger, L. (1957). *A theory of cognitive dissonance*. Evanston, IL: Row, Peterson.

Fishbein, M., & Ajzen, I. (1975). *Belief, attitude, intention, and behavior: An introduction to theory and research*. Reading, MA: Addison-Wesley.

Fiske, S. T., & Taylor, S. E. (1984). *Social cognition*. Reading, MA: Addison-Wesley.

Flavell, J. H. (1963). *The developmental psychology of Jean Piaget*. New York: Van Nostrand.

Fletcher, J. M. (1938). The wisdom of the mind. *Sigma Xi Quarterly, 26*, 6–16.

Fletcher, J. M. (1942). Homeostasis as an explanatory principle in psychology. *Psychological Review, 49*, 80–87.

Franzoi, S. L. (1983). Self-concept differences as a function of private self-consciousness and social anxiety. *Journal of Research in Personality, 17*, 275–287.

Freeman, G. L. (1948). *The energetics of human behavior*. Ithaca: Cornell University Press.

Freud, S. (1954). *Standard edition of the complete psychological works of Sigmund Freud*. (J. Strachey, Ed. 2nd Trans.) London: Hogarth.

Galassi, J. P., Frierson, H. T., & Sharer, R. (1981). Behavior of high, moderate, and low test anxious students during an actual test situation. *Journal of Consulting and Clinical Psychology, 49*, 51–62.

Gantt, W. H. (1944). *Experimental basis for neurotic behavior*. New York: Hoeber.

Gentry, W. D., & Kobasa, S. C. (1984). Social and psychological resources mediating stress-illness relationships in humans. In W. D. Gentry (Ed.), *Handbook of behavioral medicine* (pp. 87–113). New York: Guilford.

Giddens, A. (1984). *The constitution of society: Outline of the theory of stratification*. Berkeley: University of California Press.

Glaser, A. N. (1982). Drive theory of social facilitation: A critical reappraisal. *British Journal of Social Psychology, 21*, 265–282.

Glick, M., & Zigler, E. (1985). Self-image: A cognitive-developmental approach. In R. Leahy (Ed.), *The development of the self* (pp. 1–53). New York: Academic Press.

Goldstein, K. (1940). *Human nature in light of psychopathology*. Cambridge: Harvard University Press.

Grinker, R. R., & Spiegel, J. (1945). *Men under stress*. Philadelphia: Blakiston.

Hamlyn, D. (1977). Self knowledge. In T. Mischel (Ed.), *The self: Psychological and philosophical issues*. Totowa, NJ: Rowman & Littlefield.

Harré, R. (1983). *Personal being*. Oxford: Blackwell.

Harter, S. (1978). Effectance motivation reconsidered: Toward a developmental model. *Human Development, 21*, 34–64.

Harter, S. (1985). Competence as a dimension of self-evaluation: Toward a comprehensive model of self-worth. In R. Leahy (Ed.), *The development of the self* (Vol. 1, pp. 55–121). New York: Academic Press.

Harter, S. (1986). Processes underlying the construction, maintenance, and enhancement of the self-concept in children. In J. Suls & A. G. Greenwald (Eds.), *Psychological perspectives on the self* (Vol. 3, pp. 137–181). Hillsdale, NJ: Erlbaum.

Heider, F. (1946). Attitudes and cognitive organization. *Journal of Psychology, 21*, 107–112.

Heider, F. (1958). *The psychology of interpersonal relations*. New York: Wiley.

Helson, H. (1953). *Perception and personality: A critique of recent experimental literature*. (Randolph Field, Tex.: Proj. Rep. No. 1, Proj. 21-0202-0007, Air University, USAF, School of Aviation Medicine)

Helson, H. (1959). Adaptation-level theory. In S. Koch (Ed.), *Psychology: A study of a science* (Vol. 1, pp. 565–621). New York: McGraw-Hill.

Helson, H. (1964). *Adaptation-level theory: An experimental and systematic approach to behavior*. New York: Harper.

Helson, H. (1967). Some problems in motivation from the point of view of the theory of adaptation level. In D. Levine (Ed.), *Nebraska symposium on motivation, 1966* (pp. 138–182). Lincoln: University of Nebraska Press.

Helson, H. (1971). Adaptation-level theory: 1970 and after. In M. H. Appley (Ed.), *Adaptation-level theory: A symposium* (pp. 5–17). New York: Academic Press.

Henry, J. (1955). Homeostasis, society, and evolution: A critique. *Scientific Monthly, 81*, 300–309.

Higgins, E. T., Klein, R., & Strauman, T. (1985). Self-concept discrepancy theory: A psychological model for distinguishing among different aspects of depression and anxiety. *Social Cognition, 3*, 51–76.

Hobfoll, S. E. (1989). Conservation of resources: A new attempt to conceptualize stress. *American Psychologist, 44*, 513–524.

Honess, T., & Yardley, K. (1987). Cognitive, affective and contextual aspects of self: An introductory review. In K. Yardley & T. Honess (Eds.), *Self and identity: Psychosocial perspectives* (pp. 149–156). New York: Wiley.

Horrocks, J., & Jackson, D. W. (1972). *Self and role: A theory of self-process and role behavior*. Boston: Houghton Mifflin.

Hunt, J. McV. (1965). Intrinsic motivation and its role in psychological development. In D. Levine (Ed.), *Nebraska symposium on motivation, 1965* (pp. 189–282). Lincoln: University of Nebraska Press.

Hunt, J. McV. (1981). Experiential roots of intention, initiative, and trust. In H. I. Day (Ed.), *Advances in intrinsic motivation and aesthetics*. New York: Plenum.

Ilgen, D. R., & Klein, H. J. (1989). Organizational behavior. *Annual Review of Psychology, 40,* 327–351.

Izard, C. E. (1977). *Human emotions.* New York: Plenum.

Janis, I. L. (1959). Motivational factors in the resolution of decisional conflicts. In M. R. Jones (Ed.), *Nebraska symposium on motivation, 1959* (pp. 198–231). Lincoln: University of Nebraska Press.

Janis, I. L. (1982). Decisionmaking under stress. In L. Goldberger & S. Breznitz (Eds.), *Handbook of stress: Theoretical and clinical aspects* (pp. 69–87). New York: Free Press/Macmillan.

Janis, I. L., & Mann, L. (1977). *Decision making: A psychological analysis of conflict, choice, and commitment.* New York: Free Press.

Jones, E. E. (1985). Major developments in social psychology during the past five decades. In G. Lindsay & E. Aronson (Eds.), *The handbook of social psychology* (Vol. 1, pp. 47–108). New York: Random House.

Jones, E. E., & Davis, K. E. (1965). From acts to dispositions: The attribution process in person perception. In L. Berkowitz (Ed.), *Advances in experimental social psychology* (Vol. 2, pp. 220–266). New York: Academic Press.

Jones, E. E., Rhodewalt, F., Berglas, S., & Skelton, J. A. (1981). Effects of strategic self-presentation on subsequent self-esteem. *Journal of Personality and Social Psychology, 41,* 407–421.

Jones, R. A. (1977). *Self-fulfilling prophecies: Social, psychological and physiological effects of expectancies.* Hillsdale, NJ: Erlbaum.

Jung, C. G. (1953). The psychic nature of the alchemical work. In *Collected works* (Vol. 12) (H. Read, M. Fordham, & G. Adler, Eds.). Princeton: Princeton University Press.

Kagan, J. (1972). Motives and development. *Journal of Personality and Social Psychology, 22,* 51–66.

Kagan, J., Hans, J., Markowitz, A., Lopez, D., & Sigal, H. (1982). Validity of children's self-reports of psychological qualities. In B. Maher & W. Maher (Eds.), *Progress in experimental personality research* (Vol. 11, pp. 171–211). New York: Academic Press.

Kelly, G. A. (1955). *A theory of personality: The psychology of personal constructs.* New York: Norton.

Kendall, P. C. (1983). Stressful medical procedures: Cognitive-behavioral strategies for stress management and prevention. In D. Meichenbaum and M. E. Jaremko (Eds.), *Stress reduction and prevention* (pp. 159–190). New York: Plenum.

Kessen, W. (1971). Early cognitive development: Hot or cold? In T. Mischel (Ed.), *Cognitive development and epistemology* (pp. 287–309). New York: Academic Press.

Kihlstrom, J. F., & Cantor, N. (1984). Mental representations of the self. In L. Berkowitz (Ed.), *Advances in experimental social psychology* (Vol. 15, pp. 1–47). New York: Academic Press.

Kihlstrom, J. F., Cantor, N., Albright, J. M., Chew, B. R., Klein, S. B. & Niedenthal, P. M. (1988). Information processing and the study of the self. In

L. Berkowitz (Ed.), *Advances in experimental social psychology* (Vol. 21, pp. 145–178). New York: Academic Press.

Kobasa, S. C. (1979). Stressful life events, personality, and health: An inquiry into hardiness. *Journal of Personality and Social Psychology, 37*, 1–11.

Korchin, S. J. (1967). Discussion. In M. H. Appley & R. Trumbull (Eds.), *Psychological stress: Issues in research* (p. 311). New York: Appleton-Century-Crofts.

Kreitler, S., & Kreitler, H. (1982). The theory of cognitive orientation: Widening the scope of behavior prediction. In B. Maher & W. Maher (Eds.), *Progress in experimental personality research* (Vol. 11, pp. 101–169). New York: Academic Press.

Kreitler, S., & Kreitler, H. (1987). The psychosemantic aspects of the self. In T. Honess & K. Yardley (Eds.), *Self and identity: Perspectives across the life span* (pp. 338–358). London: Routledge & Kegan Paul.

Kuhl, J. (1986). Motivation and information processing: A new look at decision making, dynamic change, and action control. In R. M. Sorrentino & E. T. Higgins (Eds.), *Handbook of motivation and cognition: Foundations of social behavior* (pp. 404–434). New York: Guilford.

Kukla, A. (1972). Foundations of an attributional theory of performance. *Psychological Review, 79*, 454–470.

Lacey, J. I. (1967). Somatic response patterning and stress: Some revisions of activation theory. In M. H. Appley & R. Trumbull (Eds.), *Psychological stress: Issues in research* (pp. 14–37). New York: Appleton-Century-Crofts.

Lamont, D. J. (1983). A three-dimensional test for White's effectance motive. *Journal of Personality Assessment, 47*, 91–99.

Laux, L. (1986). A self-presentational view of coping and stress. In M. H. Appley & R. Trumbull (Eds.), *Dynamics of stress: Physiological, psychological, and social perspectives* (pp. 233–254). New York: Plenum.

Lazarus, R. S. (1966). *Psychological stress and the coping process.* New York: McGraw-Hill.

Lazarus, R. S. (1967). Cognitive and personality factors underlying threat and coping. In M. H. Appley & R. Trumbull (Eds.), *Psychological stress: Issues in research* (pp. 151–169). New York: Appleton-Century-Crofts.

Lazarus, R. S., & Folkman, S. (1984). *Stress, appraisal, and coping.* New York: Springer.

Leahy, R. L. (1985). The development of the self: Conclusions. In R. L. Leahy (Ed.), *The development of the self* (pp. 295–304). New York: Academic Press.

Lecky, P. (1945). *Self-consistency: A theory of personality.* New York: Island Press.

Levenson, H. (1981). Differentiation among internality, powerful others, and chance. In H. Lefcourt (Ed.), *Research with the locus of control concept* (pp. 15–63). New York: Academic Press.

Leventhal, H., & Tomarken, A. J. (1986). Emotion: Today's problems. *Annual Review of Psychology, 37*, 565–600.

Lewin, K. (1935). *A dynamic theory of personality: Selected papers* (Trans. D. K. Adams & K. E. Zener). New York: McGraw-Hill.

Lewin, K. (1936). *Principle of topological psychology*. New York: McGraw-Hill.

Lewin, K. (1938). *The conceptual representation and the measurement of psychological forces*. Durham, NC: Duke University Press.

Lewin, K. (1948). *Resolving social conflicts*. New York: Harper.

Lewin, K. (1951). *Field theory in social science*. New York: Harper.

Lewis, M., & Brooks-Gunn, J. (1981). The self as social knowledge. In M. D. Lynch, A. A. Norem-Hebeisen, & K. J. Gergen (Eds.), *Self-concept: Advances in theory and research* (pp. 101–118). Cambridge, MA: Ballinger.

Lindner, R. M. (1945). Psychopathic personality and the concept of homeostasis. *Journal of Clinical Psychopathology and Psychotherapy, 6,* 517–521.

Loevinger, J. (1976). *Ego development: Conceptions and theories*. San Francisco: Jossey-Bass.

Lord, R. G., & Hanges, F. J. (1987). A control system model of organizational motivation: Theoretical development and applied implications. *Behavioral Sciences, 32,* 161–178.

Lynch, M. D., Norem-Hebeisen, A. A., & Gergen, K. J. (Eds.). (1981). *Self-concept: Advances in theory and research*. Cambridge, MA: Ballinger.

Mace, C. A. (1953). Homeostasis, needs and values. *British Journal of Psychology, 44,* 200–210.

Magnusson, D. (1976). *Consistency and coherence in personality: A discussion of lawfulness at different levels*. (Reports from the Department of Psychology, University of Stockholm, no. 472.)

Magnusson, D. (1982). Situational determinants of stress: An interactional perspective. In L. Goldberger & S. Breznitz (Eds.), *Handbook of stress: Theoretical and clinical aspects* (pp. 231–253). New York: Free Press.

Maier, N. R. F. (1949). *Frustration: The study of behavior without a goal*. New York: McGraw-Hill.

Mandler, G. (1982). Stress and thought processes. In L. Goldberger & S. Breznitz (Eds.), *Handbook of stress: Theoretical and clinical aspects* (pp. 88–104). New York: Free Press.

March, J. G., & Simon, H. A. (1958). *Organizations*. New York: Wiley.

Markus, H. (1977). Self-schemata and processing information about the self. *Journal of Personality and Social Psychology, 35,* 63–78.

Markus, H., & Nurius, P. (1987). Possible selves: The interface between motivation and the self-concept. In K. Yardley & T. Honess (Eds.), *Self and identity: Psychosocial perspectives* (pp. 157–172). New York: Wiley.

Markus, H., & Sentis, K. (1982). The self in social information processing. In J. Suls (Ed.), *Psychological perspectives on the self* (Vol. 1, pp. 41–70). Hillsdale, NJ: Erlbaum.

Markus, H., & Smith, J. (1981). The influence of self-schemata on the perception of others. In N. Cantor & J. F. Kihlstrom (Eds.), *Personality, cognition, and social interaction* (pp. 233–262). Hillsdale, NJ: Erlbaum.

Markus, H., & Wurf, E. (1987). The dynamic self-concept: A social psychological perspective. *Annual Review of Psychology, 38,* 299–337.

Maslow, A. H. (1954). *Motivation and personality*. New York: Harper.

Maslow, A. H. (1955). Deficiency motivation and growth motivation. In M.

R. Jones (Ed.), *Nebraska symposium on motivation, 1955* (pp. 1–30). Lincoln: University of Nebraska Press.

McCall, R. B., & McGhee, P. E. (1977). The discrepancy hypothesis of attention and affect in infants. In I. C. Uzgiris & F. Weizmann (Eds.), *The structuring of experience* (pp. 179–210). New York: Plenum.

McCaul, K. D. (1983). Observer attributions of depressed students. *Personality and Social Psychology Bulletin, 9,* 74–82.

McGrath, J. E. (Ed.). (1970). *Social and psychological factors in stress.* New York: Holt, Rinehart & Winston.

McGuire, W. J. (1984). Search for the self: Going beyond self-esteem and the reactive self. In R. A. Zucker, J. Aranoff, & A. I. Rabin (Eds.), *Personality and the prediction of behavior* (pp. 73–120). New York: Academic Press.

McGuire, W. J., & McGuire, C. V. (1981). The spontaneous self-concept as affected by personal distinctiveness. In M. D. Lynch, A. A. Norem-Hebeisen, & K. Gergen (Eds.), *Self-concept: Advances in theory and research* (pp. 147–171). Cambridge, MA: Ballinger.

McReynolds, P. (1987). Self-theory, anxiety and intrapsychic conflicts. In N. Cheshire & H. Thomae (Eds.), *Self, symptoms and psychotherapy* (pp. 197–223). New York: Wiley.

Mead, G. H. (1934). *Mind, self, and society.* Chicago: University of Chicago Press.

Menninger, K. A. (1954). Psychological aspects of the organism under stress, I: The homeostatic regulatory function of the ego. *Journal of the American Psychoanalytical Association, 2,* 67–106.

Merton, R. K. (1949). *Social theory and social structure.* Glencoe, IL: Free Press.

Miller, D. T., & Turnbull, W. (1986). Expectancies and interpersonal processes. *Annual Review of Psychology, 37,* 233–256.

Miller, G. A., Galanter, E., & Pribram, K. H. (1960). *Plans and the structure of behavior.* New York: Holt.

Murphy, G. (1947). *Personality: A biosocial approach to origins and structure.* New York: Harper.

Natale, M., & Hantas, M. (1982). Effects of temporary mood states on selective memory about the self. *Journal of Personality and Social Psychology, 42,* 927–934.

Neisser, U. (1980). *Cognitive psychology.* New York: Appleton-Century-Crofts.

Nisbett, R. E., & Ross, L.(1980). *Human inference: Strategies and shortcomings of social judgment.* Englewood Cliffs, NJ: Prentice-Hall.

Nygard, R. (1977). *Personality, situation and persistence: A study with emphasis on achievement motivation.* Universitetsforlaget, Oslo.

Oatley, K., & Johnson-Laird, P. N. (1987). Towards a cognitive theory of emotions. *Cognition and Emotion, 1,* 29–50.

Overmire, T. G. (1974). Homeostasis. In *Encyclopaedia Britannica* (15th ed.) (pp. 1014–1017). Chicago: Helen Hemingway Benton.

Pavlov, I. P. (1927). *Conditioned reflexes* (G. V. Anrep, Trans.). Oxford: Clarendon Press.

Perlmuter, L. C., & Monty, R. A. (Eds.). (1979). *Choice and perceived control.* Hillsdale, NJ: Erlbaum.

Pervin, L. A. (1983). The status and flow of behavior: Toward a theory of goals. In M. M. Page (Ed.), *Nebraska symposium on motivation, 1982* (pp. 1–53). Lincoln: University of Nebraska Press.

Piaget, J. (1952). *The origins of intelligence in children.* New York: International Universities Press.

Pittman, T. S., & D'Agostino, P. R. (1985). Motivation and attribution: The effect of control deprivation on subsequent information processing. In G. Weary & J. Harvey (Eds.), *Attribution: Basic issues and applications* (pp. 117–141). New York: Academic Press.

Pittman, T. S., & Heller, J. F. (1987). Social motivation. *Annual Review of Psychology, 38*, 461–489.

Pittman, T. S., & Pittman, N. L. (1980). Deprivation of control and the attribution process. *Journal of Personality and Social Psychology, 39*, 377–389.

Porter, C., Markus, H., & Nurius, P. (1984). *Possible selves and coping with crises.* Unpublished manuscript, University of Michigan.

Powers, W. T. (1973a). *Behavior: The control of perception.* Chicago: Aldine.

Powers, W. T. (1973b) Feedback: Beyond behaviorism. *Science, 179*, 351–356.

Pribram, K. H. (1971). *Languages of the brain.* Englewood Cliffs, NJ: Prentice-Hall.

Pyszczynski, T. A., & Greenberg, J. (1981). Role of disconfirmed expectancies in the instigation of attributional processing. *Journal of Personality and Social Psychology, 40*, 31–38.

Pyszczynski, T. A., & Greenberg, J. (1983). Determinants of reduction in intended effort as a strategy for coping with anticipated failure. *Journal of Research in Personality, 17*, 412–422.

Rabkin, J. G. (1982). Stress and psychiatric disorders. In L. Goldberger & S. Breznitz (Eds.), *Handbook of stress: Theoretical and clinical aspects* (pp. 566–584). New York: Free Press.

Raup, R. B. (1925). *Complacency: The foundation of human behavior.* New York: Macmillan.

Raynor, J. O. (1982). A theory of personality functioning and change. In J. O. Raynor & E. E. Entin (Eds.), *Motivation, career striving, and aging* (pp. 249–302). Washington, DC: Hemisphere.

Raynor, J. O., & McFarlin, D. B. (1986). Motivation and the self-system. In R. M. Sorrentino & E. T. Higgins (Eds.), *Handbook of motivation and cognition: Foundations of social behavior* (pp. 315–349). New York: Guilford.

Reeve, J., & Cole, S. G. (1987). Integration of affect and cognition in intrinsic motivation. *Journal of Psychology, 121*, 441–449.

Richter, C. P. (1937). Hypophyseal control of behavior. *Cold Spring Harbor Symposium on Quantitative Biology, 5*, 258–268.

Richter, C. P. (1942–1943). Total self-regulatory functions in animals and human beings. *Harvey Lectures, 38*, 63–103.

Rignano, E. (1923). *The psychology of reasoning.* New York: Harcourt, Brace.

Rogers, C. R. (1959). A theory of therapy, personality, and interpersonal relationships, as developed in the client-centered framework. In S. Koch (Ed.), *Psychology: A study of a science* (Vol. 3, pp. 184–256). New York: McGraw-Hill.

Rosenberg, M. (1965). *Society and the adolescent self-image*. Princeton: Princeton University Press.

Rosenberg, M. (1969). The conditions and consequences of evaluation apprehension. In R. Rosenthal & R. L. Rosnow (Eds.), *Artifacts in behavioral research* (pp. 279–349). New York: Academic Press.

Rosenberg, M. (1979). *Conceiving the self*. New York: Basic Books.

Rosenberg, M. (1986). Self-concept from middle childhood through adolescence. In J. Suls & A. G. Greenwald (Eds.), *Psychological perspectives on the self* (Vol. 3, pp. 107–136). Hillsdale, NJ: Erlbaum.

Rosenzweig, N. (1955). A mechanism in schizophrenia: A theoretical formulation. *AMA Archives of Neurology and Psychiatry, 74*, 544–555.

Rotter, J. B. (1966). Generalized expectancies for internal versus external control of reinforcement. *Psychological Monographs, 80* (Whole No. 609).

Ruvolo, A. P., & Markus, H. (1986). Possible selves and motivation. Presented at 94th Annual Meeting of the American Psychological Association, Washington, DC.

Sanders, G. S. (1981). Driven by distraction: An integrative review of social facilitation theory and research. *Journal of Experimental Social Psychology, 17*, 227–251.

Sarason, I. G. (1975). Anxiety and self-preoccupation. In I. G. Sarason & C. D. Spielberger (Eds.), *Stress and anxiety* (Vol. 2, pp. 27–44). Washington, DC: Hemisphere.

Scheuch, K. (1986). Theoretical and empirical considerations in the theory of stress from a psychophysiological point of view. In M. H. Appley & R. Trumbull (Eds.), *Dynamics of stress: Physiological, psychological and social perspectives* (pp. 117–140). New York: Plenum.

Schlenker, B. R. (Ed.). (1985). *The self and social life*. New York: McGraw-Hill.

Schlenker, B. R., & Leary, M. R. (1982). Social anxiety and self-presentation: A conceptualization and model. *Psychological Bulletin, 92*, 641–669.

Schultz, D. P. (Ed.). (1964). *Panic and behavior: Discussion and readings*. New York: Random House.

Selye, H. (1936). A syndrome produced by diverse nocuous agents. *Nature, 138*, 32.

Selye, H. (1950). *The physiology and pathology of exposure to stress*. Montreal: Acta.

Selye, H. (1956). *The stress of life*. New York: McGraw-Hill.

Selye, H. (1974). *Stress without distress*. New York: J. B. Lippincott.

Selye, H. (1980). *Selye's guide to stress research* (Vol. 1). New York: Van Nostrand Reinhold.

Selye, H. (Ed.). (1983). *Selye's guide to stress research* (Vols. 2 & 3). New York: Van Nostrand Reinhold.

Shane, M., & Shane, E. (1980). Psychoanalytic developmental theories of the self: An integration. In A. Goldberg (Ed.), *Advances in self psychology* (pp. 23–46). New York: International Universities Press.

Sherif, M., & Cantril, H. (1947). *The psychology of ego involvement*. New York: Wiley.

Sherman, S. J., Judd, C. M., & Park, B. (1989). Social cognitions. *Annual Review of Psychology, 40*, 281–326.

Sibly, R., & McFarland, D. J. (1974). A state-space approach to motivation. In D. J. McFarland (Ed.), *Motivational control systems analysis* (pp. 213–250). London: Academic Press.

Siegel, P. S. (1965). Motivation: Second act. *Contemporary Psychology, 10*, 97–98.

Simon, H. A. (1955). A behavioral model of rational choice. *Quarterly Journal of Economics, 69*, 99–118.

Singer, J. L., & Kolligian, J., Jr. (1987). Personality: Developments in the study of private experience. *Annual Review of Psychology, 38*, 533–574.

Snyder, C. R., & Smith, T. W. (1982). Symptoms as self-handicapping strategies: The virtues of old wine in a new bottle. In G. Weary & H. L. Mirels (Eds.), *Integration of clinical and social psychology* (pp. 104–127). New York: Oxford University Press.

Sorrentino, R. M., & Higgins, E. T. (1986a). Motivation and cognition. In R. M. Sorrentino & E. T. Higgins (Eds.), *Handbook of motivation and cognition: Foundations of social behavior* (pp. 3–19). New York: Guilford.

Sorrentino, R. M., & Higgins, E. T. (Eds.). (1986b). *Handbook of motivation and cognition: Foundations of social behavior*. New York: Guilford.

Sorrentino, R. M., & Short, J-A. C. (1986). Uncertainty orientation, motivation, and cognition. In R. M. Sorrentino & E. T. Higgins (Eds.), *Handbook of motivation and cognition: Foundations of social behavior* (pp. 379–403). New York: Guilford.

Stagner, R. (1951). Homeostasis as a unifying concept in personality theory. *Psychological Review, 58*, 5–17.

Stagner, R. (1954). Homeostasis: Corruptions or misconceptions? A reply. *Psychological Review, 61*, 205–208.

Stagner, R. (1961). Homeostasis, need reduction, and motivation. *Merrill-Palmer Quarterly, 7*, 49–68.

Stagner, R. (1977). Homeostasis, discrepancy, dissonance: A theory of motives and motivation. *Motivation and Emotion, 1*, 103–138.

Stagner, R., & Karwoski, T. F. (1952). *Psychology*. New York: McGraw-Hill.

Stagner, R., & Solley, C. M., Jr. (1970). *Basic psychology: A perceptual-homeostatic approach*. New York: McGraw-Hill.

Sullivan, H. S. (1947). *Conceptions of modern psychiatry*. Washington, DC: Wm. Alanson White Psychiatric Foundation.

Sullivan, H. S. (1953). *The interpersonal theory of psychiatry*. New York: Norton.

Suls, J. M. (Ed.). (1982). *Psychological perspectives on the self* (Vol.1). Hillsdale, NJ: Erlbaum.

Suls, J. M., & Greenwald, A. G. (Eds.). (1983). *Psychological perspectives on the self* (Vol. 2). Hillsdale, NJ: Erlbaum.

Suls, J. M., & Greenwald, A. G. (Eds.). (1986). *Psychological perspectives on the self* (Vol. 3). Hillsdale, NJ: Erlbaum.

Tallman, I. (1967). The balance principle and normative discrepancy. *Human Relations, 20*, 341–355.

Teitelbaum, H. A. (1956). Homeostasis and personality. *AMA Archives of Neurology and Psychiatry, 76*, 317–324.

Tetlock, P. E., & Levi, A. (1982). Attribution bias: On the inconclusiveness of the cognition-motivation debate. *Journal of Experimental Social Psychology, 18*, 68–88.

Trumbull, R., & Appley, M. H. (1967). Some pervading issues. In M. H. Appley & R. Trumbull (Eds.), *Psychological stress: Issues in research* (pp. 400–412). New York: Appleton-Century-Crofts.

Trumbull, R., & Appley, M. H. (1986). A conceptual model for the examination of stress dynamics. In M. H. Appley & R. Trumbull (Eds.), *Dynamics of stress: Physiological, psychological, and social perspectives* (pp. 21–45). New York: Plenum.

Turner, J. H. (1987). Toward a sociological theory of motivation. *American Sociological Review, 52*, 15–27.

Ulvund, S. E. (1980). Cognition and motivation in early infancy: An interactionist approach. *Human Development, 23*, 17–32.

Van Sommers, D. (1974). Studies in learned behavioural regulation. In D. J. McFarland (Ed.), *Motivational control systems analysis* (pp. 283–350). New York: Academic Press.

Van Vorst, R. (1947). Some responses of the psychopath as interpreted in light of Lindner's suggested application of the concept of homeostasis. *Journal of Clinical Psychopathology, 8*, 827–830.

Vickers, G. (1973). Motivation theory—a cybernetic contribution. *Behavioral Science, 18*, 242–249.

Weiner, B. (1972). *Theories of motivation: From mechanism to cognition.* Chicago: Markham.

Weiner, B. (1980). *Human motivation.* New York: Holt, Rinehart & Winston.

Weiner, B. (1986). Attribution, emotion, and action. In R. M. Sorrentino & E. T. Higgins (Eds.), *Handbook of motivation and cognition: Foundations of social behavior* (pp. 281–312). New York: Guilford.

White, R. W. (1959). Motivation reconsidered: The concept of competence. *Psychological Review, 66*, 297–333.

White, R. W. (1960). Competence and the psychosexual stages of development. In M. R. Jones (Ed.), *Nebraska symposium on motivation, 1960* (pp. 97–140). Lincoln: University of Nebraska Press.

Wicklund, R. A., & Gollwitzer, P. M. (1982). *Symbolic self-completion.* Hillsdale, NJ: Erlbaum.

Wiener, N. (1948). *Cybernetics.* New York: Wiley.

Wiener, N. (1954). *The human use of human beings: Cybernetics and society.* New York: Doubleday.

Wilcox, B. L. & Vernberg, E. M. (1985). Conceptual and theoretical dilemmas facing social support. In G. Sarason & B. R. Sarason (Eds.), *Social support: Theory, research and applications* (pp. 3–20). The Hague: Nijhoff.

Wylie, R. C. (1979). *The self-concept* (rev. ed.) (Vols. 1 & 2). Lincoln: University of Nebraska Press.

Yardley, K., & Honess, T. (Eds.). (1987). *Self and identity: Psychosocial perspectives*. New York: Wiley.

Yarrow, L. J., & Pederson, F. A. (1976). The interplay between cognition and motivation in infancy. In M. Lewis (Ed.), *Origins of intelligence: Infancy and early childhood* (pp. 379–399). New York: Wiley.

Young, J. Z. (1971). *An introduction to the study of man*. New York: Oxford University Press.

Zajonc, R. B. (1980). Feeling and thinking: Preferences need no inferences. *American Psychologist, 35,* 151–175.

Self-Regulation of Motivation Through Anticipatory and Self-Reactive Mechanisms

Albert Bandura
Stanford University

Motivation is a general construct linked to a system of regulatory mechanisms that are commonly ascribed both directive and activating functions. At the generic level it encompasses the diverse classes of events that move one to action. Level of motivation is typically indexed in terms of choice of courses of action and intensity and persistence of effort. Attempts to explain the motivational sources of behavior therefore primarily aim at clarifying the determinants and intervening mechanisms that govern the selection, activation, and sustained direction of behavior toward certain goals.

Social cognitive theory distinguishes three broad classes of motivation (Bandura, 1986). One class of motivators is biologically based and includes biological conditions arising from cellular deficits and external aversive events that activate consummatory and protective behavior through physical discomfort. The early psycho-

Material contained in major portions of this chapter has been revised and expanded from chapters previously published in the following works: *Cognitive Perspectives on Emotion and Motivation* (pp. 37–61), edited by V. Hamilton, G. H. Bower, and N. H. Frijda (Dordrecht: Kluwer Academic Publishers, 1988) (copyright 1982 by Kluwer Academic Publishers; adapted by permission of Kluwer Academic Publishers), and *Goal Concepts in Personality and Social Psychology* (pp. 19–85), edited by L. A. Pervin (Hillsdale, NJ: Erlbaum, 1989) (copyright 1989 by Lawrence Erlbaum Associates, Inc.; adapted by permission).

logical theorists conceptualized motivation largely in terms of the energizing and directive functions of physiological activators. However, the activating potential of physiological states is under substantial anticipatory and generative cognitive control. For example, infants become active when they expect to be fed rather than solely when they are hungry (Marquis, 1941). Humans can be sexually stirred by erotic fantasies more than by hormonal injections (Beach, 1969). Similarly, the activating and directive influence of external aversive stimulation can be markedly altered by the way the aversive events and resulting sensations are construed (Bandura, 1991a; Cioffi, 1991; McCaul & Malott, 1984). Thus, even in the so-called biological motivators, human behavior is extensively activated and regulated by anticipatory and generative cognitive mechanisms rather than simply impelled by biological urges.

The second class of motivators operates through social incentives. In the course of development, physically positive experiences often occur in conjunction with expressions of others' interest and approval, whereas unpleasant experiences are associated with disapproval or censure. Through such correlative experiences, social reactions themselves become predictors of primary rewarding and punishing consequences and thereby become incentives. People will do things to gain approval and refrain from activities that arouse others' displeasure or wrath. By reversing the physical correlates, one could make smiles forebode suffering and scowls forewarn pleasure. The effectiveness of social reactions as incentives thus derives from their predictive value rather than inhering in the reactions themselves. For this reason the approval and disapproval of people who have power to reward and punish operate as stronger incentives than similar expressions by individuals who cannot affect one's life. Indiscriminate praise that never carries any tangible effects becomes an empty reward, and disapproval that is never backed up with any tangible consequences becomes devoid of motivating power.

Several factors contribute to the durability of social incentives. The same expressions can predict an array of possible rewarding or punishing experiences. Disapproval, for example, may result in such unpleasant effects as physical punishment, loss of privileges, monetary penalties, dismissal from a job, or ostracism. An event that signifies diverse possible consequences will have greater potency than one that portends only a single effect. Moreover, social reactions are not invariably accompanied by primary experiences: praise does not always bring material benefits, and reprimands do not always result in physical suffering. Unpredictability protects social and symbolic incentives from losing their effectiveness (Mowrer, 1960). Because of intermittency and diversity of correlates, social reactions retain their incentive function even with minimal primary support.

The third major source of motivators is cognitively based. In cognitively generated motivation, people motivate themselves and guide their actions anticipatorily by exercising forethought. They anticipate likely outcomes of prospective actions, they set goals for themselves, and they plan courses of action designed to realize valued futures. The capability for self motivation and purposive action is rooted in cognitive activity. Future events cannot be causes of current motivation or action, but by cognitive representation in the present, conceived future events are converted into current motivators and regulators of behavior. Forethought is translated into incentives and action through self-regulatory mechanisms. This chapter addresses cognitive motivators because most human behavior is activated and regulated over extended periods by anticipatory and self-reactive mechanisms.

One can distinguish three forms of cognitive motivators around which different theories have been built. These include *causal attributions, outcome expectancies,* and *cognized goals.* The corresponding theories are attribution theory, expectancy-value theory, and goal theory. Figure 1 summarizes schematically these alternative conceptions of cognitive motivation. We shall see later that certain basic mechanisms of personal agency, such as perceived self-efficacy, operate in all of these variant forms of motivation.

Attribution Theory

According to the attribution theory of motivation (Weiner, 1985), retrospective judgments of the causes of one's performance have motivational effects. People who credit their successes to personal capabilities and their failures to insufficient effort will undertake difficult tasks and persist in the face of failure, because they see their out-

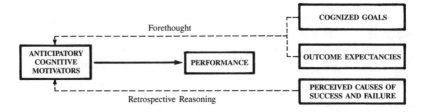

FIGURE 1. Schematic representation of conceptions of cognitive motivation based on cognized goals, outcome expectancies, and causal attributions.

comes as being influenced by how much effort they expend. In contrast, those who ascribe their failures to deficiencies in ability and their successes to situational factors will display low striving and give up readily when they encounter obstacles.

Some writers have argued that reasons offered retrospectively should not be regarded as causes. This is obviously true for past actions, which precede ascribed causes and would therefore involve backward causation. But reasons for past performances that affect beliefs about personal control can cause future actions. Thus people who believe they failed because they did not work hard enough are likely to strive harder, whereas those who believe they failed because they lack ability are apt to slacken their efforts and easily become discouraged. However, causal attributions can serve different purposes. For example, Covington and Omelich (1979) provide evidence that causal attributions may sometimes function as self-serving excuses that do not change performance rather than as motivators. The question of when causal attributions function as excuses and when they are motivators warrants investigation.

The role of attributional processes in human motivation is clarified by research in which causal attributions for ongoing performances are systematically varied by arbitrary attributional feedback and then changes in perceived self-efficacy and performance are measured. The results indicate that causal attributions can influence achievement strivings, but the effect is mediated almost entirely through changes in perceived self-efficacy (Relich, Debus, & Walker, 1986; Schunk & Gunn, 1986; Schunk & Rice, 1986).

Ability attributions are accompanied by strong self-beliefs of efficacy, which in turn predict subsequent performance. *Effort* attributions have variable effects on self-efficacy beliefs. These diverse findings raise the issue of the concept of ability in attribution theory. Attribution theorists usually treat ability as a fixed or stable internal property. High effort needed to achieve an outcome is taken as indicating low ability (Kun, 1977). In actuality, people vary in their conceptions of ability and alter their views on the relation between effort and ability with increasing experience (M. Bandura & Dweck, 1988; Dweck & Elliot, 1983; Nicholls & Miller, 1984). The presumptions of attributional theory fit the subgroup of people who regard ability as a stable entity. However, many individuals construe ability as an acquirable skill that is developed through effort. The harder you try, the more capable you become. For them, errors reflect inexperience in the activity that effort rectifies, rather than basic inability. High effort that begets rising accomplishments can thus enhance self-beliefs of efficacy (Schunk & Cox, 1986).

In judging their efficacy from performance, people use much more varied sources of enactive efficacy information than the four causal factors (effort, ability, task difficulty, chance) routinely assessed in attributional research. In addition to perceptions of task difficulty and amount of effort expended, they consider whether they performed under favorable or unfavorable conditions, the amount of external aid they received, their physical and emotional state at the time, and the pattern of their successes and failures with continued engagement in the activity. Positive or negative biases in the self-monitoring, cognitive representation, and retrieval of past successes and failures also affect self-efficacy judgments (Bandura, 1986).

The effect of effort attributions on self-efficacy beliefs will vary with different conceptions of ability and different configurations of efficacy-relevant information. Given these complicating factors, it is not entirely surprising that effort attributions do not bear a uniform relationship to self-efficacy beliefs. Regardless of whether effort attributions correlate positively or negatively with perceived efficacy, however, the stronger the self-efficacy belief, the better the subsequent performance (Schunk & Cox, 1986; Schunk & Gunn, 1986; Schunk & Rice, 1986).

The overall evidence reveals that causal attributions, whether in the form of ability, effort, or task difficulty, generally have weak or no independent effect on achievement motivation. The types of factors singled out by attributional theory convey efficacy-relevant information and influence performance attainments mainly by altering people's belief in their efficacy. Occasionally, ability attribution emerges as an independent contributor to achievement motivation, but such direct effects tend to be small and equivocal.

Subjective weighting of attributional factors and self-efficacy appraisal involves bidirectional, rather than unidirectional, causation. The relative weight given to information regarding adeptness, effort, task complexity, and situational circumstances will affect self-efficacy appraisal. Self-beliefs of efficacy, in turn, bias causal attributions. Thus, people who regard themselves as highly efficacious tend to ascribe their failures to insufficient effort, whereas those who regard themselves as inefficacious view their failures as stemming from low ability (Collins, 1982; Silver, Mitchell, & Gist, 1989). Self-efficacy belief influences causal attributions for outcomes in social transactions as well as in cognitive activities (Alden, 1986).

Expectancy-Value Theory

People also motivate themselves and guide their actions anticipatorily by the outcomes they expect to flow from given courses of behavior. Expectancy-value theory was designed to account for this form of incentive motivation (Ajzen & Fishbein, 1980; Atkinson, 1964; Rotter, 1982; Vroom, 1964). These various formulations all assume that strength of motivation is governed jointly by the expectation that particular actions will produce specified outcomes and by the value placed on those outcomes. They differ mainly in what additional determinants are combined with expectancy and outcome value. Atkinson adds an achievement motive; Rotter adds a generalized expectancy that actions control outcomes; Ajzen and Fishbein add perceived social pressures to perform the behavior and proneness to compliance; Vroom adds belief that the behavior is achievable through effort.

In its basic version, the expectancy-value theory predicts that the higher the expectancy that certain behavior can secure specific outcomes and the more highly those outcomes are valued, the greater is the motivation to perform the activity. The findings generally show that outcome expectations obtained by adding or multiplying these cognitive factors predict performance motivation (Feather, 1982; Mitchell, 1974; Schwab, Olian-Gottlieb, & Heneman, 1979). The amount of variance in performance motivation explained by this model is generally smaller than might be expected, however. This has stimulated spirited debates about the scope of the expectancy-value theory, its major assumptions, and the methods used for assessing and combining the cognitive factors.

According to maximizing expectancy models, people seek to optimize their outcomes. Questions have been raised, however, concerning the assumptions about how decisions are usually made. As several authors have correctly observed, people are not as systematic in considering alternative courses of action and in weighing their likely consequences as expectancy-value models assume (Behling & Starke, 1973; Simon, 1976). Alternatives are often ill defined. People rarely examine all the feasible alternatives or give detailed thought to all the consequences of even the options they do consider. More typically they pick, from a limited array of possibilities, the course of action that looks satisfactory rather than searching studiously for the optimal one. Moreover, they are sometimes inconsistent in how they order alternatives, they have difficulty assigning relative weights to different types of outcomes, they let the attractiveness of the outcomes color their judgments of how difficult it might be to attain them, and they opt for lesser outcomes because they can get them sooner. When faced with many alternatives and complexly contingent outcomes, they use simplifying decision strategies that may lead them to select alternatives that differ from those they would have chosen had they weighted and ordered the various factors as presupposed by the maximizing model.

The issue in question is not the rationality of the judgmental process. People often have incomplete or erroneous information about alternatives and their probable consequences, they process information through cognitive biases, and what they value may be rather odd. Decisions that seem subjectively rational to the performer, given the basis on which they were made, may appear irrational to others. Subjective rationality often sponsors faulty choices. There are too many aspects to a judgmental process where one can go astray to permit objective rationality (Brandt, 1979). The main issue in dispute concerns the correspondence between the postulated judgmental process and how people actually go about appraising and weighting the probable consequences of alternative courses of action.

The types of anticipated incentives singled out for attention is another dimension on which expectancy-value theory often departs from actuality. Some of the most valued rewards of activities are in the self-satisfaction derived from fulfilling personal standards. The satisfaction yielded by personal accomplishments may be valued more highly than tangible payoffs. When these two sources of incentives conflict, self-evaluative outcomes often override the influence of tangible rewards (Bandura, 1986). Because incentive theories of motivation tend to neglect affective self-evaluative outcomes, self incentives rarely receive the consideration they deserve in the option/outcome calculus. Predictiveness is sacrificed if influential self incentives are overlooked. With regard to the scope of the expectancy-value model, even the elaborated versions include only a few cognitive motivators. In actuality, forethought about outcomes influences effort and performance through additional intervening mechanisms.

People act on their beliefs about what they can do as well as on their beliefs about the likely effects of various actions. The motivating potential of outcome expectancies is partly governed by people's beliefs about their capabilities. There are many activities that, if done well, guarantee valued outcomes, but they are not pursued by those who doubt they can do what it takes to succeed (Beck & Lund, 1981; Betz & Hackett, 1986; Dzewaltowski, Noble, & Shaw, 1990; Wheeler, 1983). Self-perceived inefficacy can thus nullify the motivating potential of alluring outcome expectations. Conversely, a strong sense of personal efficacy can sustain efforts over extended periods in the face of uncertain or repeatedly negative outcomes. Indeed, because ordinary social realities are strewn with impediments, failures, adversities, setbacks, frustrations, and inequities, it requires a resilient sense of personal efficacy to sustain the perseverant effort needed to succeed (Bandura, 1989).

In activities that call upon competencies, self-efficacy beliefs affect the extent to which people act on their outcome expectations. Some expectancy-value theories include an expectancy that effort will beget the requisite performance (Vroom, 1964). It should be noted, however, that perceived self-efficacy encompasses much more than beliefs about how effort determines performance. Effort is only one of many factors that govern the level and quality of performance. People judge their capability for challenging activities more in terms of their perceptions of the knowledge, skills, and strategies they have at their command than solely on how much they can exert themselves. Performances that call for ingenuity, resourcefulness, and adaptability depend more on adroit use of skills, specialized knowledge, and analytic strategies than on sheer effort (Wood & Bandura, 1989a). Moreover, people who cope poorly with stressors expect that marred performances in intimidating situations will be determined by their self-debilitating thought patterns rather than by how much effort they mount. The harder they try, the more they may impair their execution of the activity. Expectancy theorists probably singled out effort as the sole cause of performance because the theory has usually been concerned with how hard people work at routine activities unimpeded by obstacles or threats. Hence, the aspect of self-efficacy that is most germane to how much is accomplished is people's perceived perseverant capabilities—that is, their belief that they can exert themselves sufficiently to attain designated levels of productivity.

Some confusion has been introduced into the expectancy literature by misconstruing the specifying criteria of a performance level as its outcomes. A *performance* is conventionally defined as "an accomplishment" or "something done"; an *outcome*, as "something that follows as a result or consequence of an activity." Three major classes of outcomes can be distinguished—material consequences, social reactions, and self-reactions. Thus, in a high-jump field event performance levels are defined in terms of height of jumps. A six-foot leap is the realization of a particular performance, not the outcome that flows from it. The outcomes are the results a six-foot leap produces—the social recognition, applause, trophies, monetary prizes, and self-satisfaction if it represents a superior attainment, or the social disappointment, forfeiture of material rewards, and self-criticism if it represents a deficient level of attainment. Similarly, in assessments of academic performance, letter grades of *A, B, C, D, F* are the specifying criteria of performance level, not the outcomes. Remove the letter indicants of performance level, and one is left with an indefinite or indescribable performance. The social reactions, personal benefits, costs, and affective self-reactions anticipated for an *A*-level performance, or for an *F*-level performance, constitute the outcome expectations. To conceptualize a performance level as the outcome of itself is to destroy the conventional meanings of performance and outcome.

The degree to which outcome expectations contribute independently to performance motivation varies depending on how tightly contingencies between actions and outcomes are structured, either inherently or socially, in a given domain of functioning. Because activities vary in their structural contingencies, there is no single relationship between judgments of self-efficacy and outcome expectations. For many activities, outcomes are determined by level of competence. Hence the types of outcomes people anticipate depend largely on how well they believe they can perform in given situations. Students do not expect to be showered with academic honors or prizes regardless of the adequacy of their scholarship. In most social, intellectual, and physical pursuits, those who judge themselves highly efficacious will expect favorable outcomes, whereas those who expect poor performances of themselves will conjure up negative outcomes. Thus, in activities in which outcomes are highly contingent on quality of performance, self-judged efficacy accounts for most of the variance in expected outcomes. When variations in perceived self-efficacy are partialed out, the outcomes expected for given performances do not have much of an independent effect on behavior (Barling & Abel, 1983; Barling & Beattie, 1983; Godding & Glasgow, 1985; Lee, 1984a, 1984b; Williams & Watson, 1985).

Self-efficacy beliefs account for only part of the variance in expected outcomes when outcomes are not completely controlled by quality of performance. This occurs when extraneous factors also affect outcomes, or when outcomes are socially tied to a minimum level of performance so that some variations in quality above or below the standard do not produce differential outcomes. In work situations, for example, compensation is fixed to some normative performance standard, but a higher level of productivity does not bring larger weekly paychecks. Perceived self-efficacy to fulfill the minimal standard will produce better expected outcomes than perceived self-inefficacy to reach that level. But variations in perceived self-efficacy above the minimal standard would not give rise to different expected outcomes. And finally, expected outcomes are independent of perceived self-efficacy when contingencies are restrictively structured so that no level of competence by certain groups can produce desired outcomes. This occurs in pursuits that are rigidly segregated by sex, race, age, or some other factor. In such circumstances, people in the disfavored group expect poor outcomes however efficacious they judge themselves to be. Thus, for example, when athletes were rigidly segregated by race, black baseball players could not gain entry to the major leagues and the attendant benefits no matter how well they pitched or batted.

Recent efforts to increase the predictiveness of expectancy-value models have added an efficacylike factor to the usual set of predictors (Ajzen, 1985). In the Ajzen and Fishbein (1980) model of reasoned action, the intention to engage in a course of action is governed by a personal determinant in the form of perceived outcomes and their valuation as well as a subjective normative determinant comprising perceived social pressures by significant others and one's motivation to comply with their expectations. Ajzen and his colleagues have shown that perceived control makes a significant independent contribution to performance within the expanded model, both directly and indirectly through its effects on intention (Ajzen & Madden, 1986; Schifter & Ajzen, 1985). Indeed, in activities that are not subject to much social pressure, perceived self-efficacy carries most of the explanatory power (Dzewaltowski, et al. 1990). The predictiveness of other versions of expectancy-value theory is enhanced by including the self-efficacy determinant (de Vries, Dijkstra, & Kuhlman, 1988; McCaul, O'Neill, & Glasgow, 1988; Schwarzer, 1990; Wheeler, 1983).

There has been some dispute between goal theorists and expectancy-value theorists on the causal ordering of motivational determinants. Expectancy theorists contend that high goals enhance motivation because they have greater incentive value (Matsui, Okada & Mizuguchi, 1981). Goal theorists contend that expectancy-value factors exert their impact on motivation by their effects on personal goal setting. Studies testing these competing conceptions reveal that perceived capability and level of personal goals predict performance motivation (Mento, Cartledge, & Locke, 1980). Success expectancy and outcome valuation enhance performance indirectly by promoting goal adoption, rather than by operating directly on performance. When success expectancy also affects performance directly, its independent contribution is small compared with personal goals (Garland, 1984).

Goal Theory

The capacity to exercise self-influence by personal challenge and evaluative reaction to one's own attainments provides a major cognitive mechanism of motivation and self-directedness. Motivation through pursuit of challenging standards has been the subject of extensive research on goal setting. Evidence from numerous laboratory and field studies involving heterogeneous task domains shows that enhancement of motivation by explicit challenging goals is a remarkably robust effect replicated across heterogeneous activity domains, settings, populations, social levels, and time spans (Locke & Latham, 1990; Mento, Steel, & Karren, 1987). Goals operate largely through self-referent processes rather than regulating motivation and action directly. The self-reactive influences by which personal standards create powerful motivational effects are analyzed in some detail in the sections that follow.

SELF-REACTIVE INFLUENCES AS MEDIATORS OF GOAL MOTIVATION

Motivation based on standards involves cognitive comparison. By making self-satisfaction conditional on matching adopted goals, people give direction to their actions and create self incentives to persist in their efforts until their performances match their goals. The anticipated self-satisfaction gained from fulfilling valued standards provides one source of incentive motivation for personal accomplishments. Perceived negative discrepancies between performance and the standard individuals seek to attain creates dissatisfaction that serves as another incentive motivator for enhanced effort. The motivational effects do not stem from the goals themselves, but rather spring from the fact that people respond evaluatively to their own behavior. Goals specify the conditional requirements for positive self-evaluation.

Activation of self-evaluation processes through internal comparison requires both comparative factors—a personal standard and knowledge of one's performance level. Neither performance knowledge without standards nor standards without performance knowledge can provide a basis for self-evaluative reactions. Studies in which goals and performance feedback are systematically varied yield results consistent with this formulation, whatever the nature of the pursuit (Bandura & Cervone, 1983; Becker, 1978; Strang, Lawrence, & Fowler, 1978). Simply adopting a goal, whether an easy or a challenging one, without knowing how one is doing, or knowing how one is doing in the absence of a goal, has no lasting motivational impact. In marked contrast, the combined influence of goals with performance feedback heightens motivation substantially. This is shown in Figure 2, which summarizes the level of self motivation in the presence of both, only one, or none of the comparative factors.

Although performance feedback alone is not a dependable motivator, it produces substantial variance in motivation that is explainable by the comparative structures individuals create for themselves. When they engage in an ongoing activity and are informed of their attainments, some set goals for themselves spontaneously (Bandura, & Cervone, 1983). Variations in personal goal setting are reflected in diversity in motivation (Figure 3). Those who set no goals for themselves achieve no change in effort and are surpassed by those who aim to match their previous level of effort, and they in turn are outperformed by those who set themselves the more challenging goal of bettering their past endeavor. However, self-set goals alone do not in themselves have any continuing motivational impact on activities that provide little inherent feedback of performance level. These results from self-created comparative structures lend further support for the influential role of cognitive comparison in motivation through personal standards or goals.

Cognitive motivation based on goal intentions is mediated by three types of self-influences: they include affective self-evaluation, perceived self-efficacy for goal attainment, and ongoing adjustment of personal standards. As I have already pointed out, goals motivate by enlisting self-evaluative involvement in the activity. People seek self-satisfaction from fulfilling valued standards and are prompted to intensify their efforts by discontent with substandard perfor-

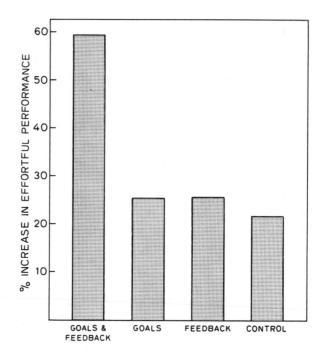

FIGURE 2. Mean percentage change in level of motivation under conditions combining goals with performance feedback, goals alone, feedback alone, or none of these factors. From Bandura, & Cervone, 1983, p. 1021. Copyright 1983 by the American Psychological Association. Reprinted by permission of the publisher.

mance. Both the positive and negative affective self-motivators operate in human pursuits, although discontent is more salient when performances fall short of what one seeks. But without the prospect of self-satisfaction from personal accomplishments, unremitting discontent would eventually take its toll on self motivation.

Perceived self-efficacy is another cognitive factor that plays an influential role in the exercise of personal control over motivation. It is partly based on their self-belief of efficacy that people choose what challenges to undertake, how much effort to expend in the endeavor, how long to persevere in the face of difficulties, and how much stress and despondency they experience in the face of difficulties and failures (Bandura, 1986, 1989). Whether negative discrepancies between personal standards and attainments are motivating or discouraging is partly determined by people's belief that they can

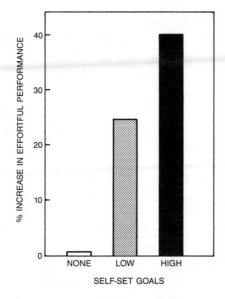

FIGURE 3. Mean increases in motivational level under conditions of performance feedback alone depending on whether people continue to perform the activity without goals or spontaneously set low or high goals for themselves. Drawn from data in Bandura & Cervone, 1983.

attain the goals they set for themselves. Those who harbor self-doubt about their capabilities are easily dissuaded by failure. Those who are assured of their capabilities intensify their efforts when they fail to achieve what they seek, and they persist until they succeed.

That strong belief in one's efficacy heightens level of effort and perseverance in difficult pursuits is corroborated by evidence across diverse domains of functioning for both children and adults (Bandura, & Cervone, 1986; Brown & Inouye, 1978; Cervone, & Peake, 1986; Jacobs, Prentice-Dunn & Rogers, 1984; Schunk, 1984; Weinberg, Gould, & Jackson, 1979). Several paradigms have been used to verify that self-efficacy beliefs operate as causal factors in motivation. Some of these tests of causality introduce a trivial factor that is devoid of information to affect competency but can alter perceived self-efficacy. The impact of the altered self-efficacy beliefs on level of motivation is then measured. For example, studies of anchoring influences show that arbitrary reference points from which judgments are adjusted either upward or downward can bias the judgments because the adjustments are usually insufficient. Cervone and Peake (1986) used arbitrary anchor values to influence self-efficacy judgments. Judgments made from an arbitrary high starting point biased students' perceived self-efficacy as problem solvers in the positive direction, whereas an arbitrary low starting point lowered students' judgments of their efficacy (Figure 4). The higher the instated perceived self-efficacy, the longer they persevered on difficult and unsolvable problems before they quit.

In a related study (Peake & Cervone, 1989), efficacy judgment was biased simply by having people judge their self-efficacy in relation to ascending or descending levels of possible attainment. The initial levels in these respective sequences served as anchoring influences that lowered or raised self-efficacy beliefs. Elevated self-beliefs of efficacy heightened effort, whereas lowered self-beliefs lessened effort on troublesome problems. In a further study, Cervone (1989) biased self-efficacy judgment through differential cognitive focus on things about the task that might make it troublesome or tractable. Dwelling on formidable aspects weakened people's belief in their efficacy, but focusing on doable aspects raised self-judgment of capabilities. The higher the altered self-efficacy beliefs, the longer people persevered in the face of repeated failure. In these various experiments, perceived self-efficacy predicts variance in motivation within treatment conditions as well as across treatments. Mediational analyses reveal that neither anchoring influence nor cognitive focus has any impact on motivation when variations in self-efficacy beliefs are controlled. These external influences thus exerted their effect on motivation entirely by mediating changes in self-efficacy beliefs.

A number of studies have been conducted in which self-efficacy beliefs are altered by bogus feedback unrelated to one's actual performance. People partly judge their capabilities through social comparison. Using this type of induction procedure, Weinberg, Gould, and Jackson (1979) showed that physical stamina in competitive situations is mediated by perceived self-efficacy. They raised the self-efficacy beliefs of one group by telling subjects they had triumphed in a competition of muscular strength. They lowered the self-efficacy beliefs of another group by telling subjects they had been outperformed by their competitors. The higher the illusory beliefs of phys-

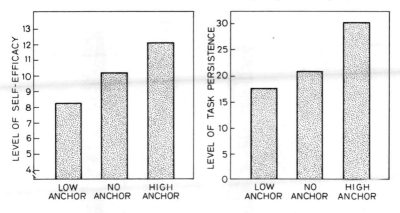

FIGURE 4. Mean changes induced in perceived self-efficacy by anchoring influences and the corresponding effects on level of subsequent perseverant effort. From Cervone & Peake, 1986, p. 495. Copyright 1986 by the American Psychological Association. Reprinted by permission.

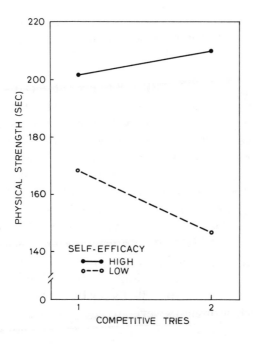

FIGURE 5. Mean level of physical stamina mobilized in competitive situations as a function of illusorily instated high or low self-percepts of physical efficacy. Drawn from data in Weinberg, Gould, & Jackson, 1979.

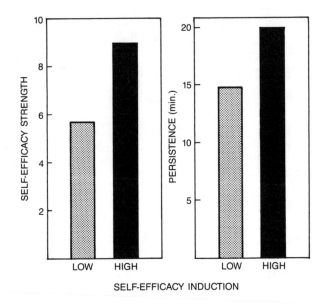

FIGURE 6. Mean changes in perceived self-efficacy induced by arbitrary normative comparison and the corresponding effects on level of subsequent perseverant effort. Drawn from data in Jacobs, Prentice-Dunn, & Rogers, 1984.

ical strength, the more physical endurance subjects displayed during competition on a new task measuring physical stamina (Figure 5). Failure in the subsequent competition spurred those with a high sense of perceived self-efficacy to even greater physical effort, whereas failure impaired the performance of those whose perceived self-efficacy had been undermined. Self-beliefs of physical efficacy illusorily heightened in females and illusorily weakened in males obliterated large preexisting sex differences in physical strength.

Jacobs et al. (1984) used another variant of social self-appraisal—bogus normative comparison—as a way of altering self-efficacy beliefs. Individuals are led to believe, regardless of their actual performance, that they performed at high or low percentile ranks of an ostensibly normative group. Self-efficacy beliefs heightened by this means produce stronger perseverant effort (Figure 6). The regulatory role of self-efficacy beliefs, instated by arbitrary normative comparison, is replicated in perseverance in markedly different domains of functioning (Litt, 1988).

The combined evidence that divergent modes of efficacy induction produce convergent effects on motivation across a variety of pursuits adds to the explanatory and predictive generality of the efficacy mediator. Perceived self-efficacy determines not only level of effort expenditure, but how productively that effort is deployed. People who have a strong sense of efficacy engage in more efficient analytic thinking than do self-doubters (Wood & Bandura, 1989a). When faced with complex decisions, those who distrust their efficacy become erratic in their analytic thinking. Perceived self-efficacy can thus enhance performance through its effects on thought processes and deployment of strategies as well as on motivation. Moreover, in activities in which deficient performances can have untoward consequences, perceived self-inefficacy can impair functioning by generating disruptive cognitions and avoidant actions. The efficacy-activated cognitive and affective processes will be addressed later.

The goals people set for themselves at the outset of an endeavor are likely to change, depending on how they construe the pattern and level of progress they are making and readjust their aspirations accordingly (Campion & Lord, 1982). They may maintain their original goal, lower their sights, or adopt an even more challenging goal. Thus the third constituent self-influence in the ongoing regulation of motivation concerns readjusting personal goals in light of one's attainments. Csikszentmihalyi (1979) examined what it is about activities that fosters continuing deep engrossment in life pursuits. The common factors found to be conducive to enduring motivation include adopting personal challenges in accordance with one's perceived capabilities and having informative feedback on progress.

Studies in which discrepancy levels are varied systematically and the self-reactive influences are measured before motivational change shed light on how these influences operate in concert in regulating motivation through goal systems. One experiment examined how self-evaluative and efficacy mediators contribute to motivation under a moderate negative goal discrepancy (Bandura, & Cervone, 1983). As shown in Figure 7, affective self-evaluation and perceived self-efficacy are good predictors of the degree of change in motivation when attainments fall short of the goal being pursued. Discontent over a substandard performance combined with high perceived self-efficacy for goal attainment produces a marked heightening of effort. A low sense of self-efficacy with low discon-

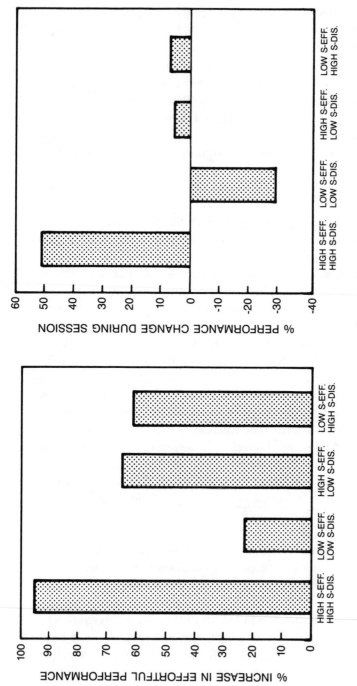

FIGURE 7. Mean percentage changes in motivational level under conditions combining goals and performance feedback as a function of different combinations of levels of self-dissatisfaction (S-DIS) and perceived self-efficacy for goal attainment (S-EFF). The left-hand panel shows the mean change in motivation for the entire session; the right-hand panel shows the mean motivational change between the initial and the final segment of the session. From Bandura & Cervone, 1983, p. 1024. Copyright 1983 by the American Psychological Association. Adapted by permission of the publisher.

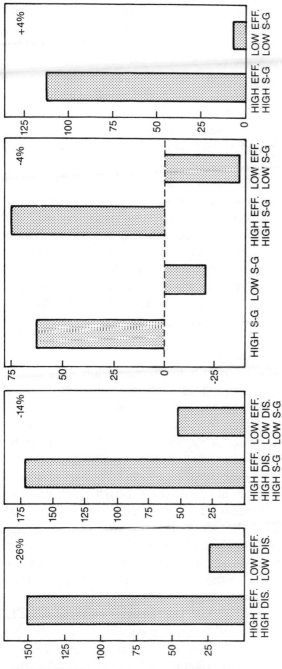

FIGURE 8. Mean percentage changes in motivational level by people who are high or low in the self-reactive influences identified by hierarchical regression analyses as the critical motivators at each of four levels of preset discrepancy between a challenging standard and level of performance attainment. EFF signifies strength of perceived self-efficacy to attain a 50% increase in effort; DIS, the level of self-dissatisfaction with the same level of attainment as in the prior attempt; and S-G, the goals people set for themselves for the next attempt. The second set of graphs at the –4% discrepancy level summarize the results of the regression analysis performed with perceived self-efficacy averaged over the 30%–70% goal attainment range. From Bandura & Cervone, 1986, p. 108. Reprinted by permission of Academic Press, Inc.

tent over a substandard performance mobilizes little effort. Either high discontent or high perceived self-efficacy alone results in a moderate increase in motivation. The joint operation of the self-re-active influences even predicts whether motivation is enhanced, sustained, or debilitated over the course of a given attempt. Discontented self-efficacious subjects intensified their effort as time went on, whereas those who judged themselves unable to reach the goal and were satisfied with a substandard performance slackened their efforts and displayed a substantial decline in motivation as they continued the activity.

The three self-reactive influences exert differential impact on motivation when attainment diverges from the comparative standard over a wide range of discrepancies (Bandura & Cervone, 1986). After performing a strenuous task, individuals received prear-ranged feedback that their effort either fell markedly, moderately, or minimally short of the adopted standard or exceeded the standard. They then recorded their perceived self-efficacy for goal attainment, their self-evaluation, and their self-set goals, whereupon their motivational level was measured. Figure 8 portrays graphically how this set of self-influences operates in concert at each discrepancy level in the regulation of motivation.

Perceived self-efficacy contributes to motivation at all discrepancy levels. The stronger people's self-efficacy beliefs that they can meet challenging standards, the more they intensify their efforts. Discontent operates as an influential affective motivator when attainment falls substantially or moderately short of a comparative standard. The more self-dissatisfied people are with substandard attainment, the more they heighten their efforts. If they are quite satisfied with approximating or matching the standard again, however, self motivationt invest increased effort. As people approach or surpass the initial standard, the new goals they set for themselves serve as an additional motivator. The higher the self-set goals, the more effort is invested in the endeavor. Taken together this set of self-reactive influences accounts for the major share of variation in motivation.

Self-reactive influences predict the impact of success, as well as of failure, on motivation. When attainments surpass challenging goals, people's belief in their efficacy and their self-set goals determine their level of motivation (Figure 8). Those who hold a strong belief in their efficacy motivate themselves by setting even higher goal challenges that create new discrepancies to be mastered. Thus, notable attainments bring temporary satisfaction, but people enlist new challenges as personal motivators for further accomplishment. Those who doubt they could muster the same level of effort again lower their goals. Their motivation declines.

SELF-REGULATION AND THE NEGATIVE FEEDBACK MODEL

Many theories of self-regulation are founded on a negative feedback control system (Carver & Scheier, 1981; Lord & Hanges, 1987; Miller, Galanter, & Pribram, 1960). The basic structure of this type of regulatory system includes a behavior monitoring operation, a comparator, and an error correction routine. The system functions as a motivator and regulator of action through a discrepancy reduction mechanism. Perceived discrepancy between performance and the reference standard automatically triggers action to reduce the incongruity. Discrepancy reduction clearly plays a central role in any system of self-regulation, but in the negative feedback control system, self motivationmatches the standard the person does nothing. A regulatory process in which matching a standard begets inertness does not characterize human self motivation. Such a feedback control system would produce circular action that leads nowhere. Nor could people be stirred to action until they receive feedback of a shortcoming.

Although comparative feedback is essential in the ongoing regulation of motivation, people can initially raise their level of motivation by adopting goals before they receive any feedback regarding their beginning effort (Bandura & Cervone, 1983). Negative feedback may help to keep them going, but it is not present antecedently to start them. That different self-regulatory systems operate in the initiation and continued control of motivation is shown in Figure 9. In the initial phase of the endeavor, individuals who had adopted a challenging goal enlisted a higher level of effort than those who performed with no goal other than to do their best. As they went on with the activity, those who continued to perform it with goals only or without goals displayed no further increases in motivation,

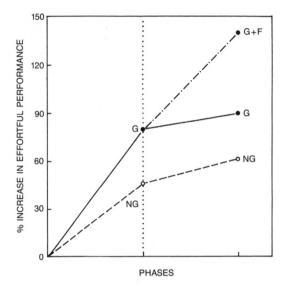

FIGURE 9. Portrayal of how proactive systems and reactive feedback systems operate in the initiation and continued regulation of motivation. Initially, subjects performed with goals (G) or no goals (NG). In the next phase, the goal subjects continued to perform with goals only (G) or with goals and performance feedback (GF). Drawn from data in Bandura & Cervone, 1983.

whereas the individuals who had the benefit of goals and performance feedback raised their level of motivation substantially. A theory of motivation control must explain how each new goal adoption motivates from the outset before the first performance feedback. The motivating starter is the anticipatory estimate of the level of effort needed to match the goal. Subsequent feedback provides instructive information on the corrective adjustments in motivation needed to attain or surpass the goal.

Human self motivation relies on both *discrepancy production* and *discrepancy reduction*. It requires *proactive control* as well as *reactive control*. People initially motivate themselves through proactive control by setting themselves valued performance standards that create a state of disequilibrium and then mobilizing their effort based on anticipatory estimation of what it would take to reach them. Feedback control comes into play in subsequent adjustments of effort expenditure to achieve desired results. As previously shown, after people attain the standard they have been pursuing, those who have a strong sense of efficacy generally set a higher standard for themselves. Adopting further challenges creates new motivating discrepancies to be mastered. Similarly, surpassing a standard is more likely to raise aspiration than to lower subsequent performance to conform to the surpassed standard. Self motivation thus involves a dual control process of disequilibrating discrepancy production followed by equilibrating discrepancy reduction.

An evaluative executive control system with a proactive component can, of course, be superimposed on a negative feedback operation that keeps changing aspirational standards either upward or downward depending on how performance attainment is construed. To capture the complexity of human self-regulation, such an executive control system must be invested with the evaluative agentive properties previously shown to play an important role in self-directedness. These include (1) predictive anticipatory control of effort expenditure, (2) affective self-evaluative reactions to one's performance rooted in a value system, (3) self-appraisal of personal efficacy for goal attainment, and (4) self-reflective metacognitive activity concerning the adequacy of one's efficacy appraisals and the suitability of one's standard setting. Evaluation of perceived self-efficacy relative to task demands indicates whether the standards being pursued are attainable or beyond one's reach.

In human endeavors, goal adjustments do not follow a neat pattern of ever-rising standards after personal accomplishments, nor do failures necessarily lower aspirations. Rather, because of interacting cognitive and affective factors, feedback of discrepancy has diverse effects on the self-reactive influences that mediate motivation and standard setting. This is shown in the study previously cited (Bandura & Cervone, 1986), in which people were led to believe that their attainments diverged from their original goal over a wide range of discrepancies. The variations in perceived self-efficacy and self-set goals at each discrepancy level are plotted in Figure 10.

Impact of Goal Discrepancy on Perceived Self-Efficacy. When people fail to fulfill a challenging standard, some become less sure of their efficacy and others lose faith in their capabilities, but many remain unshaken in their belief that they can attain the standard (Figure 10). Surpassing a taxing standard through sustained strenuous effort does not necessarily strengthen self-beliefs of efficacy. Al-

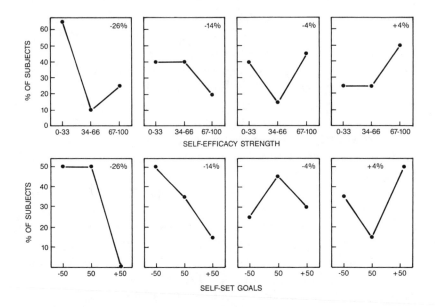

FIGURE 10. Patterns of perceived self-efficacy to attain a 50% increase in effort and whether this difficult goal was adhered to, abandoned for a lower goal, or raised to an even more challenging goal at each of four levels of preset discrepancy (–26%, –14%, –4%, +4%) between the difficult goal and level of performance attainment. Drawn from data in Bandura & Cervone, 1986.

though for most people high accomplishment strengthens self-beliefs, a sizable number who drive themselves to hard-won success doubt they can duplicate the feat.

The latter findings raise the important issue of resiliency of self-beliefs of efficacy in the face of difficulties. There is a growing body of evidence that human accomplishment and positive well-being require an optimistic and resilient sense of personal efficacy (Bandura, 1986). This is because ordinary social realities are usually fraught with difficulties. They are full of impediments, adversities, failures, setbacks, frustrations, and inequities. Success usually comes through renewed effort following failed attempts. To abort efforts prematurely limits personal accomplishment. Therefore people must have a robust sense of personal efficacy to sustain the perseverant effort needed to succeed. White (1982) vividly documents that the striking common characteristic of people who eventually achieved eminence in their respective fields was an inextinguishable sense of self-efficacy that enabled them to override innumerable rejections of their early work. Their resilient self-efficacy was combined with a steadfast belief in the worth of what they were doing.

Affective and achievement benefits of optimistic self-efficacy belief. It is widely believed that misjudgment produces dysfunction. Certainly, gross miscalculation can get one into trouble. But optimistic self-appraisals of efficacy that are not unduly disparate from what is possible can be advantageous, whereas veridical judgments can be self-limiting. Human skill is a generative capability, not a fixed property. What people can do in different situations depends on how well they orchestrate their subskills and stratagems and how hard they work at the task. Therefore the same capability can give rise to performances that are subpar, ordinary, or extraordinary for a particular person. When people err in their self-appraisal they tend to overestimate their capabilities. This is a benefit rather than a cognitive failing to be eradicated. If self-efficacy beliefs always reflected only what people can do routinely, they would rarely fail, but they would not mount the extra effort needed to surpass their ordinary performance.

Evidence suggests that it is often the so-called normals who are distorters in self-appraisal, but they distort in the positive direction. Anxious and depressed people have been compared in their skills and their self-beliefs with those who are unburdened by such problems. The groups differ little in their actual skills, but they differ substantially in their beliefs about their efficacy. People who are socially anxious are often just as socially skilled as the more sociable ones. But socially active people judge themselves much more adept than they really are (Glasgow & Arkowitz, 1975). Schwartz and Gottman (1976) have similarly shown that unassertive people know what to do but lack the efficacy to translate their knowledge into assertive action.

Depressed persons usually display realistic self-appraisals of their social competencies. The nondepressed view themselves as much more adroit than they really are. As depressed people improve in treatment, they show the self-enhancing biases that characterize the nondepressed (Lewinsohn, Mischel, Chaplin, & Barton, 1980). A similar pattern of advantageous self-appraisal is revealed in laboratory tasks in which people perform actions and outcomes occur, but the actions exert no control over the outcomes. The depressed are quite realistic in judging they lack control. In contrast, nondepressed people believe they are exercising a good deal of control in such situations (Alloy & Abramson, 1979). After nondepressed people are made temporarily depressed, they become realistic in judging their personal control. When depressed people are made to feel happy, they overestimate the extent to which they exercise control (Alloy, Abramson, & Viscusi, 1981). Thus the depressed appear as realists, the nondepressed as confident distortionists.

Social reformers strongly believe that they can mobilize the collective effort needed to bring social change (Bandura, 1986; Muller, 1979). Although their beliefs and the collective sense of efficacy they instill in others are rarely fully realized, they sustain reform efforts that achieve lesser, but important, gains. Were social reformers to be entirely realistic about the prospects of transforming social systems, they would either forgo the endeavor or fall easy victim to discouragement. Realists may adapt well to existing realities, but those with a tenacious optimistic self-efficacy are likely to change those realities.

The emerging evidence indicates that the achievers, the innovators, the sociable, the nonanxious, the nondespondent, and the social reformers take an optimistic view of their personal efficacy to exercise influence over events that affect their lives. If not unrealistically exaggerated, such self-beliefs sustain the motivation needed for personal and social accomplishments.

Effect of goal discrepancy on personal goal setting. Self-beliefs of capability affect personal goal setting. The more capable people judge themselves to be, the higher the goals they set for themselves (Bandura & Cervone, 1986; Taylor, Locke, Lee, & Gist, 1984; Wood & Bandura, 1989a), and the more firmly committed they remain to their goals (Locke, Latham, & Erez, 1988). Hence the variable impact of discrepancy feedback on perceived self-efficacy is also reflected in personal goal setting. As can be seen in Figure 10, variation in the size of the performance discrepancy produced substantially different patterns of personal goal setting. When people receive prearranged feedback that their efforts fell markedly or moderately short of the goal they were pursuing, they either adhere to or lower their goal. A strenuous effort that falls just short of a difficult standard has diverse effects on personal goal setting. Many continue to strive for it, others lower their sights, and still others set themselves an even greater challenge.

It is widely assumed that accomplishment raises performance standards. Studies of level of aspiration show that, indeed, people generally set their goals slightly above their preceding attainment (Festinger, 1942; Ryan, 1970). However, the use of simple tasks that call for little effort limits the generality of the results from this line of research. This is because in everyday life, significant accomplishments usually require arduous effort over an extended period. In such endeavors many interacting determinants, including fortuitous factors, contribute to achievement. Therefore people do not necessarily expect to outdo each past accomplishment in an ever-rising series of triumphs. Knowledge of having surpassed a demanding standard through laborious effort does not automatically lead people to raise their aspirations (Figure 10). Those who have a high sense of self-efficacy set themselves more challenging goals to accomplish. But some doubt they can muster the same level of laborious effort again, and they set their sights on simply trying to match the standard they had previously pursued. Having driven themselves to success, others judge themselves inefficacious to repeat a demanding feat, and they lower their aspirations.

NEGATIVE DISCREPANCY AS AUTOMOTIVATOR

Self motivation has been explained by some theorists in terms of an inborn automotivator operating through cognitive incongruity reduction. According to Piaget (1960), discrepancies between the cognitive schemata children already possess and perceived events create internal conflict that motivates exploration of the source of discrepancy until the internal schemata are altered to accommodate the contradictory information. In this view, moderately discrepant experiences, rather than markedly or minimally discrepant ones, presumably arouse the cognitive perturbations regarded as necessary for cognitive change.

The conceptual and empirical problems associated with this equilibration model have been addressed elsewhere in some detail and will not be reviewed here (Bandura, 1986; Kupfersmid & Wonderly, 1982). Studies of the relation between discrepancy level and inquisitiveness are inconsistent in their findings (Wachs, 1977). With regard to cognitive changes, people are inclined to adopt views that involve only small shifts from their own, but highly discrepant influences can be as effective, or even more so (Arbuthnot, 1975; Matefy & Acksen, 1976; Walker, 1982). These findings are in accord with substantial evidence in social psychology showing that the more discrepant others' views are from one's own the more one's views change (McGuire, 1985). Although discrepant influences foster cognitive changes, the changes are unrelated to level of cognitive conflict (Haan, 1985; Zimmerman & Blom, 1983). The impact of divergent influences seems to stem more from how persuasive they are than from how internally conflictful they happen to be. Social factors exert a powerful influence on how discrepant conceptions are cognitively processed and received. Simply demonstrating that children are bored by what they already know and easily discouraged by information that exceeds their cognitive-processing capabilities is a mundane finding that can be explained by any theory without requiring an automotivating mismatch mechanism.

As the preceding findings show, arousal of interest is not confined to events that differ only slightly from what one already knows; a moderate discrepancy of experience alone does not guarantee cognitive learning, nor is acquisition of knowledge dependent solely on internal cognitive conflict. There are many other motivators for bettering one's knowledge and thinking skills. The substantial benefits of being able to predict the occurrence of events and to exercise control over those that affect one's own well-being or that of significant others provide positive incentives for acquiring knowledge and cognitive and social competencies (Bandura, 1986). The self-satisfaction gained from progressive mastery and fulfillment of personal challenges serves as another enduring motivator. People often drive themselves for material gain, for social recognition, or in the pursuit of excellence.

There are other reasons why an automotivational system of the type proposed by Piaget might be viewed with considerable skepticism. An automatic self-motivator explains more than has ever been observed. If disparities between perceived events and mental structure were, in fact, automatically motivating, learning would be unremitting and much more unselective than it really is. As a rule, people do not persist in exploring most activities that differ moderately from what they know or can do. Indeed, if they were driven by every moderately discrepant event encountered in their daily lives they would be rapidly overwhelmed by innumerable imperatives for cognitive change. Effective functioning requires selective deployment of attention and inquiry. When faced with contradictions between evidence and their conceptions, people are much more likely to discount or reinterpret the "evidence" than to change their way of thinking. If people were motivated by an innate drive to know powered by negative discrepancy reduction, they should all be highly knowledgeable about the world around them and continually advancing to ever higher levels of reasoning. The evidence does not bear this out.

In the social cognitive view, people function as active agents in their own motivation rather than simply being reactive to discordant events that produce cognitive perturbations. Self motivation through cognitive comparison requires distinguishing between standards of what one knows and standards of what one desires to know. It is the latter standards, together with perceived self-efficacy, that exert selective influence over which of many activities will be actively pursued. Aspirational standards determine which discrepancies are motivating and which activities people will strive to master. Strength of self motivation varies curvilinearly with the level of discrepancy between standards and attainments: relatively easy standards are not sufficiently challenging to arouse much interest or effort; moderately difficult ones maintain high effort and produce satisfaction through subgoal achievements; standards set well beyond a person's reach can be demotivating by fostering discouragement and a sense of inefficacy.

GOAL PROPERTIES AND SELF MOTIVATION

Goal intentions do not automatically activate the self-reactive influences that govern level of motivation. Certain properties of goal structures determine how strongly the self system will become enlisted in any given endeavor. The relevant goal properties are addressed next.

Goal specificity. The extent to which goals create personal incentives and guides for action is partly determined by their specificity. Explicit standards regulate performance by designating the type and amount of effort required to attain them, and they generate self-satisfaction and build self-efficacy by furnishing unambiguous signs of personal accomplishment. General intentions, which are indefinite about the level of attainment to be reached, provide little basis for regulating one's efforts or evaluating how one is doing. In studies of the regulative function of goals differing in specificity, clear, attainable goals produce higher levels of performance than general intentions to do one's best, which usually have little or no effect (Bandura & Cervone, 1983; Locke & Latham, 1990). Specific performance goals serve to motivate the unmotivated and to foster positive attitudes toward the activities (Bryan & Locke, 1967).

Goal challenge. The amount of effort and satisfaction that accompanies variations in goals depends on the level at which they are set. Strong interest and involvement in activities is sparked by challenges. When self-satisfaction is contingent on attainment of challenging goals, more effort is expended than if easy ones are adopted as sufficient. Locke postulates a positive linear relationship between goal level and performance motivation. A large body of evidence does show that the higher the goals, the harder people work to attain them and the better is their performance (Locke & Latham, 1990). However, the linear relationship is assumed to hold only if performers accept the goals and remain strongly committed to them. Most people, of course, eventually reject performance goals they consider unrealistically demanding or well beyond their reach. But people often remain surprisingly steadfast to goals they have little chance of fulfilling, even when given normative information that others reject them as unrealistic (Erez & Zidon, 1984). When assigned goals are beyond their reach and failure to attain them carries no cost, people try to approximate high standards as closely as they can rather than abandoning them altogether (Garland, 1983; Locke, Zubritzky, Cousins, & Bobko, 1984). As a result, they achieve notable progress even though the accomplishment of distal goal aspirations eludes them.

The generality of evidence of unshaken pursuit of unreachable goals must be qualified, however, by the fact that laboratory simulations may differ from actual conditions on several important dimensions: the endeavor usually involves only a brief effort, failure carries no costs, and no opportunities exist for alternative pursuits. Unattainable goals are more likely to be abandoned when the activities require extensive investment of effort and resources, failure to meet the goals brings aversive consequences, and other activities are available in which one's efforts might be more fruitfully invested. When goals are set unrealistically high, strong effort produces repeated failure that can eventually weaken motivation by undermining perceived self-efficacy.

Much of the experimentation on level of goal challenges involves a single effort to achieve an individual goal. Social cognitive theory distinguishes between complementary regulative functions of distal goals and a graduated system of proximal subgoals in ongoing endeavors (Bandura, 1986). Superordinate distal goals give purpose to a domain of activity and serve a general directive function, but subgoals are better suited to serve as the proximal determinants of specific choice of activities and how much effort is devoted to them. Self motivation is best sustained through a series of proximal subgoals that are hierarchically organized to ensure successive advances to superordinate goals. The relation between probability of goal attainment and effort expenditure will differ for subgoals and for end goals. Pursuit of a formidable distal goal can sustain a high level of motivation if it is subdivided into subgoals that are challenging but clearly attainable through extra effort (Bandura & Schunk, 1981). To strive for unreachable subgoals is to drive oneself to unrelenting failure. By making complex tasks easier through subdivision into more manageable units, one can perhaps retain the power of goals that tend to have lesser impact on complex than on simpler activities (Wood, Mento, & Locke, 1987). It is not that challenging goals are necessarily ineffective or debilitating for complex pursuits, but that complex activities must be structured in ways that goals enhance and must helpfully channel efforts rather than misdirect them. When complex tasks are aidfully structured, challenging goals are transformed from debilitators to enhancers of performance (Earley, Connolly, & Ekegren, 1989; Earley, Connolly, & Lee, 1990).

The complementary regulation of motivation by hierarchical goals of differential achievability characterizes most of the strivings of everyday life. Long-range aspirations may remain unfulfilled, but personal and social advancements are realized in the process of successful striving. In an ongoing pursuit, of course, the perceived difficulty of a superordinate goal does not remain constant. Progress toward a superordinate goal in the distant future alters subjective estimates of eventual success. As one comes closer to realizing distal goals, the task appears less formidable than when originally viewed from far down the line.

Goal proximity. As I suggested in the preceding discussion, the effectiveness of goal intentions in regulating motivation and action depends greatly on how far into the future they are projected. A proximate standard serves to mobilize self-influences and direct what one does in the here and now. Distal goals alone are too far removed in time to provide effective incentives and guides for present action. In the face of many competing attractions, focus on the distant future makes it easy to put off matters in the present on the belief that there is always ample time to mount the effort later.

Subgoals not only enlist self-reactive motivators, they also figure prominently in the development of self-efficacy (Bandura & Schunk, 1981). Without standards against which to measure their performance, people have little basis for gauging their capabilities. Subgoal attainment provides rising indicants of mastery for enhancing self-percepts of efficacy. By contrast, distal goals are too far removed in time to serve as favorable markers of progress along the way to ensure a growing sense of personal efficacy.

The standards against which attainments are compared also contribute, in several ways, to the development of intrinsic interest in the things being pursued. People develop enduring interest in activities at which they feel self-efficacious and from which they derive satisfaction. Challenging standards enlist sustained involvement in tasks needed to build competencies that foster interest. Moreover, when people aim for and master valued levels of performance, they experience a sense of satisfaction (Bandura & Cervone, 1983; Bandura & Jourden, 1991; Locke, Cartledge, & Knerr, 1970). The satisfactions derived from goal attainment build intrinsic interest, but when distal goals are used as the comparative standard, current attainments may prove disappointing because of wide disparities with lofty future standards. As a result, interest fails to develop even though skills are being acquired in the process. To the extent that proximal subgoals promote and authenticate a sense of efficacious agency, they heighten interest by enhancing perceived personal causation (Bandura & Schunk, 1981). Perceived self-efficacy is thus a better predictor of intrinsic interest than is actual ability (Collins, 1982).

These diverse effects of proximal self-motivation are revealed in a study in which children who were grossly deficient and uninterested in mathematics pursued a program of self-directed learning under conditions involving either proximal subgoals leading to a distal goal, only the distal goal, or no reference to goals (Bandura & Schunk, 1981). Within each of the goal conditions, children could observe how many units of work they had completed in each session and their cumulative attainment. Under proximal subgoals children progressed rapidly in self-directed learning, achieved substantial mastery of mathematical operations, and developed an increased sense of efficacy (Figure 11). Distal goals had no demonstrable effects. Subgoal attainments also created intrinsic interest in arithmetic initially holding little attraction for the children (Figure 12). The value of proximal subgoals in cultivating intrinsic interest and promoting academic attainment is further corroborated by Morgan (1985) in an extended field experiment designed to improve the academic competence of college students. People not only perform better under goal proximity, but they much prefer a proximal to a distal focus (Jobe, 1984).

Like any other form of influence, goals can be applied in ways that breed dislike rather than nurture interests. Goals have their strongest positive psychological effects when they serve as mastery devices rather than as onerous dicta. As already noted, personal standards that subserve valued aspirations promote interest. But if goals assigned by others impose severe constraints and burdensome performance requirements, the pursuit can become oppressive. Because the effects of goals depend on their properties, propositions about the impact of goals on interest must be qualified by the nature and structure of the goals and the purposes they serve. Mossholder (1980) reports that goals enhance interest in dull tasks by infusing them with challenge but reduce interest on interesting tasks. Self-development would be poorly served if aspirations and challenges became dysfunctional for activities that normally hold some interest. Fortunately, this is not the case. An interesting activity with

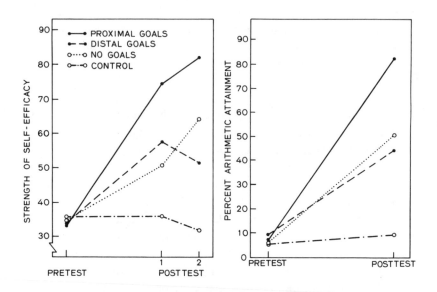

FigURE 11. The left panel shows the strength of children's perceived arithmetic efficacy at the beginning of the study (pretest), after they completed the self-directed learning (Post 1), and after they took the arithmetic posttest (Post 2). Children in the control group were assessed without the intervening self-directed learning. The right panel displays the children's level of arithmetic achievement before and after the self-directed learning. From Bandura & Schunk, 1981, p. 592. Copyright 1981 by the American Psychological Association. Reprinted by permission of the publisher.

a rising standard for success, which continues to present challenges, enhances intrinsic interest, whereas the same activity with a low level of challenge does not (McMullin & Steffen, 1982). If subgoals for an interesting activity are easily attainable, then more distal goals, which pose more of a challenge, may hold greater interest (Manderlink & Harackiewicz, 1984). Routine successes with no corresponding growth of competence create little enjoyment. Doing more of a tedious activity under the influence of performance goals will not increase liking for it (Latham & Yukl, 1976; Umstot, Bell, & Mitchell, 1976). In the studies in which proximal goals cultivate perceived self-efficacy and intrinsic interest, each subgoal presents new challenges in mastery of new subskills (Bandura & Schunk, 1981).

The combination of perceived self-inefficacy, self-devaluation, and diminished interest creates a state of self-demoralization. Subgoal structuring of pursuits can reduce the risk of such self-demor-

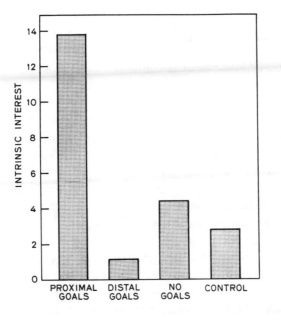

FIGURE 12. Level of intrinsic interest in arithmetic activities shown by children in different goal conditions when given free choice of activities. From Bandura & Schunk, 1981, p. 593. Copyright 1981 by the American Psychological Association. Reprinted by permission of the publisher.

alization through high aspiration. Significant performance gains judged against lofty distal standards do not provide much of a sense of accomplishment because of the wide disparity between current attainment and aspiration. Thus, people can be making good progress but downplaying their accomplishments and getting discouraged. Hierarchical subgoals minimize disspiriting mismatches. I shall return shortly to the self-debilitating affective consequences of unfulfilled striving.

Goal proximity should be distinguished from specificity of planning, which includes not only temporal variation in goals but a host of other factors. For example, in studies comparing daily specific plans with monthly general plans, the detailed proximal system prescribes more onerous busywork in creating daily flow charts of when and where activities will be performed and in monitoring and recording one's performances than does the distal general system (Kirschenbaum, Humphrey, & Mallet, 1981; Kirschenbaum, Tomarken, & Ordman, 1982). Self-influence requiring excess busywork is usually less faithfully applied and has less beneficial results. The motivating potential of goal proximity is best revealed by varying only whether attainment is compared with close or distant standards without confounding proximal goals with more bothersome and time-consuming overseeing routines.

Efforts to clarify how goal proximity operates in self-regulatory mechanisms often encounter methodological obstacles because of spontaneous goal transformations during the course of pursuits. When encouraged to set themselves distal goals, many people quickly improvise their own more helpful proximal goals. They simply partition desired future attainments into more easily realizable subgoals (Bandura & Simon, 1977; Dubbert & Wilson, 1984; Weinberg, Bruya, & Jackson, 1985). Performance becomes the product of self-created goals rather than of externally assigned ones. The effects of proximal goals are untestable if uncontrolled personal goal setting largely eliminates experimentally assigned temporal variation in goals. Similarly, even when people simply monitor their performance, without any reference to goals, many begin to create goals for themselves (Bandura & Cervone, 1983). Self-set goals predict subsequent levels of performance motivation. The motivational advantage of goal proximity becomes most evident under conditions that minimize transformation of distal goals into proximal ones (Bandura & Schunk, 1981).

Variations in personal goal setting under prescribed distal goals illustrate the dual self-processes of exercising and undergoing influence. Regardless of whether studies of self-regulatory processes focus on self-monitoring of progress or on goal setting, people are not simply reactors to situational influences. They often transform them into self-influences that differ from what others intend. Theories that attempt, through regressive causal analysis, to reduce self-regulatory processes to situational control overlook the fact that people are not merely objects of change; they act as agents who give new form to situational influences. Such bidirectionality of influence supports a reciprocal model of self-regulation (Bandura, 1986).

HIERARCHICAL STRUCTURE OF GOAL SYSTEMS

Thus far, the discussion has centered on goal systems as a directive and motivational device and on the self-referent mechanisms through which they exert their effects. Goal systems, of course, usually involve a hierarchical structure in which the goals that operate as the proximal regulators of motivation and action serve broader goals reflecting matters of personal import and value. However, proximal goals are not simply subordinate servitors of valued loftier ones, as commonly depicted in machinelike hierarchical control systems. Through engagement of the self-system, subgoals invest acself motivationersonal significance. As I have previously shown, proximal goals generate self-satisfaction from personal accomplishment that operates as its own reward during the pursuit of higher level goals. When the reward of personal accomplishment is linked to indicants of progress, individuals contribute a continuing source of self motivation quite apart from the incentive of the loftier goal. Indeed, subgoal challenges often outweigh the lure of superordinate goals as ongoing motivators (Bandura & Schunk, 1981). In this motivational process, people gain their satisfaction from progressive mastery of an activity rather than suspending any sense of success in their endeavors until the superordinate goal is attained. In short, the reward is in the ongoing process of mastery rather than solely in the attainment of the end goal. The model of self motivation as a process of recurrent proximal self-challenge and evaluative reward differs from one in which a linear series of subordinate goals is powered entirely by a superordinate one. Self motivation through proximal self-influence does not imply any restriction in the future time perspective of aspirations. Progress toward valued futures is best achieved by combining distal aspirations with proximal self-guidance.

GENERIC GOAL ORIENTATIONS

People impose goal preferences on activities that reflect their basic orientations to achievement across a wide range of situations. This process has been the focus of research on how people's conceptions of ability affect the goals they pursue, which in turn determines the quality of their intellectual functioning (M. Bandura & Dweck, 1988; Dweck & Leggett, 1988; Nicholls, 1984). Two major conceptions have been identified. In one perspective, intelligence is construed as an *incremental skill* that can be continually enhanced by acquiring knowledge and perfecting one's competencies. People with this conception adopt a learning goal. They seek challenging tasks providing opportunities to expand their knowledge and develop their competencies. Errors are regarded as a natural, instructive part of an acquisition process—one learns from mistakes. Such an outlook sustains task-oriented, perseverant effort in the face of failures. Capabilities are judged more in terms of personal progress than by comparison against the achievements of others. Mastery through effort is rewarding, whereas easy successes are boring or disappointing.

In the contrasting perspective, intelligence is construed as a more or less *stable entity*. Because quality of performance is regarded as diagnostic of intellectual capability, errors and performance insufficiencies carry personal threat and arouse concern over social evaluation of incompetence. Consequently, people adopting the entity view tend to favor goals of exhibiting established skills and to prefer tasks that minimize the risk of errors at the expense of learning something new. Prolonged expenditure of effort, which is the way most competencies are built, also poses threats because high effort is taken to indicate low ability. Those aiming to look smart through proficient performance are prone to measure their capabilities by comparison with the achievements of others. Effort is rewarded by a feeling of pride or relief over validation of intellectual status without having had to expend much effort.

The effect of these differential goal orientations on psychological functioning is revealed in experiments in which children have to cope with failure (Elliott & Dweck, 1988). Those who view intelligence as an entity and perceive themselves as deficient in it are easily debilitated by failure, whereas those subscribing to an incremental view take failure in their stride. It should be noted that the processes and correlates discussed here concern goal orientations, not types of people. Thus, when children who construe ability as a fixed attribute are encouraged to adopt a learning goal by portraying intelligence as an acquirable skill, they manage failure much more effectively. Even the same individual may construe ability as a fixed aptitude in some domains of functioning and as an acquired aptitude in others.

SELF-REGULATORY DYNAMICS IN COLLECTIVE ENDEAVORS

Virtually all of the research on cognitive motivators has been concerned with how self-regulatory dynamics operate in personal accomplishment. Many human endeavors are directed at group goals that are achieved in organizational structures through socially mediated effort. In exercising control over collective outcomes, decision makers have to rely on the concerted efforts of others, whereas at the individual level they need regulate only their own efforts. Socially mediated regulation of a group endeavor involves considerably more complex paths of influence than does direct self-regulation. Therefore functional relationships established at the individual level may require qualification at the group level.

Much of the research on human decision making examines discrete judgments in static environments under nontaxing conditions (Beach, Barnes, & Christensen-Szalanski, 1986; Hogarth, 1981). By contrast, in naturalistic environments decisions must be made from a wide array of information within a continuing flow of activity, under time constraints and with significant social and evaluative consequences. Actions taken at one point affect the options and effects of later decisions. Moreover, many of the decisional rules for exercising control over dynamic environments must be learned through exploratory experiences in the course of managing the ongoing organizational activities. Under these more complex transactional conditions, self-regulative, affective, and motivational factors can exert substantial influence on quality of sociocognitive functioning.

Because organizational outcomes must be achieved through the coordinated efforts of others, some of the most important managerial decisions concern how best to use human talent and how to guide and motivate human effort. In executing this role, managers have to cope with numerous obstacles, failures, and setbacks, which often carry perturbing self-evaluative implications as well as social consequences. These affective factors can undermine self-conceptions and motivation in ways that impair good use of decision making skills. Effective decision making thus involves more than applying a set of cognitive operators to existing knowledge for desired solutions. Self-regulatory influences have considerable impact on how well cognitive-processing systems operate (Bandura, 1986).

The mechanisms and outcomes of managerial decision making do not lend themselves readily to experimental analysis in actual organizational settings. The governing processes are usually influenced by a multiplicity of interacting factors that are difficult to identify, let alone control experimentally. Advances in this complex field can be achieved by experimental analyses of decision making in simulated organizational environments. One such computer simulation encompasses the types of decisional activities required in complex dynamic environments (Wood & Bailey, 1985). It permits experimental variation of organizational properties and belief systems that can enhance or undermine self-regulatory determinants of motivation and action. People serve as managerial decision makers in situations where they have to match employee attributes to organizational subfunctions and to learn a complex set of decision rules on how best to guide and motivate those they oversee. The managerial rules concern the optimal use of goals, supervisory feedback, and social incentives to enhance organizational performance. Some of the factors involve nonlinear and compound decision rules combining incentive and social equity elements, making them especially difficult to discern (Brehmer, Hagafors, & Johansson, 1980). The set of rules must be integrated into a cognitive model of organizational functioning that could serve as a guide for decisions regarding different group members. Knowing rules does not ensure optimal implementation of them. The managers also have to gain proficiency in tailoring the applications of the rules to individual members of the group and to apply them in concert to achieve desired group results. The self-regulatory factors are measured at periodic intervals as the managerial task is performed over a series of trials.

In the management of such dynamic environments, self-regulatory mechanisms govern organizational attainments much as they do individual accomplishments (Wood & Bandura, 1989a). Perceived managerial self-efficacy enhances organizational performance both directly and indirectly through its influence on analytic strategies. The higher the perceived self-efficacy, the more systematic people are in applying analytic thinking to discover optimal decision rules. Analytic strategies contribute to organizational attainments beyond that of perceived self-efficacy.

The multifaceted nature of managerial activities and their mazy linkage to organizational accomplishments, however, introduces complexities in the relation between personal goals and group attainment. Personal goals are readily translatable into performance attainments when people have the knowledge and means to exercise control. Goals can affect performance directly by channeling attention and by mobilizing effort and sustaining it in the face of obstacles (Locke & Latham, 1990). In most of the research demonstrating enhancement of accomplishments through goal setting, the performers already possess the means of control and need only intensify their efforts. Even on tasks that are directly controllable by effort alone, goal effects are weaker for more complex activities (Wood, Mento, & Locke, 1987). Sheer managerial effort alone does not ensure attainment of group goals. Until the optimal managerial rules are identified, goals can produce more effortful and discerning cognitive processing of outcome information, but not necessarily immediate improvements in organizational performance. To complicate further the effects of goals on group performance, efforts to enhance the level of organizational functioning often require constituent changes in particular aspects of the social structure and the way social resources are allocated. If grounded in sound judgment, such fractional changes would eventually raise organizational attainments without necessarily producing sizable gains in the short run. Learning in an ambiguous probabilistic environment is made even more difficult when the effectiveness of decisional actions is reflected in distal rather than proximal outcomes.

In studies of the management of group efforts, personal goals influence group performance by promoting effective managerial rule-learning strategies. However, they do not have a direct effect on performance. When one is faced with the task of managing a complex social environment, assigned goals that are exceedingly difficult to fulfill may even detract from organizational attainment by undermining perceived self-efficacy (Wood, Bandura, & Bailey, 1990).

The way people construe ability has substantial influence on the self-regulatory mechanisms that govern ongoing motivation and group accomplishments (Wood & Bandura, 1989b). Substandard performance is likely to carry markedly different diagnostic implications depending on whether ability is construed as an acquirable skill or as a relatively stable aptitude. When performance is viewed as skill acquisition in which one learns from mistakes, perceived self-efficacy is unlikely to be adversely affected by substandard performance, because errors become normative instructive elements in the acquisition of competencies rather than indicators of basic personal deficiencies. Construing performance as diagnostic of underlying cognitive aptitude greatly increases vulnerability to the adverse effects of failure on self-beliefs of efficacy.

Managers who perform the challenging managerial task under an experimentally induced entity conception of ability are beset by increasing doubts about their managerial efficacy. They become more and more erratic in their analytic thinking, lower their organizational aspirations, and achieve progressively less with the organization they are managing (Figure 13). In marked contrast, an induced conception of ability as an acquirable aptitude fosters a highly resilient sense of personal efficacy. Even though taxing goals are assigned that elude the managers, they remain steadfast in their perceived managerial self-efficacy, continue to set themselves challenging organizational goals, and use analytic strategies in ways that aid discovery of optimal managerial decision rules. Such a self-efficacious orientation, which is well suited for handling adversity, pays off in uniformly high organizational attainment.

Induced differential conceptions of ability bias how similar substandard performances at the outset are cognitively processed. Construing insufficient attainment as indicating personal deficiencies gradually creates an inefficacious self-schema in the particular domain of functioning, whereas construing substandard attainments as instructive guides for enhancing personal competencies fosters an efficacious self-schema. Such evolving self-beliefs further bias cognitive processing of outcome information and promote actions that create behavioral evidence confirming them. This produces an exacerbation cycle of motivational and performance impairment under the entity cognitive set and highly proficient functioning under the acquirable skill set.

Two aspects of the exercise of control are especially relevant to organizational change (Bandura, 1986; Gurin & Brim, 1984). The first concerns the level of personal efficacy to effect changes by productive use of capabilities and enlistment of effort. This constitutes the

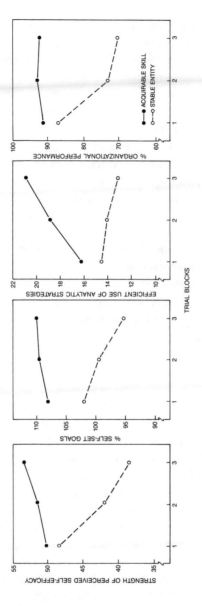

Figure 13. Changes in perceived managerial self-efficacy, self-set goals relative to the preset standard, effective analytic strategies, and achieved level of organizational performance across blocks of trials under acquirable skill and entity conceptions of capability. Each trial block comprises six different production orders. From Wood & Bandura, 1989b, pp. 411–413. Copyright 1981 by the American Psychological Association. Reprinted by permission of the publisher.

personal side of the transactional control process. The second aspect concerns the changeability or controllability of the environment. This facet represents the level of system constraints and opportunities to exercise personal efficacy. Human behavior is of course governed by perceptions of personal efficacy and social environments rather than simply by their objective properties. Thus, individuals who believe they are inefficacious are likely to effect little change even in environments that provide many opportunities and are highly responsive to the exercise of personal competence. Conversely, those who have a strong sense of efficacy, through ingenuity and perseverance, figure out ways to exercise some measure of control in environments containing limited opportunities and many constraints.

In the transactions of everyday life, beliefs regarding self-efficacy and environmental controllability are not divorced from experiential realities. Rather, they are products of reciprocal causation (Bandura, 1986). Thus, when people believe the environment is controllable on matters of import to them, they are motivated to exercise their personal efficacy fully, which enhances the likelihood of success. Experiences of success, in turn, provide behavioral validation of personal efficacy and environmental controllability. Repeated affirmation of personal effectiveness in difficult circumstances produces unshakable persisters. If people approach situations as largely uncontrollable, they are likely to exercise their efficacy weakly and abortively, which breeds failure. Over time, failure takes an increasing toll on perceived self-efficacy and beliefs about how much environmental control is possible.

Organizational simulation research underscores the influential impact of perceived controllability on the self-regulatory factors governing group attainments (Bandura & Wood, 1989). People who manage the simulated organization under a cognitive set that organizations are not easily changeable quickly lose faith in their managerial capabilities, even when performance standards are within easy reach, and they lower their sights for the organization (Figure 14). Those who operate under a cognitive set that organizations are controllable display a resilient sense of managerial efficacy, set themselves increasingly challenging goals, and use good analytic thinking to discover effective managerial rules. The divergent

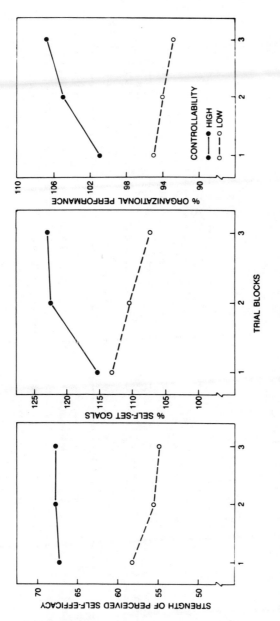

FIGURE 14. Changes in strength of perceived managerial self-efficacy, the performance goals set for the organization, and level of organizational attainment for managers who operated under a cognitive set that organizations are controllable or difficult to control. Drawn from data in Bandura & Wood, 1989.

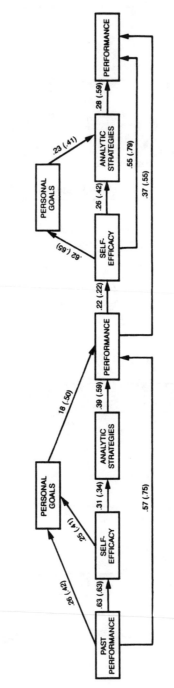

FIGURE 15. Path analysis of causal structures. The initial numbers on the paths of influence are the significant standardized path coefficients (*ps* < .05); the numbers in parentheses are the first-order correlations. The network of relations on the left half of the figure are for the initial managerial efforts, and those on the right half are for later managerial efforts. From Wood & Bandura, 1989a, p. 379. Reprinted by permission of The Academy of Management.

changes in these self-regulatory factors are accompanied by large differences in organizational attainment.

Path analyses reveal that as managers begin to form a self-schema concerning their efficacy through further experience, the performance system is powered more extensively and intricately by self-conceptions of efficacy (Figure 15). Perceived self-efficacy influences performance both directly and through its strong effects on personal goal setting. Personal goals, in turn, enhance organizational attainment directly and via the mediation of analytic strategies.

Social comparison operates as a primary factor in the self-appraisal of capabilities (Festinger, 1954; Suls & Miller, 1977), because most activities do not provide objective, nonsocial standards for gauging level of ability. People must therefore appraise their capabilities in relation to the performance of others. Most of the research on self-appraisal via social standards has centered on why people engage in social comparison, whom they choose to compare themselves with, and the attributes of the social referents that are singled out for the comparative self-appraisal (Suls & Miller, 1977; Suls & Mullen, 1982; Wood, 1989). Under the ordinary conditions of everyday life, people are continually confronted with comparative information, whether they seek it or not. To complicate further the process of self-appraisal, the patterns of comparative information often change across settings and over time.

The research on organizational management corroborates the influential role self-regulatory factors play in mediating the impact of social-comparative influences on motivation and collective attainments (Bandura & Jourden, 1991). Individuals managed the simulated organization under prearranged conditions in which they performed as well as their managerial comparators, consistently surpassed them, performed below the comparison group at the outset but gradually closed the gap and eventually surpassed them, or performed as well as their comparators but began to fall behind and ended up well below them. Feedback that one is as able as or superior to one's comparators sustained an efficacious self-regulatory orientation, although easy comparative triumphs incurred some demotivating effects through complacent self-assurance. Of special psychological interest are the comparative patterns of progressive mastery and progressive decline, which had striking contrasting effects on self-regulatory factors and organizational performance attainments (Figure 16).

Seeing oneself increasingly surpassed by similar social referents undermined perceived self-efficacy, disrupted analytic thinking, created unremitting discontent, and produced a sharp decline in organizational performance. By contrast, seeing oneself gain progressive mastery enhanced a sense of personal efficacy, fostered efficient analytic thinking, and transformed self-evaluation from discontent to satisfaction with accelerating progress. These positive self-regulatory changes were accompanied by a large rise in organizational attainment. Path analysis confirms that the contrasting performance trajectories are mediated by the changes in self-regulatory factors.

ASPIRATIONAL STANDARDS, ACHIEVEMENT MOTIVES, AND EXTERNAL INCENTIVES

Self motivation through self-reactive influence is a significant ingredient in a variety of motivational effects that come under different names. Achievement motivation is one such instance. High achievers tend to invest their self-satisfaction in attaining challenging goals; low achievers adopt easy goals as sufficient. The higher the aspirational standards people set for themselves, the harder they strive to fulfill them and the more likely they are to excel.

Personality theories often portray human strivings and accomplishments as products of achievement needs or motives. The achievement motive is usually inferred from responses to items containing cues relevant to achievement. Theories in which motives are inferred from the types of behavior they supposedly cause create problems of circularity. The motive is inferred from a given class of behavior and is then used to explain the activation of that class of behavior. The functional properties ascribed to the achievement motive are much the same as those that characterize aspirational standards. Both are said to direct and activate courses of action that lead to desired accomplishments. However, there is a major conceptual difference between a motive force and self-generated incentives arising from internal standards and self-reactive influence. Motives impel behavior; self-incentives motivate and direct behavior through cognitive anticipatory mechanisms.

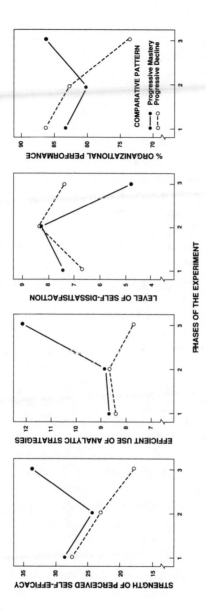

FIGURE 16. Changes in perceived self-efficacy, effective use of analytic strategies, affective self-evaluation, and achieved level of organizational performance across blocks of production orders for individuals who received social-comparative information indicating progressive mastery or progressive decline relative to their comparators. Each trial block comprises six different production orders. Drawn from data in Bandura & Jourden, 1991.

Research in which achievement motive and aspirational standards are measured sheds some light on these alternative motivational mechanisms. High need for achievement is associated with high goal setting; but need for achievement has no influence on performance independent of personal goals. The relationship between need for achievement and performance disappears when level of self-set goals is controlled (Dossett, Latham, & Mitchell, 1979; Latham & Marshall, 1982; Matsui, Okada, & Kakuyama, 1982). The goals people set for themselves predict their performance level and self-satisfaction better than do the traditional personality measures of need for achievement (Arvey & Dewhirst, 1976; Ostrow, 1976; Yukl & Latham, 1978).

The inclination of high need achievers to select high goals does not necessarily mean that performance standards are the products of an underlying motive, as is commonly assumed. Personal standards of excellence may lead people to endorse achievement statements or to produce achievement imagery on personality tests rather than such endorsements' verifying an achievement motive fueling aspiring standards. Evidence that standard setting is a better predictor of ongoing level of performance than are indexes of achievement motives lends causal priority to standard setting. Moreover, goal theory can explain rapid shifts in motivational level through changes in mediating self-processes, whereas quick changes pose explanatory difficulties for a dispositional motive determinant.

Self-influence through internal standards also contributes to the motivational effects of extrinsic feedback and incentives. Extrinsic incentives can motivate partly by activating personal goals for progressive improvement. Indeed, research on the mediating role of goals shows that incentives increase performance to the extent that they encourage people to set motivating goals for themselves (Locke, Bryan, & Kendall, 1968; Wright, 1989). In studies reporting mixed results on whether incentives influence performance predominantly or partially by their effect on self-set goals, subjects were given no information about their level of performance (Pritchard & Curtis, 1973). Self-evaluative motivators are not effectively activated in goal pursuits in the absence of knowledge of how one is doing (Bandura & Cervone, 1983). People are certainly motivated by the prospect of valued extrinsic outcomes, but by applying evaluative standards to their ongoing performances, they create motivating challenges and fulfill them to please themselves as well. Even simple feedback of progress or trivial extrinsic incentives can enhance performance motivation once self-satisfaction becomes invested in the activity. Satisfaction in personal accomplishment becomes the reward.

AFFECTIVE CONSEQUENCES OF GOAL DISCREPANCIES

Self-regulatory processes produce emotional effects that can alter level of performance motivation. Negative discrepancies between attainment and standards selected as indexes of personal merit can give rise to self-devaluation and despondent mood. Given stringent standards, even notable achievements appear trivial and undeserving of self-satisfaction. A growing body of evidence reveals that negative cognitive biases in the constituent processes of self-regulation increase vulnerability to depression (Kanfer & Hagerman, 1981; Rehm, 1981). Of special interest is evidence that faulty goal setting may be conducive to despondency and performance debilitation. Compared with nondepressed persons, the depressed tend to set higher standards for themselves relative to their attainments and to react less positively to similar successes and more self-critically to similar failures (Golin & Terrill, 1977; Loeb, Beck, Diggory, & Tuthill, 1967; Schwartz, 1974; Simon, 1979). Goal stringency is a relational characteristic reflecting the match between personal capabilities and goals, not a matter of absolute level. Depression is most likely to arise when personal standards of merit are set well above one's perceived self-efficacy to attain them (Kanfer & Zeiss, 1983).

Negative discrepancies in self-appraisal of capabilities by social comparison can also breed despondency. Perceived inability to accomplish valued performances that others find readily attainable creates a depressive mood and impairs cognitive functioning (Davies & Yates, 1982). Much attention has been given to the adverse effects of unfavorable social comparison. In studies that vary the social performance standard for comparative appraisal, the higher the accomplishments of similar others, the less satisfied people are with their own performance (Simon, 1979). The self-belittling effect of adverse social comparison is especially evident in persons who are prone to depression. When exposed to high attainments of others, the depressed judge their own accomplishments as less praiseworthy than do the nondepressed (Ciminero & Steingarten, 1978). Self-devaluative reaction to adverse social comparative appraisal is even more pronounced in depressed women (Garber, Hollon, & Silverman, 1979).

To mitigate the deleterious effects of social comparison, it is often recommended that human endeavors be structured so that people judge themselves in reference to their own standards and progress rather than by comparing themselves against others. Self-comparative standards provide the benefits of personal challenge and success experiences for self-development without the cost of invidious social comparison. However, striving to meet one's own standards of excellence can be a source of self-devaluation if they are too stringent. In competitive, individualistic systems, social comparison inevitably intrudes on self-appraisal. Social arrangements in which one person's success is another person's loss or hindrance force social comparison unless one gives up competitive pursuits. But some leeway exists in how much weight individuals give to self-comparison and to social comparison in their self-appraisals (Bandura, 1990a; Frey & Ruble, 1990).

Continued progress in a valued activity does not necessarily ensure perpetual self-fulfillment. The pace at which activities are mastered can drastically alter self-evaluative reactions (Simon, 1979). Subjects received prearranged feedback of a decelerating pattern of improvement (improve fast initially but then taper off), or an accelerating pattern of improvement (improve slowly at first but then make large gains). Different rates of improvement produced strikingly different patterns of self-evaluation (Figure 17). Accomplishments that surpass earlier ones bring a continued sense of self-satisfaction. But people derive little satisfaction from smaller accomplishments, or even devalue them, after having made larger strides. People who are prone to depression display even greater affective reactivity to their rate of progress. They are more self-satisfied with accelerating strides, but they find even less satisfaction in modest improvements after large attainments. Early spectacular accomplishments reflecting notable proficiency can thus be conductive to later self-dissatisfaction even in the face of continuing personal attainment.

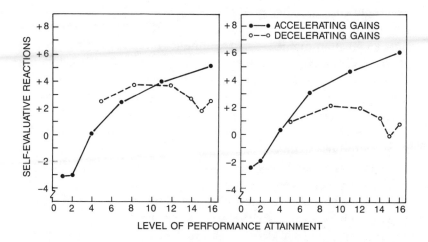

FIGURE 17. Strength of self-evaluative reactions exhibited by individuals who received feedback of a decelerating pattern of improvement (improve fast initially but then taper off) or an accelerating pattern (improve slowly at first but then make large gains). Positive numbers represent strength of self-approval; negative numbers indicate self-criticism. The graphs in the left panel are the self-evaluative reactions of normal individuals, and those in the right panel are for individuals prone to depression. In both the accelerating and decelerating patterns of improvement the individuals received the same performance score on the last trial to determine how rate of progress influences affective self-evaluation to the same eventual accomplishment. Drawn from data in Simon, 1979.

With success comes pressure to fulfill not only rising personal standards but social expectations. A noted composer put it well when he once remarked that, "The toughest thing about success is that you've got to keep on being a success." Those who experience spectacular early successes often find themselves wrestling with self-doubt and despondency if their later work falls short of their earlier triumphs. The Nobel Laureate Linus Pauling prescribed the absolute remedy for the woes of belittling self-comparison. When asked what one does after winning a Nobel Prize, he replied, "Change fields, of course!" The self-evaluation problem with spectacular accomplishments is by no means confined to creative endeavors. After a phenomenal long jump that shattered the existing world record by two feet, Bob Beamon avoided disappointment by never jumping again.

Self-regulatory theories of motivation and of depression make seemingly contradictory predictions regarding the effects of negative discrepancies between attainments and standards. Standards that exceed attainments are said to enhance motivation through goal challenges, but negative discrepancies are also invoked as activators of despondent mood. Moreover, when negative discrepancies do have adverse effects, they may give rise to apathy rather than to despondency. A conceptual scheme is needed that differentiates the conditions under which negative discrepancies will motivate, depress, or induce apathy.

Social cognitive theory posits that the directional effects of negative goal discrepancies are predictable from the relationship between perceived self-efficacy for goal attainment and level of self-set goals (Bandura, 1986). Whether negative discrepancies are motivating or depressing will depend on one's belief that one can match them. Negative disparities are likely to give rise to high motivation and low despondent mood for people who believe they have the efficacy to fulfill a difficult goal and continue to strive for it. Negative disparities are likely to diminish motivation and generate despondent mood for people who judge themselves unable to attain a difficult goal but continue to demand it of themselves for any sense of satisfaction or success. People who judge they lack the efficacy for goal attainment and abandon the difficult goals as unrealistic for themselves are likely to display the apathetic reaction. This would be reflected in lowered motivation without despondent mood.

Evidence for these differential processes comes from a study in which students received arbitrary feedback that their attainment on an intellectual task fell considerably short of a goal they had initially adopted (Bandura & Abrams, 1986). Their perceived self-efficacy for goal attainment, self-set goals, mood, and subsequent level of motivation were then measured. Different subgroups were identified in terms of whether they judged their efficacy for goal attainment to be high or low and whether they held to the difficult goal or abandoned it. The subgroups did not differ initially in mood or performance motivation. Figures 18 and 19 show how they changed in despondent mood and motivation after feedback that they had failed to fulfill the standard.

Continued adherence to the stringent goal with perceived inability to fulfill it induced despondent mood (Figure 18). The same

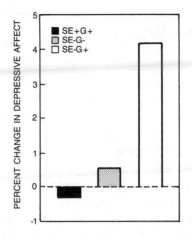

FIGURE 18. Percentage change in depressive mood for people combining strong perceived self-efficacy with goal adherence (SE + G +); weak perceived self-efficacy with goal adherence (SE–G +); and weak perceived self-efficacy with goal abandonment (SE–G–). Drawn from data in Bandura & Abrams, 1986.

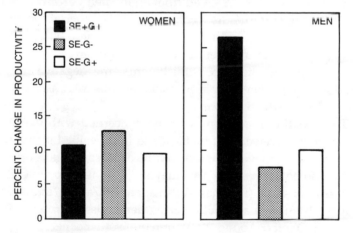

FIGURE 19. Percentage change in level of motivation for people combining strong perceived self-efficacy with goal adherence (SE + G +); weak perceived self-efficacy with goal adherence (SE–G +); and weak perceived self-efficacy with goal abandonment (SE–G–). Drawn from data in Bandura & Abrams, 1986.

level of failure did not create despondency in students who judged they could attain the difficult goal and continued to pursue it, or those who viewed the goal as beyond their capabilities and thus lowered their aim.

For men, failure heightened motivation in the perceived self-efficacious goal adherers but attenuated the efforts of the perceived self-inefficacious ones, regardless of whether they were goal adherers or goal abandoners (Figure 19). Failure had a more generalized adverse impact on women. Not only did the perceived self-inefficacious ones find it hard to motivate themselves, but even the self-efficacious goal strivers had difficulty mounting a high level of effort. Other data from control conditions in which students judged their level of productivity in the absence of performance feedback shed some light on the differential gender effects of failure. Women were realists in judging their productivity, whereas men had an inflated view of how much they had produced. This self-enhancing bias in males may account for the gender differences in the motivational impact of failure. Viewed from an inflated perceived level of accomplishment, the failure feedback would be especially jarring for men. The self-efficacious ones redoubled their efforts; the self-inefficacious ones could not get more out of themselves. For women, who downplayed their accomplishments, the negative feedback would simply validate their impression that this was an exceedingly difficult task at which to excel.

Thus far the discussion has been concerned with depression arising from perceived self-inefficacy to fulfill valued standards of achievement. Perceived inability to control other things people long for can also be depressing. This may involve inefficacy to cultivate social relationships (Holahan & Holahan, 1987a, 1987b; Stanley & Maddux, 1986), manage child rearing demands (Cutrona & Troutman, 1986; Olioff & Aboud, 1991), or handle other aspects of life that mean a great deal (Devins et al., 1982; Rosenbaum & Hadari, 1985). The greater the perceived self-inefficacy, the greater the depression.

Two biasing processes have been postulated in explaining how mood can affect self-efficacy judgment. According to the affective priming theory proposed by Bower, past successes and failures are stored as memories along with their affect (Bower, 1983). The set of memories provides the data base on which judgmental processes operate. Mood activates, through an associative mood network, the subset of memories congruent with it. Thus negative mood activates the failure subset, whereas a positive mood activates the success subset. The spread of activation from the emotion node makes mood-congruent memories salient. Self-appraisal of efficacy is enhanced by selective recall of past successes but diminished by recall of failures. In the cognitive priming view, specific successes or failures that induce the affect also produce cognitions that cue thoughts of other past successes and failures. This view places greater emphasis on the thought content of the inducing event than on the aroused affect as the primer of other positive or negative thoughts. Cognitive availability biases self-efficacy judgment.

Kavanagh and Bower (1985) have shown that, indeed, induced positive mood enhances perceived self-efficacy, whereas despondent mood diminishes it (Figure 20). The effect of induced mood on self-efficacy judgment is widely generalized across diverse domains of functioning.

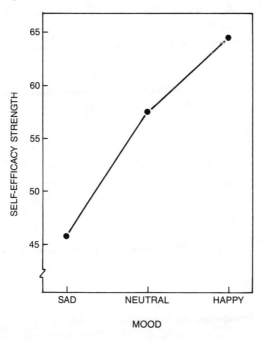

FIGURE 20. Mean strength of self-perceived efficacy across heterosexual, social, and athletic domains of functioning when efficacy judgments were made in a positive, neutral, or negative mood state. From Kavanagh & Bower, 1985, p. 515. Reprinted by permission of Plenum Publishing Corporation.

Mood and perceived self-efficacy undoubtedly influence each other bidirectionally. Kavanagh (1983) tested whether inducing events exert their effects on self-efficacy judgment through affective or cognitive priming. Happy and sad moods were induced by vivifying either a personal triumph or failure or a positive or negative fortuitous experience devoid of successful or failed efforts. The results, though qualified by gender differences, indicate that affect, rather than thought content, is the main carrier of the effect. Self-appraisal of efficacy was raised in a positive affect state and lowered in a negative affect state, regardless of whether the affect was induced fortuitously or through succeeded or failed effort. People then acted in accordance with their mood-altered efficacy beliefs, choosing more challenging tasks in a self-efficacious frame of mind than if they doubted their efficacy. The relation between perceived efficacy and challenge seeking is strongest under fortuitously induced affect. Despondency can thus lower self-efficacy beliefs, which weaken motivation and spawn poor performance, breeding even deeper despondency. In contrast, by raising perceived self-efficacy that heightens motivation and performance accomplishments, good mood can set in motion an affirmative reciprocal process.

Self-Regulatory Mechanisms in Anxiety-Related Motivation

Theories of motivation have traditionally emphasized the motivating influence of fear or anxiety (Dollard & Miller, 1950; Mowrer, 1960). Most of the research on anxiety as a motivator has been conducted within the framework of the two-factor theory. In this view, painful paired experiences create threats capable of arousing an anxiety drive that motivates defensive behavior. Defensive behavior that forestalls or removes the threat is reinforced by the resultant anxiety reduction.

Considerable research using a variety of procedures shows both aspects of the dual-process theory to be seriously wanting (Bandura, 1988b; Bolles, 1975; Herrnstein, 1969; Schwartz, 1978). Autonomic arousal is the principal index of a state of anxiety. The evidence reveals that anxiety is not the motivator of defensive behavior, nor does removal of threats by defensive behavior necessarily strengthen it. More recently, anticipation of anxiety is invoked as the motivator. However, anticipated anxiety is ill equipped to assume the motivational function in that visualization of a bodily state can hardly serve as a motivator when the actual state does not do so.

It is interesting to speculate on why the belief that anxiety arousal controls avoidant behavior remains firmly entrenched in psychological thinking despite substantial evidence to the contrary. A possible answer lies in the force of confirmatory biases in judgments of causality (Nisbett & Ross, 1980). Confirming instances in which anxiety and avoidance occur jointly remain highly salient, whereas nonconfirming instances in which anxiety and approach behavior occur together or avoidance occurs without anxiety tend to be disregarded. It is not that the nonconfirming instances are any less prevalent. Quite the contrary. People commonly perform risky activities in spite of high anxiety. Thus, for example, actors with acute stage fright strut on stage, athletes engage in dangerous competitive activities while in a state of agitated apprehension, and students take intimidating examinations although beset by intense anticipatory anxiety. Similarly, people regularly take self-protective action without waiting for anxiety to impel them to action. They strap on seat belts to prevent injury, disinfect things to protect against infections, and disconnect electrical appliances before repairing them without having to conjure up an anxious state to move them to action. These types of disconfirming occurrences tend to be ignored in judging the relation between anxiety and avoidant behavior.

PERCEIVED SELF-EFFICACY IN ANXIETY AROUSAL

In social cognitive theory (Bandura, 1986), perceived ability to control potentially threatening events plays a central role in anxiety arousal and coping behavior. Threat is not a fixed property of situational events. Nor does appraisal of the likelihood of aversive happenings rely solely on reading external signs of danger or safety. Rather, threat is a relational property concerning the match between perceived coping abilities and potentially aversive aspects of the environment. Therefore, to understand people's appraisals of external threats and their affective and behavioral reactions to them it is necessary to analyze their judgments of their coping abilities, which in large part determine the subjective perilousness of environmental events.

People who believe they can control potential threats do not conjure up perturbing cognitions. But those who believe they cannot experience high levels of anxiety arousal. They dwell on their coping deficiencies, view many aspects of their environment as fraught with danger, magnify possible threats, and worry about perils that rarely, if ever, happen. Through such inefficacious thought they distress themselves and constrain and impair their level of functioning (Lazarus & Folkman, 1984; Meichenbaum, 1977; Sarason, 1975).

Several converging lines of evidence corroborate the influential role of perceived control in anxiety and stress reactions (Averill, 1973; Levine & Ursin, 1980; Miller, 1980). A sense of personal control can be achieved either behaviorally or cognitively. In behavioral control, individuals do things that forestall or attenuate aversive events. In cognitive control, they operate under the belief that they can manage threatening situations should they arise. Although actual and perceived control are clearly distinguishable at the operational level, there is often substantial variance between perception and actuality. Perceived self-efficacy operates anticipatorily in regulating anxiety arousal in both forms of control.

Being able to control potential threats can diminish anxiety because the ability is used to reduce or prevent painful experiences. But stress reduction by behavioral control involves much more than simply curtailing painful events. The experiences accompanying the exercise of behavioral control produce substantial cognitive changes in perceived self-efficacy that continue to affect autonomic arousal after the behavioral episodes have ceased (Bandura, Cioffi, Taylor, & Brouillard, 1988). In the study cited, perceived self-efficacy was strengthened by exercise of full control over problem solving demands and substantially weakened by inability to wield adequate control. People who perceived themselves as efficacious exhibited little stress during the problem solving, whereas the perceived self-inefficacious ones experienced a high level of subjective stress and autonomic arousal (Figure 21). Simply appraising one's capabilities after the problem solving activity was over activated divergent autonomic reactions—a rise in autonomic arousal in the perceived self-

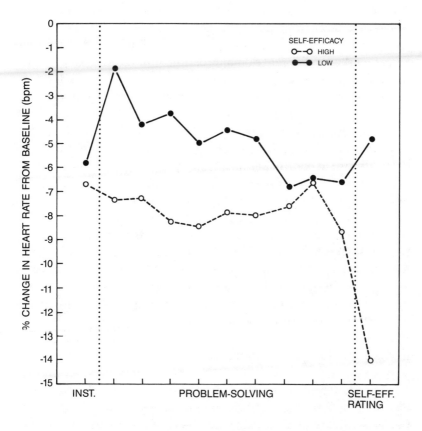

FIGURE 21. Percentage changes in heart rate displayed by perceived self-efficacious and perceived self-inefficacious subjects while they received instructions for the problem solving task, coped with the task demands, and later appraised their perceived self-efficacy. From Bandura, Cioffi, Taylor, & Brouillard, 1988, p. 484. Copyright 1988 by the American Psychological Association. Reprinted by permission of the publisher.

inefficacious group and a sharp drop in the perceived self-efficacious group. The greater the increase in perceived self-efficacy the larger the drop in autonomic arousal.

In some studies of behavioral control, threatening events occur undiminished but are promptly transformed to nonaversive ones when their occurrence is personally controlled (Gunnar–von Gnechten, 1978). Here it is simply the exercise of initiatory control, not the curtailment of the events themselves, that reduces anxiety.

The anxiety-reduction effects stem from the sense of personal control rather than from increased predictability of aversive events (Gunnar, 1980). That a sense of control can diminish anxiety, even across markedly different domains of functioning, is strikingly demonstrated by Mineka, Gunnar, and Champoux (1986) in a developmental study. Monkeys who had been reared from birth under conditions in which they exercised control over access to food showed little fear or avoidance of novel threats months later, whereas the same threats were highly frightening to monkeys who could not develop a sense of control because food had been given to them independent of their actions. In situations in which the opportunity to wield behavioral control exists but is not exercised, it is the self-knowledge that one can exercise control should one choose rather than its application that reduces anxiety reactions (Glass, Reim, & Singer, 1971). The power of unexercised illusory behavioral control to attenuate anxiety arousal was corroborated by Sanderson, Rapee, and Barlow (1989) in a study in which agoraphobics were equally exposed to panic-provoking stimuli. Exposure to the stimuli when subjects had freedom to use an illusory mode of control but never applied it rarely induced panic attacks, whereas under conditions of uncontrollability panic attacks and catastrophic cognitions were very frequent.

The converging lines of evidence indicate that much of the anxiety-reducing effects of behavioral control stem anticipatorily from perceived ability to control aversive events rather than simply from attenuating them when they occur. Therefore perceived control even without the actuality reduces anxiety. People who are led to believe they have some control over painful stimuli display lower autonomic arousal and less performance impairment than do those who believe they lack personal control, even though they are equally subjected to the painful stimuli (Geer, Davison, & Gatchel, 1970; Glass, Singer, Leonard, Krantz, & Cummings, 1973). Repeated failures arouse anxiety when ascribed to personal incapability, but the same painful experiences leave people unperturbed if ascribed to situational factors (Wortman, Panciera, Shusterman, & Hibscher, 1976).

That perceived self-efficacy operates as a cognitive mediator of anxiety arousal has been tested by creating different levels of perceived efficacy in phobics and relating them at a microlevel to different manifestations of anxiety as the subjects cope with phobic threats. People display little affective arousal while coping with potential threats they regard with high efficacy. But as they confront threats for which they distrust their coping efficacy, subjective stress mounts, heart rate accelerates, and blood pressure rises (Bandura, Reese, & Adams, 1982). Understanding of the physiological mechanisms through which self-percepts of efficacy affect anxiety arousal was carried one step further by linking strength of perceived self-efficacy to release of catecholamines (Bandura, Taylor, Williams, Mefford, & Barchas, 1985). As in the previous research, after the range of perceived self-efficacy in phobics was expanded by modeling, phobics were presented with coping tasks they judged to be in their perceived low, medium, or high self-efficacy range. Epinephrine, norepinephrine, and dopac levels were low when phobics coped with tasks in their high perceived self-efficacy range (Figure 22). Self-doubt about coping efficacy produced substantial increases in these catecholamines. When presented with tasks that exceeded their perceived coping capabilities, the phobics instantly rejected them. Catecholamines dropped sharply. The dopac response differs markedly from that of the other catecholamines. Whereas epinephrine and norepinephrine dropped upon rejection of the threatening task, dopac rose to its highest level, even though the phobics had no intention of coping with the task. Dopac seems to be triggered by the mere apperception that environmental demands overwhelm one's perceived coping capabilities.

In each of the preceding experiments, after level of anxiety is measured as a function of perceived self-efficacy, a guided mastery procedure is used to strengthen perceived coping self-efficacy to the maximum level for all previous levels of threat. When the different coping tasks are readministered, the previously intimidating threats no longer elicit differential autonomic or catecholamine reactivity. The combined results are consistent in showing that anxiety reactions to coping tasks differ when perceived self-efficacy differs but that anxiety reactions to the identical tasks are the same when perceived self-efficacy is raised to the same maximum level. Thus, perceived mismatch between perceived coping capabilities and task demands rather than the properties inherent in the tasks themselves is the source of variation in anxiety reactions. Perceived coping efficacy determines the subjective perilousness of environmental situa-

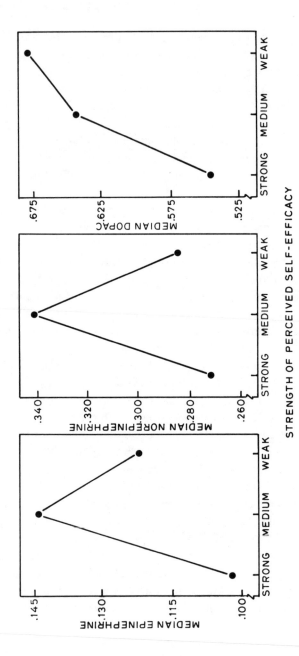

FIGURE 22. Median level of plasma catecholamine secretion as a function of perceived coping self-efficacy. From Bandura, Taylor, Williams, Mefford, & Barchas, 1985, p. 410. Copyright 1985 by the American Psychological Association. Reprinted by permission of the publisher.

tions. People view contact with potential threats as hazardous when they believe they cannot manage them safely, but they regard such encounters as nondangerous when they believe they can wield control over them.

THOUGHT CONTROL EFFICACY IN ANXIETY AROUSAL

Human activities are rarely devoid of risk. Moreover, many deleterious events are not completely under personal control. For example, even highly self-efficacious drivers may experience some apprehension on busy thoroughfares because they cannot always spot reckless drivers or forestall others from ramming them. It is therefore natural to give some thought to potential risks in any undertaking and to feel uneasy about them. But where the risks are extremely low, it is dysfunctional to magnify subjective dangers or to ruminate apprehensively to the point where it creates self-inflicted misery and impairs psychosocial functioning.

Perceived self-efficacy in thought control is a key factor in regulating cognitively generated arousal. Reducing vulnerability to distress through control over one's own consciousness is summed up well in the proverb: "You cannot prevent the birds of worry and care from flying over your head. But you can stop them from building a nest in your head." Studies of the effects of different properties of cognitions reveal that it is not the sheer frequency of disturbing cognitions, but the perceived inability to turn them off that is a major source of distress (Churchill & McMurray, 1990; Kent, 1987; Salkovskis & Harrison, 1984). Thus, the frequency of aversive cognitions is unrelated to anxiety level when variations in perceived thought control efficacy are partialed out, whereas perceived thought control is strongly related to anxiety level when frequency of frightful cognitions is partialed out (Kent & Gibbons, 1987). That perceived inefficacy to control highly intrusive thoughts is the major source of distress receives additional support in the research of Dickerson and his associates (Edwards & Dickerson, 1987; England & Dickerson, 1988). They found that a sense of inefficacy to turn off positive intrusive thoughts is just as distressing and attentionally disruptive as perceived inefficacy to turn off negative ones.

PERCEIVED SELF-EFFICACY AND AVOIDANT BEHAVIOR

Perceived coping self-efficacy regulates avoidance behavior in risky situations as well as anxiety arousal. The stronger the perceived coping self-efficacy, the more venturesome the behavior, regardless of whether self-beliefs of efficacy are strengthened by guided mastery experiences, modeling of coping strategies, or cognitive simulations of successful management of threats (Bandura, 1988a). The role of perceived self-efficacy and anxiety arousal in the causal structure of avoidant behavior has been examined in a number of studies. The results show that people base their actions on self-beliefs of efficacy in situations they regard as risky. Williams and his colleagues (Williams, 1987; Williams, Dooseman, & Kleifield, 1984; Williams, Kinney, & Falbo, 1989; Williams & Rappoport, 1983; Williams, Turner, & Peer, 1985) have analyzed by partial correlation numerous data sets from studies that measured perceived self-efficacy, anticipated anxiety, and phobic behavior. Perceived self-efficacy accounts for a substantial amount of variance in phobic behavior when anticipated anxiety is partialed out, whereas the relation between anticipated anxiety and phobic behavior essentially disappears when perceived self-efficacy is partialed out (Table 1). Studies of other threatening activities similarly demonstrate the predictive superiority of perceived self-efficacy over perceived dangerous outcomes in level of anxiety arousal (Hackett & Betz, 1989; Leland, 1983; McAuley, 1985; Williams & Watson, 1985).

The dual control of anxiety arousal and behavior by perceived coping efficacy and thought control efficacy is revealed in a study of the mechanisms governing personal empowerment over pervasive social threats (Ozer & Bandura, 1990). Sexual violence toward women is a prevalent problem. Because any woman may be a victim, the lives of many women are distressed and constricted by a sense of inefficacy to cope with the threat of sexual assault. To address this problem at a self-protective level, women participated in a mastery modeling program in which they mastered the physical skills to defend themselves effectively against sexual assailants. Mastery modeling enhanced perceived coping self-efficacy and cognitive control efficacy, decreased perceived vulnerability to assault, and reduced the incidence of intrusive aversive thoughts and anxi-

Table 1

Comparison of the Relation Between Perceived Self-Efficacy and Coping Behavior When Anticipated Anxiety Is Controlled, and the Relation Between Anticipated Anxiety and Coping Behavior When Perceived Self-Efficacy Is Controlled

	Coping Behavior	
	Anticipated Anxiety With Self-Efficacy Controlled	Perceived Self-Efficacy With Anticipated Anxiety Controlled
Williams & Rappoport (1983)		
Pretreatment 1†	−.12	.40*
Pretreatment 2	−.28	.59**
Posttreatment	.13	.45*
Follow-up	.06	.45*
Williams, Dooseman, & Kleifield (1984)		
Pretreatment	−.36*	.22
Posttreatment	−.21	.59***
Williams, Turner, & Peer (1985)		
Pretreatment	−.35*	.28*
Posttreatment	.05	.72***
Follow-up	−.12	.66***
Telch et al. (1985)		
Pretreatment	−.56***	−.28
Posttreatment	.15	.48**
Follow-up	−.05	.42*
Kirsch et al. (1983)		
Pretreatment	−.34*	.54***
Posttreatment	−.48**	.48**
Arnow et al. (1985)		
Pretreatment	.17	.77***
Posttreatment	−.08	.43*
Follow-up	−.06	.88**
Williams, Kinney, & Falbo (1989)		
Midtreatment	−.15	.65***
Posttreatment	.02	.47**
Follow-up	−.03	.71***

*p<.05.   **p<.01.   ***p<.001.

†The pretreatment phases of some of these experiments include only subjects selected for severe phobic behavior. They have a uniformly low sense of coping efficacy. In such instances, the highly restricted range of self-efficacy scores tends to lower the correlation coefficients in pretreatment phases.

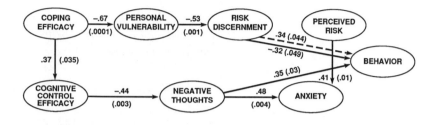

FIGURE 23. Path analysis of the causal structure. The numbers on the paths of influence are the significant standardized path coefficients; the numbers in parentheses are the significance levels. The solid line to behavior represents avoidant behavior, the broken line represents participant behavior. From Ozer & Bandura, 1990, p. 483. Copyright 1990 by the American Psychological Association. Reprinted by permission of the publisher.

ety arousal. These changes were accompanied by increased freedom of action and decreased avoidant social behavior. Path analysis of the causal structure revealed a dual path of regulation of behavior by perceived self-efficacy: one path of influence was mediated through the effects of perceived coping self-efficacy on perceived vulnerability and risk discernment; the second path of influence operated through the effect of perceived cognitive control self-efficacy on intrusive aversive thoughts (Figure 23). A strong sense of coping efficacy rooted in performance capabilities enhanced perceived self-efficacy to abort the escalation or perseveration of perturbing cognitions. Belief in personal capability to exercise control over potential threats makes it easier to dismiss intrusive aversive thoughts.

The evidence taken as a whole indicates that anxiety arousal and avoidant behavior are largely coeffects of perceived coping inefficacy rather than being causally linked. People avoid potentially threatening situations and activities not because they experience anxiety arousal or anticipate they will be anxious, but because they believe they will be unable to cope with situations they regard as risky. They take self-protective action regardless of whether they happen to be anxious at the moment. They often engage in risky activities at lower strengths of perceived self-efficacy despite high anxiety arousal as long as they entertain some prospect of success (Bandura, 1988b).

Self-Regulatory Mechanisms in Moral Motivation

The earlier discussion analyzed the mechanisms through which aspirational standards regulate motivation and personal accomplishments. In areas of functioning involving achievement striving and cultivation of competencies, the internal standards that are selected as a mark of adequacy are progressively altered as skills and knowledge are acquired and challenges are met. In many areas of social and moral behavior, the internal standards that serve as the basis for regulating one's conduct are relatively stable. That is, people do not change from week to week in what they regard as right or wrong or as good or bad. Moreover, violating moral standards is likely to generate much stronger affective self-reactions than is falling short of achievement standards.

Until recently, psychological interest in the domain of morality has centered almost exclusively on analyses of moral thought (Kohlberg, 1984). The conspicuous neglect of moral conduct reflects both the rationalistic bias of many theories of morality and the convenience of investigatory method. It is much easier to examine how people reason about hypothetical moral dilemmas than to study their actual conduct. But it is the morality reflected in conduct rather than that stated in moral pretensions that should be of central concern. People suffer from the wrongs done to them, however perpetrators might justify their harmful actions. A comprehensive theory of morality must explain how moral reasoning, in conjunction with other psychosocial factors, governs moral motivation and conduct.

Space does not permit a detailed exposition of moral motivation. The social cognitive theory of moral motivation has been presented elsewhere (Bandura, 1991b), and will only be summarized briefly here. In this theory, transgressive conduct is regulated by two major sources of sanctions: social sanctions and internalized self-sanctions. Both mechanisms operate anticipatorily. In motivators arising from social sanctions, people refrain from transgressing because they anticipate that such conduct will bring them social censure and other adverse consequences. In motivators rooted in self-reactive control, people behave in prosocial ways that give them a sense of satisfaction and self-respect, and they refrain from transgressing because it gives rise to self-reproach. Societal codes and sanctions articulate collective moral imperatives as well as influencing social conduct. However, external sanctions are limited in their deterrent power because most transgressions go socially undetected. But people continuously preside over their own behavior in countless situations presenting little or no threat of external sanctions. So the exercise of self-sanction must play a central role in regulating moral conduct.

CONCEPTION OF MORAL AGENCY IN TERMS OF SELF-REGULATORY MECHANISMS

In the course of socialization, people develop moral standards from a variety of influences (Bandura, 1986). They base standards for judging their own conduct partly on how significant persons in their lives react to it. Standards are influenced through direct instruction in the precepts of conduct as well as through the evaluative reactions of others toward one's actions. People not only prescribe self-evaluative standards for others, they also exemplify them in responding to their own behavior. The power of modeling in influencing standards of conduct is well documented.

The development of personal standards is a dynamic process (Bandura, 1991b). People do not passively absorb standards of conduct from whatever influences happen to impinge upon them. Rather, they construct generic standards from the numerous evaluative rules that are prescribed, modeled, and taught. The process is complicated because people often differ in the standards they model, and even the same person may model different standards in different social settings and domains of conduct. Moreover, those who serve as socialization influencers, whether designedly or unintentionally, often display inconsistencies between what they practice and what they preach. Personal standards must therefore be constructed within a network of conflicting social influences. Once standards are acquired, they guide and deter conduct by the consequences people produce for themselves (Bandura, 1986; Kurtines & Gewirtz, 1984).

Explanation of the relation between moral reasoning and conduct must specify the psychological mechanisms by which moral standards get translated into actions. In the stage theory of moral maturity (Kohlberg, 1971), the form of moral thought is not linked to particular conduct. Level of moral maturity determines the type of reasons given for actions, not what actions should be taken. Thus each level of moral reasoning can be used to support or to disavow transgressive conduct. People may act prosocially or transgressively out of mutual obligation, for social approval, out of duty to a social order, or for reasons of principle. Immorality can be served as well— or better—by sophisticated reasoning as by simpler reasoning. Indeed, when people reason about moral conflicts they actually face in their environment, Kohlberg and his associates find that moral reasoning is more a function of the social influences operating in the situation than of stages of "moral competence" (Higgins, Power, & Kohlberg, 1984).

In social cognitive theory, moral conduct is regulated mainly by mechanisms of self-reactive influence. Moral agency operates through a set of psychological subfunctions. To influence their own conduct people have to monitor what they do. However, self-monitoring alone provides little basis for self-directed reactions. Actions give rise to self-reactions through a judgmental function in which conduct is evaluated in relation to personal standards and environmental circumstances. Situations with moral implications contain many judgmental ingredients that not only vary in importance but may be given lesser or greater weight depending upon the particular constellation of events in a given moral predicament. Among the many factors that enter into judging conduct are the nature of the transgression, its base rate of occurrence, and the degree of norm violation; the contexts in which it is performed and the perceived situational and personal motivators for it; the immediate and long-range consequences of the actions; whether it produces personal injury or property damage; whether it is directed at faceless agencies and organizations or at individuals; the characteristics of the wrongdoers, such as their age, sex, and ethnic and social status; and the characteristics of the victims and their perceived blameworthiness.

The integrative rules of moral decision making have been studied most extensively by researchers who analyze moral thinking as a process of information integration (Kaplan, 1989; Lane & Anderson, 1976; Leon, 1982; Surber, 1985). In dealing with moral dilemmas, therefore, people must extract, weight, and integrate the morally relevant information in the situations confronting them. Factors that weigh heavily under some combinations of circumstances may be disregarded or considered of lesser import under a different set of conditions. This process of moral reasoning is guided by multi-dimensional rules for judging conduct.

Self-regulation of moral conduct involves more than moral thought. Moral judgment sets the occasion for self-reactive influence. Evaluative self-reactions provide the mechanism by which standards regulate conduct. The anticipatory self-pride and self-censure for actions that correspond to or violate personal standards serve as the regulatory influences. People do things that give them satisfaction and a sense of self-worth. They ordinarily refrain from behaving in ways that violate their moral standards because it will bring self-condemnation. Anticipatory self-sanctions thus keep conduct in line with internal standards.

INTERPLAY BETWEEN PERSONAL AND SOCIAL SANCTIONS

The self-regulation of conduct is not entirely an intrapsychic affair, nor do people operate as autonomous moral agents impervious to the social realities in which they are enmeshed. In the interactionist perspective of social cognitive theory, moral conduct is regulated by a reciprocity of influence between thought and self-sanctions, conduct, and a network of social influences. Social factors affect the operation of the self system in at least three major ways (Bandura, 1986). We saw earlier that they contribute importantly to the development of self-regulatory functions. Analyses of regulation of moral action through affective self-reaction distinguish between two sources of incentive motivation operating in the process. There are the conditional evaluative self incentives that provide guides and proximal motivators for moral courses of action. Then there are the more distal social incentives for holding to a moral system. Thus, the second way social influences contribute to morality is by providing collective support for adherence to moral standards. The third way social realities affect moral functioning is by promoting selective activation and disengagement of moral self-regulation. I shall return to this issue later.

After standards and self-reactive functions are developed, behavior usually produces two sets of consequences: self-evaluative reactions and social effects. These two sources of consequences may operate as complementary or opposing influences on behavior. Conduct is most congruent with moral standards when transgressive behavior is not easily self-excusable and the evaluative reactions of significant others are compatible with personal standards. Under conditions of shared moral standards, socially approvable acts are a source of self-pride and socially punishable ones are self-censured. To enhance the compatibility between personal and social sanctions, people generally select associates who share similar standards of conduct and thus ensure social support for their own system of self-evaluation (Bandura & Walters, 1959; Emmons & Diener, 1986). Diversity of standards in a society therefore does not necessarily create personal conflict. Selective association can forge consistency out of diversity.

Behavior is especially susceptible to external influences in the absence of strong countervailing internal standards. People who are not much committed to personal standards adopt a pragmatic orientation, tailoring their behavior to fit whatever the situation seems to call for (Snyder & Campbell, 1982). They become adept at reading social situations and guiding their actions by expediency.

One type of conflict between social and self-produced consequences arises when individuals are socially punished for behavior they highly value (Bandura, 1973). Principled dissenters and nonconformists often find themselves in this predicament. Here the relative strength of self-approval and social censure determines whether the behavior will be restrained or expressed. Should the threatened social consequences be severe, people hold self-praiseworthy acts in check in risky situations but perform them readily in relatively safe settings. There are individuals, however, whose sense of self-worth is so strongly invested in certain convictions that they will submit to prolonged maltreatment rather than accede to what they regard as unjust or immoral.

People commonly experience conflicts in which they are socially pressured to engage in behavior that violates their moral standards. When self-devaluative consequences outweigh the benefits of socially accommodating behavior, the social influences do not have much sway. The self-regulation of conduct operates through conditional application of moral standards, however. Self-sanctions can be weakened or nullified by exonerative moral reasoning and social circumstances. People display different levels of detrimental behavior and offer different types of moral reasons for it depending on whether they find themselves in social situations that are conducive to humane or injurious conduct (Bandura, Underwood, & Fromson, 1975).

SELECTIVE ACTIVATION AND DISENGAGEMENT OF INTERNAL STANDARDS

Development of self-regulatory functions operating through moral standards does not create a fixed internal regulator of conduct, as suggested by theories of internalization incorporating entities such as conscience or superego as continuous overseers of actions. Self-regulatory mechanisms do not operate unless they are activated, and there are many processes by which self-sanctions can be disengaged from inhumane conduct (Bandura, 1986, 1991b). Selective activation and disengagement of internal control permit different types of conduct with the same moral standards. Figure 24 shows the points in the self-regulatory process at which internal moral control can be disengaged from detrimental control.

These mechanisms of moral disengagement have been examined most extensively in the expression of aggressive conduct. But selective disengagement of moral self-sanctions is by no means confined to extraordinary inducements to aggression. People often experience conflicts in which behavior they themselves devalue can serve as the means for securing valued benefits. As long as self-sanctions override the force of external inducements, behavior is kept in line with personal standards. But in the face of strong external inducements, such conflicts are often resolved by selective disengagement of self-sanctions. This enables otherwise considerate people to perform self-serving activities that have detrimental social effects.

One set of disengagement practices operates on the construal of the behavior itself. People do not ordinarily engage in reprehensible conduct until they have justified to themselves the morality of their actions. What is culpable can be made righteous through cognitive reconstrual. In this process of *moral justification*, detrimental conduct is made personally and socially acceptable by portraying it in the service of moral purposes (Bandura, 1990b; Sanford & Comstock, 1971).

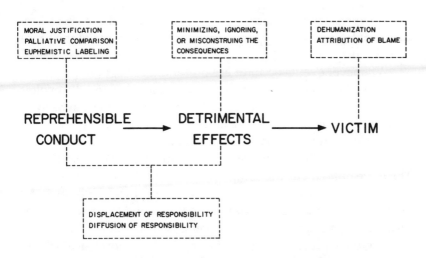

FIGURE 24. Mechanisms through which moral control is selectively activated or disengaged from detrimental conduct at different points in the self-regulatory process. From Bandura, 1986, p. 376. Reprinted by permission of Prentice Hall, Inc., Englewood Cliffs, New Jersey.

People then act on a moral imperative. Over the years, much reprehensible and destructive conduct has been perpetrated by ordinary, considerate people in the name of religious principles, righteous ideologies, and nationalistic imperatives (Rapoport & Alexander, 1982). Voltaire described this process well when he noted that "Those who can make you believe absurdities can make you commit atrocities."

Language shapes people's thought patterns, on which they base many of their actions. Activities can take on a very different appearance depending on what they are called. *Euphemistic labeling* thus provides a convenient device for masking reprehensible activities or even conferring a respectable status upon them. Through convoluted and sanitizing verbiage, detrimental conduct is made benign, and those who engage in it are relieved of a sense of personal agency. Laboratory studies attest to the disinhibitory power of euphemistic language. People behave much more inhumanely when reprehensible behavior is given a sanitized label than when it is called what it is (Diener, Dineen, Endresen, Beaman, & Fraser, 1975). In an insightful analysis of the language of nonresponsibility, Gambino (1973) identifies the different varieties of euphemisms. Palliative expressions, the agentless passive form, and the specialized jargon of legitimate enterprises are widely used to make the reprehensible respectable.

Whenever events occur or are presented contiguously, the first one colors how the second one is perceived and judged. By exploiting the contrast principle, moral judgments of conduct can be influenced by expedient structuring of what it is compared against (Bandura, 1991b). Acts that one would ordinarily deplore can be made righteous by *advantageous comparison* with flagrant inhumanities. The more outrageous the comparison practices, the more likely it is that one's own destructive conduct will appear trifling or even benevolent. Advantageous historical comparisons are also often invoked to reconstrue and justify reprehensible conduct.

Cognitive restructuring of behavior through moral justifications and palliative characterizations is the most effective psychological mechanism for promoting conduct that violates personal standards. This is because moral restructuring not only eliminates self-deterrents but engages self-approval in the service of deleterious conduct. What was once morally condemnable becomes a source of self-valuation. After harmful practices become invested with high moral purpose, people work hard to become proficient at them and take pride in accomplishments achieved deleteriously.

Self-sanctions are activated most strongly when personal agency for detrimental effects is not ambiguous. Another set of dissociative practices operates by obscuring or distorting the relationship between actions and the effects they cause. People will behave in ways they normally repudiate if a legitimate authority accepts responsibility for the consequences of the conduct (Diener et al., 1975; Milgram, 1974). Under *displacement of responsibility,* people view their actions as springing from the dictates of authorities rather than feeling personally responsible for them. Since they do not regard themselves as the actual agents of their actions, they are spared self-prohibiting reactions. Displacement of responsibility not only weakens restraints over one's own deleterious actions but diminishes social concern over the well-being of those mistreated by others (Milgram, 1974; Tilker, 1970).

In laboratory studies of disengagement of self-sanctions through displacement of responsibility, authorities explicitly authorize injurious actions and hold themselves fully accountable for the harm caused (Milgram, 1974). However, in the sanctioning practices of everyday life responsibility for detrimental conduct is rarely assumed so explicitly, because only obtuse authorities would leave themselves accusable of authorizing reprehensible acts. Sanctioners create self-absolving operations to escape not only adverse social consequences to themselves should advocated courses of action miscarry, but the loss of self-regard for sanctioning harmful practices. Therefore authorities usually invite and support detrimental conduct in insidious ways that minimize personal responsibility for what is happening.

Obedient functionaries do not cast off all responsibility for their behavior as though they were mindless extensions of others. It requires a strong sense of responsibility to be a good functionary. In situations involving displaced responsibility, people carry out orders partly to honor the obligations they have undertaken (Mantell & Panzarella, 1976). Therefore one must distinguish two levels of responsibility—duty to one's superiors and accountability for the effects of one's actions. The self system operates most efficiently in the service of authority when followers assume personal responsibility for being dutiful executors while relinquishing personal responsibility for the harm caused by their behavior. Followers who disowned responsibility without being bound by a sense of duty would be quite unreliable.

The deterrent power of self-sanctions is weakened when the link between conduct and its consequences is obscured by *diffusion of responsibility* for deleterious behavior. This is achieved in several ways. Responsibility can be diffused by division of labor. Most enterprises require the services of many people, each performing fragmentary jobs that seem harmless in themselves. The fractional contribution is easily isolated from the eventual function, especially when participants exercise little personal judgment in carrying out a subfunction that is related to the end result by remote, complex links. After activities become routinized into programmed subfunctions, attention shifts from the moral import of what one is doing to efficient engrossment in the details of one's fractional job (Kelman, 1973).

Group decision making is another common bureaucratic practice that enables otherwise considerate people to behave inhumanely, because no single individual feels responsible for policies arrived at collectively. Where everyone is responsible no one really feels responsible. Collective action is still another diffusion expedient for weakening self-restraints. Any harm done by a group can always be ascribed, in large part, to the behavior of other members. People therefore act more harshly when responsibility is obfuscated by a collective instrumentality than when they hold themselves personally accountable for what they do (Bandura, Underwood, & Fromson, 1975; Diener, 1977; Zimbardo, 1969).

Additional ways of weakening self-deterring reactions operate through *disregard for or distortion of consequences of action.* When people choose to pursue activities harmful to others for personal gain or because of social inducements, they avoid facing the harm they cause or they minimize it. They readily recall information given them about the potential benefits of the behavior but are less able to remember its harmful effects (Brock & Buss, 1962, 1964). People are especially prone to minimize injurious effects when they act alone and thus cannot easily escape responsibility (Mynatt & Herman, 1975). In addition to selective inattention and cognitive distortion of effects, the misrepresentation may involve active efforts to discredit evidence of harmful effects. As long as the detrimental results of one's conduct are ignored, minimized, distorted, or disbelieved, there is little reason for self-censure to be activated. Most social systems involve hierarchical chains of command in which superiors formulate plans and intermediaries transmit them to executors, who then carry them out. Disengagement of personal control is easiest for the intermediaries in a hierarchical system—they neither bear responsibility for major decisions nor are party to their execution or personal witnesses of the effects (Kilham & Mann, 1974).

The final set of disengagement practices operates on the victims of deleterious acts through *dehumanization* and *attribution of blame.* The strength of self-evaluative reactions to harmful conduct partly depends on how the perpetrators view the people acted upon. To perceive another as human enhances empathetic or vicarious reactions through perceived similarity (Bandura, 1991c). The joys and suffering of similar persons are more vicariously arousing than are those of strangers or individuals who have been divested of human qualities. As a result, it is difficult to mistreat humanized persons without risking self-censure.

Self-sanctions against harmful conduct can be disengaged or blunted by divesting people of human qualities. Once dehumanized, they are no longer viewed as persons with feelings, hopes, and concerns but rather are seen as subhuman objects. If dispossessing antagonists of humanness does not blunt self-reproof, it can be eliminated by attributing bestial qualities to them (Gibson & Haritos-Fatouros, 1986; Ivie, 1980). When persons are given punitive power, they treat dehumanized individuals much more punitively than those who have been invested with human qualities (Bandura, Underwood, & Fromson, 1975).

Under certain conditions, exercising institutional power changes the agents in ways that are conducive to dehumanization. This happens most often when persons in positions of authority have coercive power over others and adequate safeguards for constraining the behavior of powerholders are lacking. Powerholders come to devalue those they control (Kipnis, 1974). Systematic tests of relative influences similarly show that social influences conducive to punitiveness exert considerably greater sway over aggressive conduct than do personal characteristics (Larsen, Coleman, Forges, & Johnson, 1971). The overall findings from research on the different mechanisms of moral disengagement corroborate the historical chronicle of large-scale inhumanities: it takes conducive social conditions rather than monstrous people to produce heinous deeds. Given appropriate social conditions, decent, ordinary people can be led to do extraordinarily cruel things.

Psychological research tends to focus extensively on how easy it is to bring out the worst in people through dehumanization and other self-exonerative means. However, of considerable theoretical and social significance is the power of humanization to counteract cruel conduct. Studies examining this process reveal that it is difficult for individuals to behave cruelly toward others when they are humanized or even personalized a bit. Such maltreatment would activate strong self-condemning reactions (Bandura, Underwood, & Fromson, 1975).

Imputing blame to one's antagonists is still another expedient that can serve in self-exoneration. In this process, people regard themselves as faultless self-defenders compelled to coercive action by forcible provocation. Injurious conduct thus becomes a justifiable defensive reaction to willful or foolish provocation. Self-exoneration can be similarly achieved by viewing one's injurious conduct as forced by circumstances rather than as a personal decision. By blaming others or circumstances, not only are one's own actions made excusable, but one can even feel self-righteous.

Most of the research on attributional analysis of moral judgment is concerned with whether people view their behavior as determined by external circumstances or hold themselves responsible for it (Ross & DiTecco, 1975; Rule & Nesdale, 1976). Perceptions of causal responsibility are reduced if the harmful consequences of actions are viewed as unintended or unforeseeable, or if the actions arose from the dictates of the situation. Within the attributional framework, these factors are usually studied as mitigators of moral judgment rather than as disengagers of moral self-sanctions.

CONCLUDING COMMENT

The converging lines of evidence reviewed in this chapter testify to the paramount role self-regulatory mechanisms play in human motivation across diverse realms of functioning. Self-regulation is a multifaceted phenomenon operating through a number of subsidiary cognitive processes, including self-monitoring, standard setting, evaluative judgment, self-appraisal, and affective self-reaction. Cognitive regulation of motivation relies extensively on an anticipatory proactive system rather than simply on a reactive negative feedback system. The human capacity for forethought, reflective self-appraisal, and self-reaction gives prominence to cognitively based motivators in the exercise of personal agency.

REFERENCES

Ajzen, I. (1985). From intentions to actions: A theory of planned behavior. In J. Kuhl & J. Beckman (Eds.), *Action-control: From cognition to behavior* (pp. 11–39). Heidelberg: Springer-Verlag.

Ajzen, I., & Fishbein, M. (1980). *Understanding attitudes and predicting social behavior.* Englewood Cliffs, NJ: Prentice-Hall.

Ajzen, I., & Madden, T. J. (1986). Prediction of goal-directed behavior: Attitudes, intentions, and perceived behavioral control. *Journal of Experimental Social Psychology, 22,* 453–474.

Alden, L. (1986). Self-efficacy and causal attributions for social feedback. *Journal of Research in Personality, 20,* 460–473.

Alloy, L. B., & Abramson, L. Y. (1979). Judgment of contingency in depressed and nondepressed students: Sadder but wiser? *Journal of Experimental Psychology, 108*, 441–487.

Alloy, L. B., Abramson, L. Y., & Viscusi, D. (1981). Induced mood and the illusion of control. *Journal of Personality and Social Psychology, 41*, 1129–1140.

Arbuthnot, J. (1975). Modification of moral judgment through role playing. *Developmental Psychology, 11*, 319–324.

Arnow, B. A., Taylor, C. B., Agras, W. S., & Telch, M. J. (1985). Enhancing agoraphobia treatment by changing couple communication patterns. *Behavior Therapy, 16*, 452–467.

Arvey, R. D., & Dewhirst, H. D. (1976). Goal-setting attributes, personality variables, and job satisfaction. *Journal of Vocational Behavior, 9*, 179–190.

Atkinson, J. W. (1964). *An introduction to motivation.* Princeton, NJ: Van Nostrand.

Averill, J. R. (1973). Personal control over aversive stimuli and its relationship to stress. *Psychological Bulletin, 80*, 286–303.

Bandura, A. (1973). *Aggression: A social learning analysis.* Englewood Cliffs, NJ: Prentice-Hall.

Bandura, A. (1986). *Social foundations of thought and action: A social cognitive theory.* Englewood Cliffs, NJ: Prentice-Hall.

Bandura, A. (1988a). Perceived self-efficacy: Exercise of control through self-belief. In J. P. Dauwalder, M. Perrez, & V. Hobi (Eds.), *Annual series of European research in behavior therapy* (Vol. 2, pp. 27–59). Lisse (NL): Swets & Zeitlinger.

Bandura, A. (1988b). Self-efficacy conception of anxiety. *Anxiety Research, 1*, 77–98.

Bandura, A. (1989). Perceived self-efficacy in the exercise of personal agency. *The Psychologist: Bulletin of the British Psychological Society, 2*, 411–424.

Bandura, A. (1990a). Reflections on nonability determinants of competence. In R. J. Sternberg & J. Kolligian, Jr. (Eds.), *Competence considered* (pp. 315–362). New Haven: Yale University Press.

Bandura, A. (1990b). Mechanisms of moral disengagement. In W. Reich (Ed.), *Origins of terrorism: Psychologies, ideologies, theologies, states of mind* (pp. 162–191). Cambridge: Cambridge University Press.

Bandura, A. (1991a). Self-efficacy mechanism in physiological activation and health-promoting behavior. In J.Madden, IV, S. Matthysse, & J. Barchas (Eds.), *Adaptation, learning and affect.* New York: Raven Press.

Bandura, A. (1991b). Social cognitive theory of moral thought and action. In W. M. Kurtines & J. L. Gewirtz (Eds.), *Handbook of moral behavior and development:* (Vol. 1, pp. 45–103). Hillsdale, NJ: Erlbaum.

Bandura, A. (1991c). Social cognitive theory and social referencing. In S. Feinman (Ed.), *Social referencing and the social construction of reality in infancy.* New York: Plenum.

Bandura, A., & Abrams, K. (1986). *Self-regulatory mechanisms in motivating, apathetic, and despondent reactions to unfulfilled standards.* Unpublished manuscript, Stanford University.

Bandura, A., & Cervone, D. (1983). Self-evaluative and self-efficacy mechanisms governing the motivational effects of goal systems. *Journal of Personality and Social Psychology, 45,* 1017–1028.

Bandura, A., & Cervone, D. (1986). Differential engagement of self-reactive influences in cognitive motivation. *Organizational Behavior and Human Decision Processes, 38,* 92–113.

Bandura, A., Cioffi, D., Taylor, C. B., & Brouillard, M. E. (1988). Perceived self-efficacy in coping with cognitive stressors and opioid activation. *Journal of Personality and Social Psychology, 55,* 479–488.

Bandura, A., & Jourden, F. J. (1991). Self-regulatory mechanisms governing social-comparison effects on complex decision making. *Journal of Personality and Social Psychology.*

Bandura, A., Reese, L., & Adams, N. E. (1982). Microanalysis of action and fear arousal as a function of differential levels of perceived self-efficacy. *Journal of Personality and Social Psychology, 43,* 5–21.

Bandura, A., & Schunk, D. H. (1981). Cultivating competence, self-efficacy and intrinsic interest through proximal self-motivation. *Journal of Personality and Social Psychology, 41,* 586–598.

Bandura, A., & Simon, K. M. (1977). The role of proximal intentions in self-regulation of refractory behavior. *Cognitive Therapy and Research, 1,* 177–193.

Bandura, A., Taylor, C. B., Williams, S. L., Mefford, I. N., & Barchas, J. D. (1985). Catecholamine secretion as a function of perceived coping self-efficacy. *Journal of Consulting and Clinical Psychology, 53,* 406–414.

Bandura, A., Underwood, B., & Fromson, M. E. (1975). Disinhibition of aggression through diffusion of responsibility and dehumanization of victims. *Journal of Research in Personality, 9,* 253–269.

Bandura, A., & Walters, R. H. (1959). *Adolescent aggression.* New York: Ronald Press.

Bandura, A., & Wood, R. E. (1989). Effect of perceived controllability and performance standards on self-regulation of complex decision-making. *Journal of Personality and Social Psychology, 56,* 805–814.

Bandura, M. M., & Dweck, C. S. (1985). *The relationship of conceptions of intelligence and achievement goals to achievement-related cognition, affect and behavior.* Unpublished manuscript, Harvard University.

Barling, J., & Abel, M. (1983). Self-efficacy beliefs and performance. *Cognitive Therapy and Research, 7,* 265–272.

Barling, J., & Beattie, R. (1983). Self-efficacy beliefs and sales performance. *Journal of Organizational Behavior Management, 5,* 41–51.

Beach, F. A. (1969, July). It's all in your mind. *Psychology Today,* 33–35, 60.

Beach, L. R., Barnes, V. E., & Christensen-Szalanski, J. J. J. (1986). Beyond heuristics and biases: A contingency model of judgmental forecasting. *Journal of Forecasting, 5,* 143–157.

Beck, K. H., & Lund, A. K. (1981). The effects of health threat seriousness and personal efficacy upon intentions and behavior. *Journal of Applied Social Psychology, 11,* 401–415.

Becker, L. J. (1978). Joint effect of feedback and goal setting on performance: A field study of residential energy conservation. *Journal of Applied Psychology, 63,* 428–433.

Behling, O., & Starke, F. A. (1973). The postulates of expectancy theory. *Academy of Management Journal, 16,* 373–388.

Betz, N. E., & Hackett, G. (1986). Applications of self-efficacy theory to understanding career choice behavior. *Journal of Social and Clinical Psychology, 4,* 279–289.

Bolles, R. C. (1975). *Learning theory.* New York: Holt, Rinehart, & Winston.

Bower, G. H. (1983). Affect and cognition. *Philosophical Transactions of the Royal Society of London* (ser. B), *302,* 387–402.

Brandt, R. B. (1979). *A theory of the good and the right.* Oxford: Clarendon.

Brehmer, B., Hagafors, R., & Johansson, R. (1980). Cognitive skills in judgment: Subject's ability to use information about weights, function forms, and organizing principles. *Organization and Human Performance, 26,* 373–385.

Brock, T. C., & Buss, A. H. (1962). Dissonance, aggression, and evaluation of pain. *Journal of Abnormal and Social Psychology, 65,* 197–202.

Brock, T. C., & Buss, A. H. (1964). Effects of justification for aggression and communication with the victim on postaggression dissonance. *Journal of Abnormal and Social Psychology, 68,* 403–412.

Brown, I., Jr., & Inouye, D. K. (1978). Learned helplessness through modeling: The role of perceived similarity in competence. *Journal of Personality and Social Psychology, 36,* 900–908.

Bryan, J. F., & Locke, E. A. (1967). Goal-setting as a means of increasing motivation. *Journal of Applied Psychology, 51,* 274–277.

Campion, M. A., & Lord, R. G. (1982). A control systems conceptualization of the goal-setting and changing process. *Organizational Behavior and Human Performance, 30,* 265–287.

Carver, C. S., & Scheier, M. F. (1981). *Attention and self-regulation: A control-theory approach to human behavior.* New York: Springer-Verlag.

Cervone, D. (1989). Effects of envisioning future activities on self-efficacy judgments and motivation: An availability heuristic interpretation. *Cognitive Therapy and Research, 13,* 247–261.

Cervone, D., & Peake, P. K. (1986). Anchoring, efficacy, and action: The influence of judgmental heuristics on self-efficacy judgments and behavior. *Journal of Personality and Social Psychology, 50,* 492–501.

Churchill, A. C., & McMurray, N. E. (1990). *Self-efficacy and unpleasant intrusive thought.* Manuscript submitted for publication.

Ciminero, A. R., & Steingarten, K. A. (1978). The effects of performance standards on self-evaluation and self-reinforcement in depressed and nondepressed individuals. *Cognitive Therapy and Research, 2,* 179–182.

Cioffi, D. (1991). Beyond attentional strategies: A cognitive-perceptual model of somatic interpretation. *Psychological Bulletin, 109,* 25–41.

Collins, J. L. (1982, March). *Self-efficacy and ability in achievement behavior.* Paper presented at the annual meeting of the American Educational Research Association, New York.

Covington, M. V., & Omelich, C. L. (1979). Are causal attributions causal? A path analysis of the cognitive model of achievement motivation. *Journal of Personality and Social Psychology, 37*, 1487–1504.

Csikszentmihalyi, M. (1979). Intrinsic rewards and emergent motivation. In M. R. Lepper & D. Greene (Eds.), *The hidden costs of reward* (pp. 205–216). Morristown, NJ: Erlbaum.

Cutrona, C. E., & Troutman, B. R. (1986). Social support, infant temperament, and parenting self-efficacy: A mediational model of postpartum depression. *Child Development, 57*, 1507–1518.

Davies, F. W., & Yates, B. T. (1982). Self-efficacy expectancies versus outcome expectancies as determinants of performance deficits and depressive affect. *Cognitive Therapy and Research, 6*, 23–35.

Devins, G. M., Binik, Y. M., Gorman, P., Dattel, M., McCloskey, B., Oscar, G., & Briggs, J. (1982). Perceived self-efficacy, outcome expectations, and negative mood states in end-stage renal disease. *Journal of Abnormal Psychology, 91*, 241–244.

de Vries, H., Dijkstra, M., & Kuhlman, P. (1988). Self-efficacy: The third factor besides attitude and subjective norm as a predictor of behavioural intentions. *Health Education Research, 3*, 273–282.

Diener, E. (1977). Deindividuation: Causes and consequences. *Social Behavior and Personality, 5*, 143–156.

Diener, E., Dineen, J., Endresen, K., Beaman, A. L., & Fraser, S. C. (1975). Effects of altered responsibility, cognitive set, and modeling on physical aggression and deindividuation. *Journal of Personality and Social Psychology, 31*, 328–337.

Dollard, J., & Miller, N. E. (1950). *Personality and psychotherapy.* New York: McGraw-Hill.

Dossett, D. L., Latham, G. P., & Mitchell, T. R. (1979). Effects of assigned versus participatively set goals, knowledge of results, and individual differences on employee behavior when goal difficulty is held constant. *Journal of Applied Psychology, 64*, 291–298.

Dubbert, P. M., & Wilson, G. T. (1984). Goal-setting and spouse involvement in the treatment of obesity. *Behaviour Research and Therapy, 22*, 227–242.

Dweck, C. S., & Elliott, E. S. (1983). Achievement motivation. In P. H. Mussen (General Ed.) & E. M. Heatherington (Vol. Eds.), *Handbook of child psychology: Socialization, personality and social development* (4th ed., Vol. 4, pp. 644–691). New York: Wiley.

Dweck, C. S., & Leggett, E. L. (1988). A social-cognitive approach to motivation and personality. *Psychological Review, 95*, 256–273.

Dzewaltowski, D. A., Noble, J. M., & Shaw, J. M. (1990). Physical activity participation: Social cognitive theory versus the theories of reasoned action and planned behavior. *Journal of Sport and Exercise Psychology, 12*, 388–405.

Earley, P. C., Connolly, T., & Ekegren, C. (1989). Goals, strategy development and task performance: Some limits on the efficacy of goal-setting. *Journal of Applied Psychology, 74*, 24–33.

Earley, P. C., Connolly, T., & Lee, C. (1990). Task strategy interventions in goal setting: The importance of search in strategy development. *Journal of Management*.

Edwards, S., & Dickerson, M. (1987). On the similarity of positive and negative intrusions. *Behaviour, Research and Therapy, 25*, 207–211.

Elliott, E. S., & Dweck, C. S. (1988). Goals: An approach to motivation and achievement. *Journal of Personality and Social Psychology, 54*, 5–12.

Emmons, R. A., & Diener, E. (1986). Situation selection as a moderator of response consistency and stability. *Journal of Personality and Social Psychology, 51*, 1013–1019.

England, S. L., & Dickerson, M. (1988). Intrusive thoughts: Unpleasantness not the major cause of uncontrollability. *Behaviour Research and Therapy, 26*, 279–282.

Erez, M., & Zidon, I. (1984). Effect of goal acceptance on the relationship of goal difficulty to performance. *Journal of Applied Psychology, 69*, 69–78.

Feather, N. T. (Ed.). (1982). *Expectations and actions: Expectancy-value models in psychology*. Hillsdale, NJ: Erlbaum.

Festinger, L. (1942). A theoretical interpretation of shifts in level of aspiration. *Psychological Review, 49*, 235–250.

Festinger, L. (1954). A theory of social comparison processes. *Human Relations, 7*, 117–140.

Frey, K. S., & Ruble, D. N. (1990). Strategies for comparative evaluation: Maintaining a sense of competence across the lifespan. In R. J. Sternberg & J. Kolligian, Jr. (Eds.), *Competence considered* (pp. 167–189). New Haven: Yale University Press.

Gambino, R. (1973, November–December). Watergate lingo: A language of nonresponsibility. *Freedom at Issue* (No. 22), 7–9, 15–17.

Garber, J., Hollon, S. D., & Silverman, V. (1979, December). *Evaluation and reward of self vs. others in depression*. Paper presented at the meeting of the Association for the Advancement of Behavior Therapy, San Francisco.

Garland, H. (1983). Influence of ability, assigned goals, and normative information on personal goals and performance: A challenge to the goal attainability assumption. *Journal of Applied Psychology, 68*, 20–30.

Garland, H. (1984). Relation of effort-performance expectancy to performance in goal-setting experiments. *Journal of Applied Psychology, 69*, 79–84.

Geer, J. H., Davidson, G. C., & Gatchel, R. I. (1970). Reduction of stress in humans through nonveridical perceived control of aversive stimulation. *Journal of Personality and Social Psychology, 16*, 731–738.

Gibson, J. T., & Haritos-Fatouros, M. (1986, November). The education of a torturer. *Psychology Today*, 50–58.

Glasgow, R. E., & Arkowitz, H. (1975). The behavioral assessment of male and female social competence in dyadic heterosexual interactions. *Behavior Therapy, 6*, 488–498.

Glass, D. C., Reim, B., & Singer, J. (1971). Behavioral consequences of adaptation to controllable and uncontrollable noise. *Journal of Experimental Social Psychology, 7*, 244–257.

Glass, D. C., Singer, J. E., Leonard, H. S., Krantz, D., & Cummings, H. (1973). Perceived control of aversive stimulation and the reduction of stress responses. *Journal of Personality, 41,* 577–595.

Godding, P. R., & Glasgow, R. E. (1985). Self-efficacy and outcome expectations as predictors of controlled smoking status. *Cognitive Therapy and Research, 9,* 583–590.

Golin, S., & Terrill, F. (1977). Motivational and associative aspects of mild depression in skill and chance tasks. *Journal of Abnormal Psychology, 86,* 389–401.

Gunnar, M. R. (1980). Control, warning signals, and distress in infancy. *Developmental Psychology, 16,* 281–289.

Gunnar–von Gnechten, M. R. (1978). Changing a frightening toy into a pleasant toy by allowing the infant to control its actions. *Development Psychology, 14,* 147–152.

Gurin, P., & Brim, O. G., Jr. (1984). Change in self in adulthood: The example of sense of control. In P. B. Baltes & O. G. Brim, Jr. (Eds.), *Life-span development and behavior* (Vol. 6, pp. 281–334). New York: Academic Press.

Haan, N. (1985). Processes of moral development: Cognitive or social disequilibrium? *Developmental Psychology, 21,* 996–1006.

Hackett, G., & Betz, N. E. (1989). An exploration of the mathematics self-efficacy/mathematics performance correspondence. *Journal for Research in Mathematics Education, 20,* 261–273.

Herrnstein, R. J. (1969). Method and theory in the study of avoidance. *Psychological Review, 76,* 49–69.

Higgins, A., Power, C., & Kohlberg, L. (1984). Student judgments of responsibility and the moral atmosphere of high schools: A comparative study. In W. Kurtines & J. L. Gewirtz (Eds.), *Morality, moral behavior and moral development: Basic issues in theory and research* (pp. 74–106). New York: Wiley-Interscience.

Hogarth, R. (1981). Beyond discrete biases: Functional and dysfunctional aspects of judgmental heuristics. *Psychological Bulletin, 90,* 197–217.

Holahan, C. K., & Holahan, C. J. (1987a). Self-efficacy, social support, and depression in aging: A longitudinal analysis. *Journal of Gerontology, 42,* 65–68.

Holahan, C. K., & Holahan, C. J. (1987b). Life stress, hassles, and self-efficacy in aging: A replication and extension. *Journal of Applied Social Psychology, 17,* 574–592.

Ivie, R. L. (1980). Images of savagery in American justifications for war. *Communication Monographs, 47,* 270–294.

Jacobs, B., Prentice-Dunn, S., & Rogers, R. W. (1984). Understanding persistence: An interface of control theory and self-efficacy theory. *Basic and Applied Social Psychology, 5,* 333–347.

Jobe, L. D. (1984). *Effects of proximity and specificity of goals on performance.* Unpublished doctoral dissertation, Murdoch University, Western Australia.

Kanfer, F. H., & Hagerman, S. (1981). The role of self-regulation. In L. P.

Rehm (Ed.), *Behavior therapy for depression: Present status and future directions* (pp. 143–180). New York: Academic Press.

Kanfer, R., & Zeiss, A. M. (1983). Depression, interpersonal standard-setting, and judgments of self-efficacy. *Journal of Abnormal Psychology, 92,* 319–329.

Kaplan, M. F. (1989). Information integration in moral reasoning: Conceptual and methodological implications. In N. Eisenberg, J. Reykowski, & E. Staub (Eds.), *Social and moral values: Individual and societal perspectives* (pp. 117–135). Hillsdale, NJ: Erlbaum.

Kavanagh, D. J. (1983). *Mood and self-efficacy.* Unpublished doctoral dissertation, Stanford University, Stanford, CA.

Kavanagh, D. J., & Bower, G. H. (1985). Mood and self-efficacy: Impact of joy and sadness on perceived capabilities. *Cognitive Therapy and Research, 9,* 507–525.

Kelman, H. C. (1973). Violence without moral restraint: Reflections on the dehumanization of victims and victimizers. *Journal of Social Issues, 29,* 25–61.

Kent, G. (1987). Self-efficacious control over reported physiological, cognitive and behavioural symptoms of dental anxiety. *Behaviour Research and Therapy, 25,* 341–347.

Kent, G., & Gibbons, R. (1987). Self-efficacy and the control of anxious cognitions. *Journal of Behavior Therapy and Experimental Psychiatry, 18,* 33–40.

Kilham, W., & Mann, L. (1974). Level of destructive obedience as a function of transmitter and executant roles in the Milgram obedience paradigm. *Journal of Personality and Social Psychology, 29,* 696–702.

Kipnis, D. (1974). The powerholders. In J. T. Tedeschi (Ed.), *Perspectives on social power* (pp. 82–122). Chicago: Aldine.

Kirsch, I., Tennen, H., Wickless, C., Saccone, A. J., & Cody, S. (1983). The role of expectancy in fear reduction. *Behavior Therapy, 14,* 520–533.

Kirschenbaum, D. S., Humphrey, L. L., & Malett, S. D. (1981). Specificity of planning in adult self-control: An applied investigation. *Journal of Personality and Social Psychology, 40,* 941–950.

Kirschenbaum, D. S., Tomarken, A. J., & Ordman, A. M. (1982). Specificity of planning and choice applied to adult self-control. *Journal of Personality and Social Psychology, 42,* 576–585.

Kohlberg, L. (1971). From is to ought: How to commit the naturalistic fallacy and get away with it in the study of moral development. In T. Mischel (Ed.), *Cognitive development and epistemology* (pp. 151–232). New York: Academic Press.

Kohlberg, L. (1984). *The psychology of moral development* (Vol. 2). New York: Harper & Row.

Kun, A. (1977). Development of the magnitude-covariation and compensation schemata in ability and effort attributions of performance. *Child Development, 48,* 862–873.

Kupfersmid, J. H., & Wonderly, D. M. (1982). Disequilibrium as a hypothetical construct in Kohlbergian moral development. *Child Study Journal, 12,* 171–185.

Kurtines, W. M., & Gewirtz, J. L. (Eds.). (1984). *Morality, moral behavior, and moral development*. New York: Wiley.

Lane, J., & Anderson, N. H. (1976). Integration of intention and outcome in moral judgment. *Memory and Cognition, 4*, 1–5.

Larsen, K. S., Coleman, D., Forges, J., & Johnson, R. (1971). Is the subject's personality or the experimental situation a better predictor of a subject's willingness to administer shock to a victim? *Journal of Personality and Social Psychology, 22*, 287–295.

Latham, G. P., & Marshall, H. A. (1982). The effects of self-set, participatively set and assigned goals on the performance of government employees. *Personnel Psychology, 35*, 399–404.

Latham, G. P., & Yukl, G. A. (1976). Effects of assigned and participative goal setting on performance and job satisfaction. *Journal of Applied Psychology, 61*, 166–171.

Lazarus, R. S., & Folkman, S. (1984). *Stress, appraisal, and coping*. New York: Springer.

Lee, C. (1984a). Accuracy of efficacy and outcome expectations in predicting performance in a simulated assertiveness task. *Cognitive Therapy and Research, 8*, 37–48.

Lee, C. (1984b). Efficacy expectations and outcome expectations as predictors of performance in a snake-handling task. *Cognitive Therapy and Research, 8*, 509–516.

Leland, E. I. (1983). Self-efficacy and other variables as they relate to precompetitive anxiety among male interscholastic basketball players. (Doctoral dissertation, Stanford University, 1983). *Dissertation Abstracts International, 44*, 1376A.

Leon, M. (1982). Rules in children's moral judgments: Integration of intent, damage, and rationale information. *Developmental Psychology, 18*, 835–842.

Levine, S., & Ursin, H. (Eds.). (1980). *Coping and health*. New York: Plenum.

Lewinsohn, P. M., Mischel, W., Chaplin, W., & Barton, R. (1980). Social competence and depression: The role of illusory self-perceptions. *Journal of Abnormal Psychology, 89*, 203–212.

Litt, M. D. (1988). Self-efficacy and perceived control: Cognitive mediators of pain tolerance. *Journal of Personality and Social Psychology, 54*, 149–160.

Locke, E. A., Bryan, J. F., & Kendall, L. M. (1968). Goals and intentions as mediators of the effects of monetary incentives on behavior. *Journal of Applied Psychology, 52*, 104–121.

Locke, E. A., Cartledge, N. D., & Knerr, C. S. (1970). Studies of the relationship between satisfaction, goal setting, and performance. *Organizational Behavior and Human Performance, 5*, 135–158.

Locke E. A., & Latham, G. P. (1990). *A theory of goal setting and task performance*. Englewood Cliffs, NJ: Prentice-Hall.

Locke E. A., Latham, G. P., & Erez, M. (1988). The determinants of goal commitment. *Academy of Management Review, 13*, 23–39.

Locke, E. A., Zubritzky, E., Cousins, E., & Bobko, P. (1984). Effect of previously assigned goals on self-set goals and performance. *Journal of Applied Psychology, 69,* 694–699.

Loeb, A., Beck, A. T., Diggory, J. C., & Tuthill, R. (1967). Expectancy, level of aspiration, performance, and self-evaluation in depression. *Proceedings of the 75th Annual Convention of the American Psychological Association, 2,* 193–194.

Lord, R. G., & Hanges, P. J. (1987). A control system model of organizational motivation: Theoretical development and applied implications. *Behavioral Science, 32,* 161–178.

Manderlink, G., & Harackiewicz, J. M. (1984). Proximal versus distal goal setting and intrinsic motivation. *Journal of Personality and Social Psychology, 47,* 918–928.

Mantell, D. M., & Panzarella, R. (1976). Obedience and responsibility. *The British Journal of Social and Clinical Psychology, 15,* 239–246.

Marquis, D. P. (1941). Learning in the neonate: The modification of behavior under three feeding schedules. *Journal of Experimental Psychology, 29,* 263–282.

Matefy, R. E., & Acksen, B. A. (1976). The effect of role-playing discrepant positions on change in moral judgments and attitudes. *Journal of Genetic Psychology, 128,* 189–200.

Matsui, T., Okada, A., & Kakuyama, T. (1982). Influence of achievement need on goal setting, performance and feedback effectiveness. *Journal of Applied Psychology, 67,* 645–648.

Matsui, T., Okada, A., & Mizuguchi, R. (1981). Expectancy-theory prediction of the goal theory postulate, "The harder the goals, the higher the performance." *Journal of Applied Psychology, 66,* 54–58.

McAuley, E. (1985). Modeling and self-efficacy: A test of Bandura's model. *Journal of Sport Psychology, 7,* 283–295.

McCaul, K. D., & Malott, J. M. (1984). Distraction and coping with pain. *Psychological Bulletin, 95,* 516–533.

McCaul, K. D., O'Neill, K., & Glasgow, R. E. (1988). Predicting the performance of dental hygiene behaviors: An examination of the Fishbein and Ajzen model and self-efficacy expectations. *Journal of Applied Social Psychology, 18,* 114–128.

McGuire, W. J. (1985). Attitudes and attitude change. In G. Lindzey & E. Aronson (Eds.), *The handbook of social psychology* (3rd ed., Vol. 2, pp. 233–346). Hillsdale, NJ: Erlbaum.

McMullin, D. J., & Steffen, J. J. (1982). Intrinsic motivation and performance standards. *Social Behavior and Personality, 10,* 47–56.

Meichenbaum, D. H. (1977). *Cognitive-behavior modification: An integrative approach.* New York: Plenum Press.

Mento, A. J., Cartledge, N. D., & Locke, E. A. (1980). Maryland vs. Michigan vs. Minnesota: Another look at the relationship of expectancy and goal difficulty to task performance. *Organizational Behavior and Human Performance, 25,* 419–440.

Mento, A. J., Steel, R. P., & Karren, R. J. (1987). A meta-analytic study of the effects of goal setting on task performance: 1966–1984. *Organizational Behavior and Human Decision Processes, 39,* 52–83.

Milgram, S. (1974). *Obedience to authority: An experimental view.* New York: Harper & Row.

Miller, G. A., Galanter, E., & Pribram, K. H. (1960). *Plans and the structure of behavior.* New York: Holt.

Miller, S. M. (1980). Why having control reduces stress: If I can stop the roller-coaster I don't want to get off. In J. Garber & M. E. P. Seligman (Eds.), *Human helplessness: Theory and research* (pp. 71–95). New York: Academic Press.

Mineka, S., Gunnar, M., & Champoux, M. (1986). Control and early socio-emotional development: Infant rhesus monkeys reared in controllable versus uncontrollable environments. *Child Development, 57,* 1241–1256.

Mitchell, T. R. (1974). Expectancy models of job satisfaction, methodological, and empirical appraisal. *Psychological Bulletin, 81,* 1053–1077.

Morgan, M. (1985). Self-monitoring of attained subgoals in private study. *Journal of Educational Psychology, 77,* 623–630.

Mossholder, K. W. (1980). Effects of externally mediated goal setting on intrinsic motivation: A laboratory experiment. *Journal of Applied Psychology, 65,* 202–210.

Mowrer, O. H. (1960). *Learning theory and the symbolic processes.* New York: Wiley.

Muller, E. N. (1979). *Aggressive political participation.* Princeton: Princeton University Press.

Mynatt, C., & Herman, S. J. (1975). Responsibility attribution in groups and individuals: A direct test of the diffusion of responsibility hypothesis. *Journal of Personality and Social Psychology, 32,* 1111–1118.

Nicholls, J. G. (1984). Achievement motivation: Conceptions of ability, subjective experience, task choice, and performance. *Psychological Review, 91,* 328–346.

Nicholls, J. G., & Miller, A. T. (1984). Development and its discontents: The differentiation of the concept of ability. In J. G. Nicholls (Ed.), *Advances in motivation and achievement: Vol. 3. The development of achievement motivation* (pp. 185–218). Greenwich, CT: JAI Press.

Nisbett, R. E., & Ross, L. (1980). *Human inference: Strategies and shortcomings of social judgment.* Englewood Cliffs, NJ: Prentice-Hall.

Olioff, M., & Aboud, F. E. (1990). Predicting postpartum dysphoria in primiparous mothers: Roles of perceived parenting self-efficacy and self-esteem. *Journal of Cognitive Psychotherapy.*

Ostrow, A. C. (1976). Goal-setting behavior and need achievement in relation to competitive motor activity. *Research Quarterly, 47,* 174–183.

Ozer, E., & Bandura, A. (1990). Mechanisms governing empowerment effects: A self-efficacy analysis. *Journal of Personality and Social Psychology, 58,* 472–486.

Peake, P. K., & Cervone, D. (1989). Sequence anchoring and self-efficacy: Primacy effects in the consideration of possibilities. *Social Cognition, 7,* 31–50.

Piaget, J. (1960). Equilibration and development of logical structures. In J. M. Tanner & B. Inhelder (Eds.), *Discussions on child development* (Vol. 4). New York: International Universities Press.

Pritchard, R. D., & Curtis, M. I. (1973). The influence of goal setting and financial incentives on task performance. *Organizational Behavior and Human Performance, 10,* 175–183.

Rapoport, D. C., & Alexander, Y. (Eds.). (1982). *The morality of terrorism: Religious and secular justification.* Elmsford, NY: Pergamon Press.

Rehm, L. P. (1981). A self-control therapy program for treatment of depression. In J. F. Clarkin & H. Glazer (Eds.), *Depression: Behavioral and directive treatment strategies* (pp. 68–110). New York: Garland Press.

Relich, J. D., Debus, R. L., & Walker, R. (1986). The mediation role of attribution and self-efficacy variables for treatment effects on achievement outcomes. *Contemporary Educational Psychology, 11,* 195–216.

Rosenbaum, M., & Hadari, D. (1985). Personal efficacy, external locus of control, and perceived contingency of parental reinforcement among depressed, paranoid, and normal subjects. *Journal of Personality and Social Psychology, 49,* 539–547.

Ross, M., & DiTecco, D. (1975). An attributional analysis of moral judgments. *Journal of Social Issues, 31,* 91–109.

Rotter, J. B. (1982). Social learning theory. In N. T. Feather (Ed.), *Expectations and actions: Expectancy-value models in psychology* (pp. 241–260). Hillsdale, NJ: Erlbaum

Rule, B. G., & Nesdale, A. R. (1976). Moral judgments of aggressive behavior. In R. G. Geen & E. C. O'Neal (Eds.), *Perspectives on aggression* (pp. 37–60). New York: Academic Press.

Ryan, T. A. (1970). *Intentional behavior.* New York: Ronald Press.

Salkovskis, P. M., & Harrison, J. (1984). Abnormal and normal obsessions—a replication. *Behaviour Research and Therapy, 22,* 549–552.

Sanderson, W. C., Rapee, R. M., & Barlow, D. H. (1989). The influence of an illusion of control on panic attacks induced via inhalation of 5.5% carbon dioxide-enriched air. *Archives of General Psychiatry, 46,* 157–162.

Sanford, N., & Comstock, C. (1971). *Sanctions for evil.* San Francisco: Jossey-Bass.

Sarason, I. G. (1975). Anxiety and self-preoccupation. In I. G. Sarason & D. C. Spielberger (Eds.), *Stress and anxiety* (Vol. 2, pp. 27–44). Washington, DC: Hemisphere.

Schifter, D. E., & Ajzen, I. (1985). Intention, perceived control, and weight loss: An application of the theory of planned behavior. *Journal of Personality and Social Psychology, 49,* 843–851.

Schunk, D. H. (1984). Self-efficacy perspective on achievement behavior. *Educational Psychologist, 19,* 48–58.

Schunk, D. H., & Cox, P. D. (1986). Strategy training and attributional feedback with learning disabled students. *Journal of Educational Psychology, 78,* 201–209.

Schunk, D. H., & Gunn, T. P. (1986). Self-efficacy and skill development: Influence of task strategies and attributions. *Journal of Educational Research,* *79*, 238–244.

Schunk, D. H., & Rice, J. M. (1986). Extended attributional feedback: Sequence effects during remedial reading instruction. *Journal of Early Adolescence, 6*, 55–66.

Schwab, D. P., Olian-Gottlieb, J. D., & Heneman, H. G., III. (1979). Between-subjects expectancy theory research: A statistical review of studies predicting effort and performance. *Psychological Bulletin, 86*, 139–147.

Schwartz, B. (1978). *Psychology of learning and behavior.* New York: Norton.

Schwartz, J. L. (1974). Relationship between goal discrepancy and depression. *Journal of Consulting and Clinical Psychology, 42*, 309.

Schwartz, R. M., & Gottman, J. M. (1976). Toward a task analysis of assertive behavior. *Journal of Consulting and Clinical Psychology, 44*, 910–920.

Schwarzer, R. (1990). *Initiation and maintenance of health behaviors: A review of theoretical approaches.* Unpublished manuscript, Freie University of Berlin.

Silver, W. S., Mitchell, T. R., & Gist, M. E. (1989). *The impact of self-efficacy on causal attributions for successful and unsuccessful performance.* Unpublished manuscript, University of Washington.

Simon, H. A. (1976). *Administrative behavior: A study of decision-making processes in administrative organization* (3rd ed.). New York: Free Press.

Simon, K. M. (1979). *Effects of self comparison, social comparison, and depression on goal setting and self-evaluative reactions.* Unpublished manuscript, Stanford University.

Snyder, M., & Campbell, B. H. (1982). Self-monitoring: The self in action. In J. Suls (Ed.), *Psychological perspectives on the self* (pp. 185–207). Hillsdale, NJ: Erlbaum.

Stanley, M. A., & Maddux, J. E. (1986). Investigation of a combined protection motivation and self-efficacy model. *Basic and Applied Psychology, 40*, 101–114.

Strang, H. R., Lawrence, E. C., & Fowler, P. C. (1978). Effects of assigned goal level and knowledge of results on arithmetic computation: Laboratory study. *Journal of Applied Psychology, 63*, 446–450.

Suls, J. M., & Miller, R. L. (1977). *Social comparison processes: Theoretical and empirical perspectives.* Washington, DC: Hemisphere.

Suls, J. M., & Mullen, B. (1982). From the cradle to the grave: Comparison and self-evaluation across the life-span. In J. Suls (Ed.), *Psychological perspectives on the self* (Vol. 1, pp. 97–125). Hillsdale, NJ: Erlbaum.

Surber, C. F. (1985). Applications of information integration to children's social cognitions. In J. B. Pryor & J. D. Day (Eds.), *The development of social cognition* (pp. 59–94). New York: Springer-Verlag.

Taylor, M. S., Locke, E. A., Lee, C., & Gist, M. E. (1984). Type A behavior and faculty research productivity: What are the mechanisms? *Organizational Behavior and Human Performance, 34*, 402–418.

Telch, M. J., Agras, W. S., Taylor, C. B., Roth, W. T., & Gallen, C. C. (1985).

Combined pharmacological and behavioral treatment of agoraphobia. *Behaviour Research and Therapy, 23*, 325–335.

Tilker, H. A. (1970). Socially responsible behavior as a function of observer responsibility and victim feedback. *Journal of Personality and Social Psychology, 14*, 95–100.

Umstot, D. D., Bell, C. H., Jr., & Mitchell, T. R. (1976). Effects of job enrichment and task goals on satisfaction and productivity: Implications for job design. *Journal of Applied Psychology, 61*, 379–394.

Vroom, V. H. (1964). *Work and motivation*. New York: Wiley.

Wachs, T. D. (1977). The optimal stimulation hypothesis and early development: Anybody got a match? In I. C. Uzgiris & F. Weizmann (Eds.), *The structuring of experience* (pp. 153–177). New York: Plenum.

Walker, L. J. (1982). The sequentiality of Kohlberg's stages of moral development. *Child Development, 53*, 1330–1336.

Weinberg, R. S., Bruya, L., & Jackson, A. (1985). The effects of goal proximity and goal specificity on endurance performance. *Journal of Sport Psychology, 7*, 296–305.

Weinberg, R. S., Gould, D., & Jackson, A. (1979). Expectations and performance: An empirical test of Bandura's self-efficacy theory. *Journal of Sport Psychology, 1*, 320–331.

Weiner, B. (1985). An attributional theory of achievement motivation and emotion. *Psychological Review, 92*, 548–573.

Wheeler, K. G. (1983). Comparisons of self-efficacy and expectancy models of occupational preferences for college males and females. *Journal of Occupational Psychology, 56*, 73–78.

White, J. (1982). *Rejection*. Reading, MA: Addison-Wesley.

Williams, S. L. (1987). On anxiety and phobia. *Journal of Anxiety Disorders, 1*, 161–180.

Williams, S. L., Dooseman, G., & Kleifield, E. (1984). Comparative power of guided mastery and exposure treatments for intractable phobias. *Journal of Consulting and Clinical Psychology, 52*, 505–518.

Williams, S. L., Kinney, P. J., & Falbo, J. (1989). Generalization of therapeutic changes in agoraphobia: The role of perceived self-efficacy. *Journal of Consulting and Clinical Psychology, 57*, 436–442.

Williams, S. L., & Rappoport, A. (1983). Cognitive treatment in the natural environment for agoraphobics. *Behavior Therapy, 14*, 299–313.

Williams, S. L., Turner, S. M., & Peer, D. F. (1985). Guided mastery and performance desensitization treatments for severe acrophobia. *Journal of Consulting and Clinical Psychology, 53*, 237–247.

Williams, S. L., & Watson, N. (1985). Perceived danger and perceived self-efficacy as cognitive mediators of acrophobic behavior. *Behavior Therapy, 16*, 136–146.

Wood, J. V. (1989). Theory and research concerning social comparisons of personal attributes. *Psychological Bulletin, 106*, 231–248.

Wood, R. E., & Bailey, T. (1985). Some unanswered questions about goal effects: A recommended change in research methods. *Australian Journal of Management, 10,* 61–73.

Wood, R. E., & Bandura, A. (1989a). Social cognitive theory of organizational management. *Academy of Management Review, 14,* 361–384.

Wood, R. E., & Bandura, A. (1989b). Impact of conceptions of ability on self-regulatory mechanisms and complex decision making. *Journal of Personality and Social Psychology, 56,* 407–415.

Wood, R. E., Bandura, A., & Bailey, T. (1990). Mechanisms governing organizational performance in complex decision-making environments. *Organizational Behavior and Human Decision Processes, 46,* 181–201.

Wood, R. E., Mento, A. J., & Locke, E. A. (1987). Task complexity as a moderator of goal effects: A meta-analysis. *Journal of Applied Psychology, 72,* 416–425.

Wortman, C. B., Panciera, L., Shusterman, L., & Hibscher, J. (1976). Attributions of causality and reactions to uncontrollable outcomes. *Journal of Experimental Social Psychology, 12,* 301–316.

Wright, P. M. (1989). Test of the mediating role of goals in the incentive-performance relationship. *Journal of Applied Psychology, 74,* 699–705.

Yukl, G. A., & Latham, G. P. (1978). Interrelationships among employee participation, individual differences, goal difficulty, goal acceptance, goal instrumentality, and performance. *Personnel Psychology, 31,* 305–324.

Zimbardo, P. G. (1969). The human choice: Individuation, reason, and order versus deindividuation, impulse, and chaos. In W. J. Arnold & D. Levine (Eds.), *Nebraska symposium on motivation, 1969* (pp. 237–309). Lincoln: University of Nebraska Press.

Zimmerman, B. J., & Blom, D. E. (1983). Toward an empirical test of the role of cognitive conflict in learning. *Developmental Review, 3,* 18–38.

On Perceiving the
Other as Responsible

Bernard Weiner
University of California,
Los Angeles

I am very pleased to write a chapter for the *Nebraska Symposium on Motivation*, fulfilling one of my graduate school dreams. But I must admit that I view the field of motivation with ambivalence. On the one hand, I feel some despair. The lofty place that motivation once occupied in the research enterprise of psychology is no longer held. At one time motivation was the dominant field of study; that is no longer the case. During the 1950s and 1960s, the *Nebraska Symposium on Motivation* was one of the most prestigious publications in psychology and commanded great attention as well as changing the direction and dreams of graduate students like me; that is no longer true. One year Clark Hull was cited in almost 70% of the published experimental articles; there no longer are figures of such dominance.

At the other pole of my mixed reaction, I feel optimistic about our future. Interest in motivation and articles about it are increasing, and for the first time in about twenty years a *Nebraska Symposium* volume is to be devoted to motivation. Why the recent resurgence inter-

I want to thank Sandra Graham and Jaana Juvonen for their comments on an earlier draft of this chapter. In addition, Serena Clayton is responsible for much of the discussion on consciousness raising.

est? To what do we attribute this unexpected and important success? Here are some of my biased answers to this question.

The emergence of the study of affect. In earlier eras, the major theoretical arguments in motivation concerned whether learning should be captured with mechanistic or cognitive concepts, and whether energizing constructs such as drive and arousal are needed in a theory of motivation. In the disagreements between Hull and Tolman, and between Spence and Atkinson, the role of affect as a motivator was neglected. It seemed to fall through the "drive versus cognition" crack. Affect was weakly incorporated in that all the motivation theories tended to perceive hedonism as the mainspring of action, so that pleasure was approached and pain was avoided. There also were some associations postulated between specific affects and actions, as exemplified in the "fight or flight" reaction to fear and in the association between anger and aggression. But no serious thought had been given to the motivational role of affective experience.

We are now witnessing a tremendous increase in studies of emotion. Much of this research has little to do with motivation, such as the search for universal emotional expressions. But there also is an increasing interest in the role of affects as "push" or "pull" mechanisms, or in the conceptualization of affects as giving instructions to the organism regarding what class of behaviors to undertake. In my own work, for example, I postulate that pity elicits altruistic actions and promotes behavior that tends to equalize the plight of the receiver and the state of the giver. The enormous recent interest in the study of affect has very positive implications for the field of motivation.

The broadening of the cognitive antecedents of motivation. For many years the only cognitive component in theories of motivation was the expectancy of success, or the subjective likelihood of reaching a desired goal. But now many cognitions are recognized as important for motivated behavior. For example, in the early years of psychology it was believed that a reward would automatically increase the probability of the immediately prior response. But it now appears that if reward is perceived as controlling, then it undermines future effort, whereas reward perceived as positive feedback is motivating. Further, reward for success at an easy task is a cue to the receivers of this feedback that they are low in ability, a belief that inhibits activity, whereas reward for success at a difficult task indicates that hard work also was expended in conjunction with high ability—beliefs that augment motivation. And reward in a competitive setting is based on social comparison information, signaling that one has high ability and is better than others, whereas reward in a cooperative context signals that one has bettered oneself and has tried hard. Hence it is now recognized that reward has quite a variety of meanings and that each connotation will give rise to a different set of actions. The broadening of the cognitive base of motivation has had a very facilitative influence on the field. We will see that the cognition central to my concerns is causal attribution—the perceived reason why a particular outcome has occurred.

The rise (and fall) of individual differences. The initial systematic studies of motivation used nonhuman subjects, particularly rats, and examined their behavior in a straight alley or maze as a function of some motivational manipulation, such as hours of deprivation or amount and type of reward. As long as the study of motivation was linked with lower organisms, it was unlikely that individual differences would be assessed.

But this dramatically changed when motivation began to be studied in human populations. There were then attempts to combine individual differences with the study of process. Atkinson was perhaps the first to include personality dispositions within a formal theory of motivation. The use of the Thematic Apperception Test (TAT) as well as self-report instruments to assess need for achievement became one of the dominant research themes in the 1960s. This was closely followed by the development of the Manifest Anxiety Scale to assess individual differences in level of drive (emotional reactivity) as well as other anxiety tests, particularly the Mandler-Sarason Test Anxiety Questionnaire. These also gave rise to many research studies in the 1960s. In the next decade it was the locus of control measure developed by Rotter as well as other indicators of perceived control that became the focus of attention. The Rotter (1966) monograph describing the so-called I-E (internal-external) scale was one of the most-cited articles between 1965 and 1980. And more recently, attributional style has become an often-used measure in studies related to motivation. In sum, the change from infrahuman to human research led to the inclusion of individual difference measures in the research, and this was an important stimulus for studies in motivation.

You might have noticed, however, that I included the phrase "rise and fall" in the description of individual differences. The individual difference approach has not, in my opinion, given rise to lasting and reliable contributions to the field of motivation. This is not the appropriate context in which to defend such a bold statement. I will briefly point out, for example, that there is no sufficient evidence to conclude that the choice behavior of individuals high in need for achievement differs from the choices of persons measured as low in achievement strivings, and the alleged correlates of locus of control have little to do with social learning theory. Thus I believe that the focus on individual differences, as opposed to a concern with general laws, at this time is not the better research strategy. And following this dictum, my own research program has eschewed the search for interactions, concentrating instead on main effects.

The concern about the self. The decline in the individual difference approach in motivation has been replaced, or at least supplemented, by the vast number of studies that include some concept related to the self. Clearly, both these research streams have their roots in the desire to include the person in the study of motivation. But the self studies often examine self-related processes that are considered generalizable across subjects. Among the popular self-related themes with motivational significance are self-actualization, self-concept, self-consistency, self-efficacy, self-esteem, self-evaluation, self-focus, self-handicapping and on and on, through the rest of the alphabet.

I also view the focus on the self as promoting research in motivation, for it combines the study of the person with motivational processes, identifies a new set of pertinent cognitions, includes a number of affects that are distinctly tied to the self (such as pride and shame), and attracts the attention of researchers in diverse fields of psychology. As an attribution theorist, I make the self a central concept in my approach in part because attributing an outcome to the self (such as ability or effort) results in quite different affects and actions than does ascribing an outcome to factors that reside outside the self (such as help from others).

The ascendency of achievement motivation. I have already noted the use of nonhuman rather than human participants in early research on motivation. When research with humans was initiated, it primarily examined achievement strivings. Lewin, for example, conducted many studies of level of aspiration; Atkinson was primarily interested in choice between achievement tasks that differed in difficulty; McClelland examined the economic significance of achievement needs; Rotter looked at expectancy shifts in skill-related tasks; Heider considered the attributions made for success and failure; and a number of theorists are now contrasting competitive and cooperative reward structures in terms of their effects in classroom settings. Thus achievement strivings have been the research site for many theorists with different theoretical orientations and different research agendas, providing the focus for the study of motivation. I believe the concentration on achievement played an important role in the growth of motivational research, in part because it attracted the attention of researchers with an interest in education and in part because it is so obviously important in everyday life.

As with the study of individual differences, however, I now think this exclusive focus also has had some negative consequences. Other important sources of human motivation have been relatively neglected, such as affiliative tendencies. As a consequence, the generality of the laws developed for achievement contexts has not been sufficiently examined. My own research from an attributional perspective also has had achievement motivation as its center, and the research in achievement-related contexts provided the data for our initial theoretical growth. I have attempted to generalize the findings in achievement settings to other motivational contexts, including altruism, reactions to the stigmatized, and impression management techniques. These nonachievement areas will be examined in depth below.

These historical trends, or perhaps biased perceptions of historical trends, played an important role in the selection of the research to be discussed now: the role of responsibility judgments in motivation. The rest of the chapter has two distinct sections. First, I will present an overview of my general theoretical orientation, reviewing the theory of motivation and emotion that I have developed with my colleagues and other researchers over the past twenty-five years.

Then I will concentrate on judgments of responsibility as a unifying theme for some areas of motivational concern.

An Attributional Theory of Motivation and Emotion

The attributional theory that guides my thinking is depicted in Figure 1, which shows that an attributional sequence is initiated after the outcome of an event, such as success or failure at an achievement task or social acceptance or social rejection. Thus the theory has a postdictive flavor in that what is to be explained has already occurred (as in, for example, theories of evolution). However, this explanation then has predictive value. If the prior outcome was positive, the actor experiences a general positive affective state such as happiness; if the outcome was negative, the general affective reaction is labeled sadness or frustration (Weiner, Russell, & Lerman, 1978, 1979). Consistent with this position, Ellsworth and Smith (1988) concluded, "Happiness appears to be a generic, undifferentiated response to pleasant circumstances" (p. 326). Further affective experiences require more cognitive differentiation than just interpretation of the outcome. One should also note that there is a bidirectional relation between outcome and affect. Much research suggests that current affective state influences interpretation of prior events, so that it is likely an ambiguous outcome will be interpreted as a success when one is happy and as a failure when one is sad.

After the outcome, in certain circumstances there is a search to determine why that outcome occurred. This search is not undertaken in all conditions, for it does place demands on the cognitive system. Rather, search is most likely given an unexpected, negative, and important outcome. For example, if an A student gets a poor grade on an important exam, there certainly will be thoughts about why this happened. A high grade by the same student is much less likely to initiate attributional activity (see Weiner, 1985).

A large number of factors determine what is selected as the most likely cause(s). For example, Kelley (1967) has identified consistency of behavior and social consensus as two important attributional cues. Thus, if one fails an exam and has failed in the past, and if others succeed at this task, the likely cause of the outcome is the failing person. A more general rule is that the selected cause is omitted

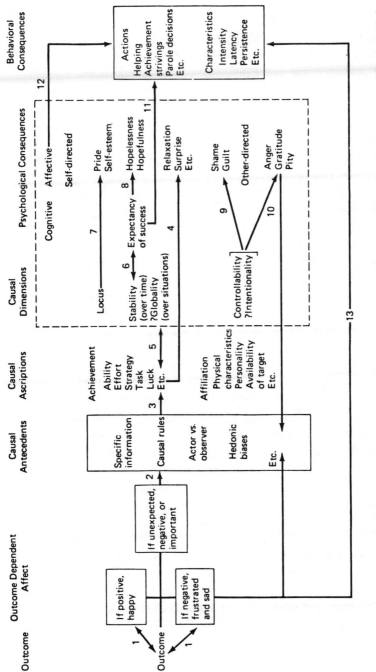

FIGURE 1. An attributional theory of motivation and emotion (adapted from Weiner, 1986, p. 240). Reprinted by permission of Springer-Verlag.

from the generalization (in the example above, all persons succeed except the actor; see Jaspers, 1983). Kelley (1973) also has identified causal schemata that influence the attributions selected. For example, if one succeeds at a difficult task and has expended high effort, then high ability also is perceived as a causal factor (multiple necessary causality). On the other hand, if one has high ability and succeeds at an easy task, it is inferred that little effort was expended (sufficient causality; Kun & Weiner, 1973; also see McClure, Lalljee, Jaspers, & Abelson, 1989). There also is a great deal of evidence that individuals take more credit for success than they do personal blame for failure (the hedonic bias) and that actors and observers tend to make different attributions because of disparities in what is perceptually salient (the perspective bias).

In addition, other-directed affects also influence attributional inferences. Studies indicate, for example, that if a teacher communicates that "she is sorry for" students who fail, then the students infer that they are low in ability (Graham, 1984). Behaviors such as unrequested help and praise for success at an easy task also communicate to others that they are low in ability (see Graham, 1990). In contrast, anger reactions following failure convey that students have not tried hard enough, and the students tend to make lack of effort attributions for failure after this feedback (Graham, 1984).

Based on specific information, biases, schemata, communications from others, and a variety of additional antecedents, individuals reach a causal ascription. In the achievement domain, there are an infinite number of causes of success and failure, the most prominent being ability, effort, strategy, task difficulty, luck, and help or hindrance from others. But among these causes, ability and effort dominate. Thus success typically is ascribed to high ability or high effort, or both, and failure is attributed to low ability or low effort or both (see review in Weiner, 1986).

In a similar manner, there are many causes of affiliative acceptance or rejection, but again a few are most salient, including physical characteristics and personality. Consistent with the general situation in motivation, however, relatively little research has been conducted on perceived causality in domains outside achievement.

It is evident that the perceived causal alternatives differ qualitatively—that is, ability as a cause of success is not the same as effort as a cause of success, and low ability as a cause of achievement failure differs qualitatively from poor personality as a cause of affiliative rejection. To make comparisons possible, it is essential to identify the underlying properties or shared characteristics of causes. One is then able to compare and contrast causes quantitatively, making scientific progress more feasible. Attribution theory has thus followed the lead of other theories (such as personality) in progressing from description to taxonomy.

The identification of these underlying dimensions has been at the very center of the attribution theory I espouse. A number of studies, using techniques including factor analysis, multidimensional scaling, and concept formation, have identified three causal dimensions: locus (internal or external to the actor), stability (enduring or not lasting over time), and controllability (someone is able or not able to volitionally alter the cause). Other dimensions of phenomenal causality including globality (cross-situational generality) and intentionality also have been suggested, but they have met with either empirical or theoretical uncertainty (see Weiner, 1986).

All perceived causes therefore are classifiable within a $2 \times 2 \times 2$ matrix, considering for now the underlying placement on a dimension as dichotomous rather than continuous. For example, aptitude as a cause of an achievement outcome is generally perceived as internal to the actor, stable, and uncontrollable. Indeed, that is what aptitude "means." Being rejected for an affilliative engagement because one is too tall or too short has exactly the same causal properties. Hence, although intellectual aptitude and height obviously differ phenotypically, they can be compared quantitatively and have much in common. Conversely, rejection because the partner already has a date is external to the actor, unstable, and also not controllable. Thus it can be seen that height and a prior engagement differ on two dimensions of causality. And it is possible to ascertain exactly the extent to which they differ.

The three causal dimensions have far-reaching psychological significance that has enabled us to pass from the second stage of theory development (taxonomy) to a third stage, the genotypic analysis of psychological phenomena. The first characteristic mentioned, causal locus, affects self-esteem, self-worth, and pride in accomplishment. Specifically, success ascribed internally to, for example, ability and effort results in enhanced self-worth and pride relative to success ascribed externally (see review in Weiner, 1986). The opposite holds for failure, where an internal ascription especially lowers self-esteem. Individuals have an intuitive understanding of a locus-esteem relation, and it often is used in contexts of impression management. For example, when rejecting someone for an affiliative engagement, females tend to give a reason that is external to the requestor so that his self-esteem is not damaged (Folkes, 1982). Thus they say: "I have a date tonight" rather than "You are boring" when refusing an invitation even when the latter is the true (but withheld) reason.

The dimension of stability influences expectancy of success. There is overwhelming evidence that if an outcome is ascribed to a stable cause, then one expects that outcome to be repeated in the future. One the other hand, an attribution to an unstable cause leads to future uncertainty. For example, failing an exam because of perceived low aptitude generates low expectations of future success compared with failure ascribed to unstable causes such as lack of effort or bad luck (see review in Weiner, 1986). Many achievement change programs have been based on this principle and attempt to alter perceptions of failure from lack of ability to insufficient effort among students who exhibit poor responses in the face of failure (see Foersterling, 1988). Note that there is also a bidirectional association between stability and expectancy, for prior expectancies influence perceived causal stability. For example, failure at a task for which one has a high expectancy of success will tend to be ascribed to an unstable cause.

Finally, causal controllability influences a variety of social affects, including anger, pity, guilt, and shame. I will defer discussion of these associations, since they form a main theme of this chapter and will soon be examined in detail.

Motivated behavior is then directly determined by expectancies (which are linked with causal stability) and affects (including pride, guilt, shame, and the like). Hence this theory follows in the tradition of expectancy-value theory as outlined by Lewin, Tolman, Atkinson, and others. However, incentive value within this conception is considered an affect that already has been experienced and functions to push the organism toward the goal. In contrast, other expectancy-value theorists consider anticipated affective states that pull the organism toward a goal.

In sum, it is now possible to present a behavioral episode from the perspective of attribution theory. Clearly, a historical sequence will be represented; motivation is not conceived as an ahistorical problem. Let us consider the historical episode in the context of the following contrived (but quite reasonable) scenario: A man asks a woman for a date and is rejected. He then withdraws socially and does not appear at other social functions or ask that woman out again.

To explain this behavior, we must look to the processes that intervene between the aversive stimulus (the rejection) and the response (withdrawal). Figure 1 reveals that after rejection the rejected person will feel sad and frustrated. Because this is a negative event, there will be a search for causality. Let us assume that this person has been rejected in the past, whereas friends are dating others. Thus he makes an attribution to himself—he is physically unattractive. When he tells others about the rejection, they express pity, increasing his belief that the rejection was due to something about him.

Unattractiveness as a cause of social rejection is conceived as internal to the rejected party. The person's self-esteem therefore will be lowered. In addition, this characteristic typically is perceived as stable. Thus there will be high expectancy of future failure. Also, because the cause is construed as uncontrollable, he will feel ashamed of himself (humiliated, embarrassed) while others convey pity. Feelings of sadness (outcome determined), low self-esteem, shame, and low expectancy of success result in his withdrawal from social activities. Hence expectancy and affect mediate between stimulus and response associations.

The interpretation above included virtually all the linkages in the theory. I now want to restrict attention to the associations labeled 10 and 12 in Figure 1; that is, the sequence between perceived controllability, affective reactions (especially pity and anger), and action. This will be the focus of the rest of this chapter, which examines judgments of responsibility and their effects on social behavior. Following my earlier dicta, we will see that cognitions and affects determine motivated behavior, that there is a search for general laws rather than interactions with individual differences, that there is concern with the self, and that the theory is extended beyond achievement strivings to address altruism, responses to the stigmatized, achievement evaluation, and impression management.

To examine the motivational consequences of perceived responsibility, I will first consider the role of responsibility attributions in eliciting emotions (anger and pity), then turn to the effects of responsibility judgments and affects on motivated behavior. It will be seen that a wide variety of phenotypically disparate behaviors can be subject to the same theoretical interpretation.

Attributions of Responsibility Related to Anger and Sympathy (Pity)

The emotions of anger and sympathy (pity) are in part determined by how an event or outcome is construed (appraised). The critical dimension of thought that determines which of these two emotions is aroused is perceived causal controllability. In this context, I use controllability as linked with personal responsibility—given a controllable cause, the person is held responsible for an outcome. Thus, when discussing causes I will use the concept of controllability; when discussing persons I will employ the concept of responsibility.

Consider, for example, an investigation by Weiner, Graham, and Chandler (1982) that involved the recall of life incidents. The researchers asked college students to describe occasions in their lives when they had experienced anger or pity. After recounting two experiences for each emotion, the subjects rated the controllability of the events instigating these reactions. For anger, almost 90% of the situations involved a cause or reason that they believed was controllable by the transgressor. Two typical anger-arousing experiences were:

1. My roommate brought her dog into our no-pets apartment without asking me first. When I got home, she wasn't there, but the barking dog was. . . . Also, the dog relieved itself in the middle of the entry.
2. I felt angry toward my boyfriend for lying to me about something he did (Weiner et al., 1982, p. 228).

The connection between violation of an "ought" or "should" and anger has been noted by many investigators. For example, in one of the very early studies, Pastore (1952) demonstrated that the relation between frustration and aggression is mediated by perceptions of responsibility and control. His data suggest that anger does not merely result from failing to attain a desired goal, but follows only when a barrier imposed by others is "arbitrary" (e.g., "Your date phones at the last minute and breaks an appointment without adequate explanation"), not when the action is "nonarbitrary" (e.g., "Your date . . . breaks an appointment because he [she] has suddenly become ill"). More recently, a thorough analysis of anger has been offered by Averill (1982, 1983). In describing his own research, which also made use of the recall of critical incidents, Averill concluded: "Over 85% of the episodes described by angry persons involved either an act that they considered voluntary and unjustified (59%) or else a potentially avoidable accident (e.g., due to negligence or lack of foresight, 28%). . . . More than anything else, anger is an attribution of blame" (Averill, 1983, p. 1150).

In contrast to the linkage between controllability (personal responsibility) and anger, uncontrollable causes are associated with sympathy and the related affect of pity. In the research by Weiner et al. (1982), approximately 75% of the sympathy stories involved an uncontrollable cause. Two typical reports were:

1. A guy on campus is terribly deformed. I pity him because it would be so hard to look so different and have people stare at you.
2. My great-grandmother lives in a rest home, and everytime I go there I see these poor old half-senile men and women. . . . I feel pity when I go there (Weiner et al., 1982, p. 228).

Inasmuch as anger is associated with perceptions of responsibility, whereas sympathy and pity are linked with perceptions of nonresponsibility and adverse differences, communicating these emotions to others has differential cue functions. As already indicated, communicating anger conveys: "You have not tried hard enough; you should [could, ought to] have done better" (see Graham, 1984). Thus an expression of anger may promote guilt. On the other hand, pity serves as a cue enhancing self-perception of nonresponsibility and specific attributions to, for example, lack of aptitude or an unfavorable and uncontrollable environment (see Graham, 1984; Weiner, Graham, Stern, & Lawson, 1982).

In sum, a great deal of evidence supports the contention that beliefs about responsibility guide the emotional reactions of anger and sympathy toward others. I will now document how causal attributions regarding personal responsibility and their linked emotions are central in determining helping behavior, reactions to the stigmatized, achievement appraisal, and excuse giving. In these diverse fields of study, inferences about personal responsibility of the other determine the emotions elicited and, in turn, the judgments made and the behavior undertaken toward the other. The general message in all four areas of research is that perceptions of responsibility, which augment anger, may have adverse consequences. On the other hand, attributions of nonresponsibility, which promote sympathy, may bring many benefits.

The analyses of the four topics of study indicated above also have implications for a broad array of applied issues. These concerns include the family dynamics that coexist with depression and hyperactivity, policy decisions regarding alcoholics and the needy, changing reactions toward individuals with AIDS, government funding for the social sciences, and even the process of consciousness raising. Applied issues are examined in the last part of this chapter.

Help Giving (Altruism)

A number of investigations have demonstrated directly or indirectly that perceptions of responsibility for the need for help influence whether a needy person is aided or neglected. Some of these studies have also examined the role that affective reactions of anger and sympathy play in help giving. Consider, for example, an experiment by Weiner (1980a). In that study, subjects were given the following scenario (based on Piliavin, Rodin, & Piliavin, 1969): "At about 1:00 in the afternoon you are riding a subway car. There are a number of other individuals in the car and one person is standing, holding on to the center pole. Suddenly, this person staggers forward and collapses. The person apparently is drunk. He is carrying a liquor bottle wrapped in a brown bag and smells of liquor. (Alternate form: The person is carrying a black cane and apparently is ill.)" (p. 120). After reading each scenario, subjects rated the responsibility for (the controllability of) the cause of the need, affective reactions of anger and sympathy (pity), and the likelihood of help giving.

The data revealed a positive association between responsibility and anger ($r = .77$) and a negative association between perceived responsibility and sympathy ($r = -.55$). This pattern is consistent with the earlier discussion of attribution-affect relations. Concerning the helping judgments, there were negative associations between responsibility and imagined help giving ($r = -.37$) as well as between anger and help ($r = -.71$). Conversely, sympathy was positively related to judgments of help ($r = .46$). These relations also are in accord with conceptions of the motivational role of emotion. For example, it has been contended that "anger educates the . . . individual by frightening him with immediate harm or with future harm of no more aid," whereas pity "motivates altruistic behavior as a function of the plight of the recipient of such behavior" (Trivers, 1971, p. 49). In general, the disabled individual was perceived as not responsible for his plight, sympathy but not anger was expressed, and help was indicated. On the other hand, the drunk was perceived as personally responsible for falling; subjects reported that they would feel more anger than sympathy and would withhold help.

A number of replication experiments examining these issues have been conducted, using other vignettes and more powerful statistical techniques such as structural equation modeling. For example, in one investigation by Schmidt and Weiner (1988), the investigators pursued whether the strengths of the observed relations could be altered by means of experimental instructions at times used in helping studies that emphasize attention to facts ("try to be as ob-

Table 1

Correlations and Structural Paths in Four Experimental Conditions

Condition	N	Correlation Coefficient					Path Coefficient		
		R×A[1]	R×S[2]	R×H[3]	A×H	S×H	R→H	A→H	S→H
Control	127	.41	−.58	−.37	−.55	.56	NS[4]	−.48	.55
Self focus	126	.28	−.70	−.25	−.64	.36	NS	−.67	.14
Other focus (empathy)	123	.38	−.62	−.23	−.58	.41	NS	−.62	.37
Objective	120	.33	−.66	−.29	−.54	.52	NS	−.49	.52
$\bar{X}$		.35	−.64	−.29	−.58	.47	NS	−.55	.42

Source: Adapted from Schmidt and Weiner, 1988, p. 617.
[1]R = responsibility; A = anger. [2]S = sympathy. [3]H = help. [4]NS = not significant.

jective as possible") versus emotional self focus ("imagine how you would react in this situation") and emotional other focus ("imagine how the other person feels"). The vignette used by Schmidt and Weiner (1988) involved borrowing class notes. One of those asking said he needed the notes because he had eye problems (not responsible), whereas the other said he needed them because "he went to the beach" (personal responsibility; from Weiner, 1980b).

The left columns in Table 1 show the correlations between the responsibility, affect, and the behavioral judgments. It is immediately evident that in all four conditions the identical pattern of data prevailed—perceived responsibility related positively to anger and negatively to sympathy, while responsibility and anger were negatively associated with help and sympathy related positively to helping judgments. Turning next to the within-condition path analyses, Table 1 documents that in all four conditions there were significant paths from affective reactions to judgments of aid, but not from responsibility to aid. A multigroup path analysis combining the data

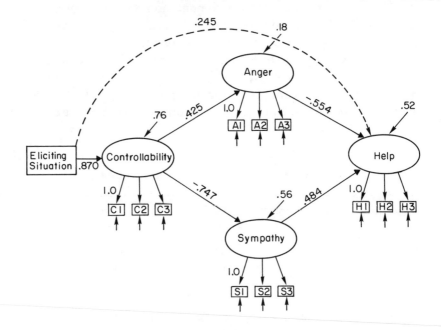

FIGURE 2. Structural model combining subjects in all experimental conditions (from Schmidt & Weiner, 1988, fig. 1, p. 618). Copyright 1988 by Sage Publications. Reprinted by permission of Sage Publications, Inc.

in all four conditions ($N = 496$) is shown in Figure 2. It is quite evident from Figure 2 that an attribution (responsibility)–affect (anger and sympathy)–action conception is strongly supported by the data (also see Betancourt, 1983; Meyer & Mulherin, 1980; Reisenzein, 1986).

Although the two reviewed studies by Weiner (1980a) and Schmidt and Weiner (1988) were simulational, behavioral observations support the conclusions that have been offered. For example, it has been found that drunks are less often helped on subways than are those who are physically ill (Piliavin et al., 1969), and that students seeking to borrow class notes because of lack of effort are helped less often than those who need notes because of low ability (Barnes, Ickes, & Kidd, 1979). In these situations it is reasonable to suggest that the key mediating variables determining the helping judgments related to perceived responsibility and to the emotions elicited by responsibility attributions.

REACTIONS TO THE STIGMATIZED: FURTHER EXAMINATION OF HELP GIVING

Reactions to social stigmas also are amenable to the analyses suggested above—that is, an interpretation that includes responsibility and affective reactions as determinants of intended or actual behavior. Indeed, stigmas already have been introduced; in the Weiner (1980a) investigation reviewed above, responsibility was manipulated by portraying the person as drunk or ill—two stigmas.

A great deal of research has revealed that both the stigmatized person and others search for the origin of a stigma and the possible presence of personal responsibility. As documented by Wright (1983), physically handicapped persons often ask themselves the existential attribution question: "Why me?" and frequently are confronted with the question "How did this happen?" This search is not limited to physical abnormalities; one hears such queries as: "Why is he drinking so much?" or "What caused the nervous breakdown?" In many instances, however, the stigma itself implies a cause, thus negating the need for further information. For example, drug abuse may automatically be linked with "moral weakness" and AIDS with promiscuous or aberrant sexual behavior. According to the previous analysis, judged responsibility for having the stigma should then guide affective reactions toward the stigmatized person and a variety of behavioral responses including, for example, the help-related actions of charitable donations and personal assistance.

A number of investigations have examined perceived responsibility for a stigma, or what is sometimes referred to as a "social mark" (Jones et al., 1984). For example, Beckman (1979) asked both alcoholic and nonalcoholic respondents to rate a number of statements concerning the causes of excessive drinking. Among both groups, the drinking individual was held responsible for drunkenness. In a similar manner, there also have been many reports of connections between obesity and personal responsibility. For example, Mackenzie (1984) stated that fat and thin people share the opinion that fatness indicates a loss of personal control, which is "considered the ultimate moral failure in our culture."

Numerous investigations also have documented that disparate stigmas elicit differential liking and help giving and that those reactions are related to suppositions about personal responsibility for the stigma. For example, obese people often are least likely to be chosen in sociometric studies of friendship and are ranked low on liking when depicted in drawings (Richardson, Hastorf, Goodman, & Dornbusch, 1961; Staffieri, 1967). DeJong (1980) found, however, that when obesity was attributed to a thyroid condition, the overweight individual was relatively liked.

My colleagues and I (Weiner, Perry, & Magnusson, 1988) directly examined the relations between stigma, perceived responsibility, affect, and intended action. In these investigations, ten stigmas (AIDS, Alzheimer's disease, blindness, cancer, child abuse, drug addiction, heart disease, obesity, paraplegia, and Vietnam War syndrome) were rated on responsibility and blame for these conditions, affective reactions of liking, anger, and pity, and help-related actions of charitable donations and personal assistance. Ratings were made on 9-point scales anchored at the extremes with labels such as entirely responsible–not responsible at all and no anger–a great deal of anger.

The data from one representative study are given in Table 2. Table 2 shows that six of the stigmas were rated low on perceived personal responsibility and blame (Alzheimer's disease, blindness, cancer, heart disease, paraplegia, and Vietnam War syndrome), whereas the remaining four (AIDS, child abuse, drug addiction, and

Table 2

Mean Values on Responsibility-Related Variables

Stigma	Respons-ibility	Blame	Liking	Pity	Anger	Assis-tance	Charitable Donations
Alzheimer's disease	0.8[a]	0.5[a]	6.5[bc]	7.9[a]	1.4[a]	8.0[a]	6.9[bc]
Blindness	0.9[a]	0.5[a]	7.5[a]	7.4[a]	1.7[e]	8.5[a]	7.2[abc]
Cancer	1.6[ab]	1.3[ab]	7.6[a]	8.0[a]	1.6[e]	8.4[a]	8.1[a]
Heart disease	2.5[b]	1.6[b]	7.5[a]	7.4[a]	1.6[e]	8.0[a]	7.5[ab]
Paraplegia	1.6[ab]	0.9[ab]	7.0[ab]	7.6[a]	1.4[e]	8.1[a]	7.1[abc]
Vietnam War syndrome	1.7[ab]	1.5[b]	5.7[c]	7.1[a]	2.1[e]	7.0[b]	6.2[cd]
AIDS	4.4[c]	4.8[c]	4.8[d]	6.2[b]	4.0[c]	5.8[c]	6.5[bc]
Child abuse	5.2[c]	6.0[de]	2.0[f]	3.3[d]	7.9[a]	4.6[d]	4.0[f]
Drug abuse	6.5[d]	6.7[e]	3.0[e]	4.0[d]	6.4[b]	5.3[cd]	5.0[e]
Obesity	5.3[c]	5.2[cd]	5.7[c]	5.1[c]	3.3[d]	5.8[c]	4.0[f]

Source: Adapted from Weiner, Perry, and Magnusson, 1988, p. 740.
Note: Means within columns not sharing a superscript differ at the $p < .01$ level.

obesity) were rated high on these variables. Hence stigmatized persons were generally not held responsible for physical problems, whereas stigmas for which individuals were held responsible were primarily behavioral/mental problems. Clearly, whether the "victim is blamed" (a phrase often accepted among psychologists) depends on the answer given to the question "Blamed for what?"

Table 2 also reveals that individuals not held responsible for their stigmas were rated high on liking, elicited pity but not anger, and generated high ratings on judgments of helping. Conversely, persons with stigmas for which they were held responsible were rated relatively low on liking, evoked little pity and relatively high anger, and elicited comparatively low help-giving responses. The correlations between these variables are shown in Table 3. In that table, stigmas were treated as a dichotomous variable; one index was derived for responsibility (responsibility + blame), positive affect (liking + pity – anger), and helping (personal assistance + charity). Table 3 shows significant correlations between the four variables. Considering the proposed sequence of stigma origin → perceived responsibility → affect → action, Table 3 indicates that the more steps between the variables in the postulated order, the lower the correla-

Table 3

Correlations Between Perceived Responsibility and Related Variables

	Stigma Source[1]	Perceived Responsibility[2]	Positive Affect	Help
Stigma source		.59[3]	.50	.38
Perceived responsibility			.66	.38
Positive affect				.65
Help				

Source: Data from Weiner, Perry, and Magnusson, 1988.
[1] Physically based stigmas = 2; mental/behavioral stigmas = 1.
[2] High values indicate lack of perceived responsibility.
[3] All p's < .01.

tion between those variables. Specifically, when there are three steps in the path (stigma source to help), then the correlation between the two variables is .38; when the path involves two series steps (stigma source to affect, perceived responsibility to help), the average r = .44; and for the correlations between adjacent path variables (stigma source to perceived responsibility, responsibility to affect, affect to help), the average r = .63. In this study, as in the research about helping reported earlier, help was most associated with affect (beta = .68) rather than with perceived responsibility or stigma source (respective betas = .14 and .12).

It is also of interest that the degree of moral condemnation and the associated affects and behaviors can be altered by communicating further information. For example, when subjects are told that heart disease was caused by smoking and drinking, and that AIDS was due to a blood transfusion, AIDS is perceived as uncontrollable and heart disease as controllable. This changes the affects and behavioral judgments toward individuals with these stigmas. However, not all stigmas are subject to attributional change. For example, we have not found any way to make a child abuser be perceived as not responsible!

In sum, reactions to the stigmatized are in part based on moral evaluations. Stigmatized people held responsible for their marks are construed as moral failures, which generates morality-related negative affects and correspondent negative thoughts and behaviors. On the other hand, stigmatized individuals not held responsible for the stigma are considered "innocent victims" and elicit altruism-generating affects as well as positive actions.

Achievement Appraisal

I shall now turn to an earlier period of my research interest—back to the achievement domain. We will see that achievement evaluation is subject to the same analyses as that given for helping behavior and general reactions to the stigmatized.

A voluminous literature exists regarding the determinants of the evaluation of individuals in achievement contexts (at school, in sporting competition, on the job). In some of this research, the perceived responsibility for success and failure has been varied, and the influence of this causal property on evaluation has been assessed. A series of investigations by Weiner and Kukla (1970) provided the prototypical evaluation method. Students were described as succeeding or failing on an exam. This outcome information was factorially combined with descriptions of each one's ability level and effort expenditure. Thus, for example, in one condition a student was described as high in ability, low in effort, and failing an exam, whereas in a contrasting condition another student was characterized as low in ability, high in effort, and succeeding. The subjects were asked to evaluate (provide feedback to) each of these students.

It is presumed here that students are perceived as responsible for their effort expenditure, in that effort is subject to volitional control and change. Lack of effort particularly activates thoughts of responsibility, since not trying is carried out "knowingly and recklessly" (Fincham & Jaspers, 1980). On the other hand, it also is presumed that students are not perceived as responsible for their level of ability, which in this research was intimated to be a fixed characteristic.

The data from one investigation reported by Weiner and Kukla (1970) are shown in Figure 3. In that figure, the outcomes represented ranged from excellent (exc) through fair, borderline (border), moderate failure (mod fail) and clear failure (clear fail). Furthermore, evaluation ranged from maximum reward (+5) to maximum punishment (–5). Figure 3 reveals, as one would expect, that positive outcomes were rewarded more (punished less) than negative

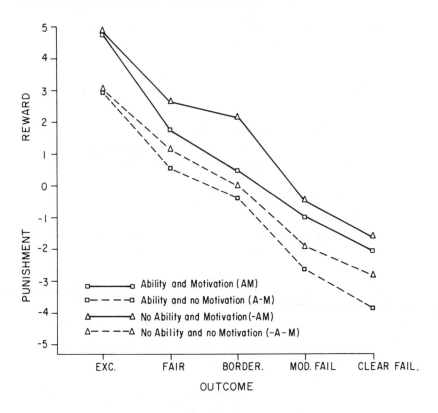

FIGURE 3. Evaluation as a function of outcome, effort, and ability (from Weiner & Kukla, 1970, p. 3). Copyright 1970 by the American Psychological Association. Reprinted by permission of the publisher.

outcomes. Of greater importance in the present context, high effort or motivation (M) was rewarded more for success and punished less for failure than was lack of effort or motivation (–M). Lack of effort accompanied by high ability (A–M), which is the causal configuration in which the student is clearly responsible for failure, elicited the greatest punishment. These data suggest that it is most immoral not to utilize one's capacity. The general pattern of data shown in Figure 3 has been replicated in many cultures, including Brazil, England, Germany, India, and Iran. The findings have also been documented in actual classrooms, work environments, and athletic settings (see review in Weiner, 1986, pp. 146–147).

The investigation by Weiner and Kukla (1970) and others guided by that paradigm have not collected affective data, so the mediating role of anger and sympathy cannot be determined. Nonetheless, there is an abundance of evidence that students who do not try evoke anger, whereas students low in ability elicit pity (see, for example, Weiner, Graham, Stern, & Lawson, 1982). In a recent investigation, Stahelski, Patch, & Enochson (1987) replicated the Weiner and Kukla procedure but also obtained affective ratings. They found that surprise was the dominant affective reaction by others given failure paired with both high ability and high effort; sympathy and pity dominated the ratings when there was failure paired with low ability and high effort; and anger and disgust were the most evident emotions given high ability, low effort, and failure. Although these data do not directly address the issue of affect as a mediating variable, they are consistent with the argument that has been put forth.

Excuse Giving (Impression Management)

It is evident from the data presented thus far that there are advantages to not being considered personally responsible for needing aid, for having a particular stigma, or for failing an exam. It would therefore be functional for the needy, the stigmatized, and the failing to manipulate perceptions regarding responsibility and in so doing to control or alter affective reactions and their correlated consequences. For example, one might want to make potential lenders think one has tried when one needs class notes, to make potential friends think one's obesity is due to a glandular dysfunction rather than to overeating, and to make teachers believe failure was due to temporary illness. One way this impression management might be accomplished is by consciously providing false public information or reasons for a need, stigma, outcome, or such. In this context, substituting a false cause for a true cause in a public setting will be called an excuse (*ex* = from, *cuse* = cause). Reducing responsibility, blame, and anger has been identified as among the main purposes of excuse giving (Weiner, Amirkhan, Folkes, & Verette, 1987).

The role of responsibility, blame, and anger in excuse giving can be readily illustrated in the breaking of a social contract—for example, not appearing for a social engagement or arriving late. This behavior typically elicits attributional search; the "wronged" person is likely to ask: "Why didn't you show up?" or "Why are you so late?" In addition, that person may display irritation or anger. The issue raised here is, What does the transgressor do to mitigate this anger?

To explore this question, my colleagues and I (Weiner et al., 1987) asked college students to recall recent occasions when social contracts had been broken and to provide the true and false reasons that were communicated, as well as any uncommunicated (withheld) reasons. The participants also were asked how angry the recipients of the communication actually did feel when receiving the reason and how they might have felt had the withheld reason been known.

Analysis of the withheld (true) reasons revealed that they were ones for which the social transgressor would be held responsible. These reasons primarily were negligence (forgetting) and intentional actions (e.g., "Decided to go to another party instead"). On the other hand, the communicated false reasons (lies) absolved the wrongdoer of responsibility. The four main categories of excuses were transportation problems (e.g., "My car broke down"), work/school demands (e.g., "I had to do homework"), prior commitments (e.g., "I had to take my parents to the airport"), and illness. Other data also revealed that the recipient of the communication was rated higher on anger when assuming that the withheld (real) explanation was known, as opposed to the actual reaction when the false communication (the excuse) was given. Data confirming an association between responsibility for a social transgression, anger, and response withholding have been reported among children ages 5–12 (Weiner & Handel, 1985; Yirmiya & Weiner, 1986).

Laboratory investigations have confirmed these findings. In one pertinent study reported by Weiner et al. (1987), subjects were detained by the experimenter so that they would arrive late for an experiment in which another student was participating. In three experimental conditions, the instructions to the tardy subject were to (1) give an excuse that would make the waiting person angry; (2) give a "good" excuse; and (3) give any excuse. Classification of the excuses revealed that "bad" excuses conveyed that the transgressor was personally responsible for being late (see Table 4). The content of these excuses again primarily involved forgetting and intended actions. On the other hand, the "good" excuses communicated that the transgressor was not responsible for being tardy. These excuses

Table 4

Excuse Classification as a Function of Experimental Condition

Excuse Classification	Experimental Condition		
	Bad Excuse	Good Excuse	Any Excuse
Not Responsible	2	15	11
Accept Responsibility	13	0	2

Source: Data from Weiner, Amirkhan, Folkes, & Verette, 1987.

primarily concerned transportation problems, other commitments, and so forth. Finally, when instructions were to give any excuse, "good" excuses were given. Other ratings gathered in the study revealed that those giving bad excuses (ones for which they were held responsible) elicited more unfavorable emotions, negative personality evaluations, and social rejection than persons giving a "good" excuse or "any" excuse.

In sum, there is a naive belief that anger is in part influenced by causal ascriptions concerning why a social contract has not been fulfilled. To ward off these negative consequences, people may withhold the truth (lie), substituting explanations they anticipate will lessen anger. These good or functional excuses relieve the transgressor of personal responsibility. That is, excuses for a broken social contract are given to foster the perception that the wrongdoer is a "moral person." This certainly increases the likelihood that the relationship will be maintained. Hence the motivational sequence apparently is: behavior (social transgression) → perceived or actual personal responsibility → anticipated anger from other → excuse → offset of personal responsibility → offset of anger → increased likelihood of social bonding.

Research Summary

A basic theme of this chapter is that responsibility judgments constitute a fundamental category or dimension of attributions that is activated in a variety of contexts. Thus the concept of responsibility fostered some unification between the diverse research areas of helping, reactions to the stigmatized, achievement appraisal, and excuses. Those held responsible for a negative state or event elicit anger and little sympathy; help is withheld, and they are disliked and appraised negatively. On the other hand, those not held responsible evoke little anger and a great deal of sympathy; help is given, and they are liked and appraised positively.

Applications and Implications

Distinctions between sin and sickness, willful miscondust and disease, needy and truly needy, and lazy and unable are made daily by family members, teachers, and the government to determine how to judge others and how much help to offer. In this section I examine some representative dilemmas in everyday interaction and a few policy decisions that are illuminated by the prior discussion of psychological research related to perceptions of responsibility. I very briefly consider depression, hyperactivity, alcoholism, and AIDS, then make some general comments about funding in the social sciences and current trends in psychology. Finally, I end with some observations about consciousness raising, since that highlights some of the complexities raised when reaching a responsible versus not responsible resolution of an attributional conflict.

DEPRESSION AND HYPERACTIVITY

There are many situations in which there is disagreement about the perceived causes of a negative event or outcome, and this disagreement often concerns responsibility and blame. The attributional disparity could be between observers of an event or between observers and the actor. For example, Coates and Wortman (1980) have documented that those interacting with depressives often experience anger, thereby implying that depressed persons should be able to control (i.e., change) their affective state and maladaptive behavior (also see Hooley, Richters, Weintraub, & Neal, 1987; Sacco, Milana, & Dunn, 1985). But at times depressed individuals believe their emotional valley is not subject to volitional control and change. Hence sympathy and concern are "deserved" and are emotional supports that they "should" be receiving. That is, there is a discrepancy between their affective anticipations and the emotion that actually is communicated from others. The effects of such incongruent emotional fits might enter into the dynamics of depression, resulting in a feedback loop that exacerbates the condition. On the other hand, depressed persons often also believe that their sadness is controllable—that they are responsible for their negative affective state and actions. In this case the communicated anger is another cue substantiating this belief. Of course, the anger also might be the information that actually instigates the self-blame belief. In either case, accepting the communication of anger and self-attribution of responsiblity would then augment experienced guilt, which is one of the consequences of accepting responsibility for negative events. This discussion does not "take sides" on whether it is "better" to blame or not to blame (to hold responsible or not hold responsible) the depressed person. But these judgments will have disparate implications that are likely to influence interpersonal interaction, both experienced and communicated affects, and perhaps even the course of the problem.

Attributions of responsibility for hyperactivity have equal ambiguity. Among teachers, hyperactive children are perceived as responsible for their misbehavior and tend to elicit anger and no help, in contrast to children with problems that do not affect the teacher, such as shyness. Shy pupils are offered help and support (Brophy & Rohrkemper, 1981).

However, the prescription of medication for hyperactivity implies that the problem is one that the person cannot control without outside aid. Whalen and Henker (1976) point out that when hyperactivity is attributed to inborn, neurological factors for which neither the parents nor the children are responsible, they both experience less guilt and personal blame. However, it is suggested that reducing personal responsibility also discourages self-initiated actions toward alleviating the problem. There may be no escaping from this predicament. But the dilemma posed does highlight both the positive and the negative consequences of reducing (or augmenting) responsibility perceptions.

ALCOHOLICS AND THE NEEDY

The issue of whether alcoholics are responsible for their plight recently received a great deal of attention. Many in the health profession view alcoholism as a "disease." This approach was first espoused by Alcoholics Anonymous in the 1930s and subsequently was accepted by both the American Medical Association and the American Psychological Association. The genetic component of alcoholism, psychological explanations related to early deprivation, and sociological evidence shifting etiology outside the person—to social class and urban environments—all tend to absolve the alcoholic of personal responsibility.

As noted earlier, however, both alcoholics and nonalcoholics perceive that one is responsible for one's drinking behavior. Indeed, massive guilt among alcoholics often has been reported (see, for example, Tuite & Luiten, 1986). Recently, in agreement with laypersons, the courts have ruled that alcoholism should be considered "willful misconduct." Thus alcoholics have not been able to receive the government benefits accorded to others with "diseases." This reaction is to be anticipated, given the research evidence regarding the neglect elicited by perceived responsibility.

A similar responsibility decision can be seen in the government's handling of welfare recipients. A differentiation has been made between the "needy" and the "truly needy." The latter, unable to care for themselves, are considered deserving of aid and benefits. The former are seen as responsible for their current predicaments and thus are judged not worthy of support.

AIDS

There have been great shifts in the government's and the public's reactions toward persons with AIDS. The concept of perceived responsibility sheds light on this fluctuation and perhaps allows one to make some future (grave) predictions. When AIDS was initially acknowledged as a serious problem, the response of the government and the population was primarily neglect. From the discussion in this chapter, such a reaction was to be expected, since the perceived cause of AIDS was homosexual activity (and later drug use). Table 2 shows that both AIDS and drug abuse are perceived as controllable and thus elicit relatively high anger, low pity, and few indications of desire to help (see Triplet & Sugarman, 1987). Subsequently, however, the known population of AIDS victims began to include recipients of blood transfusions, infants of mothers with AIDS, and heterosexuals. Hence AIDS also began to elicit perceptions of nonresponsibility (Staff, 1987). These perceptions evoke relatively high pity, low anger, and altruistic help (see Weiner et al., 1988). It now appears that AIDS contracted from transfusions has been greatly reduced because of blood testing; there are increased abortions of children of AIDS-infected mothers; and there is some suggestive evidence that the spreading of AIDS among heterosexuals is less than anticipated. Thus altruistically motivated help should decrease (see Sheer, 1987). Of course help might still be given, but motivated by fear or cost-benefit concerns, rather than generated by sympathy and care.

GOVERNMENT FUNDING FOR MENTAL/BEHAVIORAL PROBLEMS

The discussion regarding stigmas has negative implications for the mental health profession in terms of solicitation of charitable donations, public support, and government funding, inasmuch as mental/behavioral problems such as alcoholism and drug abuse arouse little sympathy, particularly compared with stigmas that have a clear somatic component, such as paraplegia or blindness. One course for psychologists and researchers to take is to alter perceptions of these illnesses toward uncontrollability so that they are perceived or labeled as "diseases." Indeed, research in mental illness has become strikingly biological in orientation. It might be argued that merging mental/behavioral problems with biology and genetics will greatly benefit researchers in terms of ultimate funding because the needy target population will no longer be blamed. This, of course, is not to argue that there are not biological determinants of mental illnesses such as schizophrenia and depression, or that such issues do not deserve full exploration. Rather, I am merely pointing out that support and funding, which often drive research, are likely to be more available when the subject population under study elicits pity and sympathy rather than anger and moral condemnation.

CONSCIOUSNESS RAISING AND THE DILEMMA OF RESPONSIBILITY

The typical goal of consciousness raising for females and other disadvantaged minority groups is to have personal "failure" ascribed to social and political forces that are external to group members. That is, consciousness raising attempts to alter perceptions (attributions) so that the group members no longer see themselves as personally responsible for their plight. This is evident in the manifesto of Redstockings, the radical feminist group that began consciousness raising: "We reject the idea that women consent to or are to blame for their own oppression. Women's submission is . . . the result . . . of . . . continual, daily pressure from men" (Rosenthal, 1984, p. 315).

One desired result of this attributional shift is to decrease guilt and self-blame and increase self-worth. The externalization of responsibility and the consequent affective change also have been noted in work with other minority groups. For example, in discussions regarding their struggle in Mexico, Werner and Bower (1982) write: "Critically aware persons come to realize that only by changing the norms and procedures of organized society can the most serious ills . . . be corrected. . . . As their awareness deepens, persons also begin to feel better about themselves" (p. 26).

The goal of decreasing responsibility, however, creates a paradox: If one is not responsible, how can change be accomplished? This dilemma is inherent in all the topics discussed here. For example, if one does not accept responsibility for continual sadness, for disruptive behavior, for drunkenness, or for sexual activity that could result in harm, what will induce one to change?

There are a few solutions to this dilemma, and the solutions at the group level may not be applicable to resolutions at the individual level. For example, consciousness raising is based on the philosophy that awareness of obstacles will promote group action: "Redstockings argued that the source of women's problems lies in the organization of patriarchal society, and the solution to these problems will spring out of the acquisition of a true picture of oppression. . . . Once women connect information about themselves and their lives with these ideas, militance will inevitably follow, just as the acquisition of class consciousness, in the Marxist view, reaches its culmination in revolutionary activity" (Rosenthal, 1984, p. 315). In a similar manner, Freire (1970) states: "In order for the oppressed to be able to wage the struggle for their liberation, they must perceive the reality of oppression not as a closed world from which there is no exit, but as a limiting situation which they can transform" (p. 34).

Note, however, that these solutions imply personal responsibility at some level. The members of the group are responsible for militancy or for transforming society. Thus it appears that responsibility is accepted for the offset, but not the onset, of the problem (Brickman et al., 1982). This may decrease the negative consequences that accompany responsibility attributions (guilt, self-blame, low esteem, and lack of help from others) while maintaining the positive products of responsibility ascription (continued instrumental action toward the goal).

Concluding Comment

I shall end this chapter by emphasizing the richness of an attributional approach to motivation. Many, many motivational issues appear to be amenable to an attributional analysis. This approach cannot readily incorporate the speed of a hungry rat running down a maze for food or one's unconscious aggressive desires toward a sibling or parent. But it is able to shift easily from the interpretation of achievement strivings to social phenomena ranging from help giving to excuse making and to everyday problems ranging from government funding to consciousness raising. Thus I think it provides the language to unify many diverse effects of interest to motivational theorists.

REFERENCES

Averill, J. R. (1982). *Anger and aggression: An essay on emotion.* New York: Springer-Verlag.
Averill, J. R. (1983). Studies on anger and aggression. *American Psychologist, 38,* 1145–1160.

Barnes, R. D., Ickes, W. J., & Kidd, R. (1979). Effects of perceived intentionality and stability of another's dependency on helping behavior. *Personality and Social Psychology Bulletin, 5*, 367–372.

Beckman, L. J. (1979). Beliefs about the causes of alcohol-related problems among alcoholic and non-alcoholic women. *Journal of Clinical Psychology, 35*, 663–670.

Betancourt, H. (1983). *Causal attributions, empathy, and emotions as determinants of helping behavior: An integrative approach.* Unpublished doctoral dissertation, University of California, Los Angeles.

Brickman, P., Rabinowitz, V. C., Karuza, J., Coates, D., Cohn, E., & Kidder, L. (1982). Models of helping and coping. *American Psychologist, 37*, 368–384.

Brophy, J. E., & Rohrkemper, M. M. (1981). The influence of problem ownership on teachers' perceptions of strategies for coping with problem students. *Journal of Educational Psychology, 73*, 295–311.

Coates, D., & Wortman, C. B. (1980). Depression maintenance and interpersonal control. In A. Baum & J. E. Singer (Eds.), *Advances in environmental psychology: Vol. 2. Applications of personal control* (pp. 149–182). Hillsdale, NJ: Erlbaum.

DeJong, W. (1980). The stigma of obesity: The consequences of naive assumptions concerning the causes of physical deviance. *Journal of Health and Social Behavior, 21*, 75–87.

Ellsworth, P. C., & Smith, C. A. (1988). Shades of joy: Patterns of appraisal differentiating pleasant emotions. *Cognition and Emotion, 2*, 301–332.

Fincham, F. D., & Jaspers, J. M. (1980). Attribution of responsibility: From man the scientist to man as lawyer. In L. Berkowitz, (Ed.), *Advances in experimental social psychology* (Vol. 13, pp. 82–139). New York: Academic Press.

Foersterling, F. (1988). *Attribution theory in clinical psychology.* New York: Wiley.

Folkes, V. S. (1982). Communicating the causes of social rejection. *Journal of Experimental Social Psychology, 18*, 235–252.

Freire, P. (1970). *Pedagogy of the oppressed.* New York: Seabury.

Graham, S. (1984). Communicated sympathy and anger to black and white children: The cognitive (attributional) consequences of affective cues. *Journal of Personality and Social Psychology, 47*, 40–54.

Graham, S. (1990). Communicating low ability in the classroom: Bad things good teachers sometimes do. In S. Graham & V. S. Folkes, (Eds.), *Attribution theory: Applications to achievement, mental health, and interpersonal conflict.* Hillsdale, NJ: Erlbaum.

Hooley, J. M., Richters, J. E., Weintraub, S., & Neal, J. M. (1987). Psychopathology of marital distress: The positive side of positive symptoms. *Journal of Abnormal Psychology, 96*, 27–33.

Jaspers, J. M. (1983). The process of causal attribution in common sense. In M. Hewstone (Ed.), *Attribution theory: Social and functional extensions* (pp. 28–44). Oxford: Basil Blackwell.

Jones, E. E., Farino, A., Hastorf, A. H., Markus, H., Miller, D. T., & Scott, R. A. (1984). *Social stigma*. New York: Freeman.

Kelley, H. H. (1967). Attribution theory in social psychology. In D. Levine (Ed.), *Nebraska Symposium on Motivation, 1967* (pp. 192–238). Lincoln: University of Nebraska Press.

Kelley, H. H. (1973). Causal schemata and the attribution process. *American Psychologist, 28*, 107–123.

Kun, A., & Weiner, B. (1973). Necessary versus sufficient causal schemata for success and failure. *Journal of Research in Personality, 7*, 197–207.

McClure, J., Lalljee, M., Jaspers, J. M., & Abelson, R. P. (1989). Conjunctive explanations of success and failure: The effect of different types of causes. *Journal of Personality and Social Psychology, 56*, 19–26.

Mackenzie, M. (1984). *Fear of fat*. New York: Columbia University Press.

Meyer, J. P., & Mulherin, A. (1980). From attribution to helping: An analysis of the mediating effects of affect and expectancy. *Journal of Personality and Social Psychology, 39*, 201–210.

Pastore, N. (1952). The role of arbitrariness in the frustration-agression hypothesis. *Journal of Abnormal and Social Psychology, 47*, 728–732.

Piliavin, I. M., Rodin, J., & Piliavin, J. A. (1969). Good Samaritanism: An underground phenomenon? *Journal of Personality and Social Psychology, 13*, 289–299.

Reisenzein, R. (1986). A structural equation analysis of Weiner's attribution affect model of helping behavior. *Journal of Personality and Social Psychology, 50*, 1123–1133.

Richardson, S. A., Hastorf, A. H., Goodman, N., & Dornbusch, S. M. (1961). Cultural uniformity in reaction to physical disabilities. *American Sociological Review, 26*, 241–247.

Rosenthal, N. B. (1984). Consciousness raising: From revolution to re-evaluation. *Psychology of Women Quarterly, 8*, 309–326.

Rotter, J. B. (1966). Generalized expectancies for internal versus external control of reinforcement. *Psychological Monographs, 80*, 1–28.

Sacco, W. P., Milana, S., & Dunn, V. K. (1985). Effect of depression level and length of acquaintance on reactions of others to a request for help. *Journal of Personality and Social Psychology, 49*, 1728–1737.

Schmidt, G., & Weiner, B. (1988). An attribution-affect-action theory of motivated behavior: Replications examining judgments of help-giving. *Personality and Social Psychology Bulletin, 14*, 610–621.

Sheer, R. (1987, August 14). AIDS: Is widespread threat an exaggeration? *Los Angeles Times*, pt. 1, pp. 1, 18.

Staff. (1987, August 30). Public is polled on AIDS. *New York Times*, pt. 1, p. 12.

Staffieri, J. R. (1967). A study of social stereotype and body image in children. *Journal of Personality and Social Psychology, 7*, 101–104.

Stahelski, A. J., Patch, M. E., & Enochson, D. E. (1987). *Differential effects of ascribed ability and effort on helping, emotion, and behavior*. Unpublished manuscript, Portland State University, Portland.

Triplet, R. G., & Sugarman, D. B. (1987). Reactions to AIDS victims: Ambiguity breeds contempt. *Personality and Social Psychology Bulletin, 13,* 265–274.

Trivers, R. L. (1971). The evolution of reciprocal altruism. *Quarterly Review of Biology, 46,* 35–57.

Tuite, D. R., & Luiten, J. W. (1986). 16PF research into addiction: Meta-analysis and extension. *International Journal of Addictions, 21,* 287–323.

Weiner, B. (1980a). A cognitive (attributional)-emotion-action model of motivated behavior: An analysis of judgments of help-giving. *Journal of Personality and Social Psychology, 39,* 186–200.

Weiner, B. (1980b). May I borrow your class notes? An attributional analysis of judgments of help-giving in an achievement-related context. *Journal of Educational Psychology, 72,* 676–681.

Weiner, B. (1985). An attribution theory of achievement motivation and emotion. *Psychological Review, 92,* 548–573.

Weiner, B. (1986). *An attribution theory of motivation and emotion.* New York: Springer-Verlag.

Weiner, B., Amirkhan, J., Folkes, V. S., & Verette, J. A. (1987). An attributional analysis of excuse-giving: Studies of a naive theory of emotion. *Journal of Personality and Social Psychology, 52,* 316–324.

Weiner, B., Graham, S., & Chandler, C. C. (1982). Pity, anger, and guilt: An attributional analysis. *Personality and Social Psychology Bulletin, 8,* 226–232.

Weiner, B., Graham, S., Stern, P., & Lawson, M. E. (1982). Using affective cues to infer causal thoughts. *Developmental Psychology, 18,* 278–286.

Weiner, B., & Handel, S. (1985). Anticipated emotional consequences of causal communications and reported communication strategy. *Developmental Psychology, 21,* 102–107.

Weiner, B., & Kukla, A. (1970). An attributional analysis of achievement motivation. *Journal of Personality and Social Psychology, 15,* 1–20.

Weiner, B., Perry, R. P., & Magnusson, J. (1988). An attributional analysis of reactions to stigmas. *Journal of Personality and Social Psychology, 55,* 738–748.

Weiner, B., Russell, D., & Lerman, D. (1978). Affective consequences of causal ascriptions. In J. H. Harvey, W. J. Ickes, & R. F. Kidd (Eds.), *New directions in attribution research* (Vol. 2, pp. 59–88). Hillsdale, NJ: Erlbaum.

Weiner, B., Russel, D., & Lerman, D. (1979). The cognition-emotion process in achievement-related contexts. *Journal of Personality and Social Psychology, 37,* 1211–1220.

Werner, D., & Bower, B. (1982). *Helping health workers learn.* Palo Alto, CA: Hesperian Foundation.

Whalen, C., & Henker, B. (1976). Psychostimulants and children: A review and analysis. *Psychological Bulletin, 83,* 1113–1130.

Wright, B. A. (1983). *Physical disability: A psychological approach* (2nd ed.). New York: Harper.

Yirmiya, N., & Weiner, B. (1986). Perceptions of controllability and anticipated anger. *Cognitive Development, 1,* 273–280.

Self-Theories and Goals: Their Role in Motivation, Personality, and Development

Carol S. Dweck
Columbia University

The early contributors to this series recognized that motivation was at the core of psychology. Whether they were learning, personality, or developmental theorists, motivation typically formed the basis and the heart of their theory: What do individuals (human or infra-human) want, need, value? How do their goals impel and organize their behavior?

In this chapter I will suggest that important aspects of personality and development can be understood in motivational terms—that is, in terms of the goals individuals are pursuing. Specifically, I will center on goals related to the self, and demonstrate (1) how individual differences in maladaptive and adaptive patterns can be understood in terms of the particular goals individuals focus on and (2) how developmental differences can be understood in terms of the particular aspects of the self that are salient to the child and that serve as the target of these goals.

Thus, in the first part of the chapter I will present our model that describes the way in which individuals' implicit theories about their self attributes (such as intelligence) orient them toward specific goals (self-judgment vs. self-development) and the way in which these goals set up characteristic patterns of maladaptive or adaptive behavior.

In the second part of the chapter I will turn to developmental issues and present the results from four new studies of young children. Much current literature depicts young children as relatively invulnerable to maladaptive motivational patterns, chiefly because they have not yet developed the conceptions of self attributes (like intelligence) that are associated with maladaptive patterns in older children. Our results repeatedly demonstrate, first, that a sizable proportion of young children in fact display point for point virtually every aspect of the maladaptive pattern found in older children. Second, the results suggest that young children do indeed have self-conceptions that are associated with maladaptive patterns. However, these conceptions do not appear to be about intelligence or any specific attribute. Rather, they appear to be about the general goodness or badness of the self. Thus it will be shown that once one identifies the locus of young children's concerns, the many motivational similarities (and differences) between older and younger children can begin to be understood.

Next, taking our body of findings as a whole, I will relate those findings to traditional theories of personality and personality development, noting that the fundamental needs these theories posit are strikingly similar to the goals we are identifying, describing, and investigating more precisely in our research. Finally, given the motivational patterns we have examined, and the ways they are linked to self theories, I will draw some general conclusions about the nature of adaptive and maladaptive belief systems.

The Motivational Model

Our model, depicted in Table 1, was developed to illuminate adaptive and maladaptive patterns in achievement situations: Given children of equal ability, why do some respond to failure with effective persistence while others deteriorate or give up? Why do some meet challenges with enthusiasm, while others approach them, if at all, with anxiety? Our early work was aimed at discovering the different facets—cognitive, affective, and behavioral—of the adaptive, persistent (mastery-oriented) pattern and the maladaptive, nonpersistent (helpless) pattern. I will begin by describing the patterns them-

Table 1

Theories, Goals, and Behavior Patterns in Achievement Situations

Theory of Intelligence	Goal Orientation	Confidence in Present Ability	Behavior Pattern
Entity (intelligence is fixed or uncontrollable)	Performance (gain positive/avoid negative judgment of competence)	Low	Helpless
		High	Mastery-oriented
Incremental (intelligence is malleable)	Learning (increase competence)	Low or high	Mastery-oriented

selves in some detail, because they remain the basic phenomena that our model seeks to predict and explain.

THE HELPLESS AND MASTERY-ORIENTED PATTERNS

In describing the basic patterns, I draw primarily on a series of studies by Diener and Dweck (1978, 1980). It was these studies that spelled out the different cognitive, affective, and behavioral components of the two patterns. In this research, late grade-school-age children worked on a concept-formation task. They succeeded on the first eight problems but failed on the next four, which were somewhat too difficult for children their age. To capture responses to failure, the task was constructed so that the child's precise hypothesis-testing strategy could be identified; thus any changes in the sophistication of that strategy could be detected as the child moved from the success trials to the failure trials. Further, in order to monitor changes in reported affect and achievement cognitions (attributions, expectancies, etc.) over the trials of interest, children were asked to verbalize aloud after the sixth success trial. The instructions encouraged them to relate any thought or feeling, whether task-relevant or not, and indeed they appeared to comply. Taken together, the strategy and the verbalization data revealed two distinct responses to failure.

Before describing the different patterns of response, I should note that prior to the experimental session children had been classified into groups (those who were likely to show the helpless pattern vs. those who were likely to show the mastery-oriented pattern) based on an attribution questionnaire that asked them to explain their failures. This questionnaire (the Intellectual Achievement Responsibility Scale of Crandall, Katkovsky, & Crandall, 1965) had been successful in predicting persistence and effectiveness in the face of failure in prior research (Dweck, 1975; Dweck & Reppucci 1973), but the Diener and Dweck research was concerned with what cognitions and what affect would emerge naturally in the situation if children themselves were in control of what they reported and when they reported it.

As I noted above, two distinct, coherent patterns emerged on the failure problems—even though the two groups had exhibited equivalent performance on the success problems.[1] The helpless children, very soon after the onset of the failure problems, appeared to define themselves as having failed, and they rapidly began to offer attributions for their failures (see Weiner, 1972, this volume). Most of these took the form of indictments of their ability. These spontaneous assertions of low ability were accompanied by a negative prognosis for their future performance. Indeed, specific probes after the failure problems revealed that a sizable proportion of the helpless children (35%) no longer believed they could solve one of the original success problems again if it were readministered. (In contrast, none of the mastery-oriented children anticipated that they would have any difficulty solving one of the earlier problems.) Interestingly, these postfailure probes also showed that the helpless children had distorted recall of their past successes and failures. They recalled only 5.14 successes, on the average (instead of the actual 8) and remembered 6.14 failures (instead of 4). (In contrast, the mastery-oriented children more accurately recalled 7.57 successes and 3.71 failures.)

Returning to the on-line self-reports and behavior, we find that, in accord with these negative appraisals, the helpless children expressed significantly more negative affect than did the mastery-oriented children and, on the performance front, exhibited far greater deterioration in their problem-solving strategies. Over 60% of the helpless children showed a decline in the sophistication of their strategies as they encountered failure and, of these, many showed a descent into completely unproductive strategies. In summary, the helpless children quickly perceived themselves to be failing, saw the failures as a measure of their ability, and became mired in them as past and future successes seemed to recede from their grasp.

The cognitive, affective, and behavioral pattern displayed by the mastery-oriented children contrasted in virtually every way. First, the mastery-oriented children did not offer attributions for the failures or ascribe any personal meaning to them. Indeed, they did not appear to see themselves as failing. Instead, they began issuing more self-instructions—planning and instructing themselves in strategies designed to overcome the failures. Second, their prognosis for future success remained highly positive, with many spontaneously expressing confidence that they would soon be successful again. In line with these constructive and optimistic cognitions, their affect remained positive. A number of them even indicated heightened positive affect, explicitly relishing the challenge and the opportunity for mastery. Finally, 80% of the mastery-oriented children maintained or improved their problem-solving strategies under failure, and 25% actually showed more sophisticated strategies during failure than they had during success. In summary, the mastery-oriented children appear to see failure as an interlude between past and future successes and as an opportunity for new learning and mastery.

The next stage in our research was aimed at understanding why helpless children react to failure as though their ability is being measured and discredited, whereas mastery-oriented children react to it as an opportunity for learning. Elliott and Dweck (see Dweck & Elliott, 1983; Elliott & Dweck, 1988) hypothesized that the two groups of children were actually focusing on different goals in the same situation and that these different goals led them to construe and react to similar events in highly discrepant ways.

GOALS

Specifically, we proposed that individuals can pursue two classes of goals in achievement situations: *performance goals*, in which the aim is to gain favorable judgments of their competence and to avoid unfavorable ones, and *learning goals*, in which the aim is to increase their competence by, for example, learning something new or mastering a new task. Although both classes of goals are natural and universal, we hypothesized that an overemphasis on performance goals would create a vulnerability to the helpless pattern. That is, when individuals focus on the performance goal of documenting their ability and they encounter failure, the failure may well be seen as calling that very ability into question—thereby setting in motion the helpless reaction of negative cognitions, negative affect, and performance disruption. In contrast, when individuals are oriented toward a learning goal, errors and obstacles should be seen as a natural part of learning and should be a spur to the mastery-oriented pattern of enhanced involvement in the face of failure.

This hypothesis—that a differential emphasis on performance versus learning goals sets up the helpless versus mastery-oriented responses—has been tested in several ways. In the first study of this type, Elliott and Dweck (1988) experimentally induced an emphasis on performance or learning goals in order to test for a causal relation between these goals and the helpless versus mastery-oriented patterns. Later studies (see Dweck & Leggett, 1988) examined naturally existing individual differences in goal preference and their relation to response patterns in the face of obstacles.

In their experimental study, Elliott and Dweck (1988) manipulated children's goal orientation by highlighting either performance goals (i.e., heightening the evaluative aspects of the situation) or learning goals (i.e., emphasizing the value of the task to be learned). They also manipulated children's perceptions of their ability via feedback on a pretest that was said to tap task-relevant skills. This was done to test the prediction that performance goals would foster the helpless pattern particularly when children had low confidence in their ability, for then failures would most readily be seen as reflecting low ability and signaling goal failure (see Table 1). In contrast, learning goals were predicted to foster the mastery-oriented pattern regardless of children's confidence in their present ability, since within a learning goal present ability is not at issue and, as noted above, obstacles should be seen as a natural part of learning new and difficult skills.

After the experimental inductions, children were given the Diener and Dweck concept-formation task, and as in that research, their strategies and verbalizations were monitored as they went from success to failure. As predicted, children who were focused on performance goals and who perceived themselves to have low ability showed all the cognitive, affective, and behavioral characteristics of the naturally occurring helpless pattern: negative self-attributions, negative affect, and strategy deterioration in the face of failure. Children in the other three groups displayed the mastery oriented pattern. Of particular interest here is the fact that children with low perceived ability were still mastery oriented when their goal was to learn rather than to perform. Thus low perceived ability is a hindrance when the goal involves a display of ability but not when it involves acquisition of ability.

Also of interest is the fact that although children with performance goals and high perceived ability were still mastery-oriented, there was a critical difference between them and the mastery-oriented children who were pursuing learning goals. When later given the opportunity, the children who were focused on performance goals rejected the chance to learn something new if it involved the risk of errors and confusion. They were, in other words, so protective of how their ability would be judged that they sacrificed a chance to develop that ability. Finally, it should be noted that a loss of confidence in their ability would place this group of children in the cell that is most vulnerable to helplessness; yet, as we will see shortly, confidence is particularly difficult to maintain within a performance goal. Not only are negative outcomes potentially seen as reflecting low ability, but so is the exertion of effort in itself.

In subsequent studies (see Dweck, 1989; Dweck & Leggett, 1988) we measured children's naturally existing goal preferences and confidence levels, and we documented the same relations to the helpless and mastery-oriented patterns. Thus, whether a child is focused on a goal because the situations increase its salience or value or because of a preexisting tendency in the child, it appears that the two classes of goals differentially foster the different motivational patterns (see also Ames, 1984; Ames & Archer, 1988; Pervin, 1983).

How, more specifically, does this occur? I have suggested (see Dweck & Leggett, 1988) that the goals create a framework within which information is processed and interpreted (cf. Pervin, 1983). Within a performance goal, information is processed in terms of its relevance for measuring or judging ability. As we saw, potential and actual failure outcomes are interpreted in terms of ability. Even performance-oriented children with high confidence sacrificed learning tasks that posed a threat of errors and jeopardized desired ability judgments. In contrast, within a learning goal, information is processed in terms of its relevance for mastering the task. Here errors provide cues for escalating effort and for varying one's strategies in the service of obtaining future success.

As implied above, even effort is interpreted entirely differently within the two frameworks—again, either as a measure of ability or as a strategy for mastery (Dweck & Leggett, 1988). For children with performance goals, effort is seen as implying low ability and as necessary only for those with low ability. Specifically, children who favor performance goals endorse such statements as: "If you have to work at something, you must not be very good at it," or "Great discoveries come easily to people who are true geniuses." For children who favor learning goals, however, effort is seen as something that activates ability and allows people to use their ability. They agree that "even geniuses have to work hard for their discoveries." Thus the same information about outcomes or effort will have entirely different meanings depending on the goal within which the individual is processing that information.

The next major aim in our research program became to understand why children emphasized such different goals in achievement settings—why some focused on proving their ability while others focused on improving it. Mary Bandura and I (M. Bandura & Dweck, 1985) hypothesized that perhaps children with different goals actually had different conceptions of ability—different implicit theories about the nature of their intelligence.

THEORIES OF INTELLIGENCE

M. Bandura and Dweck (1985) proposed that some children would regard their intelligence as a fixed trait over which they had no control, whereas others would see it as a malleable quality that could be developed through their efforts. The former we called an "entity theory," because here intelligence is conceived of as a static *thing* that you have, whereas the latter we called an "incremental theory" because here intelligence is conceived of as a more dynamic characteristic that can be increased.

Although both theories are common and defensible, we proposed that they would have different motivational consequences. Children holding an entity theory were predicted to favor performance goals. That is, if you believe an important attribute like intelligence is a fixed trait, then you will be concerned with measuring it favorably or documenting that you have a respectable amount of it. In contrast, we proposed that those holding an incremental theory would orient toward learning goals. If you believe that intelligence is a quality you can develop, then you will be more concerned with developing it and less concerned with documenting it at any given moment.

In three studies, we tested the hypothesis that children's theories of intelligence would predict their achievement goals. In two of them (one done with M. Bandura, and one with E. Leggett) (see Dweck & Leggett, 1988), children's theories were assessed by means of a questionnaire asking them to agree or disagree with such statements as, "Your intelligence is something very basic about you that you can't really change." In the third study (with Y. Tenney and N. Dinces) (see Dweck & Leggett, 1988), children's theories of intelligence were manipulated by means of reading passages that espoused an entity or incremental theory. In all cases, children's theory was a significant predictor of their choice of goals on an upcoming achievement task. In the study by Leggett and Dweck, 81.8% of the children who endorsed an entity theory also elected to pursue a performance goal on the experimental task. That is, they selected a task that would gain them a favorable ability judgment or one that would avoid a negative judgment over a task that they could learn from but not necessarily do well on. In fact, 50.0% of the entity theorists chose an easy task that completely avoided any risk of negative judgment. In contrast, 60.9% of the children who endorsed an incremental theory selected the learning goal. Another 29.3% selected the challenging performance task, and only 9.8% chose the easy performance task.

Thus the research results support the view that children's theories about their intelligence orient them toward particular goals. The entity theory, by raising concerns about the amount of fixed intelligence one has, creates a focus on performance goals, whereas the incremental theory, by portraying a valued attribute as acquirable, creates a focus on learning goals.

THEORIES AND GOALS AS SELF SYSTEMS

It is interesting to think of the different theories as different "self-concepts" and of their allied goals as ways of building and maintaining self-esteem within those self-conceptions (see Dweck & Leggett, 1988). That is, the entity theory is one way of conceptualizing the self—namely, as consisting of static traits that can be measured. The incremental theory, on the other hand, depicts the self as a more dynamic system that can be developed. When would one feel pride in (or high self-esteem regarding) each of these selves? Within the entity theory one would feel pride if the traits were measured and judged favorably—that is, if one successfully attained performance goals. In contrast, within the incremental theory one would feel pride if one pursued courses of action that allowed one to use and develop valued attributes—that is, if one pursued learning goals.

In a study germane to this issue, Dweck and Elliott (reported in Dweck & Bempechat, 1983) assessed children's theories of intelligence and then asked them to describe when they felt smart in school. As predicted, entity theorists reported feeling high self-esteem in the academic domain when optimal conditions for attaining performance goals were present: when a task was easy for them, when they didn't need to exert effort for success, when they didn't make mistakes, when they finished first. In contrast, children with incremental theories reported feeling smart when pursuing learning and mastery: when they were working on something hard, when they didn't understand something and then mastered it, when they figured out something new.

Thus the implicit theories with their allied goals may be seen as representing qualitatively different self systems, each with its own values, rules, logic, and coherence. Moreover, the fact that the theories and goals can be manipulated experimentally (that is, can be situationally induced) suggests that a person can operate within both systems. This would mean that each of us may conceive of ourselves sometimes as a fixed object that is being judged and at other times as a dynamic system whose aim is to grow. Individual differences can then be seen as predispositions to operate within one system or the other, with individuals differing, for example, in the strength with which a given implicit theory is held or in the relative availability of the different theory-goal systems.

Nonetheless, as the research suggests, the theory-goal system individuals favor can have profound effects on their behavior—on the courses of action they pursue and the effectiveness with which they pursue them. We have examined in some detail the potentially maladaptive consequences of the entity theory, and although one might point to potential pitfalls of the incremental theory (for example, if one could not accept any limits to personal development or if one paid too little heed to performance goals), the issues raised in the present section suggest another maladaptive implication of the entity self system. The entity system puts self-esteem and self-development in conflict with each other.

The entity theory not only creates a bias toward performance rather than learning goals when the two are explicitly pitted against each other, but also appears to foster a natural antagonism between them: what you do to feel smart and what you must do to learn new things are at odds with each other. That is, to the extent that entity theorists feel smart when they have tasks they can perform without effort and without errors, then many tasks that involve or foster learning will hold the danger of making them feel incompetent.

In contrast, the incremental theory creates a consonance between self-esteem and self-development: what you do to feel smart and what you do to learn are the same—namely, exert effort on a challenging task. Indeed, within this system effort is what activates ability, increases ability, and creates the subjective experience of possessing ability. Ironically, an incremental theory may at times even render one better able to pursue performance goals when necessary. Because one's fixed intelligence is not on the line, effort can be exerted in a less defensive, more effective way. In the next section I will present evidence that speaks to this issue.

IMPLICIT THEORIES PREDICT REAL-WORLD
OUTCOMES

Throughout our research program we have been concerned with demonstrating that the effects we obtain are not merely laboratory phenomena but mirror real-world processes. Therefore, all along we have conducted experiments in classrooms, measuring individual differences, giving children new material to learn (under conditions that do or do not involve obstacles to mastery), and assessing learning and mastery under the various conditions (e.g., Farrell, 1985; Licht & Dweck, 1984). We have consistently found that children with the maladaptive patterns are hampered in learning new material under conditions that involve periods of failure or confusion.

However, these same children, in grade school, are entirely equivalent in achievement to children with the more adaptive patterns. Thus, even though they show clear debilitation in the face of failure in our studies (whether conducted in the laboratory or the classroom), they show no evidence of an achievement deficit. Why might this be? One plausible hypothesis is that grade school does not present the conditions of challenge that would evoke the helpless pattern. In the typical grade school, the work, the pace, and the grading are relatively unthreatening. In this view, grade school would be akin to the initial success problems in the Diener and Dweck research—those problems required effort, concentration, and training, but although children operated at different levels, everybody did fine. However, the prediction would be that when the academic demands and task difficulty escalate, and when the evaluation becomes more stringent, as they suddenly do in junior high school, children's motivational patterns should begin to predict their achievement.

To test this hypothesis, Henderson and Dweck (1990) tracked children over the transition to junior high school. At the beginning of seventh grade, measures were taken of children's theories of intelligence and their confidence in their intellectual ability. Four groups were constituted based on their theory (entity or incremental) and their confidence level (high or low). Children's grades and achievement test scores from sixth grade were obtained from their school records. Then, given the grades they earned in seventh grade, we asked: How did the groups do compared with what would be expected on the basis of their past achievement?

As predicted, the theory groups pulled apart in their seventh grade grades. Children holding an incremental theory tended to match or exceed their projected grade point. Overall, those who had been high achievers in sixth grade remained so, and many of those who had been relatively low achievers became high achievers. Of particular interest is that many incremental theorists with low confidence who had not done especially well in the past were now earning many of the highest grades. Indeed, this group showed the most impressive gains in their relative standing.

The results for children holding an entity theory provide a dramatic contrast and speak to the vulnerability of even those entity theorists who profess to have high confidence in their ability. Overall, entity theorists who had been low achievers in the past remained so, and many of those who had been high achievers in sixth grade were now among the lowest achievers. Prominent among the latter were many high-confidence entity theorists. Although it was not predicted, this group showed the most pronounced decline of any group. It may be that the challenge and confusion of the transition are most threatening to those who believe intelligence is fixed and have been accustomed to thinking of themselves as having it.

Grades are desirable to students both as indices of learning and as performance judgments. Those students whose theories create a focus on judgments are in danger of missing out on both, whereas those whose theories orient them more toward learning seem to be attaining both.

In summary, implicit theories appear to orient individuals toward different goals. These goals, in turn, set up and organize different patterns of behavior. Although these theories, goals, and patterns are initially unrelated to actual ability, they begin to predict the acquisition and display of ability over time.

GENERALITY OF THE MODEL

Before moving on to developmental issues, I would like briefly to mention some of our recent research that is beginning to establish the generality of our model—that is, its ability to describe and predict motivational patterns in a variety of domains.

First, several studies have recently been completed that suggest the applicability of the model to the social domain. Originally, Goetz and Dweck (1980) established the existence of helpless and mastery-oriented responses to rejection that are directly analogous to the responses Diener and Dweck demonstrated in achievement situations. Now further work from our laboratory has shown that these patterns are related to the social goals children are pursuing and to the implicit theories children hold about their personalities. Specifically, an experiment by Loomis, Hines, Erdley, and Cain (1989) showed that orienting children toward the performance goal of documenting their social skills versus the learning goal of improving their social skills set up, respectively, the helpless and mastery-oriented responses to rejection. In a related vein Olshefsky, Erdley, and Dweck (1987) showed that children's implicit theories about their personalities—that is, whether they conceived of personality as a fixed trait or as a malleable quality—predicted their responses to social rejection in precisely the way that would be expected from our model. Thus implicit theories and goals appear to have utility for understanding motivational patterns in differing domains of action. Although people may hold different implicit theories in different domains, the theory they hold in any particular domain appears to have important motivational implications.

In another series of studies (Erdley & Dweck, 1989), we have shown that children's implicit theories about *others* predict important aspects of their social judgments. Specifically, we have found strong evidence that children who hold an entity theory of other people's personalities (viewing personality as something very basic about an individual that cannot be changed) are more prone to make stereotyped (global, rigid) judgments than are children who hold an incremental theory. In these studies, children watched a slide show of a target child engaging in a series of negative behaviors that could be understood as stemming in part from situational pressures. For example, in one study the target child was a new boy in school who was extremely eager to make a good impression. Toward this end, he engaged in some lying, cheating, and stealing, but of a sort that was never malicious and never harmful to others. Although no one was expected to endorse his behavior as the appropriate way to deal with the situation, the question was how severely and how rigidly he would be judged.

The results showed striking differences between entity and incremental theorists. Children holding the entity view made not only more *long-term* negative predictions, but also more *extreme* negative judgements, more *global* negative judgments (generalizing their negative ratings beyond the specific traits exemplified by the behavior to superordinate traits like "bad" and "mean"), and more *rigid* negative judgments (showing no significant change in their ratings of the depicted traits when they were exposed to direct counterinformation). In addition, entity theorists expressed less sympathy for the target child's plight and recommended harsher punishment for his transgressions.

Thus, in the same way that children holding an entity view of their own traits tended to make sweeping inferences about their intelligence or personality from a very small sample of outcomes, children with an entity view of others appear to draw sweeping conclusions about other people based on a small sample of behavior. Although further research needs to be done, it is tempting to suggest that an entity theory of others may make individuals more prone to prejudice and stereotyping. Indeed, the characteristics of stereotyped judgments are precisely the ones exhibited by the entity theorists in our research: on the basis of limited information, a group of individuals is deemed to have permanent, underlying qualities. If these qualities are negative, they are seen to justify a lack of compassion and discriminatory or even punitive behavior toward that group.

It appears, then, that our model, which was originally designed to capture achievement-related processes, may well be useful for understanding a variety of other personal and interpersonal processes as well.

Motivation and Development

It is a widely held belief in the achievement motivation literature that younger children are not susceptible to the helpless pattern. This view is supported by a wealth of empirical findings and also fits nicely with a number of theoretical frameworks, including our own. In fact, Dweck and Elliott (1983), in an extensive review of research and theory in achievement motivation and its development, concluded that younger children (before about 9 or 10 years of age) do not tend to exhibit maladaptive responses to failure.

This view makes sense theoretically in that, as we have seen, maladaptive patterns in older children are associated with viewing intelligence as a stable trait. Young children do not seem to have the notion of intelligence as a stable trait or even an understanding of what intelligence is. Therefore, it has been reasoned, failures would not be seen as calling it into question and would thus not have debilitating effects.

As noted, a large body of evidence has accrued showing that young children are highly challenge seeking and relatively undaunted by failure. For example, their expectancies, ability estimates, persistence, and performance have been found not to flag in the face of failure (Nicholls & Miller, 1984; Parsons & Ruble, 1977; Rholes, Blackwell, Jordan, & Walters, 1980; Weisz, 1981).

However, there is reason to believe that the research and theory to date have not truly reflected young children's motivational processes. First, on the research front, the procedures that are successful in eliciting debilitation and the other concomitants of the helpless pattern in older children may not be appropriate for younger children. Older children may be sensitive to a lapse from the desired standard on virtually any task one might administer, but younger children may need a visible, salient failure on a meaningful task (see Stipek, 1981). Older children may be able to ponder past, now invisible failures and reflect on the causes in terms of abstract variables like ability and effort. Younger children may need simpler, more direct questions posed with respect to still-visible outcomes. If such conditions were fulfilled, maybe young children would display an ability to be debilitated hitherto shown chiefly by older children.

Next, on the theoretical front, there is reason to believe that our focus on achievement and ability as vehicles for studying motivation may have blinded us to the domain in which young children are operating. Just as older children, who are in the thick of the academic domain, are wrestling with issues of intelligence and what events are relevant indices of it, it is likely that young children, who are in the thick of socialization, are wrestling with issues of morality—their goodness and badness—and what events are relevant indices of that. Thus it may be that young children, when they do respond to an "achievement" outcome, respond in terms of its perceived implications for the general goodness of the self rather than for the particular trait of intelligence.[2]

If young children are indeed operating within a moral framework, might they have implicit theories of goodness that are analogous to older children's implicit theories of intelligence? Would such self-conceptions be linked to motivational patterns as they are in older children? If this is the case, this too, would be at odds with much developmental literature. In the recent literature on the development of self-conceptions, young children have often been depicted as not having *any* meaningful psychological self-conceptions. Instead, their self-conceptions are said to be "physicalistic," focusing on such things as their actions, their physical characteristics, and their possessions. This, I believe, has grown out of a tendency to equate children's self-descriptions with their self-conceptions. Although there is a great deal of fascinating and informative work on children's self-descriptions and how they change with age (e.g., Barenboim, 1981; Keller, Ford, & Meacham, 1978; Livesley & Bromley, 1973; see also Damon & Hart, 1982), it is likely that there are a multitude of self-conceptions and implicit theories that cannot begin to be tapped by the kinds of questions used to elicit self-descriptions.

In the sections that follow, I describe four new studies that examine young children's motivational patterns. First I present three studies that used age-appropriate tasks and assessments to determine young children's susceptibility to helplessness. Next, I present findings from two studies (one of the previous studies and one other) suggesting that young children's concerns are in fact in the arena of goodness, and that failures are interpreted within that framework. Then I present preliminary evidence that young children have implicit theories of goodness that are tied to their motivational patterns. Following this, I discuss what it is that changes with age and what the motivational implications of these changes are.

STUDIES OF HELPLESSNESS IN YOUNG CHILDREN

Table 2 provides an overview of the variables measured in, and some of the results of, the three studies of helplessness in young children: Hebert and Dweck, in which the participants were preschoolers; Smiley and Dweck (see Smiley, 1989), in which the participants were preschoolers and kindergartners; and Cain and Dweck (see Cain, 1990), in which the participants were first graders. In each study, nonpersisters were distinguished from persisters on the experimental tasks, and the two groups were compared on a variety of measures to determine whether the nonpersisters displayed the other (cognitive and affective) components of the helpless pattern. The top row of the table indicates the percentage of participants in

Table 2

Evidence for the Helpless Pattern in Young Children

	Hebert and Dweck	Smiley and Dweck	Cain and Dweck
Nonpersisters	37%	42%	36%
Reason: avoid challenge		X	X
Equal initial ability		X	X
Postfailure expectancy		X	X
Attribution	X	X	X
Negative verbalizations	X	X	X
Negative affect	X	X	X

each study who were classified as nonpersisters. The marks in the subsequent rows indicate that the variable in question was measured in a given study. The last four variables represent the achievement cognitions and affect that distinguished the helpless and the mastery-oriented in the studies of older children. To anticipate, nonpersisters differed significantly from persisters on every one of these variables in every study (though not necessarily on every measure of that variable when several were included in a given study). Let me review, briefly, the general procedure that was followed in the three studies and then present the major results from each study in turn.

In all three of these studies, children worked on puzzles of popular cartoon characters. On each trial, they were first shown what the completed puzzle should look like and then given the puzzle to assemble. There were four puzzles in all. The first three were either insoluble or too difficult for them to complete, although they could place at least half of the pieces correctly within the allotted time. (Time limits ensured that children did not perceive the puzzles as inherently insoluble.) The fourth was solved by all. This success puzzle was placed last so the success would be salient and children's persistence choices, expectations, and attributions, as well as their appraisals of the rewards or punishments they deserved, would take place in the context of this recent success.

After all four trials were completed, the subjects' puzzles were resurrected as they had left them, and they were asked which they would like to work on again and why. This was the measure on which they were classified as nonpersisters or persisters, with those who chose to rework the already completed puzzle being categorized as nonpersisters. Over the three failure trials, spontaneous verbalizations were encouraged and recorded, and measures of affect (subject-rated, observer-rated, or both) were taken. After the fourth trial, future expectations were elicited and attributions for the failures were probed.

Eighty-nine preschoolers (four and five years old) participated in the Hebert and Dweck study. Of these, 32 (37%) were classified as nonpersisters. As noted above, nonpersisters and persisters were then compared on the other variables characteristic of the helpless pattern. (In discussing these studies of young children, I will not call the groups "helpless" and "mastery-oriented," because that would be begging the question of whether these patterns in fact exist in children of this age.)

Two attribution questions were administered to determine whether children believed they could complete any of the unsolved puzzles with further effort or whether they believed they lacked the ability to do so. The first question asked: "If you had lots of time right now, do you think you could finish any of these puzzles, or are you just not good enough at puzzles?" Table 3, panel A, shows the percentage of nonpersisters and persisters who selected each response. As one can see, the clear majority of the nonpersisters favored the lack of ability choice, whereas the majority of the persisters believed they could succeed if they persisted.

Table 3

Percentage of Nonpersisters and Persisters Making Each Attribution Choice

	A. Question 1	
	Nonpersisters	Persisters
Could finish (effort)	29.0	64.3
Not good at (ability)	71.0	35.7
	B. Question 2	
Yes (effort)	46.4	81.5
No (ability)	53.6	18.5

The second attribution question asked: "If you tried very hard right now, your very hardest, do you think you could do any of these puzzles? Yes or no?" Table 3, panel B, shows these results. This question seemed to draw more agreement overall, but again, clear differences emerged. Whereas the nonpersisters split their votes between the two choices, the persisters overwhelmingly endorsed the effort option. Thus the findings for younger children directly mirror those for older children: those who persist focus on effort as a means of attaining future success; those who give up see failure as implying inability.

Examination of children's spontaneous verbalization showed that nonpersisters made significantly more negative and non-strategic statements than did persisters. Finally, children's ratings of their affect over the three failure trials were analyzed. For each trial, children were shown their uncompleted puzzle and asked to rate how they had felt while working on it. They did so by choosing one of a series of five faces that ranged from a broad smile to a deep frown. These data were analyzed to determine what proportion of children, like the mastery-oriented older children, maintained or increased their level of affect as they encountered difficulty, and what proportion, like the helpless older children, indicated decreased positive affect. Among the nonpersisters, only 29.4% maintained their affect level, while 70.6% reported declining affect over trials. In contrast, 52.7% of the persisters maintained their affect and 47.3% reported a decline.

The Smiley and the Cain studies replicated these findings and contributed additional ones. I will mention just a few of the most relevant additional findings. Both of these studies took pre-measures of children's puzzle performance in a prior session and confirmed that nonpersisters and persisters were equivalent in their performance. Thus the different patterns, like those of the helpless and mastery-oriented children, could not be attributed to differential ability at the tasks.

Next, both of the studies confirmed that the nonpersisters were truly nonpersistent and challenge-avoidant, whereas the persisters remained truly challenge-seeking. An examination of the reasons for the puzzle choice revealed that across both studies not one of the nonpersisters gave a challenge-seeking or learning-oriented reason for opting to redo the already completed puzzle. Instead, the great majority of them (approximately two-thirds) gave explicitly challenge-avoidant reasons, citing the easiness of the task or the fact that they already knew how to do it. Thus it was not the case that these children had experienced the success puzzle as difficult and believed they were pursuing a challenge when they selected it. Further evidence comes from the Smiley and Dweck study, in which children were asked to make a second choice—that is, to indicate which puzzle they would like to work on after their first-choice puzzle. Amazingly, most of the nonpersisters (again, about two-thirds) repeated their choice of the same, already solved puzzle. In contrast, the persistent children gave challenge-seeking reasons for their original choice in both studies (citing the difficulty of the task, their curiosity, or their desire to figure it out). And, in the Smiley and Dweck study, when asked to make a second choice, virtually all of them chose a different unsolved puzzle, again because of a desire for challenge.

These studies also provide evidence that nonpersisters and persisters, like helpless and mastery-oriented children, differentially revise their expectancies in the face of failure. In the Smiley study, children who were classified as nonpersisters or persisters on the original puzzle task then worked on a second task, which required them to build a tower of blocks. Before each trial children estimated, on a yardstick calibrated to the blocks, how tall a tower they would build. Before the first trial, nonpersisters and persisters had nearly identical expectancies, and on the first trial they built towers of roughly equivalent height. As is the tendency, however, at some point in the building process the towers toppled over. Nonpersisters then showed significantly lower expectancies than persisters for the subsequent trials.

In the Cain and Dweck study, children were asked to estimate how many puzzles they could complete if they were given four more puzzles similar to the first set to work on. Almost one-third of the nonpersisters (31.2%) thought they would be able to solve none or only one of the new puzzles, whereas only 5.3% of the persisters were this pessimistic.

To summarize this section, it appears that the helpless pattern occurs point for point in an appreciable proportion of young children. These children show a marked lack of persistence in the face of failure, as well as a strong tendency (a) to express spontaneous negative thoughts and affect when they encounter obstacles, (b) to see difficulty as meaning they are incapable of performing a task (as opposed to seeing difficulty as surmountable through effort), and (c) to exhibit low expectancies of success on similar future tasks.

Thus, even though young children may have no clear understanding of "intelligence," they clearly can display the helpless pattern in all its facets. In the research I will turn to now, we have explored the possibility that these motivational patterns in young children are related not to the specific domain of intelligence, but to a more generalized moral domain—that is, to children's beliefs about and assessments of the general goodness or badness of the self.

HELPLESSNESS AND JUDGMENTS OF GOODNESS

Were the young children conceiving of their puzzle performance in terms of goodness and badness? Did the nonpersisters view themselves (or believe others would view them) as morally reprehensible or punishment-worthy? To begin to get at this question, Hebert and Dweck, in the study described earlier, taught children to role-play with dolls as a vehicle for having them enact the evaluations, rewards, and punishments they believed adults would administer for their performance. After working on the puzzles, children role-played four scenes. In three, a social agent (the mother, the father, or the teacher) individually surveyed the three uncompleted puzzles and one completed puzzle, and the child role-played that agent's evaluation. In the fourth, the mother surveyed the puzzles, then called the father on the phone to report her opinion, and the child role-played that conversation. For each agent, the child's spontaneous remarks were followed by specific probes. For these, the doll representing the child (played by the experimenter) asked such things as: Are you happy with me? Are you mad at me? Will you punish me? What should I do now?

Table 4 presents the number of punishments role-played by nonpersisters and persisters. Specifically, the table shows the percentage of children in each group who role-played punishment in most of the four scenes versus those who role-played punishment in half or fewer. Because the probes were direct, and because a very low criterion was used for scoring a child as role-playing punish-

Table 4

Percentage of Nonpersisters and Persisters Enacting Punishment in 0–2 versus 3–4 of the Four Episodes

Number of Episodes	Nonpersisters	Persisters
0–2	50.0	84.2
3–4	50.0	15.8

ment (any criticism, anger, or punishment on any of the questions), punishment from one or two agents was considered low. As can be seen, half of the nonpersisters role-played universal or near-universal punishment, whereas only 15.8% of the persisters did so. The following quotations exemplify the remarks of the nonpersisters who role-played punishment:

"She didn't finish the puzzles. I spanked her, but she keeps on hiding."

"You better do nothing but sit in your room."

"He did bad on the puzzles and messy, too."

"He did one good one and three bad ones. He's punished."

"He's punished cuz he can't do them and he didn't finish."

"Daddy's gonna be very mad and spank her."

Not only did the persisters role-play less punishment, but many of them role-played reward—for their effort or for what they had accomplished. They also portrayed constructive suggestions from the agents. Examples are:

"Our little girl did very good. I'm proud of her and I'm going to hug her."

"He worked hard but he just couldn't finish them. He wants to try them again later."

"He didn't work hard enough. He can try again after lunch."

"You did the best you could. Come sit on my lap."

"She did the puzzles beautiful. I'll give her a candy."

Interestingly, virtually no children spontaneously referred to intelligence or smartness in their evaluations.

These results provide preliminary support for the view that for young children behavior and outcomes, even on skill tasks, are evaluated on the more general dimension of goodness-badness. Nonpersisters, like older helpless children, portray themselves as unable on direct attribution questions, but for many of these younger children "unable" brings with it an expectation of criticism and punishment from adults. In the following study, the meaning and impact of adult criticism were directly investigated.

In this study, by Heyman, Dweck, and Cain (in press) young children began each trial with a highly positive self-evaluation of their product but then encountered criticism of the product from an adult. So here, in essence, we were pitting a completed mastery experience against a negative judgment. For what proportion of the children will this external judgment override their own positive evaluation? Even more interesting, how general is the inference they draw from the negative evaluation? That is, do they draw inferences just about their product or, at a more general level, about their global goodness? In other words, do they treat a specific appraisal as a valid indication of more general worthiness?

Heyman, Dweck, and Cain had 107 kindergarten children roleplay three stories. In each, with appropriate props, they pretend to create a product as a surprise for their teacher. They work long and carefully to make it look really nice, but in each case, just before bestowing it on the teacher, they notice that something is missing. In one story the house they built has no windows; in another, a figure they drew has no feet; and in a third the number eight is missing from the row of numbers one through ten. But the child, so the story goes, still very much wants to give the work to the teacher. One story, the first or the last, stopped here, and the child was asked to rate the product. The other two continued, with the teacher criticizing the flaw and expressing disappointment.

How did children rate their product after their own discovery of the flaw but before experiencing any criticism? When the no-feedback story came first, as it did for half of the children, the overwhelming majority gave their product one of the highest possible ratings. Specifically, children responded to the question, "What do you think you should get for what you did?" by indicating one of six faces ranging from a big frown to a big smile. The first row of Table 5 shows that 94.4% of the children gave their work one of the two highest ratings (the clearly smiling faces), while only 5.6% gave themselves the more neutral or negative faces. What happened on the two stories where criticism was received? As shown in the second row of the table, 60.7% still rated themselves highly, but 39.3% now gave themselves the lower ratings.

Table 5

Percentage of Children With Low and High Product Ratings Before and After Negative Feedback

	Low	High
Before feedback	5.6	94.4
After feedback	39.3	60.7

Let us now take these as our two groups: Those who, following negative evaluation, gave their products low ratings (mostly those for whom the external negative evaluation superseded what would have been their own positive evaluation) and those whose evaluations remained high despite negative evaluation.[3] How general was this negative evaluation taken to be?

To determine this, four questions were asked after each of the two stories with feedback. Children were told, for example, to "think about everything that happened with the numbers. Did everything that happened with the numbers make you feel like you were good or not good at writing numbers?" "Did everything . . . make you feel like you were a good girl/boy or not a good girl/boy?" "Did everything . . . make you feel like you were nice or not nice?" "Did everything . . . make you feel like you were smart or not smart?" Across the two stories, then, children were given eight opportunities to select the positive or negative characteristic. The scores could, and did, range from zero (not good at, good, nice, or smart for both stories) to eight (all positive choices). Comparing children who had given their products high versus low ratings following feedback, we find dramatic differences in their self-ratings on these questions.

As shown in Table 6, the high product raters gave themselves an average of 7.4 out of the possible 8 positive ratings. In contrast, the low product raters gave themselves a significantly lower 4.7, indicating a greater tendency to take the product criticism and generalize it to broader characteristics of the self. The question of how broad the generalization was can be addressed by looking at these data broken down by question. Were children (particularly the low product raters) less likely to give themselves a low self-rating on the most general question (good girl/boy) than on the most specific and task-related (good at . . .)? The answer was no: the low product raters

Table 6

Relationship Between Product Rating and Self-Rating

	Product Rating	
	Low	High
Mean self-rating (0–8)	4.7	7.4

generalized just as much to the broadest characteristic as to the most specific. Only the question about niceness showed a lower level of negative self-rating, as one would expect from the fact that the whole point of producing each product was to create a nice surprise for the teacher. Nevertheless, there was still a significant difference for this question between the high and low product raters. A sizable proportion of the low product raters (almost 40%) reported feeling that they were "not nice" after at least one of the two stories, whereas fewer than 5% of the high product raters had this reaction.

Analyses of children's free responses to more open-ended questions confirmed and extended these findings. Specifically, children were asked what they would have done or said if they were the teacher, what their parents would do or say if they knew what happened, and what would happen next in the interaction between the child and the teacher. It should be emphasized that the free responses of both groups of children reflected great concern with issues of goodness. It was not the case that the high product raters, secure in their goodness, were unconcerned with others' evaluations or with being a "good girl/boy." It was simply that they saw different things as reflecting on their goodness and took a more constructive stance toward rectifying problems.

Akin to the results of our previous research, the high product raters not only reported less punishment and criticism but also reported much more praise—for their effort, their intention, and the finished parts of their product. Indeed, as suggested by their product ratings, many of them took the criticism not as a judgment of their product, but rather as a suggestion for how it could be improved in the future. In line with this, most of them portrayed themselves in the final portion of the interaction as practicing the relevant skill, completing their product, or taking it home with them for homework. Thus these children appeared to retain an array of positive goals—both toward the task itself and toward the teacher's judgment—and to maintain an active, mastery-oriented stance toward these goals.

In contrast, the low product raters not only filled their responses with criticism, punishment, and negative affect on everyone's part, but also tended to view the product criticism as a permanent judgment. Instead of suggesting constructive solutions to the problem at hand, most of them completed the interaction by leaving the actors mired in negative affect (anger or sadness) or by having the teacher express further disdain for the project. Thus many of these children entirely abandoned the pursuit of mastery and positive judgments for their work or themselves. This is particularly striking in light of the fact that they did not in reality have to master anything, but could simply have acted out mastery and subsequent approval. Even when they suggested solutions, these were often completely task irrelevant and consisted of such strategies as inviting the teacher to dinner or buying her a candy heart.

To review thus far, the high product raters did not interpret product criticism as reflecting on themselves—either on their skills or on their moral character. They retained a sense of mastery and of pride in their work. Further, they appeared to view the criticism as a piece of information of which they could make constructive use. The low product raters, on the other hand, were more likely to take the product criticism as a general indictment of themselves and to assume a more helpless stance toward the problem, acting as though their product and their self-esteem were not salvageable.

Were these children just feeling bad about being criticized themselves, or do they tend in general to make moral inferences from product information? To determine this, children were asked, before any of the stories, "Imagine a new boy/girl is in your class. You look over at his schoolwork and see that he got lots and lots wrong and has a big frown on his paper. Does this mean that he is bad?" Table 7 contains the data from this question. As can be seen, the great majority of the high product raters (81.5%) asserted that the child was not bad because of some faulty schoolwork, whereas almost half of the low product raters (47.6%) took this as evidence that the child was in fact bad. Thus the greater tendency of low product raters to believe that product deficiencies bear on moral character

Table 7

Percentage of Low and High Product Raters Who Agreed or Disagreed that Faulty Schoolwork Implies Badness

	Product Rating	
	Low	High
Yes (bad)	47.6	18.5
No (not bad)	52.4	81.5

appears to be a more general belief that extends beyond oneself and one's immediate experience.

Is it possible that the two groups have other general beliefs that distinguish them? Might they also differ in their "theory of morality" as a fixed versus malleable attribute? To determine this, children's theories were elicited by means of a question that posed the issue in concrete terms rather than with respect to abstract concepts. Children were told: "Imagine a new girl [boy] is in your class. She steals your crayons, scribbles on your paper and spills your juice. Then she teases you and calls you names. Do you think this new girl will always act in this way?" The responses to this question can be seen in Table 8. There was a significant difference between the responses of the two groups, with the low product raters more likely than the high product raters to see the behaviors as reflecting a permanent disposition. Thus there appears to be an association between viewing badness as a fixed trait and buying into others people's negative judgments.

Table 8

Percentage of Low and High Product Raters Who Agreed or Disagreed that Misbehavior Reflects an Enduring Trait

	Product Rating	
	Low	High
Yes (always bad)	50.0	24.6
No (not always bad)	50.0	75.4

   The results from this research suggest that for young children the drama is taking place in the domain of the general moral self. And a drama it is, for children seem to be grappling with the difficult question of what makes someone good or bad. Do effort, intention, and partial mastery make one good, or does a flawed and criticized product make one bad? The Heyman, Dweck, and Cain study intentionally put two of these sources of evaluation in potential conflict, and some children clearly enacted this conflict. One boy did so particularly clearly, locating the two points of view in different parents, as he portrayed the following home scenario.

   Mother: Hello. What are you sad about?
   Subject: I gave my teacher some numbers and I skipped the number 8 and now I'm feeling sad.
   Mother: Well, there's one thing that can cheer you up?
   Subject: What?
   Mother: If you really tell your teacher that you tried your best, she wouldn't be mad at you. (Turning to father), We're not mad at [him], are we?
   Father: Oh [yes] we are!

   Unfortunately, this subject appeared to give greater weight to the father's point of view, for he gave both his products and himself extremely low ratings.

   Thus even though on many tasks young children may look (and may, on the average, be) more confident, optimistic, and satisfied with themselves than older children, it is not accurate to depict them as invulnerable. Perhaps our emphasis on achievement situations for assessing motivational patterns has led us to miss the locus of young children's vulnerability. But once we find it, it is difficult to argue that condemning one's general self as bad is a hardier thing to do than viewing oneself as merely inept.

   What does change with development, then, and how can we understand the differences between older and younger children? A study by Benenson and Dweck (1986) sheds some light on this issue. First, it appears that over the grade school years more specific social and intellectual traits become individually conceptualized and differentiated from each other. In a study of children in kindergarten through fourth grade, Benenson and Dweck examined children's explanations for social and intellectual successes and failures. We were particularly interested in the emergence of traits as explanations, and as these traits emerged, children's self-ratings in the two domains went from being correlated to being uncorrelated. Second, as the traits emerged, first in the social domain and then in the intellectual domain, children became less positive in their self-ratings in that domain and more defensive about their performance even when it was good. For example, even children who said they got "mostly A's" (the highest category they could choose), when asked to explain why they got these grades, explained a "failure,"—why they did not get all A's.

Thus it may well be the case that as specific domains and their traits become more clearly conceptualized, children grow more knowledgeable about what particular cues reflect specifically on that trait and even more sensitive to evaluative cues and lapses from standards in that domain. Hence, older children's reputation for greater vulnerability.

To conclude this section, I would like to underscore the parallels between the motivational patterns found in younger and older children. For both populations we found that the maladaptive (vs. adaptive) pattern included:

1. A heightened concern with outcomes and judgments (vs. effort and progress).
2. A heightened reaction to negative outcomes and judgments, such that these terminated and defined the episode as a failure, eradicated both past and future successes, and led to the abandonment of constructive goals (vs. a view of negative outcomes or judgments as a point in time between past and future successes).
3. A tendency to draw general inferences about important characteristics of the self from a small sample of outcomes or feedback (vs. a tendency to view outcomes and feedback as information to be used constructively).
4. A tendency to hold implicit theories that depict important characteristics of the self as immutable (vs. as qualities that can be changed or developed).

It is possible, then, that the model developed to characterize older children is also an apt description of motivational patterns in younger ones. Clearly, more research is needed to establish the nature of young children's implicit theories and their role in motivational patterns. Many interesting questions suggest themselves. For example, in what order do the variables in our model develop? Might it be that implicit theories initially grow out of existing goals and concerns but, once established, serve to heighten these concerns? Does favoring a certain theory early on in one domain foster the subsequent adoption of that theory in other domains? What remains intriguing, however, is the striking degree to which virtually every aspect of the motivational patterns found in older children is there in some form earlier.

Relation to Traditional Personality Theories

In this section I will tentatively suggest parallels between the processes depicted in our model and processes posited by a number of more traditional personality-motivational formulations.

Many past personality theories (e.g., Allport, 1961; Erikson, 1950; Horney, 1950; Maslow, 1955; Rogers, 1963) have posited a natural tendency toward self-development and individuality (perhaps akin to our learning goal, with its emphasis on development and personal mastery), as well as a need for positive regard and acceptance by others (perhaps akin to our performance goal, with its emphasis on judgment and validation) (cf. Deci & Ryan, this volume).

Most of these theories are also developmental theories and, starting with these basic needs, suggest ways in which different personality patterns may come into existence. As with our two classes of goals, these basic tendencies are not seen as necessarily in conflict; indeed, in an environment where both classes of needs can simultaneously be fulfilled, development should proceed happily, resulting in a child who spontaneously pursues self-enhancing courses of action without undue conflict, guilt, anxiety, or defensiveness.

In some environments, however, the different tendencies may well come into conflict: what one gets approval for is not what serves to express or develop the self. In other words, according to these theories the child's spontaneous displays of, or tendencies toward, self-expression, autonomy, or self-development may meet with nonacceptance or negative reactions from the environment. Now, for Freud, the guilt, anxiety, and defenses that are seen to result from this are a normal and crucial part of personality; but for the others this is an undesirable state of affairs. For them such negative judgments from the outside can lead to an unhealthy duality between inherent tendencies toward self-realization and what one does to be approved of and accepted by others. This can result in a distortion or suppression of tendencies toward growth and autonomy as individuals strive to prove themselves worthy to others. Some of these theorists even posit the formation of an alternative self designed specifically for the purpose of obtaining validation (e.g., Horney, 1950; Rogers, 1963).

It is intriguing to speculate that, although more specific and research-based, the processes I have described in our model may capture to some degree those processes postulated by past personality theorists. In children with an incremental theory, we see children who believe in a developing self, who proudly display their works-in-progress and undefensively deal with and use appraisals of their work. In contrast, in children with an entity theory, we see children who have (re)conceptualized themselves as objects for judgment, who sacrifice learning for judgments, and who wilt in the face of errors or criticism because they believe a negative judgment or a deficient product implies an unworthy self.

General Conclusions

In this chapter I have described how important, coherent motivational patterns can be understood in terms of the particular goals individuals are pursuing and the belief systems that set up these goals. I would like to conclude with a few thoughts about what makes a belief system maladaptive or adaptive.

First, maladaptive beliefs are those that put basic needs or goals in conflict with each other. We saw that the entity belief system, by focusing individuals on moment-to-moment judgments and by requiring easy, error-free tasks to ensure those judgments, created a natural antagonism between performance and learning goals. Although such belief systems may well arise in environments in which basic needs *are* in conflict with each other, these beliefs may rigidify and perpetuate the conflict, leading the individual to generalize inappropriately to new situations.

Adaptive beliefs, in contrast, are those that render basic needs compatible with each other and allow them, when possible, to be pursued in concert. Perhaps the most interesting thing revealed by the young persistent children was their simultaneous pursuit of task mastery and positive judgments via constructive mastery efforts. In the same vein, older children with incremental theories and learning goals may not perceive themselves to be sacrificing positive judgments from others when they reject the performance goal we offer them. It is interesting to consider, then, that the "conflict" we set up in our research—when we pit learning goals against performance goals or when we pit feelings of personal mastery against negative judgments from others—is indeed a conflict for children operating within one belief system but not for children operating within another.

A second characteristic of maladaptive beliefs is that they interfere with the attainment of one's chosen goals. That is, they not only may lead people to sacrifice important goals, but they may also render them less effective in pursuing the goals they have selected. We saw that an entity theory and performance goals created a vulnerability to the helpless pattern, marked by the demise of effective striving. To the extent that all important goals at some point are likely to present challenges and obstacles, it is clearly more adaptive to operate within a belief system that accepts and welcomes them and thus promotes the attainment of valued goals.

A third characteristic of maladaptive belief systems is that they lead people to traffic excessively in fictions instead of realities. Although much fine work has been done on adaptive positive illusions (such as optimism or a sense of control beyond that warranted by the data, e.g., Alloy and Abramson, 1979; Langer, 1975; Taylor & Brown, 1988), it appears from our work that the mastery-oriented children are the ones who are in touch with reality. For example, their recall of past outcomes is more accurate (Diener & Dweck, 1980), they make fuller use of the information available, and they are clearly more strategic and planful in surmounting obstacles. It is true that they are highly optimistic about future success, but they are certainly not resting on their expected laurels; they are working assiduously for that success.

In contrast, the helpless children are dealing in reified entities (their fixed "intelligence" or "goodness") that they assess through

symbols (outcomes or judgments). They make unwarranted inferences about these entities on the basis of a few outcomes or criticisms,
such that they lose contact with their own prior perceptions (e.g., of
their product or performance), with their actual experiences (e.g., their
past success), and most important, with their own true abilities.

Is it the case that positive illusions or distortions are adaptive
but negative ones are not? This is a question that remains to be explored, but it seems as though rigid, defensive positive distortions
(e.g., denial of negative outcomes or externalizing blame) that prevent individuals from dealing directly and constructively with outcomes or feedback would also be maladaptive if overused. This
might well arise within an entity belief system among high confidence entity theorists, who may strive over time to maintain their
confidence through defensive distortions and not merely through
active striving. In short, although many questions remain about the
nature and consequences of various illusions, it appears from our
work that belief systems that remove people from the realm of simple events and place them in the realm of abstractions and symbols
are fraught with maladaptive possibilities.

At the outset, I raised a fundamental motivational question:
What do individuals want, need, and value, and how do their goals
impel and organize their behavior? In addressing these issues, I have
attempted to show that a motivational analysis can illuminate systematic differences between individuals and across development.

NOTES

1. All findings or group differences reported in this chapter are statis-
tically significant, although this will not be explicitly stated in each case.

2. This position is consistent with Erikson's theory (Erikson, 1950), first
in the general sense that children's focal identity concerns are seen to
change with age, and second, in the specific sense that those of school-age
children are viewed as centering on academic and social attainment in the
world of their peers, whereas those of preschoolers are seen as centering
on right or wrong courses of action according to parental standards.

3. It is important to note that if we look back at how these two groups
had rated their product on the previous, no-feedback story, their ratings
were identical and high (approximately 5.6 on the 6-point scale). Thus it is
not the case that those who responded to criticism by giving their products
low ratings simply began with more negative self-evaluations.

REFERENCES

Alloy, L. B., & Abramson, L. Y. (1979). Judgment of contingency in depressed and non-depressed students: Sadder but wiser? *Journal of Experimental Psychology: General, 108,* 441–485.

Allport, G. W. (1961). *Pattern and growth in personality.* New York: Holt, Rinehart, and Winston.

Ames, C. (1984). Achievement attributions and self-instructions under competitive and individualistic goal structures. *Journal of Educational Psychology, 76,* 478–487.

Ames, C., & Archer, J. (1988). Achievement goals in the classroom: Student learning strategies and motivational processes. *Journal of Educational Psychology, 80,* 260–267.

Bandura, M. M., & Dweck, C. S. (1985). *The relationship of conceptions of intelligence and achievement goals to achievement-related cognition, affect and behavior.* Unpublished manuscript, Harvard University.

Barenboim, C. (1981). The development of person perception in childhood and adolescence: From behavioral comparisons to psychological constructs to psychological comparisons. *Child Development, 52,* 129–144.

Benenson, J. F., & Dweck, C. S. (1986). The development of trait explanations and self-evaluations in the academic and social domains. *Child Development, 57,* 1179–1187.

Cain, K. M. (1990). *Children's motivational patterns and conceptions of intelligence: A study of the developmental relationship between motivation and cognition.* Unpublished doctoral dissertation, University of Illinois.

Crandall, V. C., Katkovsky, W., & Crandall, V. J. (1965). Children's beliefs in their own control of reinforcement in intellectual-academic situations. *Child Development, 36,* 91–109.

Damon, W., & Hart, D. (1982). The development of self-understanding from infancy through adolescence. *Child Development, 53,* 841–864.

Deci, E. L., & Ryan, R. M. (1980). The empirical exploration of intrinsic motivational processes. In L. Berkowitz (Ed.), *Advances in experimental social psychology* (Vol. 13, pp. 39–80). New York: Academic Press.

Diener, C. I., & Dweck, C. S. (1978). An analysis of learned helplessness: Continuous changes in performance, strategy and achievement cognitions following failure. *Journal of Personality and Social Psychology, 36,* 451–462.

Diener, C. I., & Dweck, C. S. (1980). An analysis of learned helplessness: 2. The processing of success. *Journal of Personality and Social Psychology, 39,* 940–952.

Dweck, C. S. (1975). The role of expectations and attributions in the alleviation of learned helplessness. *Journal of Personality and Social Psychology, 31,* 674–685.

Dweck, C. S. (1989). Motivation. In A. Lesgold & R. Glaser (Eds.), *Foundations for a psychology of education.* Hillsdale, NJ: Erlbaum.

Dweck, C. S., & Bempechat, J. (1983). Children's theories of intelligence. In

S. Paris, G. Olsen, & H. Stevenson (Eds.), *Learning and motivation in the classroom* (pp. 239–256). Hillsdale, NJ: Erlbaum.

Dweck, C. S., & Elliott, E. S. (1983). Achievement motivation. In P. H. Mussen (Gen. Ed.) & E. M. Hetherington (Vol. Ed.), *Handbook of child psychology: Vol. 4. Social and personality development* (pp. 643–691). New York: Wiley.

Dweck, C. S., & Leggett, E. L. (1988). A social-cognitive approach to personality and motivation. *Psychological Review, 95,* 256–273.

Dweck, C. S., & Reppucci, N. D. (1973). Learned helplessness and reinforcement responsibility in children. *Journal of Personality and Social Psychology, 25,* 109–116.

Elliott, E. S., & Dweck, C. S. (1988). Goals: An approach to motivation and achievement. *Journal of Personality and Social Psychology, 54,* 5–12.

Erdley, C. A., & Dweck, C. S. (1989, April). *Childrens theories of personality as predictors of their social judgments.* Paper presented at the biennial meeting of the Society for Research in Child Development, Kansas City, MO.

Erikson, E. H. (1950). *Childhood and Society.* New York: Norton.

Farrell, E. (1985). *The role of motivational processes in transfer of learning.* Unpublished doctoral dissertation, Harvard University.

Goetz, T. E., & Dweck, C. S. (1980). Learned helplessness in social situations. *Journal of Personality and Social Psychology, 39,* 246–255.

Henderson, V., & Dweck, C. S. (1990). Adolescence and achievement. In S. Feldman & G. Elliot (Eds.), *At the threshold: Adolescent development.* Cambridge: Harvard University Press.

Heyman, G. D., Dweck, C. S., & Cain, K. M. (in press). Young children's vulnerability to self-blame and helplessness: Relationship to beliefs about goodness. *Child Development.*

Horney, K. (1950). *Neurosis and human growth.* New York: Norton.

Keller, A., Ford, L. H., & Meacham, J. A. (1978). Dimensions of self-concept in preschool children. *Developmental Psychology, 14,* 483–489.

Langer, E. J. (1975). The Illusion of control. *Journal of Personality and Social Psychology, 32,* 311–328.

Licht, B. G., & Dweck, C. S. (1984). Determinants of academic achievement: The interaction of children's achievement orientations with skill area. *Developmental Psychology, 20,* 628–636.

Livesley, W. J., & Bromley, D. B. (1973). *Person perception in childhood and adolescence.* New York: Wiley.

Loomis, C. C., Hines, F. A., Erdley, C. A., & Cain, K. M. (1989, April). *Goals and children's response to social rejection: An experimental analysis.* Paper presented at the biennial meeting of the Society for Research in Child Development. Kansas City, MO.

Maslow, A. H. (1955). Deficiency motivation and growth motivation. In M. R. Jones (Ed.), *Nebraska Symposium on Motivation.* Lincoln: University of Nebraska Press.

Nicholls, J. G., & Miller, A. T. (1984). Development and its discontents: The differentiation of the concept of ability. In J. G. Nicholls (Ed.), *The develop-*

ment of achievement motivation (pp. 185–218). Greenwich, CT: JAI Press.

Olshefsky, L., Erdley, C. A., & Dweck, C. S. (1987). Children's theories of personality and their response to social rejection. Unpublished data.

Parsons, J. E., & Ruble, D. N. (1977). The development of achievement-related expectancies. *Child Development, 48,* 1075–1079.

Pervin, L. A. (1983). The stasis and flow of behavior: Toward a theory of goals. In M. M. Page & R. Dienstbier (Eds.), *Nebraska Symposium on Motivation.* Lincoln: University of Nebraska Press.

Rholes, W. S., Blackwell, J., Jordan, C., & Walters, C. (1980). A developmental study of learned helplessness. *Developmental Psychology, 16,* 616–624.

Rogers, C. R. (1963). Actualizing tendency in relation to "motives" and to consciousness. In M. R. Jones (Ed.), *Nebraska Symposium on Motivation.* Lincoln: University of Nebraska Press.

Smiley, P. (1989, April). *Individual differences in preschoolers' task persistence.* Paper presented at the biennial meeting of the Society for Research in Child Development, Kansas City, MO.

Stipek, D. J. (1981). *Children's use of past performance information in ability and expectancy judgments for self and other.* Paper presented at the meeting of the International Society for the Study of Behavior Development, Toronto.

Taylor, S. E., & Brown, J. D. (1988). Illusion and well-being: A social psychological perspective on mental health. *Psychological Bulletin, 103,* 193–210.

Weiner, B. (1972). *Theories of motivation: From mechanism to cognition.* Chicago: Markham.

Weisz, J. R. (1981). Illusory contingency in children at the state fair. *Developmental Psychology, 17,* 481–489.

A Motivational Approach to Self: Integration in Personality

Edward L. Deci and
Richard M. Ryan

University of Rochester

Prologue

Two features characterize the dominant views of "self" within modern empirical psychology. First, the self tends to be conceptualized as a set of cognitive appraisals and schemata; second, the self tends to be understood as a reflection of social evaluations (e.g., Bandura, 1978; Greenwald, 1988; Harter, 1988; Kihlstrom & Cantor, 1984; Markus & Sentis, 1982; Scheier & Carver, 1988).

It is quite understandable, in light of the history of empirical psychology, that current "self" theories would have these characteristics. First, the use of concepts like cognitive structures and mechanisms is de rigueur in current mainstream psychology (Hilgard, 1987). Inferences and schemata, for example, enjoy wide currency in contemporary theorizing. Second, most theories of self have emerged within the areas of social and social-developmental psychology, where the concern has always been with the influence of social forces on the psychological processes of individuals. It is for this reason, perhaps, that modern self theorists have used as their point of departure the early theories that emphasize the "self" as a mirror of social evaluations (Cooley, 1902; Mead, 1934).

Preparation of this chapter was supported in part by grants from the NICHD (HD 19914) and NIMH (MH 18922) to the Human Motivation Program, Department of Psychology, University of Rochester.

In this chapter we present a very different perspective on the self. In our view the two features mentioned above are only partially true, and taken together they miss the essence of what the self is and does. For us, self goes deeper than cognition—it is not a set of cognitive mechanisms and structures but rather a set of *motivational* processes with a variety of assimilatory and regulatory functions. In addition, the self does not simply reflect social forces; rather, it represents intrinsic growth processes whose tendency is toward integration of one's own experience and action with one's sense of relatedness to the selves of others. Thus the self is not simply an outcome of social evaluations and pressures but instead is the very process through which a person contacts the social environment and works toward integration with respect to it.

One important feature of our conception of self is that it provides a framework for distinguishing, both empirically and theoretically, those internally motivated, intentional actions that represent human agency and *self-determination* from those that do not (e.g., Deci, 1980; Deci & Ryan, 1985b; Deci & Ryan, 1987). Behaviors that either are intrinsically motivated or stem from well-integrated personal values and regulatory processes can, we argue, be described as self-determined in the exacting sense of that term, whereas behaviors that emanate from nonintegrated processes such as internal pressures and socially acquired introjects cannot. More accurately, we would say that in the former case the *degree of involvement of the self* in the initiation and regulation of action would be greater than in the latter case. We will now explicate these issues within the context of self-determination theory.

Introduction: The Organismic Dialectic

There is perhaps no type of theory for which the underlying metatheory—the philosophical starting point—is more critical than for theories of the self. Because the self is the core of what we are, the characterization of self (whether explicit or implicit) reflects what the theorists assume the nature of the human being to be.

According to our perspective, a central feature of human nature is an active agency and a synthetic tendency that we ascribe to the self. From the time of birth, human beings are oriented toward the

active exercise of their capacities and interests. They seek out optimal challenges, and they attempt to master and integrate new experiences. In other words, they are engaged in a developmental process that is intrinsic to their nature and is characterized by the
tendency toward a more elaborate and extensive organization. Interestingly, this synthetic nature, which is displayed as a tendency
toward negentropy, is not unique to human personality development but is evinced by all living organisms (von Bertalanffy, 1968) at
many levels of a systems analysis. As Piaget (1971) put it, the nature
of life is always to overtake itself. In our view this nature, this tendency toward elaborated organization, is central to the definition
and development of self (Ryan, in press).

Activity and integration do not occur in a vacuum, however, nor
do the active, synthetic tendencies of the self always predominate.
Enhancing one's self involves assimilating one's world (especially
the social world), and although that world can be supportive of integrative development, it can also be resistant—even antagonistic—
to it. Our theory of self-determination is concerned with this dialectical struggle between the active self and the various forces, both
within and without, that the person encounters in the process of development. Further, it is concerned with the social context within
which those encounters occur, which can either support or forestall
development toward harmonious relations within and between persons. An obvious implication of this dialectical viewpoint is that
synthesis of personality does not invariably succeed, and that some
aspects of interpersonal and cultural environments conduce toward
fractionation rather than integration and toward alienation rather
than cohesion.

The development of self begins with intrinsic activity and the
tendency toward coherent elaboration. One implication of this view
is that there is a nascent self—a set of innate interests, potentials,
and processes (most notably the organismic integration process)—
that develops as the person engages in the dialectical interaction
with unintegrated aspects of itself and the surrounds. Stated differently, the development of self entails integrating new experiences
and regulatory processes with one's intrinsic self. To the extent that
integration fully occurs, the behaviors that are thus regulated will be
said to be self-determined. To the extent that integration does not
fully occur, however, scripts or schemata from the social world may

be taken in but not integrated. In such circumstances, these "scripts" will provide the bases for non-self-determined behavior.

Since the central elements of our theory are the active organism, the social context, and the self, we shall briefly consider each in turn.

THE ACTIVE ORGANISM

Central to organismic activity are the concepts of intrinsic motivation and organismic integration.

Intrinsic motivation is inseparably intertwined with the idea of a spontaneous or active nature. It emerged as a concept in empirical psychology about the time this annual symposium began, owing in large part to the pioneering work of Harlow (1950, 1953), a participant in the first symposium. Subsequently, the important conceptual statement by White (1959, 1960), a later symposium participant, not only introduced the closely linked idea of effectance motivation, but likened it to what the psychoanalytic ego psychologists refer to as independent ego energy (Hartmann, 1939/1958). By postulating an intrinsic need for competence, White (1959) was also placing the concept of intrinsic motivation in a tradition that can be traced to Murray (1938), whose analyses of interview data led him to postulate numerous psychological (i.e., non-drive-based) needs. And by reviewing the animal learning studies of the early 1950s (e.g., Butler, 1953; Montgomery, 1953) as well as evidence within the psychoanalytic tradition, White's work represented a landmark integrative analysis.

Increasingly through the 1950s and 1960s, the concept of intrinsic motivation gained importance and was discussed primarily in reaction to the two dominant behavioral theories of that era—operant theory (Skinner, 1953) and drive theory (Hull, 1943). Its central message was that "voluntary" behaviors are *not* all a function of operationally separable reinforcements (as the Skinnerians had asserted) and that these reinforcement-independent behaviors are *not* derivative of tissue deficits (as the Hullians had asserted). Instead, they are inherent in the nature of life, and their only necessary rewarding consequences are the spontaneous affects and cognitions that accompany them.

It has often been said that the rewards for an intrinsically motivated activity are "in the activity itself," and though that is true in the sense that there are no separable external rewards, Berlyne (1971) correctly pointed out that rewarding consequences are in people, not activities. These consequences, in our view, are the feelings and thoughts that emerge spontaneously as people engage in the activity. The nature of these consequences (or more accurately, accompaniments) will become clear as we consider the needs and affects that are central to intrinsic motivation.

The idea of intrinsic motivation as a nonderivative motivational force has been discussed and defined differently within different theoretical traditions. We will consider four of these approaches in an attempt to provide a comprehensive characterization of intrinsic motivation and to address the issue of "rewarding consequences." The first approach states that intrinsically motivated behaviors can occur in the absence of any apparent external reward. This aspect of the definition, which emerged as a reaction to operant theory, is the basis of the operational definition and the "free-choice" measure of intrinsic motivation introduced by Deci (1971, 1972). Although this definition does not shed light on the internal psychological processes involved in intrinsic motivation, it has been of considerable importance both because of its challenge to operant psychology's tenet that all behavior is a function of external reinforcements and because the "free-choice" measure has served well as a laboratory measure of intrinsic motivation for nearly two decades. As we will show later, the measure has encountered some problems as the study of internal motivational processes has become more differentiated to include consideration of internalized regulatory processes.

A second definitional approach suggests that intrinsically motivated behaviors are those the person undertakes out of *interest*. Interest is what relates the self to external and internal experiences. It is the central affect of synthesis and is fundamental to the processes of organismic contact and assimilation. Accordingly, interest is essential for understanding self-development and for explicating an aspect of the psychological processes involved in intrinsic motivation. Thus, in both laboratory and applied studies of intrinsic motivation and autonomous development, self-reports of interest have played an important role as another operational measure of intrinsic motivation (e.g., Grolnick & Ryan, 1989; Ryan, Mims, & Koestner, 1983).

The third definitional approach has focused on the idea that intrinsically interesting activities are optimally challenging. Csikszentmihalyi (1975), for example, suggested that when activities are optimally challenging for a person's capacities, the person is likely to enjoy them and have an autotelic or "flow" experience. Deci (1975) proposed, further, that when people are intrinsically motivated they will seek out and attempt to conquer optimal challenges, and he pointed out that this idea is similar to Piaget's (1952) suggestion that people naturally approach optimally assimilable situations and to Hunt's (1965) proposal that the tendency to engage stimuli that are optimally discrepant from one's cognitive structure is inherent in information processing and development. The linking of optimal challenge to assimilation and intrinsic motivation has also been a fruitful research endeavor (Danner & Lonky, 1981; Harter, 1978).

The final component of our characterization of intrinsic motivation states that intrinsically motivated behaviors are based in innate psychological needs. In particular, White (1959) spoke of the need for effectance; deCharms (1968) of the need for personal causation; and Deci and Ryan (1980) of the needs for competence and self-determination. The idea of psychological needs, as mentioned, can be traced to Murray (1938), who identified achievement and autonomy as psychological needs, and also to Maslow (1943), who suggested that people have an innate need for what Goldstein (1939) termed "self-actualization."

The needs for competence and self-determination (autonomy) provide a comprehensive explanation for a wide range of exploratory and mastery behaviors and for the idea that individuals strive to develop their interests and capacities. Thus in most contexts these two needs are emphasized as the bases of intrinsic or mastery motivation (Ryan & Connell, 1988). However, an exclusive focus on mastery motivation fails to take account of the intrinsic social need that directs people's interest toward the development of relational bonds and toward a concern for interpersonally valued and culturally relevant activities.

Harlow's (1958) interesting work on affiliation, suggesting that there is a psychological need for love as distinct from the physiological need for sex, provided some evidence about people's tendency toward social relatedness and about the developmental significance of a healthy connectedness to others, as did the work on the need for affiliation (McClelland, 1985; Shipley & Veroff, 1952) and the related-ness needs (Alderfer, 1972; Maslow, 1943).

In our own recent theorizing, we have attempted to synthesize the work on intrinsic needs by suggesting that there are three primary psychological needs. The need for *competence* encompasses people's strivings to control outcomes and to experience effectance; in other words, to understand the instrumentalities that lead to desired outcomes and to be able to reliably effect those instrumentalities. The need for *autonomy* (or self-determination) encompasses people's strivings to be agentic, to feel like the "origin" (deCharms, 1968) of their actions, and to have a voice or input in determining their own behavior. It concerns the desire to experience an internal perceived locus of causality with regard to action—that is, to experience one's actions as emanating from the self. Finally, the need for *relatedness* encompasses a person's strivings to relate to and care for others, to feel that those others are relating authentically to one's self, and to feel a satisfying and coherent involvement with the social world more generally. We believe these three innate psychological needs are reasonably exhaustive and help to explain a substantial amount of variance in human behavior and experience (e.g., Connell, 1990; Deci & Ryan, 1985b; Ryan, in press; Ryan & Lynch, 1989).

One heuristically useful consequence of specifying the human needs that relate to intrinsically motivated processes is that it allows us to predict the contextual conditions that will promote rather than undermine those processes. Contextual factors that allow the satisfaction of the basic psychological needs are theorized to promote intrinsic motivational processes, while those that thwart one or more of the basic needs are theorized to impair such processes—a point to which we will return.

Organismic integration refers to the most basic developmental strivings of the self that can be considered at two levels of analysis. First, there is the tendency toward unity in one's "self," that is, toward coherence in one's regulatory activity and experience. The process of organismic integration, operating at this level, entails differentiating aspects of one's interests and capacities and then working to bring them into a higher-order organization with other aspects of one's self. Second, there is the tendency toward interacting in a coherent and meaningful way with others so as to experience satisfying personal relationships with individuals and a harmonious relation to the larger social order. Here too one is attempting to differentiate aspects of the social world and to create an organized set of relationships and representations. This dual-level process of seeking integration and cohesion both within oneself and with others is the essence of the active agentic self in development (Ryan, in press).

The concept of integration or organized complexity is at the heart of several important theories, and it is the combination of innate activity and integration that gives a theory an *organismic* character. In Piagetian theory, for example (Piaget, 1952), the concept of organization refers to the complementary processes of differentiating cognitive structures into elaborated elements and then integrating these differentiated elements into organized totalities. In psychoanalytic theory, the integrative process is often referred to as the synthetic function of the ego (Freud, 1923/1962; Nunberg, 1931).

According to self-determination theory (Deci & Ryan, 1985b), intrinsic motivation (as organized by the needs for competence, autonomy, and relatedness) is the energizing basis for natural organismic activity. It leads people to encounter new challenges that are optimal for their self-development and that can be integrated as development proceeds naturally. Like all natural processes, however, development through integration must be nurtured, and the inputs that are theorized to nurture this development are those that allow the person to satisfy the basic psychological needs for autonomy, competence, and relatedness. Thus, specifying the inherent psychological needs not only helps to characterize the "content" of human nature but also explains what organizes and, in a sense, delimits the direction of organismic integration.

The *dialectic* of development involves the integrative tendency of the self as it meets the forces and events that arise internally from organismic conditions and externally from contextual circumstances—what Greenspan (1979) referred to as the internal and external boundaries of the self. Integration, and thus development, results when the person is able to make contact with and assimilate events and thus gain a sense of being an agent with respect to them. But if the challenges one encounters are too far beyond an optimal level, development will be impaired or inhibited.

In describing organismic integration, we do not mean to portray development as autoplastic. Development not only entails modifying oneself, it involves acting on, and thus changing, the environment to make it more consistent with oneself. Furthermore, because of the person's nature (as specified here by the needs for competence, autonomy, and relatedness), some forces cannot be integrated. For example, processes or contents of socialization that are inconsistent with basic needs cannot be fully assimilated or integrated. As such, they may lead to conflict, internal fragmentation or inconsistency, and anomie. It is in this sense that the "content" of human nature delimits organismic integration.

THE SOCIAL CONTEXT

Human activity occurs within real or imagined social contexts. As we work, play, study, perform, or relax, other people often observe us, make requests of us, or coact with us. And even when others are not actually present, we may be aware of what they would like us to do or how they would like us to do it. The quality of the others' presence (whether actual or imagined), as well as the quality of the broader social context within which we interact with others, can have an important effect not only on our behavior but also on our feelings about ourselves and our overall development.

In the motivational analysis of self-determination theory (e.g., Deci & Ryan, 1985b; Grolnick & Ryan, 1989; Grolnick, Ryan, & Deci, 1990), we have often focused on three dimensions for assessing the social context. We refer to these as autonomy support, structure, and involvement. *Autonomy support* (as opposed to control) describes a context that provides choice, minimizes pressure to perform in specified ways, and encourages initiation. Autonomy-supportive relationships are those that are responsive with respect to an actor's internal frame of reference. For example, teachers provide a social context for students, parents for children, managers for subordinates, and they—the teachers, parents, or managers—are being autonomy supportive of the target persons (the students, children, or subordinates) when they are able to promote action with respect to the target persons' perceptions and needs. *Structure* describes the extent to which behavior-outcome contingencies are understandable, expectations are clear, and feedback is provided. The degree of structure afforded by a social context directly affects one's sense of efficacy and perceived control over outcomes (Skinner, Wellborn, & Connell, 1990). *Involvement* describes the degree to which significant others (e.g., parents for children) are interested in and devote time and energy to a relationship. It concerns others' dedication of psychological resources that the target person can use as a basis of support and an aid to effectance.

Social contexts that are autonomy supportive, that provide moderate structure, and that contain involved others are optimal for encouraging self-determined engagement and promoting development, because they facilitate the target person's expression and satisfaction of his or her basic psychological needs. These are the contexts that not only will promote effective behavior but will also help the person develop the inner resources required for adaptive self-regulation. On the other hand, social contexts that are controlling, that are unstructured or overstructured, or that do not provide involvement of significant others run the risk of undermining self-determination and impairing development by thwarting both the satisfaction of basic needs and the involvement of the agentic self.

THE SELF: IN BRIEF

The idea of inherent capacities and tendencies toward development—that is, of intrinsic motivation and organismic integration—suggests that the neonate is not tabula rasa, is not empty and waiting for the world to write its script. Instead, it suggests that there is an inherent rudimentary self, a set of processes and potentials (e.g., exploratory tendencies, innate preferences, and the motivation to relate and assimilate) that represent the beginning of a developing self. As one acts from this self—exercising capacities, following interests, and relating to others within varied social contexts—the self develops. Thus, although we assert that development is intrinsically motivated (is motivated by the needs for competence, autonomy, and relatedness), we do not believe that development per se is the goal of activity; rather, it is the by-product of activity that emanates from the phenomenal core of one's experience and satisfies one's basic psychological needs.

One very important corollary of the view that a nascent self develops through mastery-oriented encounters with the physical and

social surrounds is that only to the extent that some new element—some regulatory process, say—is brought into harmony
with the characteristics of one's inherent self will that element become part of one's self. Only when an element is fully integrated
will it represent self.

The Regulation of Behavior

Within empirical psychology, two types of concepts have been pivotal to explanations of behavioral regulation. The first type, which is
a wholly mechanistic conceptualization, suggests that *associative
bonds* develop between an internal or external stimulus event and a
behavior to determine future behaviors. Terms such as conditioning
and reinforcement (e.g., Hull, 1943; Pavlov, 1927; Skinner, 1953) have
been used to describe how these associative bonds develop mecha-
nistically to provide an environmental supplement to one's genetic
endowment. The various associative theories do, of course, differ in
many important respects, but the main similarity is that none of
them gives a central causal role to experiential variables such as cognition, awareness, or consciousness. An organismic conceptualization, on the other hand, requires that some type of internal experiential variables be accorded determinative status in the regulation of
behavior, and the concept that has most often been used for this purpose is *intention*.

An intention is a conscious or preconscious formulation about
some future behavior or outcome the person will attempt to perform
or achieve. Within empirical psychology, this approach can be most
directly traced to the influence of Tolman (1932) and Lewin (1936)
and to the emergence of the field of artificial intelligence and cognitive simulation (Newell, Shaw, & Simon, 1958). The concept of intention can be treated in relatively mechanistic ways (e.g., com-
puters can be said to have intentions), or it can be used as a truly
organismic concept. It is to the latter view that we subscribe.

According to this approach, people's behavior is intended to
yield a desired outcome, whether that is a concrete, external object
such as a monetary reward or a spontaneous, internal feeling such
as enjoyment of an activity. If, because of an enduring aspect of their
personality (Rotter, 1954) or because of the way the current situation

is structured (Seligman, 1975), people believe they will not be able to achieve a desired outcome, they are expected not to engage in intentional action. Instead, they will be helpless, disorganized, and amotivated.

The theories that have evolved out of the "intentional" perspective have had two central concepts, one that refers to the desired outcome and its psychological value to the person, and one that refers to people's beliefs or expectations about being able to attain that outcome (e.g., Tolman, 1959; Vroom, 1964). Terms like valence, goals, and incentives have been used to describe outcomes, and terms like probabilities, instrumentalities, and expectancies have been used to refer to the person's attainment beliefs.

Two types of expectancies or attainment beliefs have been identified as critical for intentional behavior and have received a tremendous amount of empirical attention (e.g., Skinner, Chapman, & Baltes, 1988). The first type, *contingency expectations*, concern whether the person believes various outcomes are reliably linked to (contingent upon) particular behaviors (Rotter, 1966). The second type, *efficacy expectations*, refer to whether one believes one can competently perform the requisite instrumental actions (Bandura, 1977).

Heider (1958), in discussing the concept of intentionality, described a continuum from impersonal causation to personal causation, pointing out that only actions that are mediated by an intention can be said to be personally caused (i.e., motivated) whereas those that are not mediated by intentions are said to have impersonal causes (and are thus not properly termed motivated). DeCharms (1968), elaborating on Heider's concept of personal causation, introduced the terms internal and external perceived locus of causality to represent different types of personal causation. Internal perceived causality refers to one's seeing oneself as the locus of initiation for a behavior (and thus feeling like an "origin"), while external perceived causality describes intentional actions for which one perceives the source of initiation to be outside oneself (and thus feels like a "pawn"). DeCharms's theorizing thus suggests that one can be either an origin or a pawn and still be "intentional" in one's behavior.

The concept of an internal versus an external perceived locus of *causality* has often been confused with that of an internal versus an external locus of *control* (e.g., Weiner, 1986), yet the two have quite different referents. Locus of *control's* being internal versus external (Rotter, 1954, 1966) refers to whether a person believes that outcomes can (versus cannot) be reliably attained; in other words, it refers to contingency expectations, with efficacy expectations implicit within them. Thus locus of control allows one to predict whether a person is likely to engage in motivated (intentional) action. In contrast, the locus of *causality's* being internal versus external refers to whether the experienced locus of initiation for a motivated (intentional) action is internal versus external to one's *self* (Ryan & Connell, 1989). As such, internal versus external *control* is somewhat parallel to the Heiderian distinction between personal and impersonal *causality,* whereas internal versus external *causality* can be best understood as referring to gradations or subcategories within personal causation and thus to variations in the degree to which an intentional action is self-determined. It is worth noting, however, that although there is a structural parallel between internal versus external control (Rotter, 1966) and personal versus impersonal causation (Heider, 1958), the two sets of terminology, when properly used, have rather different theoretical flavors because the locus of control concept is anchored in a reinforcement framework while the locus of causality concept derives from a phenomenological perspective (Spiegelberg, 1972).

INTRINSIC VERSUS EXTRINSIC MOTIVATION

DeCharms (1968), in discussing internal versus external causation, used the dichotomy between intrinsic and extrinsic motivation to characterize the different loci of causality. Intrinsically motivated behaviors (those behaviors that occur in the absence of external controls) were said to represent internal causality, whereas behaviors that are coerced or seduced by external forces were said to represent external causality. The intrinsic/extrinsic distinction sparked a great many experimental investigations (e.g., Deci, 1971, 1972; Kruglanski, Friedman, & Zeevi, 1971; Lepper, Green, & Nisbett, 1973; Ross, 1975) and considerable debate (e.g., Calder & Staw, 1975; Deci, Cascio, & Krusell, 1975). The central, and now well-known, finding from the studies was that extrinsic rewards can undermine intrinsic motivation, presumably through shifting the perceived locus of causality from internal to external. This finding has been difficult to reconcile with the operant theory view that all behavior is "motivated" by extrinsic reinforcements (e.g., Reiss & Sushinsky, 1975) and with the expectancy theory view that the effects of intrinsic and extrinsic motivation are simply additive (e.g., Porter & Lawler, 1968).

BEHAVIORAL REGULATION: SELF-DETERMINATION

As the research on intrinsic motivation continued, a number of experiments began to show that extrinsic rewards do not necessarily undermine intrinsic motivation, even though the early research (e.g., Deci, 1971) indicated that on average they do. For example, Ryan (1982) found that positive feedback could either enhance or diminish intrinsic motivation, depending on the way the feedback was worded, and Ryan, Mims, and Koestner (1983) found that performance-contingent monetary rewards could either increase or decrease intrinsic motivation depending on the interpersonal context within which they were administered. Other studies (e.g., Koestner, Ryan, Bernieri, & Holt, 1984; Pallak, Costomiris, Sroka, & Pittman, 1982; Pittman, Davey, Alafat, Wetherill, & Kramer, 1980) revealed similar findings.

These and other types of evidence led us (Deci & Ryan, 1985b) to suggest that the simple intrinsic/extrinsic dichotomy had in a sense outlived its usefulness. The two types of motivation are dynamically different and need to be kept separate for some analytic purposes; but the undifferentiated approach of pitting extrinsic motivation against intrinsic motivation is misleading. In particular, we have suggested that characterizing all extrinsically motivated behavior as having a perceived external locus of causality is incorrect. Instead, whereas intrinsically motivated action is definitionally self-determined, as deCharms (1968) originally suggested, we argue that extrinsically motivated action can vary in its degree of self-determination, thus having either a relatively internal or a relatively external perceived locus of causality. Accordingly, any intentional action can be described using the perceived locus of causality continuum and thus can be said to be more or less self-determined, a point we will return to in the section on internalization.

To summarize in categorical terms, we suggest that the regulation of actions can be viewed as being *self-determined, controlled,* or *amotivated*. Both self-determined and controlled behaviors are intentional, though only self-determined behaviors involve a true sense of choice, a sense of feeling free in doing what one has chosen to do. Controlled behaviors, although undertaken with the *intent* of achieving an outcome, are not truly chosen. Rather, they are compelled by some internal or external force; one feels one *has to* do them, whether to attain a monetary payment or to appease some generalized sense of authority. Both self-determined and controlled behaviors require at least a moderate sense of being able to *control* or attain outcomes (that is, they require contingency and efficacy beliefs), though as noted they differ greatly in how the behaviors are initiated and regulated.

Amotivated actions, in contrast, are those whose occurrence is not mediated by intentionality. In other words, amotivation with respect to an action refers to the person's being ineffective in regulating it; its occurrence is thus experienced as impersonally caused.

Having differentiated intentional actions along a perceived locus of causality continuum, anchored by self-determination and control, it would be instructive to return to the concept of human agency. Agency, as we previously noted, is central to an organismic perspective; it describes the inherent tendency of organisms to originate behavior, to relate to and assimilate events, and to gain a sense of effectance. In human psychology, this spontaneous, agentic tendency is the basis of self-determination. Accordingly, in our theory, an intentional action would be said to typify human agency only to the extent that it is self-determined. Behavior that is initiated by external or internal prods and coercion lacks a sense of volition or choice and would not be said to represent true agency, even though it is intentional.

Theories that do not distinguish between self-determined and controlled behavior—that do not have the concept of autonomy (or self-determination) as an integral aspect—often confuse the meaning of agency. A case in point is a recent discussion of the topic by Bandura (1989). After summarily dismissing the concept of "autonomous agency" by defining it as action that is "wholly independent of environmental influences," Bandura ascribed agency to any intentional action, adding that self-efficacy is the central mechanism of agency. The problem in doing that, however, is that people can be intentional, with high efficacy expectations, and yet lack a sense of psychological freedom with respect to the outcomes they are competent at attaining. They can have self-efficacy and still be pawns, driven toward action or outcomes either by heteronomous forces or by introjected pressures. By equating the concepts of agency and intentionality, self-efficacy theory implicitly makes the peculiar application of the term "agency" to cases where one is a pawn, thereby continuing to miss the important distinction that is made by the concept of self-determination (or autonomy). The idea of human agency properly refers to action that is characterized by an internal perceived causality—that is self-determined—rather than to all intentional action.

This point is much more than a theoretical quibble. As we will see later, in the section on culture, it is integral to a meaningful understanding of how people can be involved yet still be free with respect to economic and political forces in their societal context.

Amotivation. Unlike self-determined and controlled behavior, amotivated action is not intentional—that is, the person does not try to do it—and as such it represents what Heider referred to as impersonal causation. A clear though uninteresting example would be someone's being unexpectedly knocked over from behind. There is movement in the affected person but no intention, and in a certain sense the movement would not even be considered a behavior. A more classic instance of amotivation is the type of passivity or disorganized action that results from the experience of not being able to achieve a desired outcome, whether because of one's own incompetence in that domain or because of some barrier such as a rigid, arbitrary authority who dispenses outcomes in an unpredictable way. In spite of wanting an outcome, one will not act in a predictable, goal-oriented fashion because of the experienced inability to attain it. There may be action, but it is likely to be disorganized and accompanied by the feelings of frustration, fear, or depression. This type of amotivation occurs at the external boundary—the boundary between the person and the external world. Amotivation at the external boundary is similar to what Seligman (1975) called helplessness.

A more interesting and complex instance of amotivation is exemplified by a man who actively intends one behavior (for example, not hitting his friend) yet behaves in a different way (he hits the friend). He has an intention to behave one way, yet he cannot control himself. Of course, the action of hitting is motivated by a dynamic, nonconscious process; but with respect to the behavior of *not hitting* there is amotivation, a helplessness with regard to execution of the intention. This represents amotivation at the internal boundary (the boundary between the self and nonintegrated internal forces). One is ineffective or amotivated with respect to forces, such as affects or impulses, that are within one rather than forces that are in the environment.

INTRINSIC/EXTRINSIC REVISITED

The dichotomy that was posed in the early studies between intrinsic motivation and extrinsic control does represent the paradigmatic example of the difference between an internal and an external perceived locus of causality (between self-determined and controlled action). Intrinsic motivation is the prototypical form of self-determination: with a full sense of choice, with the experience of doing what one wants, and without the feeling of coercion or compulsion, one spontaneously engages in an activity that interests one. The action emanates from oneself and is thus *self*-determined. By focusing on intrinsic motivation as a starting point for studying self-determination, researchers have been able to detail the characteristics of behavior that epitomizes self-determination—behavior that represents a template against which other behaviors can be compared. Thus, for operational purposes, we would say that the more closely the qualities of a behavior approximate those of intrinsically motivated behavior, the more that behavior would be said to be self-determined.

The behaviors that were referred to as "extrinsically motivated" in most of the experiments of the past two decades are those that were either coerced or seduced by externally administered consequences—the receipt of a reward or the avoidance of punishment, for example. The convincing evidence that the rewards and threats were controlling (and thus that the behaviors were controlled) was that when they were given to subjects for doing an intrinsically interesting activity, the subjects typically lost interest in the activity and were willing to continue it only if the external inducement continued. The subjects' behavior had become dependent upon those inducements, and the perceived locus of causality changed from internal to external.

As we mentioned earlier, however, the presence of an extrinsic incentive does not ensure external causality or controlled behavior. Experiments have shown, for example, that a person can be autonomous or self-determined in the presence of extrinsic rewards or structures (Ryan, Mims, & Koestner, 1983), and thus we would say that the pursuit of extrinsic goals can be fully endorsed by one's self. Accordingly, extrinsically motivated behavior may have either an external or an internal perceived locus of causality.

One process that is central for externally prompted (i.e., extrinsically motivated) behaviors' becoming self-determined is described by the idea of internalization. That term has been used by many theorists, with widely differing theoretical and metatheoretical perspectives, to describe the change from outer to inner regulation (e.g., Collins, 1977; English & English, 1958; Hartmann & Loewenstein, 1962; Lepper, 1983). Schafer's (1968) description of internalization as a process by which people *actively transform* external regulations into internal regulations is perhaps the most compatible with our own view, because it emphasizes that internalization is something the person does—something, we would say, that *the person is motivated to do*—rather than something that *is done to the person.*

In a developmental analysis we have outlined a continuum representing the degree to which the regulation of a nonintrinsically motivated behavior has been internalized (e.g., Deci & Ryan, 1985b; Ryan & Connell, 1989; Ryan, Connell, & Deci, 1985). We begin with the assumption that many behaviors and values come to be acquired in the course of socialization that were not originally interesting or intrinsically motivated but that may be important for effective functioning in the social world. Typically such behaviors have to be initially encouraged through extrinsic structures, contingent approval, or tangible incentives. The goal of socialization, however, entails acceptance by the individual of the value of such culturally transmitted practices and taking responsibility for performing them. Ultimately, a person who is fully socialized with respect to a behavior would perform it volitionally, independent of the original prompt. This requires *internalization,* and our analysis asserts that, as one more fully internalizes and accepts the regulation of behavior, one will experience a greater sense of willingness and self-initiation.

INTERNALIZATION: SELF-DETERMINED EXTRINSIC MOTIVATION

As people interact with the social order, they adapt to some aspects of it while modifying others to make them more conducive to satisfying their needs for autonomy, competence, and relatedness. Internalization is the process through which people make the adaptation—through which they accept values and regulatory processes that are endorsed by the social order but are not intrinsically appealing. In our view, internalization is a natural outcome of organismic integration that occurs as people encounter the challenge of achieving meaningful relationships with others. To be accepted as part of a dyad, family, group, or culture, people must share social practices and ideals, whether or not the practices are interesting or their personal value is initially apparent. To a large extent, it is the need for relatedness that provides the primary impetus for internalizing values and regulatory processes. Wanting to find their place in the social order, people are motivated to connect with and accommodate to that order.

Integrating social values and regulatory processes requires more than merely accommodating, however; it requires identifying with them and bringing them into a coherent relation to other aspects of the self. Here the need for autonomy can be seen to be particularly important. To be self-determining with respect to internalized regulatory processes and structures, one must fully assimilate them; that is, one must accept them as one's own and bring them into a consistent relation to the other needs, processes, and values that represent self.

Elsewhere (Deci & Ryan, 1985b; Ryan & Connell, 1989), we have suggested that people can be more or less successful in their attempts at integration, and thus we described three types of internalized regulation that differ in the extent to which they represent autonomous self-regulation. Before any internalization has occurred, a person is likely to engage in an uninteresting activity only when requested to do so by another, with explicit or implicit rewards or sanctions accompanying the request. We label such behaviors *externally* regulated because they are done for the external inducement. The least self-determined of the three types of internalized regulation is referred to as *introjected regulation.* It occurs when one has taken in, or introjected, a value or structure but has not fully accepted it as one's own. In the classic forms of introjection, the socializing agent still figures phenomenally in the regulation of action; compliance is thus associated with a sense of the other's approval, whereas transgressions connote imagined disapproval. In the more common forms it involves establishing "shoulds" or rules for action that are associated with or enforced by the expectations of self-approval or of avoiding guilt and anxiety. In either case, when regulations are introjected there is an inherent tension because the person is still in a sense "being regulated" rather than operating with an integrated sense of volition. Introjected regulatory processes can also be more or less critical and evaluative, and more or less demanding, depending on the quality of the original external structures and the social contexts in which they were acquired. Although varied in affective tone and intensity, however, they nonetheless represent instances of internal regulatory processes that have not been fully integrated with the self and thus accepted as one's own. Accordingly, introjected regulation does not represent self-determination.

If organismic integration continues to function with respect to an introjected regulatory process, one may identify with the importance of the activity for oneself and thus accept it as one's own. The regulation that would follow is referred to as *identified* regulation and represents greater self-determination than does introjected regulation. When the person has identified with a regulatory structure, there is less experience of pressure and conflict and less salience of guilt and anxiety. What may be missing, however, is consistency between this and other identifications that may have been internalized. For example, identifications between achievement strivings and caregiving roles can be strong within an individual and yet at times be antagonistic and conflictful. Thus the most self-determined form of internalized regulation is referred to as *integrated* regulation. One comes to experience an organization among regulatory processes within which they can harmoniously coexist. This would be accompanied by the feeling of integrity in action and cohesion of the self. As one becomes more integrated, these various identifications would not remain "isolated molecules" but rather would find a smooth and balanced synthesis, being reciprocally assimilated and meaningfully hierarchically organized. When regulatory structures are well integrated one's action is experienced as personally valued and freely done. Thus integrated action is *authentic* in the full sense of emanating from the "author," of displaying full self-endorsement.

It is worth noting that even after a behavioral regulation has been fully integrated, it is typically still extrinsically motivated because it is usually still an instrumental action—done because of its importance for achieving personal goals rather than because of its inherent or intrinsic interest. Nonetheless it would be self-determined, because it would be undertaken willingly and with no sense of coercion.

To summarize, in this theoretical analysis of internalization we have attempted to show that extrinsically motivated behaviors can be more or less self-determined; that internalization, which is a natural aspect of organismic integration, is the underlying process that allows people to be self-determined with respect to extrinsic motivation; that this process is motivated by people's basic psychological needs; and that some internalized regulatory structures have not been (and may never be) integrated with the self and thus do not represent self-determination. We turn now to a theoretical consideration of emotional regulation in which we will also suggest that behavior motivated by one's emotions may also either be or not be self-determined.

EMOTIONAL INTEGRATION

Emotions have been a focus of psychological study for over a century (e.g., Lange, 1885). Most psychologists interested in the topic agree that emotions involve a physiological response to some real or imagined stimulus, accompanied by an experiential component. There is less agreement about whether, if that experiential component is blocked from awareness, there is still an emotion, though we strongly subscribe to the view that there is. Further, many theorists also agree that the physiological change and experience that constitute an emotion are associated with an inherent impulse or behavioral tendency (e.g., James, 1890) that can result in action. When one is angry, for example, the impulse may be to strike; when frightened, to flee; and when joyful, to exclaim.

Although there is disagreement about the extent of cognitive and self-relevant mediators between the referent stimulus and the subsequent emotional behavior (e.g., James, 1890; Schachter, 1966), it seems useful to consider three aspects of that mediating process. The first two, as proposed by Arnold (1960), are the immediate intuitive appraisals and the slower reflective judgments through which people interpret and give meaning to the stimulus. These processes are the antecedents of emotional experience. The third mediating element concerns the regulation of the behavior that is motivated (i.e., energized) by the emotion. In our view the development of self-determination with respect to emotions relates to both the second and third of these mediating elements. It involves learning both to reflectively interpret stimuli in more integrated ways and to regulate one's emotion-motivated behavior more autonomously.

Several current theories of emotion (e.g., Weiner, 1986) interpret reflective judgment as a self-attributional process. They posit that people assess outcomes with respect to such dimensions as internality, controllability, globality, and stability and then feel particular emotions as a function of the resulting attributions. Our understanding of the role of cognitive activity as a mediator of emotional experience is quite different, however, and can be seen to be much closer to the position expressed by Rogers (1951) when he suggested that emotions are a function of the relation of a stimulus to one's organismic and self-actualization.

From our motivational perspective, the interpretive process involves assessing the relation of events and stimuli to one's needs, goals, and expectations. The interpretation becomes the proximal antecedent of the emotion. Stimuli that threaten one's needs or goals may occasion fear or anger, for example, whereas those that satisfy them may occasion enjoyment or pride. This interpretive process, however, can operate with respect to introjects and other unintegrated aspects of a person or with respect to intrinsic and integrated aspects. When the internal state or standard against which a stimulus is appraised represents an integrated aspect of one's self, the emotional experience will be more integrated—that is, it will be more fully in awareness and will more authentically reflect the self. When the basis for appraisal is an unintegrated aspect of the person, however, as with ego involvement or contingent self-worth, the emotion will be less flexible and more pressured; it may be less fully experienced and more subject to defensive reactions such as projection. It will less fully express one's self.

The other issue concerning self-determination (or integration) with respect to emotions relates to the regulation of emotion-motivated behavior and concerns the extent to which a behavior that follows an emotion is determined by the emotion itself or is chosen by the person. Emotions are strong internal forces, with evolutionarily determined and genetically endowed behavioral tendencies (e.g., James, 1890) that can lead automatically to behaviors or can, to a greater or lesser extent, be mediated by intentional processes. As a person develops within the self a set of flexible and coherent processes and structures for regulating emotions, that person will become more self-determined with respect to emotional behaviors. The emotion will serve as an input to the process of behavioral choice rather than determining the behavior. In other words, the person will experience choice with respect to the behavior that is based on a full awareness of the emotion and of the goals and values relevant to it.

In many ways, the process of integration at the internal boundary (e.g., emotional integration) is similar to integration at the external boundary. Both involve developing integrated regulatory processes and values that relate to one's basic sense of self. Out of the need for competence (i.e., to be effective), the need for relatedness (to be involved with others in a satisfying way), and the need for autonomy (to act in accord with the self), people gradually develop and integrate processes and structures for interpreting information and regulating their experience and action.

As with other types of motivated behavior, our theory describes three broad classes of emotion-motivated behavior. Some emotional behaviors, we assert, are accompanied by a true sense of choice and freedom; they have an internal perceived locus of causality and are said to be self-determined. Other emotional behaviors are accompanied by a sense of pressure, for example, to preserve self-worth or to avoid guilt; they have an external perceived locus of causality and are referred to as being controlled. Controlled behaviors, like self-determined ones, are intentional; the person acts to achieve a desired outcome or effect. Yet with controlled behaviors the person feels compelled rather than free, and the behaviors are rigid rather than flexible. Finally, there are still other emotional behaviors in which one is overwhelmed by an emotion and its impulses; one behaves automatically because one is unable to regulate the behavior intentionally. Indeed, such behaviors may even occur in spite of one's intending not to do them. Here the regulation of the emotion-driven action is said to be amotivated, in the sense that it is not mediated, regulated, or endorsed by a sense of intentionality.

Empirical Evidence: The Integrated Self

The development of self involves an organismic integration process through which intrinsic interests and capacities become elaborated and refined. One develops a set of flexible, unified regulatory processes and values that allow one to engage more willingly in socially prompted and emotionally motivated activities, while feeling both self-determined and connected with others. Related to this view is the premise that many processes, structures, and forces that are internal to the person are not integral to the self. Introjected structures, for example, are not considered integrated with one's self, nor are emotions for which integrated interpretive and regulatory processes have not been developed.

In the past few years, we and our associates at Rochester and elsewhere have begun three types of research to test this formulation. Let us consider these in turn.

INTERNALLY CONTROLLING REGULATION: EXPERIMENTS

Ryan (1982) first argued that some internal events relevant to the initiation and regulation of behavior are controlling and pressuring and thus inhibit autonomy. The initial experimental research on this topic (Ryan, 1982) employed the concept of ego involvement, a concept that has been prominent in psychology for many years.

Sherif and Cantril (1947) defined ego involvement in terms of the contents of one's ego that provide standards of judgment or frames of reference. Both Alper (1942) and Greenwald (1982) asserted that there has been no general agreement about how best to treat the concept theoretically, although Alper (1942) suggested that experimenters who had researched the concept seem to have agreed that it means "threats to self-esteem." Greenwald (1982) later proposed that there are three types of ego involvement, agreeing that contingent self-esteem is one of the forms. Breckler and Greenwald (1986) later equated the idea of self-esteem-contingent ego involvement with achievement motivation (McClelland, Atkinson, Clark, & Lowell, 1953), a comparison we believe is inappropriate. Achievement motivation is based on the desire to match an internal standard, although, as we have argued elsewhere (e.g., Ryan, Connell, & Grolnick, in press), the standard can be highly variable in how well it is integrated. Achievement can, for example, be motivated by standards that serve to preserve contingent self-esteem or by standards that are fully and flexibly endorsed by one's self. Thus achievement motivation can be more or less self-determined.

The general strategy in the experiments on ego-involvement has been to induce an ego-involved (i.e., self-esteem contingent) orientation in some subjects and a task-involved orientation in others while they work on an interesting activity. The first agenda in this research strategy was to assess the subsequent intrinsic motivation for the target activity of ego-involved versus task-involved subjects. The idea was that if ego involvement decreased subjects' intrinsic motivation for the target activity, this would indicate that the ego-involved regulatory process is controlling and thus restricts subjects' self-determination.

To test this experimentally, Ryan (1982) reasoned that students at a competitive university could easily become ego-involved (self-esteem contingent) in their performance on achievement tasks. Thus he employed a hidden-figures task and told the "ego-involvement" subjects that performance on this task reflected creative intelligence. "In fact," he added, "hidden-figures tasks are often used in IQ tests." Ryan suggested that this would lead subjects to be contingently evaluative of themselves and thus internally controlling in their approach to the task, thus precluding true self-determination. A decrease in intrinsic motivation was predicted for ego-involved subjects relative to those who were task involved. Results supported this prediction; subjects who had been given the ego-involvement induction displayed less subsequent intrinsic motivation, as assessed by the behavioral free-choice measure, than subjects who had been given a rather neutral, task-involved induction. Plant and Ryan (1985) replicated this result, as did Koestner, Zuckerman, and Koestner (1987) and Ryan and Deci (1989). In the Ryan and Deci experiment the instructions were automated, using a tape recorder, so the subjects would not have to interact with the experimenter. That minimized the extent to which the detrimental effect could be attributed to interpersonal rather than intrapsychic controlling processes.

Plant and Ryan (1985) took a complementary approach to exploring this problem. They reasoned that if subjects are made "objectively self-aware" (Duval & Wicklund, 1972)—that is, aware of themselves as if observed from the outside—they would be more likely to be controlling in regulating themselves. In their study some subjects worked on an interesting activity in front of a mirror and some worked in front of a video camera, both procedures having previously been used to induce objective self-awareness. Comparison subjects worked on the task in conditions not expected to induce objective self-awareness. Results indicated, as predicted, that objective self-awareness decreased subjects' intrinsic motivation, thus further confirming that the regulatory process we refer to as *internally controlling* does not represent self-determination and is to some extent antagonistic to it.

Performance feedback is extremely important when people are ego-involved in achievement, because performance outcomes are the basis on which they judge their self-worth. The function of positive feedback is thus instrumental for attaining their internally controlling goal of maintaining self-esteem. When they get positive feedback, they have accomplished their goal and have no further need to persist at the activity. On the other hand, if ego-involved subjects do not get positive feedback (particularly on an ambiguous task where they cannot reliably assess their own performance), they will not have achieved the goal of succeeding and thus maintaining their sense of self-worth. Consequently, they are very likely to persist at the activity during the subsequent free-choice period, so that at least they can observe improvement in themselves and thus have some "self-administered" positive feedback. In the Ryan and Deci

(1989) experiment, ego-involved subjects received either positive feedback or no feedback after their performance on a task that involved drawing with their nondominant hand. As predicted, subjects who did not receive positive feedback persisted significantly longer than those who did, a finding opposite from the more typical pattern of positive feedback's enhancing intrinsically motivated persistence.

The study helps to clarify the conditions under which internally controlling regulation will lead people to persist at an activity— when the persistence may be instrumental to attaining their internal, controlling goal. However, it also highlights the methodological problem that free-choice behavior, long used to assess intrinsic motivation, may not be a wholly appropriate measure when used in experiments that stimulate ego-involvement. Intrinsic motivation and ego-involvement are different (in fact, incompatible) forms of internal motivation, yet they sometimes have the same behavioral manifestation of persistence (Deci & Ryan, 1985b).

ASSESSMENTS OF REASONS FOR ACTING

A second type of research that has differentiated types of internal motivation and explored the extent to which the regulation of action is autonomous focuses on the reasons people report or endorse for engaging in various actions. Reasons can vary from being very external (e.g., I do it because others make me) to being intrinsic (e.g., I do it because it's fun) and can include each of the internalized forms of regulation. Thus, the reasons people give for their actions can vary along the continuum from an external to an internal perceived locus of causality.

Ryan and Connell (1989) provided initial evidence for this conceptualization by asking children to endorse the salience of external, introjected, identified, and intrinsic reasons for doing their schoolwork. The data confirmed that the external, introjected, identified, and intrinsic scales formed a simplexlike pattern, suggesting that the four regulatory styles can be ordered along a single dimension of self-determination or autonomy. Further, the researchers found that the more autonomous styles (identification and intrinsic) were positively correlated with enjoyment of school, expenditure of effort, proactive coping, and perception of the classroom context as being autonomy supportive, while the less autonomous styles were correlated with anxiety and poor coping. Introjection in particular was strongly correlated with anxiety and with anxiety amplification following failure, thus highlighting the inner tension resulting from unintegrated proscriptions. In a study using the same survey of reasons, Grolnick and Ryan (1987) found that students who endorsed more autonomous reasons for school-related behaviors had better long-term memory for material they were exposed to in a learning task. This suggests that the relative autonomy of achievement-related behavior influences the quality of learning.

Ryan and Connell (1989) also presented a scale of prosocial self-regulation during middle childhood and adolescence that assessed external, introjected, and identified styles of regulation. These scales again showed intercorrelations conforming to a simplexlike pattern, and the researchers found that identified regulation in the prosocial domain was associated with empathy, moral reasoning, and positive relatedness to others, indicating that more autonomous self-regulation is associated with a variety of positive outcomes.

Taken together, work with the two questionnaires suggests that it is useful to understand regulatory styles in terms of a gradient of autonomy or self-determination and that the styles reflecting greater autonomy are associated with a range of variables that indicate higher levels of personal adjustment and effective functioning. The difference between the introjected style—the internal regulatory style that is quite controlling—and the identified and intrinsic styles is particularly important for illustrating that some internal regulatory processes and values are *not* fully self-determined.

Vallerand, Blais, Briere, and Pelletier (1989) developed a related scale, in French, for assessing reasons in the academic domain among college-age students and found results that complemented those of Ryan and Connell. Their scale included an amotivation subscale as well, and they found, for example, that amotivation correlated negatively with interest and with satisfaction in school, whereas identification correlated positively with both.

Blais, Sabourin, Boucher, and Vallerand (1990) assessed adults' reasons for living with their spouses by elaborating on this methodology. They included six types of reasons—amotivation, external, introjected, identified, integrated, and intrinsic—and found, in a sample of 63 heterosexual couples, that the six reason categories conformed to a simplex model (again supporting the idea of a self-determination continuum). Results also showed that the three regulatory styles constituting absence of self-determination (amotivation, external, and introjected) all correlated significantly negatively with dyadic adjustment, with agreement in 26 areas of marital relations (e.g., finances, contraception), and with general marital happiness. On the other hand, the three regulatory styles constituting higher levels of self-determination (identification, integration, and intrinsic) all correlated significantly positively with those same variables. Finally, these researchers tested a path model in which each partner's level of self-determination (i.e., regulatory style) predicted his or her perceptions of the couple's adaptive behaviors, which in turn predicted each partner's happiness/satisfaction in the relationship. This model explained 61% of the variance for the male's marital satisfaction and 55% of the variance for the female's, thereby further supporting the utility of distinguishing degrees of self-determination in one's motivation.

Ongoing work in various domains is continuing to show the importance of the continuum of relative autonomy. New results in the areas of religion (King, 1990; O'Connor & Vallerand, 1990), health care programs (Plant, 1990), and schools (Grolnick, Ryan, & Deci, 1990) indicate that the more integrated and autonomous one's motives for engagement, the more positive are the outcomes and attitudes associated with it.

INDIVIDUAL DIFFERENCES: CAUSALITY ORIENTATIONS

The third line of research relevant to organismic integration and self-determination involves the concept of general causality orientations (Deci & Ryan, 1985b). The *autonomy orientation* describes people's general tendency to orient toward inputs relevant to interest and choice (inputs that promote self-determination); the *control orientation* describes people's general tendency to orient toward salient controls in initiating and regulating their behavior; and the *impersonal orientation* describes people's general tendency to orient toward cues that signify incompetence or lack of control and are thus amotivating.

The construction and validation of an instrument to assess general causality orientations was reported in a paper by Deci and Ryan (1985a). In it we suggested that everyone is to some degree autonomy oriented, to some degree control oriented, and to some degree impersonally oriented. Thus the scale gives three subscale scores, one for each orientation, which can be used separately or together in making various predictions.

Briefly, the autonomy orientation was positively correlated with self-esteem, ego development, self-actualization, and the tendency to support other people's self-determination. The control orientation, in contrast, was positively correlated with the type-A coronary-prone behavior pattern and with public self-consciousness, and the impersonal orientation was positively related to self-derogation, social anxiety, and an external locus of control (which, as we mentioned earlier, assesses the belief about behavior-outcome independence that relates to nonintentionality). Other research using the scale has shown that cardiac patients high on the autonomy orientation viewed their surgery more as a challenge than as a threat and reported more positive postoperative attitudes than did patients low on the autonomy orientation (King, 1984). Also, the impersonal orientation discriminated restrictive anorexic patients from patients with other subtypes of eating disorders and from matched comparison subjects (Strauss & Ryan, 1987).

In a recent study of general causality orientations, Koestner, Bernieri, and Zuckerman (1991) directly explored the relation of autonomy to integration in personality. Their strategy was to convert scores on the autonomy and control orientations of their college-student subjects to z-scores and to use those scores to form an autonomy-oriented group and a control-oriented group. They then explored the consistency of behavior, attitudes, and traits among these two groups, with the general hypothesis that autonomy-oriented subjects would evince greater integration or consistency across these aspects of personality than would control-oriented subjects.

First, the authors considered the relation between the free-choice behavioral measure and the self-report-of-interest measure of intrinsic motivation, because previous studies had shown only modest correlations between these two measures (Harackiewicz,

1979; Ryan, Mims, & Koestner, 1983). Koestner et al. (1991) used the data from two intrinsic motivation laboratory experiments and looked separately at the correlations between attitudes and behavior within the autonomy-oriented group and the control-oriented group. In both experiments the correlation for the autonomy-oriented subjects was in excess of 0.6, whereas for the control-oriented subjects there was no correlation. It appears from these data that the more autonomy-oriented subjects display greater integration between behaviors and feelings than do the less self-determined subjects. The behavior of the latter group is apparently based on controlling thoughts or contingencies rather than on the subjects' feelings and interests.

In a second study, Koestner et al. (1991) had subjects come to a lab and complete a trait measure of conscientiousness. As the subjects were about to leave, the experimenter gave them a questionnaire and asked them to complete it at home and drop it off at the Psychology Department office. The researchers then correlated subjects' conscientiousness score with the behavior of returning the questionnaire and found that this trait-behavior correlation for the autonomy-oriented group was significantly greater than for the control-oriented group. Finally, the researchers had a friend of each subject rate the person on various traits, including conscientiousness, and they correlated the self- and peer ratings. Here the correlation for the autonomy-oriented subjects was marginally stronger than for the control-oriented subjects. Taken together, these studies provide initial support for the theoretical proposition that autonomy is associated with greater congruence between self-report and action and reflects greater integration in personality.

Results of a study by Lonky and Reihman (1990) complemented those of Koestner et al. (1991). These researchers developed a domain-specific causality orientations scale to examine motivational orientations toward school achievement, and they used the measure to investigate whether college students' orientations would predict cheating under varied conditions. In the study, Lonky and Reihman found an association between motivational orientation and moral reasoning, with greater autonomy predicting higher levels of moral reasoning (more principled reasoning). Furthermore, motivational orientations did predict cheating, in that subjects high in autonomy cheated less and subjects high in control and impersonal orientations cheated more. From this one could infer that subjects who were more autonomous in their orientation seemed to display greater integration or consistency between the development of moral reasoning and morally relevant behavior, thus providing further evidence for the general association between integration and self-determination.

The Role of Social Contexts: Theory and Evidence

Intrinsic growth strivings are at the core of the self and are displayed through tendencies toward integration both within and between persons. People seek optimal challenges, as well as dealing with the situations they encounter, and in doing so they attempt to satisfy their basic needs for competence, autonomy, and relatedness. Thus, in their interactions with the environment, people seek competence-enhancing feedback, they attempt to express personal choice and initiative, and they work to feel meaningfully related to others. People's success in satisfying these needs and actualizing their growth strivings depends to a considerable extent on the interpersonal dynamics of the context within which they occur.

In our view, people give meaning to inputs from the real or imagined social environment, and those psychological meanings—what we have often referred to as the *functional significance* of inputs or contexts—represent the antecedents of action. The functional significance, we suggest, is based in the relation of the inputs to the person's opportunities for satisfying the three basic needs.

PROMOTING COMPETENCE AND AUTONOMY

Our early studies on facilitating contexts explored the role of competence feedback and autonomy support in the promotion of intrinsically motivated behaviors. We reasoned that feeling competent with respect to an activity—in other words, being reliably able to achieve desired outcomes and to experience effectance in action—is necessary for intentional or motivated behavior. To the extent that circumstances afford access to competence-relevant information and clarity of contingencies, they are more likely to promote motivated, intentional action. Conversely, a context is likely to be experienced as amotivating if it ensures or signifies that one cannot attain desired outcomes. Environments with inadequate structure—in other words, those that involve behavior-outcome independence (e.g., Seligman, 1975) or blocks to competence (Deci, Cascio, & Krusell, 1973)—have been found to amotivate.

Being motivated, however, does not ensure self-determination or its prototype, intrinsic motivation. Thus, for example, although positive feedback has often been found to increase intrinsic motivation (e.g., Boggiano & Ruble, 1979; Vallerand & Reid, 1984), other studies have shown definitively that promoting or affirming competence will enhance intrinsic motivation *only* when accompanied by a noncontrolling or autonomy-supportive ambience (Fisher, 1978; Ryan, 1982). In much of our writing, we have used the term *informational* to describe contexts that both promote competence and support autonomy by providing effectance-relevant inputs in the absence of control. Promoting or affirming competence in controlling situations (i.e., in the absence of autonomy support) does not enhance intrinsic motivation; rather, it promotes controlled intentional behavior (non-self-determined extrinsic motivation).

Since our primary agenda has been to differentiate motivated activity with respect to the concept of self-determination, much of our research has focused on the autonomy-supportive versus controlling dimension. We will briefly review that work, though detailed reviews appear elsewhere (Deci & Ryan, 1980, 1985b, 1987).

The initial experiments on intrinsic motivation indicated that task-contingent rewards (Deci, 1971), good-player awards (Lepper, Greene, & Nisbett, 1973), avoidance of unpleasant stimuli (Deci & Cascio, 1972), deadlines (Amabile, DeJong, & Lepper, 1976), imposed goals (Mossholder, 1980), surveillance (Lepper & Greene, 1975), and social evaluation (Smith, 1974) all undermined intrinsic motivation. These events, we suggest, tend to be experienced as controlling because the intent behind them is usually to "motivate" or pressure people to behave, think, or feel in specific ways. Pressuring locution such as "Be a good boy (girl) and do X" or "You should do X" has also been found to be controlling and to undermine intrinsic motivation (e.g., Koestner et al., 1984). In contrast, offering people explicit choices (Zuckerman, Porac, Lathin, Smith, & Deci, 1978) and using nonpressuring locution (Ryan et al., 1983) have been found to maintain or enhance intrinsic motivation.

Field studies have yielded complementary findings. When the general interpersonal context, such as a classroom climate (Deci, Schwartz, Sheinman, & Ryan, 1981; Ryan & Grolnick, 1986) or a work-group climate (Deci, Connell, & Ryan, 1989), is experienced as autonomy supportive rather than controlling, it has been associated with greater intrinsic motivation, trust, self-worth, and satisfaction. All these studies therefore highlight the importance of autonomy support for promoting intrinsically motivated behavior.

In recent work we have also considered the contextual factor of interpersonal involvement as it affects motivation and self-determination. By involvement, we refer to significant others' devoting psychological and material resources to interactions with a target person.

For intrinsically motivated behavior, the immediate involvement of others is often not necessary. People frequently do what interests them quite by themselves, although research with children has indicated that such independent intrinsic activity (e.g., exploration and interest, without the immediate involvement of significant others) is most likely to occur if the children experience secure interpersonal attachments (e.g., Ainsworth, Blehar, Waters, & Wall, 1978). When people do not feel secure, immediate involvement may become very important, as was revealed in a recent study of 4- and 5-year-old children by Anderson, Manoogian, and Reznick (1976). The study included a so-called neutral condition in which the children were given an interesting task in the presence of an experimenter/stranger who had been instructed not to interact with them. According to the researchers, the children tried repeatedly to interact with the adult, who did not respond, and subsequently the children displayed very low intrinsic motivation for the target activity. By not being involved, the experimenter had inadvertently had a strongly negative effect on the children's intrinsic motivation for the activity.

For internalization, ongoing involvement may be even more important than for intrinsic motivation, because internalization requires the significant others to provide the regulatory structures and to endorse and demonstrate the values that become internalized. In one study of internalization, Grolnick and Ryan (1989) employed structured interviews to assess parents' involvement as well as their autonomy support and structure. The researchers reported that parental involvement predicted children's feeling able to attain their desired outcomes and that it supplemented the effects of autonomy support in predicting children's identified and autonomous self-regulation. Grolnick, Ryan, and Deci (1990) extended this by using structural equation modeling to show that children's perceptions of their parents' autonomy support and involvement predicted more autonomous self-regulation (which in turn predicted school achievement). Further, using a very different approach, Avery and Ryan (1988) examined preadolescents' "object representations" of their parents and found that perceived parental autonomy support and involvement were related to the nurturing quality of the object representation, which was also related to the children's self-esteem and positive peer relations.

Believing that significant others' autonomy support and involvement are optimal for promoting internalization and integration, Eghrari and Deci (1989) attempted, in a laboratory paradigm, to isolate specific factors that could contribute to creating that optimal context. They reasoned that internalization of regulations requires understanding or having a rationale for why the activity is important to one's personal goals. In addition, people should be more willing to identify with and accept responsibility for that important regulation if they do not feel pressured and if their own feelings or points of view are acknowledged. Results of the experiment indicated that in fact the combination of these three specific factors—rationale, low control, and acknowledgment of the person's perspective—did lead both to the highest level of subsequent behavioral self-regulation and to the highest level of feeling free and enjoying the activity (Eghrari & Deci, 1989).

AUTONOMY AND RELATEDNESS IN SOCIAL CONTEXTS

As we have said, involvement by significant others refers to the quantity of time, attention, and other resources devoted to a target person. Involvement can, however, vary in nature or quality. The others can relate to a target person in ways that acknowledge the target's individuality and frame of reference, or they can be involved as if the target were a social object, an instrument for the others' own gratification. These differences in the quality of involvement are well captured by the autonomy-support dimension, so one can see how it is the *convergence* of involvement and autonomy support that promotes integration and development. For example, when an involved parent is also autonomy supportive, the child will be able to feel both autonomous and supported. But parents' involvement can also occur in combination with pressure and control. The technique of "withdrawal of love" is an example of how parents can be involved in an interpersonally controlling way. With this type of involvement, in which approval and affection are made contingent as a means of control, the child may have to sacrifice a sense of autonomy and personal development for the sake of approval. The need to be related is fundamental and basic, and the social context in which approval is made contingent upon particular behaviors can bring a person's needs for autonomy and relatedness into opposition. The unfortunate thing about this, of course, is that the synergy of these two needs' being satisfied is what promotes optimal development.

In contrast to our viewpoint, which asserts that the needs for autonomy and relatedness are complementary but that the social context may lead them to become antagonistic, a number of other theorists have suggested or implied that needs for autonomy and relatedness are themselves antithetical. For example, Steinberg and Silverberg (1986) have argued that developing autonomy entails breaking one's ties with family members, and other writers (e.g., Hare-Mustin & Marecek, 1986) seem to suggest that being concerned with autonomy precludes a concern with relatedness and interdependence. We believe, as indicated, that there is no inherent conflict between autonomy and relatedness, and we think the apparent contradiction between our viewpoint and the ones just mentioned results from the confusion of autonomy and independence. Consistently, we have defined autonomy as referring to a sense of endorsement and initiation with regard to one's own behavior. The opposite of autonomy is heteronomy, experienced as coercion or lack of self-determination and choice. In contrast, we construe the concept of independence as referring to the fact of not utilizing interpersonal resources, of not relying on others. Clearly, therefore, it is inappropriate to equate the concepts of autonomy and independence, and when theorists have done so, it has added confusion to the literature on autonomy, relatedness, and independence.

One *can* be autonomously interdependent, thus being willingly dependent on others and authentically providing care for others. In addition, one can be nonautonomous in one's independence, by breaking relational ties to prove one's self-worth or appease some other controlling forces. The concepts that do appear to be antithetical, then, are not relatedness and autonomy, but relatedness and independence. In fact, as the earlier-mentioned Blais et al. (1990) study indicated, one is likely to feel most secure and satisfied in interdependent relationships when one feels autonomously involved and similarly experiences the other as being involved by choice. Furthermore, a study of adolescents by Ryan and Lynch (1989) showed that optimal adjustment involves maintaining relatedness with family while developing greater autonomy, and that independence or detachment involves weakening relational ties.

To summarize, we have argued that the basic needs for autonomy and relatedness are complementarily important to developing intrapsychic and interpersonal integration. Furthermore, the social context created by significant others plays a critical role in whether individuals' strivings to be both autonomous and related will be actualized. Contexts in which others are both autonomy supportive and involved allow satisfaction of the individual's basic needs and are thus optimal for development, whereas those that are controlling by virtue of contingent love and approval can pit the basic needs against each other and impair development. As research has shown, the experience of autonomy support is an important element not only in developing one's autonomous self-regulation but also in maintaining and deepening relatedness to others both during one's infancy (Frodi, Bridges, & Grolnick, 1985) and in later years (Ryan & Lynch, 1989). In short, optimal contexts allow the needs for autonomy and relatedness to work catalytically in forming and enriching intrapersonal and interpersonal development and integration (Ryan, in press).

The Self in Social Context

At the beginning of this chapter we pointed out that there are two important features to many of the current empirically based theories of self: first, that self is viewed as a set of knowledge structures and cognitive mechanisms (e.g., Greenwald, 1988; Markus & Sentis, 1982); second, that the cognitive structures are treated primarily as reflections of social evaluations (e.g., Harter, 1988; Schlenker, 1980), a view that is perhaps most clearly expressed by Cooley's (1902) idea of the "looking-glass self." The theory of self that we are presenting is substantially different from those theories, and we shall now summarize the differences.

MOTIVATIONAL PROCESSES

The processes of self are fundamentally motivational. The self is replete with knowledge, but it is not merely a set of knowledge structures, because it has at its core an energizing component that has been termed intrinsic or growth motivation. In functioning to satisfy basic needs, one's self-related processes are synthetic. They operate to reciprocally assimilate aspects of one's inner and outer environments, thus expressing one's interests, conquering challenges, and fully internalizing values, practices, and styles of being. Actions that emanate from the self are experienced as spontaneous and volitional because they stem from processes that reflect the most vital and integral aspects of one's personality.

Acting from the self, people seek harmony, though not quiescence. In other words, people strive for coherence among all the aspects of themselves and their world that are in awareness, and they seek to uncover new aspects of each that can then be differentiated and integrated. The natural tendency toward synthesis does not, however, mean that people suppress and rationalize dissonant aspects of themselves in order to achieve consistency and quiescence; rather, it means that they engage—even seek—inconsistencies and treat them as nutriments to growth, so long as the inconsistencies do not constitute challenges that are too far beyond what is optimal for their capacities. Insofar as denial, rationalization, and defensive consistency are in evidence, then processes antithetical to self-determination have been operative.

Self-related processes are characterized as agentic or self-determined. The fundamental affect underlying these processes is *interest*. Through interest one makes contact with arising emotions and needs as well as with external inputs to action, and through interest one is able to guide or regulate intentional actions in a flexible, "choiceful" manner. This aids the tendency toward unity and coherence and the resultant experience of autonomy or self-determination.

There are, of course, other regulatory processes and structures within the person that do not represent self, but these unintegrated aspects exist in a kind of hierarchical relationship to the core self and thus are not simply "other selves." Many social-cognitive theories (e.g., Gergen, 1971; Kihlstrom & Cantor, 1984) specifically eschew the concept of a core self, positing instead that there are many different selves that have no natural or inherent relation to one another. Instead these selves are said to be interconnected as a function of the way the schemata have been "programmed" by social forces. For us, that view misses the essence of self and fails to acknowledge the developmental process of organismic integration with which human beings have been endowed by nature and through which self develops. To the extent that selves are separate in experience and functioning, there has been fractionization or lack of integration in personality. This is most likely to be in evidence under social conditions that lack the enhancing qualities of autonomy support, optimal structure, and involvement.

A REFLECTION OF SOCIAL PROCESSES?

The shifting focus in the field of motivation toward recognizing intrinsic motivation and organismic integration has emphasized that there are many innate aspects of the person. Infants are born with innate psychological needs—the needs for autonomy, competence, and relatedness—and throughout their lives they seek to satisfy these needs. They are born with general interests and innate capacities that go hand in hand to motivate their continued strivings for intrapersonal and interpersonal coherence. This view is *not*, however, equivalent to the view that abilities and interests are predetermined by genetics. Rather, it means that the innate organismic integration process, combined with very general capacities and behavioral tendencies, is the starting point for an ongoing developmental process that involves interacting with the social and physical surrounds to

differentiate and integrate, to elaborate and construct, to reciprocally assimilate.

An understanding of the development of *self*, we contend, requires that one begin from the frame of reference of the individual
rather than the social world. The self is not merely conditioned by
the social context. Quite the contrary, a child actively elaborates the
"self" by using nutriments from the social context. It is the child, acting from his or her experiential core, that is the basis for the continued development of self, and the importance of the social environment is that it can afford the supports for autonomy, effectance, and
relatedness that are essential for growth and development.

The social context can, however, also thwart development and
can "implant" structures or introjects that influence and regulate behavior but are not integral to the self. Only if regulations and values
are eventually integrated through the activity of the agentic self will
they become part of the self and thus reflect autonomy. Whether
that integration occurs depends both on whether the content of the
social learning is consistent with the person's basic needs and on
whether the social context provides the nutriments required for integration.

IMPLICATIONS: THE TRUE SELF

The idea of a "true self" has fascinated people throughout the centu-
ries. It appears in a variety of writings, yet it has seldom been discussed by empirical psychologists. In one sense that is easy to understand, because empirical psychologists have tended to employ
metatheoretical assumptions and theoretical concepts that can be
readily researched. By using mechanistic metatheories and by rul-
ing concepts such as "true self" out of consideration, research can be
conducted more straightforwardly. Yet human beings are, above all
else, living organisms, and we believe it is possible to begin with a
more organismic metatheory (one that acknowledges the human being as an active, living organism) and apply empirical methods to
the study of difficult psychological concepts. Accordingly, the concept of a true self *is* open to empirical exploration, and we have begun such exploration as we have elaborated self-determination theory. The concept of true self needs more empirical explication; but

such work is possible, and the starting point is the concept of intrinsic motivation. By studying the qualities of intrinsically motivated, autonomous behavior, we have found markers that can be used to judge empirically the extent to which a nonintrinsically motivated action is self-determined and thus the extent to which it emanates from the true or integrated self. These markers include behavioral qualities that can be observed (e.g., spontaneity and creativity; Koestner et al., 1984) as well as reasons for actions (e.g., interest and personal importance; Ryan & Connell, 1989), feelings (e.g., feeling free rather than pressured; Eghrari & Deci, 1989), and psycholinguistic indicators (e.g., expressing "wants" rather than "shoulds"; Ryan, 1982). If those who are interested in the concept of true self proceed astutely, it will be possible to continue developing empirical means for studying both what it is and how it relates to the false self or nonself that is manifest in introjected values, internally controlling regulatory "schemata," and other nonintegrated aspects of the psyche.

The view of self as action and development from within, as innate processes and motivations that lead people to master themselves (the internal boundary) and their environments (the external boundary), can also, we believe, represent an empirical means of addressing what some philosophers refer to as authenticity (e.g., Sartre, 1956; Wild, 1965). Authenticity, we suggest, is a descriptor for behavior that is an expression of the true self and for which one accepts full responsibility. When an action is endorsed by its "author," the experience is that of integrity and cohesion—the experience is one of being true to one's *self*. Authenticity is thus self-determination.

CULTURE: THE DIALECTIC OF HUMANITY

Throughout history one can find examples of repressive regimes and other cultural forces that are affronts to human dignity and have wreaked havoc on the well-being of citizens. Yet in spite of these, people have persevered and in many instances have emerged victorious. From the perspective of our theory, we analyze such situations in terms of the dialectic between the person, viewed in terms of intrinsic motivation and organismic integration, and the cultural forces, viewed in terms of growth-promoting versus controlling and amotivating influences. For us, the recent events in Eastern Europe have been a palpable and heartening instance in which the need for self-determination has emerged as a strong influence in spite of having been suppressed for decades by strong controlling and amotivating forces.

A less dramatic though interesting example of the interaction of individuals and cultural influences can be seen in phenomena within the current American culture, where great value is placed on wealth and material consumption. The advertising industry is organized to imbue goods and services with value and to implant those values in people. The aim of advertising is to control behavior, and one of its primary hooks is to link self-esteem to owning and using objects and engaging in activities. (Feel good about yourself, become a blond!) The value of consumerism that is so pervasive in Madison Avenue hype can be viewed as a strong controlling force that represents a challenge to the self. To be caught up in such forces is to be controlled, whereas to resist such forces—to integrate the content that has personal meaning and to leave the rest—is to be self-determined.

In this example one can see clearly how the definition of concepts like human agency is critical for explicating people's relation to the culture they live in. To equate the concept of agency with intentional action, as is done in social-cognitive theory (e.g., Bandura, 1989), can result in ascribing agency to actions that are controlled by insidious social forces. For example, pressured dieting to look like the much-heralded models of the media and aggressive accumulation of goods do not represent human agency; rather, they represent instances where behavior is driven by outcomes or by contingent self-esteem. Hard-driving, compulsive striving for achievement and wealth can similarly be viewed as well-anchored heteronomy rather than as personal freedom. True agency means more than knowing how to attain outcomes and being competent to do so; it means feeling free by making authentic and meaningful human choices with respect to those outcomes.

The concepts of intrinsic motivation and organismic integration provide a basis for understanding agency and freedom in human behavior and for seeing how people can gradually come to identify with the unconditional value of life. Out of the need to be genuinely related to the social world and to feel free, people can naturally come to accept the true selves of others as well as their own. In so doing, they will be accepting the value of life and will be able to see the possibilities for coexistence among all people and all forms of life; they will be able to achieve synthesis even in the face of controlling and amotivating social forces. The self as it works to integrate will continually encounter non-self-consistent values in such forms as controlling introjects and amotivated hatred. Fortunately, however, it is in the nature of self to struggle against such forces, to strive for integration rather than to be controlled or amotivated by them.

Epilogue

In his explication of the self, James (1890) made an interesting distinction between the "I" and the "me." The "I," he said, is the self as subject, the self as knower, whereas the "me" is the self as object, the self as known. It is instructive to consider this distinction in light of our current discussion. We agree, of course, that the self is both knower and known. However, some theories treat the self— both the knower and the known—as if it were an agentic *subject*, whereas others treat the self—again, both the knower and the known—as a passive *object*. This difference, we suggest, derives from whether the theory begins from the frame of reference of a person's viewing him- or herself as the locus of active development or alternatively from the extraspective frame of reference of the social environment, viewing it as the locus of a person's change.

To illustrate, let us begin by considering the work of Mead (1934), who presented an extensive discussion of the concepts of "I" and "me." He suggested that the "me" is an organized set of other people's attitudes that the person has assumed, whereas the "I" is the response of the organism to those attitudes. Although the response is somewhat unpredictable, said Mead, the "I" tends to fulfill its duty to the "me." In this conceptualization, the "me" is portrayed in "looking-glass" terms (Cooley, 1902), as a reflection of social processes, and the "I" is portrayed as if it were beholden to social demands that have been taken on to form the "me." Accordingly, even the "I" becomes largely a passive object, a knower and an actor that is under the thumb of the "me."

Alternatively, consider the theory we have outlined. It begins from the perspective of the "I," the knower and actor that is intrinsically motivated and engaged in a proactive process of knowing itself. Beginning from within, with personal knowledge (Bridgman, 1959), the theory suggests that the "I" actively integrates information from the social world—digesting it rather than simply absorbing it. Thus, if one were to use the term "me" to refer to this "self that is known," one would say that the "me" is actively constructed by the "I," through organismic integration, and does not necessarily reflect other people's attitudes.

McAdams (1990) used the "I/me" distinction to organize various self-relevant theories into two categories, depending on whether they tend to emphasize the "I" (the knower) aspect or the "me" (the known) aspect of the self. McAdams classified organismic theories such as Loevinger's (1976) theory of ego development and Blasi's (1988) theory of self and identity as "I theories," whereas he presented cognitive theories such as Markus's (e.g., Markus & Nurius, 1986) schema theory and Higgins's (1987) self-discrepancy theory as "me theories."

In our view, the groupings McAdams made go beyond simply reflecting whether the theories focus on the knower or the known; they reflect the underlying nature of the theories themselves. The theories presented in the "I" category are ones that begin from the internal frame of reference, that convey a true sense of agency and acknowledge an inner tendency toward development. On the other hand, the theories presented in the "me" category are ones such as the current social cognitive theories that begin from the external frame of reference, that do not convey a true sense of agency, and that view development in terms of changes brought about by the social world.

A theory of self must, we contend, convey the essence of the human being as an active agent; it must be an "I-type" theory to be a meaningful theory of self. Nonetheless, the important point that is conveyed in the "me-type" theories is that human beings, even though active by nature, do sometimes behave as if they were controlled by introjected evaluations or social pressures. Our theory, which is both organismic and dialectic, affords people their human essence, while also accounting for the processes through which they appear to be controlled. It places the active organism in a social context that can either support or impair its natural development and self-determination.

REFERENCES

Ainsworth, M. D. S., Blehar, M. C., Waters, E., & Wall, S. (1978). *Patterns of attachment*. Hillsdale, NJ: Erlbaum.

Alderfer, C. P. (1972). *Existence, relatedness, and growth*. New York: Free Press.

Alper, T. G. (1942). Memory for completed and uncompleted tasks as a function of personality: An analysis of group data. *Journal of Abnormal and Social Psychology, 41*, 403–420.

Amabile, T. M., DeJong, W., & Lepper, M. R. (1976). Effects of externally imposed deadlines on subsequent intrinsic motivation. *Journal of Personality and Social Psychology, 34*, 92–98.

Anderson, R., Manoogian, S. T., & Reznick, J. S. (1976). The undermining and enhancing of intrinsic motivation in preschool children. *Journal of Personality and Social Psychology, 34*, 915–922.

Arnold, M. B. (1960). *Emotion and personality. Vol. 1: Psychological aspects*. New York: Columbia University Press.

Avery, R. R., & Ryan, R. M. (1988). Object relations and ego development: Comparison and correlates in middle childhood. *Journal of Personality, 56*, 547–569.

Bandura, A. (1977). *Social learning theory*. Englewood Cliffs, NJ: Prentice-Hall.

Bandura, A. (1978). The self-system in reciprocal determinism. *American Psychologist, 33*, 344–358.

Bandura, A. (1989). Human agency in social cognitive theory. *American Psychologist, 44*, 1175–1184.

Berlyne, D. E. (1971). *Aesthetics and psychobiology*. New York: Appleton-Century-Crofts.

Blais, M. R., Sabourin, S., Boucher, C., & Vallerand, R. J. (1990). Toward a motivational model of couple happiness. *Journal of Personality and Social Psychology, 59*, 1021–1031.

Blasi, A. (1988). Identity and the development of the self. In D. K. Lapsley & F. C. Power (Eds.), *Self, ego, and identity: Integrative approaches* (pp. 226–242). New York: Springer-Verlag.

Boggiano, A. K., & Ruble, D. N. (1979). Competence and the overjustification effect: A developmental study. *Journal of Personality and Social Psychology, 37*, 1462–1468.

Breckler, S. J., & Greenwald, A. G. (1986). Motivational facets of the self. In R. M. Sorrentino and E. T. Higgins (Eds.), *Handbook of motivation and cognition: Foundations of Social Behavior* (pp. 145–165). New York: Guilford Press.

Bridgman, P. W. (1959). *The way things are*. Cambridge: Harvard University Press.

Butler, R. A. (1953). Discrimination learning by rhesus monkeys to visual exploration motivation. *Journal of Comparative and Physiological Psychology, 46*, 95–98.

Calder, B. J., & Staw, B. M. (1975). The interaction of intrinsic and extrinsic motivation: Some methodological notes. *Journal of Personality and Social Psychology, 31*, 76–80.

Collins, B. E. (1977). *Internalization: Towards a micro-social psychology of socialization or enduring behavior control.* Unpublished manuscript, University of California, Los Angeles.

Connell, J. P. (1990). Context, self and action: A motivational analysis of self-system processes across the life-span. In D. Cicchetti and M. Beeghly (Eds.), *The self in transition.* Chicago: University of Chicago Press.

Cooley, C. H. (1902). *Social organization.* New York: Scribner.

Csikszentmihalyi, M. (1975). *Beyond boredom and anxiety.* San Francisco: Jossey-Bass.

Danner, F. W., & Lonky, E. (1981). A cognitive-developmental approach to the effects of rewards on intrinsic motivation. *Child Development, 52*, 1043–1052.

deCharms, R. (1968). *Personal causation: The internal affective determinants of behavior.* New York: Academic Press.

Deci, E. L. (1971). Effects of externally mediated rewards on intrinsic motivation. *Journal of Personality and Social Psychology, 18*, 105–115.

Deci, E. L. (1972). Intrinsic motivation, extrinsic reinforcement, and inequity. *Journal of Personality and Social Psychology, 22*, 113–120.

Deci, E. L. (1975). *Intrinsic motivation.* New York: Plenum.

Deci, E. L. (1980). *The psychology of self-determination.* Lexington, MA: D. C. Heath (Lexington Books).

Deci, E. L., & Cascio, W. F. (1972, April). *Changes in intrinsic motivation as a function of negative feedback and threats.* Paper presented at the Eastern Psychological Association, Boston.

Deci, E. L., Cascio, W. F., & Krusell, J. (1973, May). *Sex differences, positive feedback, and intrinsic motivation.* Paper presented at the Eastern Psychological Association, Washington, DC.

Deci, E. L., Cascio, W. F., & Krusell, J. (1975). Cognitive evaluation theory and some comments on the Calder and Staw critique. *Journal of Personality and Social Psychology, 31*, 81–85.

Deci, E. L., Connell, J. P., & Ryan, R. M. (1989). Self-determination in a work organization. *Journal of Applied Psychology, 74*, 580–590.

Deci, E. L., & Ryan, R. M. (1980). The empirical exploration of intrinsic motivational processes. In L. Berkowitz (Ed.), *Advances in experimental social psychology* (Vol. 13, pp. 39–80). New York: Academic Press.

Deci, E. L., & Ryan, R. M. (1985a). The general causality orientations scale: Self-determination in personality. *Journal of Research in Personality, 19*, 109–134.

Deci, E. L., & Ryan, R. M. (1985b). *Intrinsic motivation and self-determination in human behavior.* New York: Plenum.

Deci, E. L., & Ryan, R. M. (1987). The support of autonomy and the control of behavior. *Journal of Personality and Social Psychology, 53*, 1024–1037.

Deci, E. L., Schwartz, A. J., Sheinman, L., & Ryan, R. M. (1981). An instrument to assess adults' orientations toward control versus autonomy with children: Reflections on intrinsic motivation and perceived competence. *Journal of Educational Psychology, 73*, 642–650.

Duval, S., & Wicklund, R. A. (1972). *A theory of objective self-awareness*. New York: Academic Press.

Eghrari, H., & Deci, E. L. (1989). *Facilitating internalization: A motivational analysis*. Unpublished manuscript, University of Rochester.

English, H., & English, A. C. (1958). *A comprehensive dictionary of psychological and psychoanalytic terms*. New York: David McKay.

Fenigstein, A., Scheier, M. F., & Buss, A. H. (1975). Public and private self-consciousness: Assessment and theory. *Journal of Consulting and Clinical Psychology, 43*, 522–527.

Fisher, C. D. (1978). The effects of personal control, competence, and extrinsic reward systems on intrinsic motivation. *Organizational Behavior and Human Performance, 21*, 273–288.

Freud, S. (1962). *The ego and the id*. New York: Norton. (Original work published 1923.)

Frodi, A., Bridges, L., & Grolnick, W. S. (1985). Correlates of mastery-related behavior: A short-term longitudinal study of infants in their second year. *Child Development, 56*, 1291–1298.

Gergen, K. J. (1971). *The concept of self*. New York: Holt, Rinehart, & Winston.

Goldstein, K. (1939). *The organism*. New York. American Book Co.

Greenspan, S. I. (1979). *Intelligence and adaptation*. New York: International Universities Press.

Greenwald, A. G. (1982). Ego task analysis: An integration of research on ego-involvement and self-awareness. In A. H. Hastorf & A. M. Isen (Eds.), *Cognitive social psychology* (pp. 109–147). New York: Elsevier.

Greenwald, A. G. (1988). A social-cognitive account of the self's development. In D. K. Lapsley & F. C. Power (Eds.), *Self, ego, and identity: Integrative approaches* (pp. 30–42). New York: Springer-Verlag.

Grolnick, W. S., & Ryan, R. M. (1987). Autonomy in children's learning: An experimental and individual difference investigation. *Journal of Personality and Social Psychology, 52*, 890–898.

Grolnick, W. S., & Ryan, R. M. (1989). Parent styles associated with children's self-regulation and competence in school. *Journal of Educational Psychology, 81*, 143–154.

Grolnick, W. S., Ryan, R. M., & Deci, E. L. (1990). *The inner resources for school achievement: Motivational mediators of children's perceptions of their parents*. Unpublished manuscript, University of Rochester.

Harackiewicz, J. (1979). The effects of reward contingency and performance feedback on intrinsic motivation. *Journal of Personality and Social Psychology, 37*, 1352–1363.

Hare-Mustin, R. T., & Maracek, J. (1986). Autonomy and gender: Some questions for therapists. *Psychotherapy, 23*, 205–212.

Harlow, H. F. (1950). Learning and satiation of response in intrinsically motivated complex puzzle performance by monkeys. *Journal of Comparative and Physiological Psychology, 43,* 289–294.

Harlow, H. F. (1953). Motivation as a factor in the acquisition of new responses. In J. S. Brown et al., *Current theory and research on motivation* (pp. 24–49). Lincoln: University of Nebraska Press.

Harlow, H. F. (1958). The nature of love. *American Psychologist, 13,* 673–685.

Harter, S. (1978). Pleasure derived from optimal challenge and the effects of extrinsic rewards on children's difficulty level choices. *Child Development, 49,* 788–799.

Harter, S. (1988). The construction and conservation of the Self: James and Cooley revisited. In D. K. Lapsley & F. C. Power (Eds.), *Self, ego, and identity: Integrative approaches* (pp. 43–70). New York: Springer-Verlag.

Hartmann, H. (1958). *Ego psychology and the problem of adaptation.* New York: International Universities Press. (Originally published 1939.)

Hartmann, H., & Loewenstein, R. M. (1962). Notes on the superego. *Psychoanalytic Study of the Child, 17,* 42–81.

Heider, F. (1958). *The psychology of interpersonal relations.* New York: Wiley.

Higgins, E. T. (1987). Self-discrepancy theory: A theory relating self and affect. *Psychological Review, 94,* 319–340.

Hilgard, E. R. (1987). *Psychology in America: A historical survey.* San Diego, CA: Harcourt, Brace, Jovanovich.

Hoffman, M. L. (1960). Power assertion by the parent and its impact on the child. *Child Development, 31,* 129–143.

Hull, C. L. (1943). *Principles of behavior: An introduction to behavior theory.* New York: Appleton-Century-Crofts.

Hunt, J. McV. (1965). Intrinsic motivation and its role in psychological development. In D. Levine (Ed.), *Nebraska symposium on motivation* (Vol. 13, pp. 189–282). Lincoln: University of Nebraska Press.

James, W. (1890). *The principles of psychology.* New York: Holt.

Kihlstrom, J. F., & Cantor, N. (1984). Mental representations of the self. In L. Berkowitz (Ed.), *Advances in experimental social psychology* (Vol. 17, pp. 2–47). New York: Academic Press.

King, K. (1990). *An empirical investigation of an object relations and motivational approach to the study of religiosity and mental health.* Unpublished doctoral dissertation, University of Rochester.

King, K. B. (1984). *Coping with cardiac surgery.* Unpublished doctoral dissertation, University of Rochester.

Koestner, R., Bernieri, F., & Zuckerman, M. (1991). Self-determination and consistency between attitudes, traits and behaviors. *Personality and Social Psychology Bulletin,* in press.

Koestner, R., Ryan, R. M., Bernieri, F., & Holt, K. (1984). Setting limits on children's behavior: The differential effects of controlling versus informational styles on intrinsic motivation and creativity. *Journal of Personality, 52,* 233–248.

Koestner, R., Zuckerman, M., & Koestner, J. (1987). Praise, involvement and intrinsic motivation. *Journal of Personality and Social Psychology, 53,* 383–390.

Kruglanski, A. W., Friedman, I., & Zeevi, G. (1971). The effects of extrinsic incentive on some qualitative aspects of task performance. *Journal of Personality, 39,* 606–617.

Lange, C. (1885). *The emotions.* Translated by I. A. Haupt and edited by K. Dunlap. Baltimore: Williams and Wilkins, 1922.

Lepper, M. R. (1983). Social-control processes and the internalization of social values: An attributional perspective. In E. T. Higgins, D. N. Ruble, & W. W. Hartup (Eds.), *Social cognition and social development* (pp. 294–330). New York: Cambridge University Press.

Lepper, M. R., & Greene, D. (1975). Turning play into work: Effects of adult surveillance and extrinsic rewards on children's intrinsic motivation. *Journal of Personality and Social Psychology, 31,* 479–486.

Lepper, M. R., Greene, D., & Nisbett, R. E. (1973). Undermining children's intrinsic interest with extrinsic rewards: A test of the "overjustification" hypothesis. *Journal of Personality and Social Psychology, 28,* 129–137.

Lewin, K. (1936). *Principles of topological psychology.* New York: McGraw-Hill.

Loevinger, J. (1976). *Ego development.* San Francisco: Jossey-Bass.

Lonky, E., & Reihman, J. M. (1990). *Self-regulation and moral reasoning as mediators of moral behavior.* Unpublished manuscript, State University of New York at Oswego.

Markus, H. J., & Nurius, P. S. (1986). Self-understanding and self-regulation in middle childhood. In W. A. Collins (Ed.), *Development during middle childhood.* Washington, DC: National Academy Press.

Markus, H. J., & Sentis, K. (1982). The self in social information processing. In J. Suls (Ed.), *Psychological perspectives on the self* (Vol. 1, pp. 41–70). Hillsdale, NJ: Erlbaum.

Maslow, A. H. (1943). A theory of human motivation. *Psychological Review, 50,* 370–396.

McAdams, D. P. (1990). *The person: An introduction to personality psychology.* New York: Harcourt Brace Jovanovich.

McClelland, D. C. (1985). *Human motivation.* Glenview, IL: Scott, Foresman.

McClelland, D. C., Atkinson, J. W., Clark, R. W., & Lowell, E. L. (1953). *The achievement motive.* New York: Appleton-Century-Croft.

Mead, G. H. (1934). *Mind, self, and society.* Chicago: University of Chicago Press.

Montgomery, K. C. (1953). Exploratory behavior as a function of "similarity" of stimulus situations. *Journal of Comparative and Physiological Psychology, 46,* 129–133.

Mossholder, K. W. (1980). Effects of externally mediated goal setting on intrinsic motivation: A laboratory experiment. *Journal of Applied Psychology, 65,* 202–210.

Murray, H. A. (1938). *Explorations in personality.* New York: Oxford University Press.

Newell, A., Shaw, J. C., & Simon, H. A. (1958). Elements of a theory of human problem solving. *Psychological Review, 65,* 151–166.

Nunberg, H. (1931). The synthetic function of the ego. *International Journal of Psycho-analysis, 12,* 123–140.

O'Connor, B. P., & Vallerand, R. J. (1990). Religious motivation in the elderly: A French-Canadian replication and an extension. *Journal of Social Psychology, 130,* 53–60.

Pallak, S. R., Costomiris, S., Sroka, S., & Pittman, T. S. (1982). School experience, reward characteristics, and intrinsic motivation. *Child Development, 53,* 1382–1391.

Pavlov, I. P. (1927). *Conditioned reflexes.* New York: Dover.

Piaget, J. (1952). *The origins of intelligence in children.* New York: International Universities Press.

Piaget, J. (1971). *Biology and knowledge.* Chicago: University of Chicago Press.

Pittman, T. S., Davey, M. E., Alafat, K. A., Wetherill, K. V., & Kramer, N. A. (1980). Informational versus controlling verbal rewards. *Personality and Social Psychology Bulletin, 6,* 228–233.

Plant, R. W. (1990). *Motivation, expectation, and psychiatric severity in predicting early dropout from outpatient alcoholism treatment.* Unpublished doctoral dissertation, University of Rochester.

Plant, R. W., & Ryan, R. M. (1985). Intrinsic motivation and the effects of self-consciousness, self-awareness, and ego-involvement: An investigation of internally controlling styles. *Journal of Personality, 53,* 435–449.

Porter, L. W., & Lawler, E. E. (1968). *Managerial attitudes and performance.* Homewood, IL: Irwin-Dorsey.

Reiss, S., & Sushinsky, L. W. (1975). Overjustification, competing responses, and the acquisition of intrinsic interest. *Journal of Personality and Social Psychology, 31,* 1116–1125.

Rogers, C. R. (1951). *Client centered therapy.* Boston: Houghton-Mifflin.

Ross, M. (1975). Salience of reward and intrinsic motivation. *Journal of Personality and Social Psychology, 32,* 245–254.

Rotter, J. B. (1954). *Social learning and clinical psychology.* Englewood Cliffs, NJ: Prentice-Hall.

Rotter, J. B. (1966). Generalized expectancies for internal versus external control of reinforcement. *Psychological Monographs, 80* (1, Whole No. 609), 1–28.

Ryan, R. M. (1982). Control and information in the intrapersonal sphere: An extension of cognitive evaluation theory. *Journal of Personality and Social Psychology, 43,* 450–461.

Ryan, R. M. (in press). The nature of the self in autonomy and relatedness. In G. R. Goethals & J. Strauss (Eds.), *Multidisciplinary perspectives on the self.* New York: Springer-Verlag.

Ryan, R. M., & Connell, J. P. (1988). Mastery motivation. In T. Husen & T. N. Postlethwaite (Eds.), *International encyclopedia of education.* New York: Pergamon Press.

Ryan, R. M., & Connell, J. P. (1989). Perceived locus of causality and internalization: Examining reasons for acting in two domains. *Journal of Personality and Social Psychology, 57*, 749–761.

Ryan, R. M., Connell, J. P., & Deci, E. L. (1985). A motivational analysis of self-determination and self-regulation in education. In C. Ames & R. E. Ames (Eds.), *Research on motivation in education: The classroom milieu* (pp. 13–51). New York: Academic Press.

Ryan, R. M., Connell, J. P., & Grolnick, W. S. (in press). When achievement is *not* intrinsically motivated: A theory of self-regulation in school. In A. K. Boggiano & T. S. Pittman (Eds.), *Achievement and motivation: A social-developmental perspective*. New York: Cambridge University Press.

Ryan, R. M., & Deci, E. L. (1989). *When free-choice behavior is not intrinsically motivated: Experiments on internally controlling regulation.* Unpublished manuscript, University of Rochester.

Ryan, R. M., & Grolnick, W. S. (1986). Origins and pawns in the classroom: Self-report and projective assessments of individual differences in children's perceptions. *Journal of Personality and Social Psychology, 50,* 550–558.

Ryan, R. M., & Lynch, J. (1989). Emotional autonomy versus detachment: Revisiting the vicissitudes of adolescence and young adulthood. *Child Development, 60,* 340–356.

Ryan, R. M., Mims, V., & Koestner, R. (1983). Relation of reward contingency and interpersonal context to intrinsic motivation: A review and test using cognitive evaluation theory. *Journal of Personality and Social Psychology, 45, 736–750.*

Sartre, J.-P. (1956). *Being and nothingness.* New York: Philosophical Library.

Schachter, S. (1966). The interaction of cognitive and physiological determinants of emotional states. In C. D. Spielberger (Ed.), *Anxiety and behavior* (pp. 193–224). New York: Academic Press.

Schafer, R. (1968). *Aspects of internalization.* New York: International Universities Press.

Scheier, M. F., & Carver, C. S. (1988). A model of behavioral self-regulation: Translating intention into action. In L. Berkowitz (Ed.), *Advances in experimental social psychology* (Vol. 21, pp. 303–346). New York: Academic Press.

Schlenker, B. R. (1980). *Impression management: The self-concept, social identity, and interpersonal relations.* Monterey, CA: Brooks-Cole.

Seligman, M. E. P. (1975). *Helplessness: On depression, development, and death.* San Francisco: Freeman.

Sherif, M., & Cantril, H. (1947). *The psychology of ego involvements, social attitudes and identifications.* New York: Wiley.

Shipley, T. E., Jr., & Veroff, J. (1952). A projective measure of need for affiliation. *Journal of Experimental Psychology, 43,* 349–356.

Skinner, B. F. (1953). *Science and human behavior.* New York: Macmillan.

Skinner, E., Chapman, M., & Baltes, P. (1988). Control, means-ends, and agency beliefs: A new conceptualization and its measurement during childhood. *Journal of Personality and Social Psychology, 54,* 117–133.

Skinner, E., Wellborn, J. G., & Connell, J. P. (1990). What it takes to do well in school and whether I've got it: A process model of perceived control and children's engagement and achievement in school. *Journal of Educational Psychology, 82*, 22–32.

Smith, W. E. (1974). *The effects of social and monetary rewards on intrinsic motivation.* Unpublished doctoral dissertation, Cornell University.

Spiegelberg, H. (1972). *Phenomenology in psychology and psychiatry.* Evanston, IL: Northwestern University Press.

Steinberg, L., & Silverberg, S. (1986). The vicissitudes of autonomy in adolescence. *Child Development, 57*, 841–851.

Strauss, J., & Ryan, R. M. (1987). Autonomy disturbances in subtypes of anorexia nervosa. *Journal of Abnormal Psychology, 96*, 254–258.

Tolman, E. C. (1932). *Purposive behavior in animals and man.* New York: Century.

Tolman, E. C. (1959). Principles of purposive behavior. In S. Koch (Ed.), *Psychology: A study of a science* (Vol. 2, pp. 92–157). New York: McGraw-Hill.

Vallerand, R. J., Blais, M. R., Briere, N. M., & Pelletier, L. G. (1989). Construction et validation de l'échelle de motivation en éducation (EME). *Canadian Journal of Behavioural Sciences, 21*, 323–349.

Vallerand, R. J., & Reid, G. (1984). On the causal effects of perceived competence on intrinsic motivation: A test of cognitive evaluation theory. *Journal of Sport Psychology, 6*, 94–102.

von Bertalanffy, L. (1968). *General systems theory.* New York: G. Braziller.

Vroom, V. H. (1964). *Work and motivation.* New York: Wiley.

Weiner, B. (1986). *An attributional theory of motivation and emotion.* New York: Springer-Verlag.

White, R. W. (1959). Motivation reconsidered: The concept of competence. *Psychological Review, 66*, 297–333.

White, R. W. (1960). Competence and the psychosexual stages of development. In M. R. Jones (Ed.), *Nebraska symposium on motivation* (Vol. 8, pp. 97–141). Lincoln: University of Nebraska Press.

Wild, J. (1965). Authentic existence: A new approach to "value theory." In J. M. Edie (Ed.), *An invitation to phenomenology: Studies in the philosophy of experience* (pp. 59–78). Chicago: Quadrangle.

Zuckerman, M., Porac, J., Lathin, D., Smith, R., & Deci, E. L. (1978). On the importance of self-determination for intrinsically motivated behavior. *Personality and Social Psychology Bulletin, 4*, 443–446.

The Adaptive Base of the Neural Hierarchy: Elementary Motivational Controls on Network Function

Douglas Derryberry
Oregon State University

and Don M. Tucker
University of Oregon

Complex as well as elementary motives must be implemented by neural mechanisms, yet it has been difficult to relate such mechanisms to the psychological processes of human motivation. The difficulty in the past has been a lack of knowledge about the workings of the brain. In recent years there have been important advances in the neurosciences, but this knowledge is typically limited to specific neural mechanisms, rather than general brain function, and it is held by researchers who are seldom conversant with psychological theory.

The rediscovery of neural net models in cognitive psychology (Rumelhart & McClelland, 1986) has stimulated new efforts to cross the borders between cognitive science and neuroscience. The way information is represented in connectionist models seems similar to the way mental functions must be distributed across brain tissues. However, most of the work in the emerging field of cognitive neuroscience deals with specific model systems, such as motion perception or word recognition, and has yet to address the issues of adaptive self-control that are required for a theory of motivation.

DISEMBODIED COGNITION

Extracting a specific mental process for laboratory study has been the traditional approach of cognitive psychology. This approach has been described as "disembodied" because it often fails to appreciate the bodily context for the mind's operations. Some of the most popular psychological theories of motivation and emotion have assumed that physiological mechanisms are influential only by causing a vague visceral arousal that must be interpreted through cognitive processes before having any influence on behavior (Mandler, 1985; Schachter & Singer, 1962). These theories amount to a kind of cognitive reductionism, ascribing a rich array of psychological processes to a restricted form of cognition that is largely verbal, conscious, and propositional. If a psychological theory is to capture much of the diversity of human experience and behavior, it must have a place for the more inarticulate, bodily, motivational influences, such as feelings, postures, and urges.

Several examples of elementary motivational processes are found in the papers from the 1990 session of the Nebraska Symposium on Motivation (this volume). In Bernard Weiner's view, the cognitive attributions following an event help to shape the meaning of the event, and thus the emotional reaction to it. It is the emotional reaction that then motivates subsequent behavior. From this perspective, cognitive self-control is effective only as it achieves an emotional state that then implies an appropriate course of action.

In the studies by Carol Dweck and her associates of the development of achievement orientations in young children, the findings suggest that what appear to be enduring attitudes about the relations between talent, effort, and accomplishment may be built upon more elementary emotional reactions to success and failure. Before differentiating concepts of domains of ability, such as doing arithmetic or making friends, the child seems to respond to feedback in terms of primitive feelings about the self as good or bad. It seems quite likely that the cognitive differentiation of ideas about the self builds upon this initial affective base. Even though an older child can make finer discriminations, the emotional response to an event, and the motivation for subsequent effort, may continue to be organized around a primitive good/bad vector of self-evaluation. When this evaluative vector is highly sensitized and is not subordinated to more complex concepts of self and context, pathological responses to events may occur, as in clinical depression or in the way borderline and narcissistic personalities evaluate self and others by "splitting," seeing only the good or the bad. Even when optimal self-evaluation is guided by a complex and differentiated conceptual system, the motive power for coping efforts may draw on the primitive affective base. Features of this affective base may be described by Thayer's (1989) dimension of "energetic" arousal, and perhaps by Albert Bandura's notion of "self-efficacy" (this volume).

In research on how children internalize the achievement efforts that are initially imposed by family and cultural values, Edward Deci and his associates have emphasized the interplay between psychological development and social interaction. This research shows how a careful account of the internalization process is necessary before the nature of intrinsic motivation can be appreciated. By focusing on the discrepancies between one's self-concept and idealized values, Higgins (1987) has provided evidence that different emotional reactions may occur for discrepancies involving what people would like to be (leading to depression) versus discrepancies involving what they feel they should be (leading to anxiety). The implication may be that there are specific affective dimensions underlying domains of self-evaluation, and that psychological organization around these dimensions may figure importantly both in the internalization of cultural values for work motivation and in the development of a more autonomous, intrinsic motivation.

DIMENSIONS OF NEURAL ORGANIZATION

The study of the brain may be particularly useful for understanding the more primitive and elementary motivational influences on human behavior. In the course of its evolution, the human brain has elaborated upon certain basic systems that evaluate the significance of events and motivate the appropriate efforts. Although humans are clearly remarkable for interposing mental representations between stimulus and response, the basic control systems that regulated the brain activity and survival efforts of simpler vertebrates still operate in some form in the human brain. Understanding the anatomy of these systems may provide important insight into the hierarchical organization of psychological as well as neural processes.

The lateral dimension of brain organization has received the most attention in recent research. This research has provided important evidence that communicating emotion in everyday interaction, through facial displays or tone of voice, requires the cognitive skills of the right hemisphere (Borod, Koff, & Buck, 1986; Safer, 1981; Tucker, 1986). The left hemisphere's verbal and analytic cognition may afford greater distance from such emotional processes, yet there are suggestions that anxious persons (Tyler & Tucker, 1982) or in some cases schizophrenics (Gur, 1978; Serafetinides, 1973) may show exaggerated activation of the left hemisphere. Although the interpretation of hemispheric roles in emotion and personality remains controversial (see Davidson, 1984; Kinsbourne & Bemporad, 1984; Tucker & Frederick, 1989), it seems clear that when we do understand the significance of hemispheric specialization we will find important insights into both normal and disordered motivation.

The brain shows a major functional distinction between posterior regions, which handle perceptual information, and anterior regions, which contribute to the planning and organization of behavior. Although it has not been as popular as laterality in modern neuropsychological research, this dimension led to interesting constructs of emotion and personality in the earlier literature (Denny-Brown, Meyer, & Horenstein, 1952; Petrie, 1952). If we consider emotions as affective processes, aligned with the perceptual input, and motivations as more efferent processes, directing motor initiatives, a theoretical model of anterior-posterior specialization would be important to understanding adaptive brain function. Pribram (1981) suggested that the anterior brain may be concerned with "ethical" functions, controlling behavior in light of survival needs, whereas the posterior brain may be concerned with "aesthetic" functions, elaborating the qualities of the perceptual modalities. Although both classes of function could be seen as having motivational qualities, this line of reasoning implies that the more fundamental motivational processes must converge on the anterior brain.

Some recent accounts of adaptive control in brain systems have suggested that the lateral dimension of functional organization is not orthogonal to, but is perhaps subordinate to, the anterior-posterior dimension. Following earlier suggestions in the literature (Jackson, 1879), Tucker and Williamson (1984) proposed that the left hemisphere's cognitive specialization has involved an elaboration upon the motor readiness mechanisms of the frontal regions. Similarly, the right hemisphere's holistic skills in spatial perception suggest that its specialization has emphasized the more receptive attentional mode of the posterior brain (see also Kinsbourne & Bemporad, 1984).

Another dimension of brain organization is an obvious one, yet its functional significance in the neocortex has only recently been discovered. From the spinal cord through the brainstem to the forebrain, the central nervous system routes perceptual information through dorsal pathways, and it achieves motor control through ventral pathways. The anterior-posterior dimension must be understood as it elaborates on this more elementary dorsal-ventral plan. Furthermore, in the evolution of the neocortex, one group of networks evolved around the dorsal limbic structures, specifically the hippocampus, while another set of networks evolved around the ventral limbic olfactory cortex. Studies of visual perception (Goldberg & Robinson, 1977) and memory (Ungerleider & Mishkin, 1982) in the primate cortex have shown that the dorsal and ventral pathways from sensory neocortex to the limbic system have different functions, with the dorsal pathway specialized for spatial localization and the ventral pathway specialized for object identification. The dorsal-ventral distinction is thus another important way of understanding the functional organization of the neocortex. As with the left-right and anterior-posterior dimensions, the dorsal-ventral dimension may be closely integrated with, rather than orthogonal to, the other dimensions. For example, the left hemisphere's skill in perceptual and verbal analysis may entail a particularly strong elaboration on the object identification abilities of the ventral neocortical trend (Tucker & Derryberry, in press).

HIERARCHICAL NETWORKS

Underlying these several divisions of the neocortex is perhaps the most fundamental and yet least understood dimension of brain organization—what might be called the vertical dimension. The extensive human neocortex is only one component of a multilevel brain, each level emerging as a major advance in the evolution of neural strategies for sensorimotor control (Livesey, 1986). Each level evolved to modify and extend the functioning of the previous level, which remained in place. Each level is dependent on continuous functional support from lower levels. The large human neocortex requires intact connections to limbic structures in order to retain its network representations in memory (Squire, 1986). Both neocortical and limbic systems depend on activating and modulating influences from the brainstem (Foote & Morrison, 1987; Saper, 1987).

In this chapter we focus on the vertical dimension of brain organization. We suggest that a consideration of brain anatomy and function shows the hierarchical organization that combines both primitive and complex neural systems. As shown in Figure 1, this hierarchy might be thought of as an inverted pyramid. At the top is the neocortex, with its extensive representational networks. At the base is the brainstem, providing the most elementary controls over sleep and activation. Between these are the midbrain and limbic systems, providing support not only for bodily homeostasis, but for the most complex neocortical functions as well.

The traditional view of hierarchical control in brain systems has placed the neocortex, and often the frontal lobes, at the top of the functional hierarchy, exerting the most general control. Although there are important executive functions carried out by the frontal lobe, it is not necessarily the case that the most general control will be exerted by the most complex level of the brain's networks. One important principle of brain connections could be described in terms of computer architecture as "bottom-up, fan out": the most widespread connections—and thus the most general control influences—originate from the narrow base of the inverted pyramid, the brainstem, and fan out in an upward direction. Another principle of neural connections is reciprocity: each area receiving projections reciprocates with back projections. This leads to the complementary pattern of top-down, fan in. With information going either up or down, this architecture places a major nexus for the integration of control influences at the points of convergence in the more primitive levels of the hierarchy. The cortex itself is not a homogeneous network but comprises of several waves of increasingly differentiated networks evolving from the limbic system, with the most local and specific connections found in the most recently evolved networks

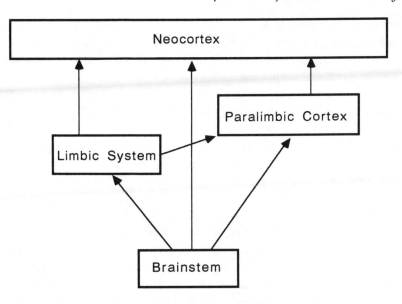

FIGURE 1. Simplified diagram illustrating ascending systems projecting upon the neocortex. The brainstem region includes projections from the locus coeruleus, raphe nuclei, ventral tegmental area, and nonspecific thalamic nuclei. The limbic system includes cortical projections from the hypothalamus, nucleus basalis, amygdala, and hippocampus. The paralimbic cortex includes neocortical projections from the orbital frontal, insula, temporal pole, cingulate, retrosplenial, and parahippocampal cortices.

(Pandya & Yeterian, 1985). The network architecture of the cortex itself is thus consistent with the principle of bottom-up, fan out.

An important theoretical problem is how to account for vertical integration within this hierarchy. Each evolutionary level seems to have its own representation of sensory space and motor control. For example, studies of the control of vocalization in monkeys by Ploog and associates (Ploog, 1981) have shown that elementary components of vocalization behavior are controlled by the lower brainstem. The integration of these components, however, requires a second hierarchical level, in the midbrain. When the midbrain areas are stimulated, the animal emits a vocalization that has the characteristic patterning of a species-specific call. However, this call lacks the concurrent behavioral expressions that accompany a spontaneous emotional vocalization. Ploog and associates showed that the midbrain vocal-pattern area must receive connections from limbic structures—such as amygdala, hippocampus, and septal area—before the vocalization is integrated with an affective display.

The cortical influences on monkey vocalization operate at a still higher level, and within the cortex itself there is a further differentiation of hierarchical layers of representation and control. Ploog and associates found that what they termed "voluntary call initiation" is controlled by the anterior cingulate gyrus, which in the human brain is interconnected with the supplementary motor area of the mediodorsal frontal cortex. This area projects to the midbrain control area and can thus initiate a patterned vocalization without requiring the spontaneous affective influence from limbic circuits. A final cortical control comes from the more recently evolved networks of the primary motor area, which project via pyramidal fibers to the lower brainstem vocalization component areas, bypassing both limbic and midbrain centers. This area provides what Ploog and associates describe as "voluntary call formation," with the patterning of the vocalization achieved within the cortical networks themselves rather than by the midbrain area. This pathway for controlling vocalization is not important for the innately patterned vocalizations of simpler primates. In humans, however, the evidence on aphasia suggests the pyramidal cortical pathway is critical to the complex control of the articulatory apparatus in speech (Buck, 1988).

An analysis of vocalization thus gives an example of parallel and overlapping circuits that must be integrated to achieve continuity and adaptive efficacy in behavior. This kind of parallel hierarchical systems analysis may seem foreign to psychological theories of motivation. It requires what is essentially an evolutionary explanation for the development of each sequence of behavior (Brown, 1987). The vertical integration across multiple control levels may best be understood by tracing the evolutionary relationships across levels that specify when a higher level operates through a lower level, and when it may operate in parallel with it.

The idea of multiple representations of sensorimotor patterns may also seem foreign to the psychology of emotions, which often seem to appear as unitary experiences. Yet there are clinical disorders in which damage to a specific level of the hierarchy produces a subjective as well as a behavioral dissociation. For example, in the neurologic condition of pseudobulbar palsy the connections from the forebrain to the pons area of the brainstem are damaged (Rinn,

1984). Released from inhibitory cortical control, the brainstem centers appear to generate spontaneous episodes of laughing or crying. Although these outbursts show the familiar patterns of laughing or crying, the patients report that they do not experience the associated emotion. Without integration within limbic and cortical circuits, the primitive affect patterns appear to be divorced from subjective experience.

Such evidence suggests that for an adequate phenomenological, as well as neurophysiological, explanation of motivated behavior, we must account for the vertical integration across the brain's hierarchical systems. In this chapter we attempt to develop concepts of motivational control that would be consistent with the bottom-up, fan out pattern of the brain's connectional architecture. The basic idea is that the primitive processes of the brainstem and limbic system exert the most general forms of motivational control, whereas the articulation of goals and means is achieved through the incorporation of subcortical controls into cortical representations. This idea is framed within an anatomical model of brainstem regulatory systems, the circuits of the limbic system and paralimbic cortex, and the pathways of the neocortex. Within this model, we consider ways that elementary motivational processes can direct cognition. The most general influences, probably beginning in the brainstem projection systems, may alter the style of cognition—its temporal flow and its scope of semantic activation. From higher, perhaps paralimbic, levels, motivational processes influence the content of cognition—the representations that shape awareness. Our argument is that cognition is neither isolated nor independent but is embedded within a multilayer motivational context, closely entrained to the ongoing background of bodily processes.

Subcortical Regulation of the Cortex

The traditional model of control in the central nervous system places the cortex at the highest level. After all, the cortex is the most recently evolved structure, it appears essential to any sophisticated form of cognition, and it demonstrates extensive descending connections to the limbic system, brainstem, and spinal cord. Nevertheless, massive ascending projections extend from the brainstem and limbic regions to modulate processing in virtually all areas of the cortex. In addition, the cortex itself includes paralimbic regions carrying out motivational and affective functions as well the neocortical regions thought to accomplish higher cognition. Several lines of evidence suggest that neocortical representations may emerge through a differentiation and articulation of ongoing activity in more primitive paralimbic circuits. In the following sections we sketch out the brain's ascending regulatory influences, moving from the general brainstem mechanisms to the increasingly specific limbic and paralimbic effects on the neocortex. The blueprint of processing architecture that emerges is that of widely distributed motivational influences fanning out from subcortical controls toward the cortex. As various combinations of the subcortical systems are recruited, unique modes of cortical processing emerge, and the contents of mental representations and the motor plan become increasingly specified. Figure 1 is a schematic of these ascending connections.

ASCENDING BRAINSTEM PROJECTIONS

The brainstem projections to the cortex were traditionally viewed in terms of the "reticular activating system," a unified arousal system thought to carry out a nonspecific regulation of the cortex in relation to states of sleep, wakefulness, or emergency reactions. However, more recent investigations have shown that the reticular formation consists of multiple and specific subsystems projecting to extensive areas of the cortex (Bloom, 1988). Some project directly to the cortex, such as the norepinephrine system arising from the nucleus locus coeruleus, several serotonergic systems from the raphe nuclei, and dopaminergic systems from the ventral tegmental area (Saper, 1987). Other systems, such as the cholinergic neurons ascending from the dorsolateral tegmental nucleus, synapse in the nonspecific thalamic nuclei before influencing the cortex. Thus, ascending brainstem systems exert more complex controls than are reflected in the traditional construct of a single arousal system.

Several of the properties of these control systems are important for a theory of motivation. These systems are highly reactive, responding to external and internal sensory inputs, to circadian rhythms, and to hormonal influences. At the sensory level they respond to various stimuli from multiple modalities, but they do so in terms of relatively general properties of the stimulus. The norepinephrine-containing locus coeruleus neurons, for example, show their greatest responsivity to signals that are "conspicuous" in some way, such as novel, intense, or aversive stimuli (Grant, Aston-Jones, & Redmond, 1988). Similarly, the dopamine-containing ventral tegmental neurons respond to a range of motivationally arousing cues (Schultz & Romo, 1990) and demonstrate enhanced activity during stressful situations (Trulson & Preussler, 1984). It should also be noted that these brainstem cell groups respond very rapidly, within 100 milliseconds, following a stimulus. This puts them in a position to influence, via their ascending projections, early information processing within the cortex.

In their cortical projections, the reticular cell groups give rise to extensive, highly collateralized terminations in virtually all cortical and forebrain regions. A single neuron appears capable of influencing numerous cortical areas by means of its branching, divergent axonal trajectories. This "one-to-many" or fan out pattern suggests a relatively general influence, perhaps affecting activity across multiple, related cortical circuits. Nevertheless, these projections should not be considered "nonspecific," since the various systems demonstrate important laminar and regional variations in their terminal distributions. For example, norepinephrine fibers appear densest in the deeper cortical levels, serotonin fibers in the middle layers, and dopamine fibers in the upper layers (Lewis & Morrison, 1989). Perhaps more important, evidence suggests that norepinephrine favors the dorsal, spatial-related areas of the cortex, whereas dopamine favors the ventral areas involved in object discrimination (Lewis & Morrison, 1989). Thus, although their effects are widespread, these systems may exert functionally distinct controls on circuits distributed through specific areas of the cortex.

The influences these systems apply to their target networks are not well understood. They have been described as forms of "modulation." The concept of a neuromodulator has been discussed by Wise (1987), who contrasted it with a neurotransmitter. Wise proposed that perceptual, cognitive, and response processing is carried out by spatially precise circuits employing the fast-acting excitatory and inhibitory amino acid neurotransmitters. The spatial and temporal resolution provided by such circuits allows for precise coding and transmission of information, with subtle impulse patterns encoding the specific details of the environment and the motor commands. In contrast, motivational processes are carried out through slower-acting and spatially diffuse neuromodulatory systems, such as those employing monoamine (serotonin, norepinephrine, and dopamine), acetylcholine, and peptide neurochemicals. Rather than transmitting information, these modulatory systems seem to enhance or attenuate the sensitivity of other circuits to incoming signals.

Thus at the cellular level norepinephrine seems to exert an inhibitory effect that suppresses spontaneous activity more than stimulus-induced activity. Researchers have proposed that such a mechanism increases the "signal-to-noise" ratio in the target cells, in this way amplifying incoming signals that are adaptively significant (Foote, Bloom, & Aston-Jones, 1983). Evidence suggests that a complementary attenuation of the signal-to-noise ratio may arise from activation of serotonergic (Waterhouse, Moises, & Woodward, 1986) and dopaminergic (Mantz, Milla, Glowinski, & Thierry, 1988) systems. Although their specific consequences depend on the nature of the target information, these modulatory effects suggest a role in attentional and alerting processes. By biasing sensory processing across a wide range of cortical circuits, these reticular subsystems may initiate an early and general tuning of the motivational state of cortical networks.

ASCENDING LIMBIC PROJECTIONS

The limbic system consists of a set of circuits linking the hypothalamus, amygdala, hippocampus, nucleus basalis, and related structures to both the cortex and the brainstem. These pathways are considered to represent an intermediate evolutionary stage between the brainstem and cortex. Traditionally, the limbic subsystems have been viewed as under the control of the cortex, with their main role in the hierarchy being to consolidate and transmit the descending control influence to the brainstem's autonomic and somatic areas. Although this effector function is important, the limbic circuits also have extensive, direct projections to the cortex, as well as projections to cortical processing loops through the thalamus and basal ganglia. These connections make the limbic circuits integral to the perceptual, memory, and attentional processes of the cortex. According to Isaacson (1980), the limbic projections do not control or "drive" the other regions. Rather, they exert a modulatory influence, biasing cells in the cortex and brainstem to be more or less responsive to inputs arriving over other pathways.

Limbic circuits and hierarchical evaluation. While specific limbic circuits mediate specific functions, the general role of the limbic system may be to evaluate the motivational significance of incoming sensory information. The brain seems to carry out its adaptive evaluations in a hierarchical fashion, with the most general evaluation performed at the most primitive level of the hierarchy. The brainstem's reticular networks appear responsive to crude features of a stimulus, such as its intensity. Within the midbrain regions, cells in the nucleus basalis and the lateral hypothalamus respond to a variety of visual food-related stimuli, but not to nonfood stimuli. Importantly, the hypothalamic and nucleus basalis responses are dependent upon the animal's internal state, increasing given hunger and decreasing given satiety (Rolls, 1987). Thus, the "significance" of the visual stimulus is coded in relation to internal states of need. More recently, reinforcement-related neurons have been found in the cholinergic nucleus basalis region that respond to visual and auditory cues signaling the availability of rewarding or aversive stimuli. These neurons reacted to a broad range of stimuli associated with both feeding and drinking, with latencies in the range of 150–200 milliseconds (Wilson & Rolls, 1990).

Although limbic projections to the cortex remain fairly general, they are more specific than those radiating from the brainstem. Four distinct systems have recently been discovered arising from the hypothalamus (Saper, 1987). Although they have not been characterized in detail, some appear to have topographically organized projections with discrete terminal fields (1.5 mm in size). More thoroughly investigated are the extensive cholinergic projections to the entire cortex from the nucleus basalis. This nucleus has been implicated in the pathology of Alzheimer's disease, and its cortical efferents have been investigated in relation to the attentional and memory impairments accompanying the dementia. The cells possess relatively short axon collaterals, innervating cortical areas roughly

1.5 mm in size (Richardson & DeLong, 1988). Selective effects are also suggested by the denser projections of these cholinergic cells to the cortical areas that are connected with the amygdala and hippocampus (Mesulam, 1988). The cholinergic effects appear to be facilitatory, biased toward enhancing selectivity of the target neuron (Sillito & Murphy, 1987). Given their responsivity to motivationally significant inputs (Rolls, 1987), the basalis neurons may prime specific cortical areas relevant to ongoing motivational states (Mesulam, 1988; Sillito & Murphy, 1987).

Within the more recently evolved telencephalic limbic regions, cells in the amygdala and hippocampus show greater specificity than the brainstem and nucleus basalis systems. For example, cells in the amygdala respond to sight of only one or a few kinds of food (Ono, Tamura, Nishijo, Nakamura, & Tabuchi, 1989), whereas those in the nucleus basalis respond to any type of food reward (Wilson & Rolls, 1990). In addition to these appetitive functions, amygdala and hippocampal neurons are also involved in processing aversive information (Fuster & Uyeda, 1971). Both the central nucleus of the amygdala (Davis, Hitchcock, & Rosen, 1987) and the hippocampus (Gray, 1982) appear closely linked to anxiety. Although these structures are usually viewed as responding to highly processed cortical inputs, evidence indicates that under certain conditions they respond before the cortex, presumably in light of direct input from the thalamus. The central amygdala has been found to respond to a shock-related auditory stimulus with a latency under 50 milliseconds (LeDoux, 1987; Supple & Kapp, 1989). The hippocampus and adjacent presubiculum respond to a relevant light flash within 100 milliseconds, considerably earlier than activity in the visual areas in the inferotemporal cortex (Coburn, Ashford, & Fuster, 1990). As in the case of the reticular systems, such short-latency responses place the amygdala and hippocampus in a position both to initiate emergency reactions and to influence the early stages of cortical processing.

This cortical influence can be exerted in a variety of ways. First, both the amygdala and hippocampus project to lower-level structures, allowing them to regulate or recruit the ascending cortical influences of raphe nuclei, the nucleus basalis, and the ventral tegmental area (Alheid & Heimer, 1988; Davis et al., 1987). Second, both of these limbic structures project to the striatum, a crucial link in the basal ganglia loops channeling information from multiple cortical regions onto response-related areas of the frontal lobe (Everitt, Cador, & Robbins, 1989; Ragsdale & Graybiel, 1988). Third, amygdala and hippocampal circuits project to the mediodorsal and anterior thalamic nuclei, respectively, allowing them to modulate processing in the corticothalamocortical loops (Gabriel, Sparenborg, & Stolar, 1986; Groenewegen, 1988). Finally, both have direct connections to the cortex. The hippocampal circuitry is primarily connected with paralimbic structures, including the parahippocampal, retrosplenial, and cingulate regions, whereas the amygdala is more closely related to the paralimbic orbital frontal, insula, and temporal pole regions (Mesulam & Mufson, 1982a). In addition, the amygdala projects to multiple neocortical regions of the frontal (Sarter & Markowitsch, 1984), temporal, and occipital (Iwai & Yukie, 1987) lobes. The temporal and occipital projections, extending to the earliest visual sensory areas, place the amygdala in a pivotal position for regulating the course of visual object processing.

Paralimbic cortex. The conventional view of cortical processing emphasizes the progressive convergence and integration of parallel channels of information. Sensory input from the thalamus is first processed in the primary sensory areas of the posterior neocortex, where perceptual features (e.g., color, form, motion) are analyzed. These parallel feature channels then converge upon unimodal association areas, resulting in integrated object-level representations for the specific sensory modality. Projections from multiple unimodal regions then converge upon higher-level association areas, giving rise to polymodal representations integrating two or more modalities. In general, it is usually assumed that this convergent, hierarchical processing within the neocortex underlies the construction of a progressively more abstract representation of the external world. At relatively late stages in this constructive process, the information is sent to the paralimbic cortices and then on to the limbic system, where its motivational significance is finally extracted (Pandya & Seltzer, 1982). Although such processing from sensory to association to paralimbic areas is undoubtedly important, recent anatomical studies demonstrate that reciprocal connections proceeding in the opposite direction also exist. Moreover, these paralimbic-neocortical pathways follow the progression of the evolutionary development of the neocortex (Pandya, Seltzer, & Barbas, 1988) and may thus suggest what new functional capacities were provided by the evolution of increasingly differentiated neural networks.

As delineated by Mesulam and Mufson (1982a), the paralimbic regions consist of a ring of primitive, transitional areas along the ventral and medial boundaries of the cortical mantle. These regions demonstrate a progressive differentiation from an allocortical to a granular isocortical architecture. The innermost paralimbic foci consist of primordial allocortex in the prepiriform and hippocampal regions. These allocortical areas are surrounded by periallocortical regions, consisting of three-layered agranular cortex. The periallocortical regions are in turn surrounded by dysgranular proisocortical regions, characterized by more differentiated architecture involving five to six layers and some granular cells. Finally, the proisocortical regions give way to six-layered isocortical fields demonstrating well-defined granular layers. Thus the paralimbic regions comprise an allocortical core surrounded by a series of concentric growth rings featuring a progressively differentiated laminar organization (Mesulam & Mufson, 1982a; Moran, Mufson, & Mesulam, 1987). As described below, this advancing differentiation continues outward into the neocortical fields, reaching its highest levels in the primary sensory areas.

The patterns of connectivity among the paralimbic regions suggest that the cortex evolved from two limbic foci. The first is centered on the hippocampus and radiates outward to include the cingulate, parahippocampal, and retrosplenial cortices. These areas are reciprocally connected with a wide range of neocortical regions, but they appear most closely associated with the dorsal neocortical pathways involved in spatial processing. At this time the evidence suggests that these networks link motivational, attentional, and spatial cognitive processes (Pandya & Yeterian, 1984; Witter, Groenewegen, Lopes da Silva, & Lohman, 1989). Mesulam has suggested that the cingulate region functions as a motivational map that interacts with a parietal-based spatial map in selecting adaptively significant spatial locations for attention (Mesulam, 1981).

The second paralimbic focus is the prepiriform cortex, which is densely interconnected with the orbital frontal cortex, insula, and temporal pole. These structures are closely related to the amygdala. Sensory convergence is particularly dense within the insula, which is in the unique position of receiving olfactory, gustatory, and visceral input via its anterior regions and somesthetic, auditory, and visual input via its posterior regions (Mesulam & Mufson, 1982b). The orbital-insula-temporopolar cortices radiate outward to the ventral neocortical pathways involved in object recognition. These ventral paralimbic cortices appear to code the motivational significance of specific objects. The orbital cortex, for example, has cells that respond conditionally to specific rewarding and aversive objects (Thorpe, Rolls, & Maddison, 1983), in a manner reflecting the animal's internal state (Nakano et al., 1984) and preferences (Yamamoto et al., 1984). The ventral structures also appear to be implicated in fear motivation. In humans, recent analyses of cerebral blood flow during anxiety suggest increased activation in the left orbital (Johanson, Risberg, Silfverskiold, & Smith, 1986) and temporal pole (Reiman, Fusselman, Fox, & Raichle, 1989) regions. The involvement of these areas in anxiety is consistent with traditional psychosurgical practice, which for many years utilized lesions of the orbital cortex as a treatment for severe anxiety (Powell, 1981).

A particularly important function of the orbital-insula temporopolar group is the representation of autonomic and visceral activity. The insula and orbital cortices seem to exert the major cortical control over the autonomic nervous system. They project to subcortical autonomic areas and, when stimulated, give rise to variety of autonomic responses (Van der Kooy, Koda, McGinty, Gerfen, & Bloom, 1984). Importantly, the insula has recently been found to be the location of the primary visceral sensory area (Krushel & Van der Kooy, 1988). A wide range of visceral information, reflecting cardiovascular, respiratory, and gastrointestinal activity, ascends from the brainstem through the thalamus to the insula. The cortical representation appears to be viscerotopic, with the gustatory, gastric, and cardiopulmonary modalities represented in adjacent but distinct areas (Cechetto & Saper, 1987). Consistent with these projections, electrical stimulation of the human insula elicits a variety of visceral sensations (Penfield & Faulk, 1955). It is also of interest that these visceral sensory areas are situated adjacent to the somatic representation of the trunk in the secondary somatosensory area (Cechetto & Saper, 1987), and that the posterior insula also provides a rich source of somatosensory information (Mesulam & Mufson, 1982a). Taken together, these findings suggest that the insula provides a high-level representation of the internal milieu, a representation that may be essential to the bodily feelings integral to human motivation and emotion (Mesulam & Mufson, 1982a).

Another intriguing aspect of the paralimbic brain is its susceptibility to regenerative and uncontrolled—that is, epileptic—electrophysiological discharges. Along with the amygdala and hippocampus, the paralimbic regions are highly excitable, perhaps as a result of their dense cholinergic input from the nucleus basalis (Mesulam & Mufson, 1982a). These areas respond strongly to seizure activity anywhere in the neocortex, as shown in kindling phenomena in animal experiments (Doane & Livingston, 1986), and as shown by the tendency of human seizure disorders to develop the major focus in the temporal lobe (Brandt, Seidman, & Kohl, 1985). Investigations of temporal lobe epilepsy have revealed that seizures may be preceded by intense emotional feelings, and that the patient's interictal behavior often shows emotional changes (Bear, 1983). Patients with right temporal lobe foci tend to show an "impulsive" or "emotive" pattern of traits such as euphoria, sadness, and aggression. In contrast, those with left foci demonstrate more "reflective" or "ideative" traits such as religiosity, a sense of personal destiny, and paranoid concerns (Bear, 1983). Given their inputs from the neocortex, the hyperexcitable paralimbic regions appear to intensify the affective components of experience, such that even trivial events become charged with significance. At the same time, their reciprocal connections may have a kindling effect on neocortical fields, serving to initiate and sustain activity related to the ideational elaboration of the affective concerns. Thus the electrical sensitivity of paralimbic cortex may have a functional parallel, such that the paralimbic core of the cortex is excited when mental representations touch on issues that are personally significant.

FUNCTIONAL ORGANIZATION OF THE CORTEX

Given the identification of primary sensory areas of the neocortex and of the multimodal association areas that are extensive in the human brain, the conventional model of the cortex assumed that the brain's hierarchical organization is achieved as information from sensory areas is combined into progressively more abstract representations in the higher association areas of the parietal, temporal, and frontal lobes. The flow of information was assumed to be posterior to anterior, with elementary perceptual analysis in posterior receptive areas and more complex cognitive processes in more anterior association areas.

Another assumption of conventional neuropsychology has been that each area serves as a "center" where certain cognitive functions can be localized, such as visuospatial processes in the parietal lobes, memory in the temporal lobes, and motor planning in the frontal lobes. The effects of brain lesions are then understood through localizing damage to the relevant centers, or through analyzing cognitive deficits in order to discern functional "disconnections" between centers (Geschwind, 1965).

Retroactivations and distributed representations. Although these assumptions have allowed neuropsychology to relate damage to functions with some empirical success, they implied that complete mental representations are held in focal centers of the cortex, and this notion has never withstood careful scrutiny. As connectionist models in cognitive science have shown how cognitive representations could be achieved by distributed networks, there have been new opportunities for a theoretical understanding of the functions of the cortex.

Damasio (1989) has taken issue with the traditional assumption that elementary perceptual analyses are completed in the posterior brain while more anterior regions form complex representations of objects and events. He points to evidence that damage to primary sensory cortices may impair recall as well as perception of information in the relevant sensory modality. This evidence suggests that storage is achieved in part by the same tissue that conducted the initial perception (see also Squire, 1986). Damasio theorizes that the brain stores a mental representation in a distributed fashion, with its perceptual features encoded in the primary sensory cortices.

How these features or "fragments" could be combined to create a coherent memory of an event is termed the "binding problem." Damasio (1989) proposes that the fragments from primary cortices are first combined in the adjacent parasensory areas. This information is then again combined in the "convergence zones" that receive information from several modalities. These include neocortical association areas, the paralimbic cortex, and the subcortical basal ganglia. What is represented in these areas is not the experience of an object or event, but the binding function that links the representational fragments in primary sensory cortices. This linkage, accomplished through "retroactivation" of the sensory fragments, integrates the mental contents—widely distributed across the sensory cortices—to achieve the unity of consciousness.

In support of his contention that processing in the cortex occurs in multiple parallel streams, Damasio points out that, with the exception of the paralimbic entorhinal cortex, no cortical area integrates projections from all other areas of cortex. In both frontal and posterior association areas, there remains a segregation of connection patterns, precluding the kind of integrated mental representation that has traditionally been attributed to these higher association areas. Although Damasio seems to discount the possibility that limbic structures and their paralimbic cortices could provide the "binding function" required to integrate mental representations, there is both anatomical and functional evidence that this may be the case.

Limbic roots of the neocortex. Recent anatomical studies suggest that the best way to understand the connectional architecture of the cortex may be to consider the course of its evolution (Pandya et al., 1988). Drawing from his studies of the cytoarchitectonics of the mammalian cortex and from earlier studies of the primitive cortex of reptiles, Sanides (1970) proposed that the mammalian neocortex evolved from two primitive limbic-related fields—the hippocampal archicortex and the amygdala-related piriform paleocortex. These primordial "spring sources" gave rise to two protogradations or trends: a medial trend originated in the hippocampal archicortex to extend upward along the medial surface of the hemisphere and then downward along the dorsolateral surface, and a lateral trend originated within the piriform paleocortex to progress across the temporal lobe and upward along the lateral surface of the hemisphere. Sanides' medial and lateral trends appear to constitute neocortical extensions of the hippocampal- and piriform-focused components of paralimbic cortex. As they differentiate and progress out from the paralimbic regions, each successive field constitutes a structurally similar version of older fields, but with an increase in laminar differentiation. In general, the newer fields within the trends show a progressive development of the more superficial cortical layers (Pandya & Yeterian, 1985).

The evolutionary approach thus uncovers two distinct processing networks in the cortex. Moreover, it shows that in both trends the neocortex has its developmental roots in the limbic system. Importantly, recent studies have revealed sequenced projections within the medial and lateral trends, proceeding from paralimbic to successively more differentiated neocortical fields (Pandya et al., 1988). Running backward compared with the conventional corticoparalimbic projections, these pathways provide a means for information of limbic origin to influence cognition at multiple levels. Through these connections the limbic roots may provide a kind of adaptive control over the formation of representations in the more articulated neocortical networks.

Several aspects of this architecture may have implications for functional representation. Within each trend, the "vertical" connections from the more differentiated fields tend to terminate in a columnar fashion in layer 4 of the adjacent more primitive field. In contrast, the projections from the more primitive to the more differentiated fields terminate primarily in layer 1. Since layer 1 contains the apical dendrites of pyramidal output neurons, back-projections from the older regions may effect a subtle modulation of the advancing sensory information.

Another key feature of cortical architecture is the organization of transcortical connections in a "horizontal" pattern, with most connections linking areas of similar architectonic differentiation. For example, the least differentiated frontal regions tend to be connected with the older temporal sensory areas, while the more differentiated frontal regions project to the newer temporal areas. This suggests that the primary units for functional integration in the cortex may not be lobes or sensory modalities but the cortical growth rings—the levels of architectonic differentiation. The most general sensory information is closely integrated with the most primitive response information, the more articulated sensory networks linked with the more recent response networks, and so forth. A simplified illustration of this horizontal and vertical connectivity is contained in Figure 2.

Furthermore, the more primitive, least differentiated regions closest to the limbic origins have the most widespread cortical

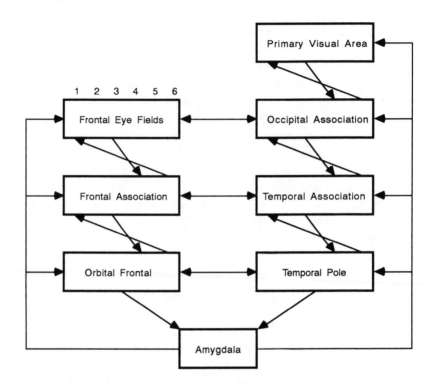

FIGURE 2. Highly simplified diagram illustrating the vertical and horizontal organization of the prefrontal (on left) and temporal (on right) components of the paleocortical trend. The orbital frontal and temporal pole regions constitute the paralimbic origins. Within the prefrontal lobe, the frontal association and frontal eye field regions correspond to vental areas 46 and 8, respectively. Within the temporal lobe, the temporal association region refers to areas 20 and 21, the occipital association region refers to areas 18 and 19, and the primary visual area is area 17. The box labeled Amygdala refers to the basolateral amygdala, which projects to layers 1 and 2 of all areas. Forward projections from the more differentiated areas (at top of trend) begin in layer 3 and terminate in layer 4. Backward projections from the less differentiated areas (at bottom of trend) begin in layers 5 and 6 and terminate in layer 1. Horizontal arrows between the vertical levels schematize the tendency for regions of similar architectonic development to be highly interconnected (based on Pandya, Seltzer, & Barbas, 1988).

connections (generally to other primitive cortex), whereas the more differentiated neocortical fields have more restricted and local interconnections. In fact, the areas with the greatest laminar differentiation, the primary sensory cortices, have few transcortical connections besides those relayed through the immediately adjacent, less differentiated parasensory areas. This reflects the same pattern evident in brainstem and limbic regions, a progressive fan out from diffuse, undifferentiated projection patterns to more specific, confined patterns of interconnection. This connection pattern implies that the most differentiated neocortical networks, even those of multimodal posterior and frontal cortex, are specialized for articulating the features of mental representations, whereas the binding function that integrates features into coherent experiences may be achieved by the more primitive, densely interconnected networks of paralimbic cortex.

Both the fan in from sensory cortices to limbic structures and the fan out from limbic system to motor cortex have become increasingly important facts of anatomy in interpreting the results of recent studies of functional pathways in the cortex. In research on primate vision, the analysis of information from primary visual cortex proceeds in parallel along the dorsal route to archicortex and the hippocampus and along the ventral route to paleocortex and the amygdala. The integrity of the connections to the limbic structures is essential to support the memory functions of these pathways, the spatial memory of the dorsal pathway and the object memory of the ventral pathway (Ungerleider & Mishkin, 1982). In studies of motor control, it has become important to understand the progressive elaboration of function through the increasingly differentiated networks of the archicortical and paleocortical trends from anterior limbic areas to primary motor cortex (Goldberg, 1985). Although the specification of motor sequences appears to occur in primary motor cortex, this specification may be the end product of a developmental process that recruits progressive stages of organization from paralimbic cortex through the increasingly articulated layers of neocortical networks (Brown, 1987; Goldberg, 1985).

Motivational Regulation of Cognition

The representations achieved by neocortical regions are thus shaped by multiple ascending control systems. The most elementary of these systems are tuned to extract the motivational significance of incoming information, showing the greatest responsivity to stimuli that are stressful, conspicuous, or related to current need states. The control exerted seems to be a kind of modulation, biasing the sensitivity of cortical cells to significant inputs. Note that the ascending systems have become increasingly specific, in both their sensory responsivity and their efferent projections, as the forebrain evolved. In a spatial sense, the highly precise neocortical circuitry can be viewed as nested within a succession of progressively broader innervation patterns arising from paralimbic regions, the telencephalic and diencephalic limbic structures, and the brainstem reticular systems. In a temporal sense as well, the succinct, finely patterned neocortical processing appears embedded within longer-lasting control biases of the subcortical projections. These properties of brain organization suggest that cortical processing must be a highly dynamic affair, shaped by a variety of fluctuating and complex modulatory states.

In addition to influences arising from subcortical systems, the organization of the cortex itself has important implications for understanding the relation of cognition to motivational and emotional processes. The large human neocortex has evolved increasingly articulated networks, yet each is linked to its predecessor. In the mammalian brain, the most differentiated networks have acquired specialized input and output connections—the thalamic projections to primary sensory cortices and the pyramidal tracts connecting motor cortex directly to specific brainstem motor nuclei. But in the architecture of the neocortex itself the highly differentiated networks have become isolated, such that their representational products can be integrated with those of other brain regions only through the transformations required to pass down through the hierarchy to the less differentiated networks, which are then integrated across lobes and regions. The anatomical evidence suggests that the greatest degree of cross-lobe interconnection, and thus the greatest functional binding of the distributed network representations, occurs at the most primitive, paralimbic level of the neocortical hierarchy. If the neocortex functions in a vertically integrated fashion—and the evidence on memory indicates that it does—then each articulate cognitive representation may be organized around a less articulate, more adaptively constrained base.

Thus, if a psychological theory of motivation is to be anatomically correct, it must begin with the general modulation of arousal state applied by the brainstem projection systems. It must also recognize multiple levels of cognitive representation, some less differentiated, yet perhaps more organismically integrated, than others. In the following sections we attempt to work toward such a theory by suggesting that the broader systems serve primarily to regulate the "stylistic" properties of cognition, whereas the more organized systems modulate its "content." More specifically, we theorize that the brainstem reticular systems set up two general modes of attentional control, one involving a tonic readiness for action and the other a phasic arousal or alertness. These general control modes are elaborated by embedded network regulatory processes that are continually recruited from limbic and paralimbic circuits. Constrained by the general states of activation and arousal, the limbic circuits act to potentiate more specific neocortical networks representing those sensory and response processes that are adaptive for the current motivational state.

INFLUENCES ON PSYCHOLOGICAL STYLE

The brainstem neuromodulator pathways alter general states of brain activity, such as the change from sleep to wakefulness. In psychological terms, such state changes are considered in the domain of "arousal." Both conventional psychological theory and the conventional notion of a reticular activating system have viewed arousal as a quantitative dimension—more or less arousal of the brain and its functions. Yet the evidence on neuromodulator effects shows qualitative influences on the nature as well as the amount of neural activity. For example, the locus coeruleus noradrenergic pathways are particularly responsive to novel external events (Foote et al., 1983) and habituate rapidly to a constant environment. Although their influence is clearly one of arousal or alerting, it seems to have a specific patterning in time. Another example is seen in the behavioral effects of the dopamine pathways projecting from midbrain nuclei to striatal, ventral limbic, and frontal cortical areas. Although they appear to facilitate behavioral initiation by increasing the activity in motor circuits, the dopaminergic pathways include qualitative effects as well, restricting the range of novel behavior, until with strong dopaminergic modulation the animal begins showing repetitive, stereo-typed behavior (Antelman & Chiodo, 1984).

Tucker and Williamson (1984) attempted to develop a model of arousal and attentional control that would capture the qualitative effects that seem to be produced by the neuromodulator pathways. They focused on the noradrenergic and dopaminergic systems that appear to be the primary "activating" neuromodulators. Their model was clearly speculative, and it addressed only certain pieces of the neuromodulator puzzle. Yet it showed how a number of specific controls on attention and working memory could follow from primitive influences on the flow of information in brain circuits.

Drawing from Pribram and McGuinness's (1975) theoretical overview of brain systems of arousal and attention, Tucker and Williamson proposed that the dopamine projections apply a form of "tonic activation" to support motor readiness, whereas the norepinephrine projections are particularly important to perceptual orienting and, because of their rapid habituation, support a mode of "phasic arousal." Each of these ways of augmenting brain activity can be seen to entail more complex cybernetic effects than are captured by the traditional notion of arousal control. Each may incorporate a form of negative feedback that applies necessary constraints to the brain's responsivity to perceptual stimulation or to the adaptive initiation of motor activity.

Consider the design of a simple perceptual arousal system that has the effect of augmenting brain activity in response to perceptual input. If part of what is augmented is the responsivity of the perceptual system itself, then this simple system has the fatal defect of a positive feedback loop, such that increased responsivity amplifies the effective stimulus, which increases responsivity still further, and so forth. The habituation bias of the brain's perceptual orienting circuitry, mediated at least in part by norepinephrine pathways, seems to correct for this potential defect by decrementing its responsivity to repetitive input. The positive control effect is a novelty bias, alerting the brain selectively to changes in the environmental flux.

An opposite bias seems to be applied by the dopaminergic pathways to the motor circuitry, such that greater modulation means greater routinization and stereotypy of the information directing the motor sequence. Tucker and Williamson speculated that the tonic activation system may entail a redundancy bias, restricting the range of motor control information. The cybernetics of this system may have evolved to deal with the design problem of priming motor activity in emergency situations. When the brainstem must suddenly energize neural circuits in a crisis, a nonspecific activation of potential motor plans would result in poorly organized behavior. The redundancy bias of the tonic activation system would engage the best-rehearsed and most routinized fight or flight sequences.

Given the qualitative cybernetics of these primitive systems, a number of psychological properties can be deduced. The phasic arousal system may support what is traditionally described as the orienting response. Because they apply a habituation bias to cortical processing, the ascending noradrenergic fibers have the net effect of selecting for novelty. As cortical cells continue to respond to novel events, working memory fills with representations of many unique environmental data, giving rise to an expansive, holistic attentional style. In the temporal domain, conversely, this rapid updating of unique, immediately present events leads to a short, present-centered attentional style.

Drawing on clinical and pharmacological evidence on the nor adrenergic system, Tucker and Williamson (1984) proposed that there are affective qualities to variations in the phasic arousal system, experienced as a positive affect dimension running from depression to elation. Thus noradrenergic phasic arousal may be a core component of positive motivational states, and positive motivational states may promote a processing style with an expansive spatial scope of attention along with a narrow, present-centered temporal span of attention.

The complementary tonic activation system is central to motor readiness. To support the rapid sequencing required by motor systems, the ascending dopaminergic systems apply a redundancy bias to processing in neural circuits, thus increasing the constancy of currently active information. As a result, working memory is restricted to a limited number of closely related representations, leading to a focused, narrow style of attention. Since these contents are integrated and enduring, however, a more continuous representation across time is possible, and attention incorporates events in the immediate past and the anticipated future. This tonic, focused attentional mode, integrating between recent events and the impending future, can be seen as essential to preparing for action under threatening conditions. In affective terms, tonic activation is hypothesized to be synonymous with a negative affect dimension running from relaxation and calmness to anxiety and hostility. Dopaminergic tonic activation may thus be fundamental to negative motivational states that require a narrow spatial focus of attention along with a bias toward stability of the contents of attention across time.

Several observations can be seen to be consistent with this proposal that specific attentional modes are inherent to certain affective states. In the case of phasic arousal, Isen and her colleagues have found that experimentally induced positive affect leads to impulsive and impressionistic as opposed to methodical and effortful problem-solving styles (Isen & Hastorf, 1982). In addition, such mild "elation" increases remote associations to neutral words in a first associates task (Isen, Daubman, & Gorgoglione, 1985). Clinical evidence also indicates an expansive attentional style during positive motivational states. Like creative artists, manic patients show a categorization style that is overinclusive (Andreasen & Powers, 1975). When taken off lithium, manic patients show enhanced remote associations on an associational fluency task, but when lithium is reinstated their associations again become restricted (Shaw, Mann, Stokes, & Manevitz, 1986). Thus a dynamic modulation of affective state seems to entail a simultaneous modulation of the scope of attention.

In the case of tonic activation, dopamine agonists such as amphetamine promote repetitive, stereotyped behaviors (Antelman & Chiodo, 1984). With repeated usage, dopamine agonists can give rise to a psychotic state characterized by paranoia, compulsive stereotyped behavior, social withdrawal, and hypervigilance. The tightly structured paranoid elaborations are accompanied in severe cases by an almost autistic internal focusing of attention (Antelman & Chiodo, 1984). Such examples of highly focused attention are consistent with a number of experimental studies indicating that anxious states involve a bias favoring central at the expense of peripheral visual information (Easterbrook, 1959; Weltman, Smith, & Egstrom, 1971). However, additional studies suggest that the narrowing of attention is not limited to central vision but can also involve a focusing on peripheral cues, particularly when they constitute a source of threat or danger (MacLeod, Mathews, & Tata, 1986; Reeves & Bergum, 1972).

Future research and theoretical work will need to clarify not only the interactions between norepinephrine and dopamine and the other major neuromodulators, but the vertical integration between these elementary brainstem controls and higher regulatory systems. Tucker and Williamson (1984) reviewed evidence that the major neuromodulator systems are asymmetrically distributed in the human brain, and they theorized that hemispheric specialization has elaborated on the primitive cybernetics of tonic activation and phasic arousal. The left hemisphere's analytic cognition may have evolved as an extension of the focal attention and sequential cognitive processing emergent from the tonic motor readiness system. The right hemisphere's holistic spatial skills and capacity for parallel processing may have evolved to elaborate on the attentional mode of the phasic perceptual arousal system.

More recently, neuroanatomical studies have shown that the noradrenergic pathways preferentially innervate the dorsal cortical regions involved in spatial perception, whereas the dopaminergic projections radiate most strongly to the ventral cortical regions involved in object perception (Lewis & Morrison, 1989). With these findings, there are new theoretical opportunities to understand the congruence of primitive control modes with unique patterns of network representation in the cortex, and thus to appreciate the interdependence of multiple dimensions of brain organization—left-right, dorsal-ventral, and hierarchical-vertical.

For example, the right hemisphere may have become specialized not only for the expansive attention of the phasic arousal system, but for the spatial localization skills of the dorsal neocortical pathways (Bear, 1983; Galaburda, 1984; Tucker & Derryberry, in press). If so, then the primitive mode of phasic arousal may facilitate perceptual and cognitive processes employing "spatial" representations, where parts are globally related to the general context, and metric "distances" between the parts are preserved. Similarly, the left hemisphere's evolution may have elaborated an entire hemisphere's processing networks to extend the object-parsing skills of the ventral neocortical trend, which in turn requires the sequencing and analytic focusing inherent to the redundancy bias of the tonic motor activation system (Galaburda, 1984; Tucker & Derryberry, in press). This redundancy bias may be integral to processing "object-like" representations, where parts are related to one another in an analytic and categorical manner.

INFLUENCES ON PSYCHOLOGICAL CONTENT

By tuning elementary properties of neural activity, the tonic activation and phasic arousal systems may alter the patterning of information processing in time, thereby achieving complementary effects on the scope of the available mental representations. Although these elementary cybernetic effects would alter the structure of concept formation, their influence on the content of thought seems limited to primitive biases toward facilitating the perception of threatening versus hedonic qualities of the information (Tucker, Vannatta, & Rothlind, in press). More specific motivations of the substance of cognition must be achieved at more differentiated levels of control, in limbic and neocortical networks.

Interpreting the processing architecture. An analysis of the architecture of the neocortex suggests that cognition must be performed through parallel representations at multiple levels of the network hierarchy, with a fan out of connections from the primitive to the more differentiated networks. A number of theoretical issues must be addressed before the organized functioning of these networks can be understood. How do the representations at the archicortical and paleocortical levels figure in the activity within the extensive neocortical networks of the human brain? What is the nature of processing across adjacent levels? How are hierarchical relations organized? What control mechanisms balance the multiple representations to allow a unified experience of the environment and an integrated behavioral act?

An evolutionary interpretation seems necessary to account for the brain's hierarchical structure and for its increasing articulation of neocortical networks. In the evolution of the primate brain, each new wave of neocortical differentiation seemed to provide a more complex representation of the external environment, culminating in what are now the primary sensory and motor cortices. To support this most complex and articulated representation of the environment, the most recently evolved networks acquired their own direct connections from receptors, such as from the thalamic projections to primary sensory cortices, and to effectors, such as through the pyramidal motor tract from primary motor cortex. With the successive waves of network differentiation, and with each outer layer refining the model of the environment, the brain is like an onion. Each new wave of network differentiation was superimposed on its predecessor, and the predecessor layer was then transformed from the role of front-line environment interface to a role of greater evaluation and integration of the environmental data.

At the base of the cortical hierarchy are the archicortical and paleocortical foci of the protomammalian general cortex. The general cortex of the ancestors of mammals did not have specified sensory modality and motor projection zones but represented an undifferentiated matrix of information on both internal states and the external context. As it developed in mammals, the general cortex seems to have provided mnemonic functions: its network architecture produced representations of need-states-in-context that allowed behavior to be integrated across increasing time spans. Instead of reptilian fixed-action patterns locked to discrete environmental releasers, mammals soon had more generalized behavioral capacities, directed by increasing spans of memory and anticipation.

In humans, the primitive cortical networks retain their undifferentiated organization, and they remain closely connected to limbic need states and the visceral milieu (Mesulam & Mufson, 1982b). Because it has the greatest density of interregional connections, this least differentiated level of representation must also yield the greatest functional integration of any level in the cortical hierarchy. In sensory processing, the information fans in from articulated networks to paralimbic regions, cascading through increasingly undifferentiated representational forms. In motor organization, the paralimbic level serves as a base for the fan out of impulses and target object representations during the developmental articulation of actions (Goldberg, 1985).

As described above, there are extensive back-projections from more primitive toward more differentiated sensory networks (Pandya et al., 1988), with a particular pattern of interlaminar connection from deep to superficial layers. Given that the same pattern of intralaminar connections across adjacent architectonic areas holds for frontal cortex (Barbas & Pandya, 1989), then the articulation of motor sequences appears to be achieved through a "forward" progression within the connections that in the sensory cortices form the "back-projections." Information flows across multiple levels toward the core of the onion, then across multiple levels back out again.

It seems unlikely that much useful information processing is achieved in one pass through the hierarchy, fanning either in or out. We suggest that an important principle for processing in the cortex may be described as "vertical recursion." The formation of a stable pattern of parallel representations across the multiple network levels may be achieved only after several waves of recursive interaction have cascaded up and down the hierarchy. Within the onion metaphor for the network architecture, this processing might be described as radial recursion, integrating the representations at the core with those of the more superficial networks. The processing is recursive in that the output from any level of the hierarchy returns to that level, either after processing by the immediately adjacent architectonic level or after eliciting links to representations at more distant networks. There are multiple representational "maps" of environmental data at the multiple levels of the hierarchy, each deeper one within a more primitive network. The two-way, recursive processing across the levels may achieve a hierarchy of congruent, linked representations, each at a different evolutionary level.

The differentiated networks at the top of the hierarchy provide articulate representations of the sensory and motor environment interface. Yet these are only the top layer of the integrated, parallel-representation hierarchy, and they cannot be formed without contributions from all lower levels. These lower levels may provide a continual evaluation of the adaptive, organismic meaning of the patterns at the sensory/motor interface level.

In the dynamics of vertical recursion, the process of concept formation may be controlled through a kind of "adaptive selection." The only concepts that survive to be instantiated in the neocortical networks are the ones that achieve some sort of adaptive resonance with the significance evaluation regions at the core of the brain. Although representations may be stored at each level of the hierarchy, this storage process, and many kinds of adaptively directed retrieval, may require the integrated patterning across all levels that is achieved through vertical recursion.

We propose that this hypothetical outline of information representation in the brain can suggest a theoretical model of motivated cognition. It may be useful to consider vertical recursion as a developmental process, in which the differentiated representations of perceptual data recruit more global organismic states, represented at the brain's core, that then facilitate further perceptual evaluation and simultaneously impel an increasingly differentiated course of action.

As described below, response organization begins with the laying out of general autonomic and endocrine patterns, followed by a selection of axial muscle groups involved in supporting adaptive postures, and finally by the more precise specification of distal motor groups controlling the extremities. At the same time, specific exteroceptive pathways carrying relevant sensory information are facilitated. Perceptual processing may begin with a global apprehension of the environmental context, but given that certain features recruit qualities of adaptive resonance in the core brain, there is a narrowing of attention on the most important environmental information. Processing in both the response and the sensory systems gives rise to interoceptive information, which serves as an internal evaluation of the significance of the sensorimotor activity. Through interoception, visceral-somatic feelings contribute to the ultimate selection of a specific stimulus-response option. Interactions among the interoceptive, exteroceptive, and response-related information are in turn constrained by the prevailing states of phasic arousal and tonic activation.

Response modulation. Many traditional approaches to motivation, including drive (Hull, 1952), ethological (Tinbergen, 1951), and incentive (Mowrer, 1960) models, have emphasized the control of response processes. From the present perspective, this control would be carried out by a hierarchy serving to progressively specify the details of the action. At the more general levels, specific patterns of autonomic and endocrine activity would be set up, providing the background support for many potential postures and actions. At intermediate levels, more specific postural orientations employing the axial and proximal musculature would be specified, in turn providing support for a variety of more specific actions. At the most specific levels, individual actions incorporating the extremities would be specified in terms of the body's distal muscles. For example, a state of anxiety would be grounded in a defensive autonomic and endocrine pattern, potentiating adaptive postural activity related to freezing, fleeing, or fighting behavior. If the general environmental circumstances favored fleeing, then distinct escape programs would be facilitated, with the specific environmental situation determining which was selected. This type of hierarchy is temporally nested; that is, the general autonomic state persists across time while several postural changes occur. Similarly, each postural state can temporally embed a number of discrete arm, leg, and eye movements.

Limbic and paralimbic efferents are consistent with this way of thinking. Limbic circuits are closely linked with lower brainstem autonomic and somatic mechanisms, as well as with the basal ganglia loops of the forebrain. Particularly important are the paralimbic projections to the neocortical response areas. If we return to Sanides' (1970) model of cortical evolution, two trends emerge from the paralimbic regions of the frontal lobe. A medial premotor trend extends from the hippocampus-related cingulate cortex to the supplementary motor area to the primary motor cortex, while a lateral trend extends from the amygdala-related orbital cortex to the arcuate premotor region to the primary motor cortex. According to Goldberg (1985), the lateral or "responsive" trend functions in a feedback mode of control to adjust ongoing behavior in light of motivationally significant objects. In contrast, the medial or "projectional" trend functions in a feed-forward mode to direct behavior in terms of an anticipatory model of the future environment. Both of these trends receive subcortical input from limbic structures and from the processing loops of the basal ganglia and cerebellum. Programming begins with activation throughout the cortex and basal ganglia loops that provides a general context. Limbic and paralimbic regions aid in focusing this activation within the premotor regions, thus transforming the general context into an intention to act (Goldberg, 1985). Given the autonomic functions of the paralimbic cortex, this initial motor envelope may be organized around autonomic, drivelike states (Brown, 1989). As the activation spirals in on the motor cortex, additional postural and distal components are progressively specified.

The developmental process of vertical recursion throughout primitive and differentiated networks may be constrained by the current state of modulation by tonic activation and phasic arousal. Given its redundancy bias, tonic activation during stressful states would serve to restrict the unfolding response options, limiting them to a relatively small set of adaptive and prepotent behaviors. With strong dopaminergic activation, the sequencing of behavior would become rigid, and repetitive and stereotyped patterns would emerge. Given the apparent involvement of ventral object processing systems and their relation to Goldberg's (1985) responsive motor system, behaviors may be selected in light of a tight set of ongoing and anticipated environmental events.

In contrast, the phasic arousal accompanying positive states would promote a more extensive potentiation of response options. As the habituation bias selects for unique environmental events, behavior would appear more spontaneous and flexible, but also more labile and impulsive. If noradrenergic systems preferentially facilitated spatial pathways, then the behavior may tend to be "projected" in terms of the spatial environment, with less reactivity to individual objects and events.

Exteroceptive content. Whereas traditional models emphasized the response consequences of motivation, recent evidence indicates there are also important motivational influences on perceptual and cognitive processes. The basic idea is that by simultaneously facilitating relevant perceptual pathways, responses can be more effectively organized and guided. Moreover, motivational facilitation of perceptual and conceptual pathways can be carried out in the absence of response processing, thus setting the stage for motivated cognition. As in the case of response modulation, motivational influences over perception begin at a general level. A wide range of potential targets is first selected, followed by a progressive narrowing and specification.

The simplest examples involve facilitation of significant stimuli in the immediate environment. For example, Gray (1982) has discussed fear motivation in terms of a hippocampal-based system responsive to signals of punishment, nonreward, and novelty. Upon detecting such a signal, the system inhibits ongoing behavior and directs attention to the threatening stimulus. By facilitating the flow of relevant sensory information, the motivational circuitry promotes a more thorough analysis of the threat and thus a more appropriate response. At the same time, irrelevant information becomes less capable of eliciting distraction or an inappropriate response. More generally, fear motivation can be viewed as organizing perceptual processing around relevant input channels (Bolles & Fanselow, 1980). Not only sources of environmental threat would be facilitated, but also sources of potential relief, such as available safe locations and escape routes. We view this as an adaptive form of modulation, functioning to bring a range of potentially useful input channels into a state of simultaneous readiness.

Based on the divergent patterns of ascending limbic projections, this form of control can be distinguished from the sequential node-to-node types of excitatory activation prevalent within semantic network models. This more diffuse, parallel facilitation of sensory channels mirrors and supports that arising in the response systems, providing links from actual and anticipated perceptual events to multiple response options.

One way of viewing this initial facilitation emerges from the distinction between global and local processing drawn within cognitive psychology. A number of theorists have suggested that perception is a two-step process. It begins with a general analysis of the global environment, providing "suggestions" that guide a subsequent and more detailed analysis of local features (Broadbent, 1977). Thus the perceptual system operates in a hierarchical fashion, with the more detailed and local features nested within the more global and general ones. Global processing would be best accomplished by the older cortical regions featuring a relatively undifferentiated architecture and diffuse efferent projections. Local processing would be consistent with the more differentiated structures and precise outputs of the newer, modality-specific neocortical regions. Motivational effects would first operate at a global level, facilitating a range of potentially important objects and locations. As a global apprehension of the environment becomes available, it would feed into the more general stages of response preparation, such as those developing under the control of autonomic and postural mechanisms. Because pathways between anterior and posterior cortical regions tend to interconnect fields at the same level of architectonic development (Pandya et al., 1988), and because the densest interconnections occur among the most primitive networks, the evaluation of exteroceptive events may begin as a general "sensorimotor" foundation is framed, within which a more focused local analysis of potential targets can be carried out.

An important aspect of adaptive facilitation is its extension beyond the immediate environment. When a motivational state becomes active, it primes the stored representations of the objects and locations that have proved significant or useful in the past. For example, Bindra (1978) proposed that a state such as hunger functions by priming the central representations of "hedonic stimuli"—in this case representations of food objects. These potentiated food representations render the individual more responsive to food-related environmental cues and may also serve as "goals" or "search images" during exploratory behavior. Deutsch (1960) proposed that hunger motivates behavior by exciting a location in the animal's cognitive map representing a previous food source. Activation then spreads out from this potentiated location in a decremental manner, setting up a gradient of activation across links in the cognitive map. Although the food source is out of sight, the animal is able to approach and close in on it by orienting up the motivational gradient. Similar use of cognitive maps may occur during fear motivation, where locations associated with safety are accentuated to facilitate escape behavior (Toates, 1983). These examples of spatial modulation are reminiscent of Mesulam's (1981) proposal that a motivational map constructed in paralimbic cingulate cortex modulates a spatial map located in neocortical parietal cortex, thus directing attention toward hedonic environmental locations.

Given its emphasis on early global processing, motivational facilitation can have a variety of effects on information processing. Consider, for example, states related to success and failure. Successful outcomes of task performance in a psychology experiment have been found to facilitate tachistoscopic recognition of success-related words, whereas failure enhances failure-related words (Postman & Brown, 1952). Success also appears to increase attention to, and memories of, positive self-relevant information (Mischel, Ebbesen, & Zeiss, 1976). Similarly, in a reaction time paradigm employing sequential feedback and target signals, success feedback speeds the processing of high-valued positive targets, whereas failure enhances high-valued negative targets (Derryberry, 1990). When an incentive signal (conveying the possibility of gaining or losing points) is presented before the target, however, an incongruent feedback effect appears: success enhances attention to negative incentives, whereas failure facilitates positive incentives (Derryberry, 1988, 1989). These findings suggest that a state such as success exerts simultaneous congruent and incongruent effects. The individual is primed for information suggesting a similar outcome, but at the same time is set to shift to information supporting the opposite outcome.

Although they may be extensive, these facilitatory influences remain relevant to the situation and the individual's state. For instance, recent studies using Stroop paradigms indicate that anxious subjects have a tendency to shift attention toward threatening conceptual information, such as that conveyed by words denoting various types of physical and social threats. When asked to name the ink color of printed words, subjects with physical concerns are disrupted by a range of words referring to physical but not social threats (Mathews & MacLeod, 1985; Mogg, Mathews, & Weinman, 1989). Similarly, patients with spider phobias have been found to show "worry-congruent" interference from words (e.g., web) specifically related to their phobic object (Watts, McKenna, Sharrock, & Trezise, 1986). Thus the facilitation may be not a general potentiation of all negative content, but a relatively constrained bias favoring motivationally relevant information.

The conventional interpretation of such anxiety effects holds that interference occurs because anxious subjects have extensive and integrated knowledge structures that represent personal threats. When activated, these threat schemata consume a disproportionate amount of processing resources, leading to an impairment in processing other information. The present approach is not necessarily incompatible with this cognitive schema interpretation. However, we suggest that the schema is better approached as a potential rather than a stable cognitive structure (Rumelhart, Smolensky, McClelland, & Hinton, 1986), to some extent a result rather than a cause of the emotional activity. Diverse perceptual and conceptual representations may be facilitated and then may coalesce into a variety of broader schematic structures. Such horizontal and vertical integration will depend upon incoming environmental information, ongoing response programming, and the current states of tonic activation and phasic arousal.

Given a state of anxiety, for example, limbic circuitry functions to potentiate information relevant to various threats and means of coping. These contents will be set within the more general state of tonic activation and thus constrained in specific ways. To the extent that anxiety augments local, analytic processing, particularly by the left hemisphere (Tyler & Tucker, 1982), the initial global appraisal of the environment may be limited, and attention quickly becomes narrow. The prevailing redundancy bias will further limit the spread of activation, leading to a relatively constricted scope of working memory and perhaps a tendency to process information in a categorical manner. As a result, the schema that emerges is likely to consist of a relatively small subset of information showing strong coherence, with the individual components acting in concert to support one another and to suppress alternative interpretations.

Such tightly bound representations are likely to be rigid and difficult to perturb once they stabilize. In extreme instances the focused rumination may be severe enough that the person locks into repetitive and stereotyped trains of thought, such as those in obsessive-compulsive disorder. In the temporal frame, the redundancy bias acts to direct attention toward the future, so the person anticipates threats. Given the tightly categorical mode of processing, some of the analogical, metric properties of time may be lost, and the person may see possible threats of the distant future as imminent and thus as requiring immediate vigilance. The anxious person thus worries how to cope with threats, ruminating within a restricted domain of cognitive associations, which are in turn constrained by a tight attentional scope (Tucker & Derryberry, in press).

Interoceptive content. From an objective perspective, a theory of motivation must describe how a person responds to, and acts upon, environmental events. Yet a complete scientific approach to motivation must also consider the internal, subjective experiences of bodily states and processes. From a physiological view, information about internal states is essential to motivate adaptive behavior. From a psychological view, most people would agree that experiences of bodily states and associated emotions are integral to the phenomenology of motivation.

Because it is subjective, interoceptive experience has been ignored in many psychological theories. In examining the nervous system, however, it is remarkable how many circuits and structures are involved in processing interoceptive information. Interoceptive pathways include brainstem nuclei, extend upward to thalamic and limbic circuits, and attain their greatest resolution in the visceral and somatic fields of the paralimbic and neocortical regions. Two aspects of interoceptive experience are not commonly recognized. First, interoception is not limited to visceral information but includes complex somatic information as well. For example, the highest level interoceptive representations may reflect cardiovascular, digestive, thermal, respiratory, pain, and sexual sensations, interwoven with information on more superficial activity within the axial, proximal, and distal musculature. Second, although these representations are often activated by input from the body itself, the connectivity within the brain suggests that they may also be activated by means of corollary discharges ascending from subcortical effector systems, or by means of direct connections from other cortical regions (Nauta, 1971). Such connections suggest that subjective feelings do not always depend upon actual motor and autonomic responses. In addition, interoceptive feelings may arise in an anticipatory manner before the response itself, thereby providing important content for somatic and autonomic imagery.

Some theorists have argued that interoceptive information is experienced in terms of a single dimension of "general arousal," thought to reflect nonspecific autonomic activation (Mandler, 1985; Schachter & Singer, 1962). However, factor analytic studies of emotional experience suggest the presence of at least two primary factors. Earlier research extracted factors related to "activation" (low arousal–high arousal) and "evaluation" (pleasant-unpleasant). More recent studies suggest that these factors are not necessarily primary and that an equally valid rotation in the factor space defines dimensions of "positive affect" (varying from sadness to pleasurable engagement) and "negative affect" (varying from calmness to unpleasurable engagement) (Tellegen, 1985; Watson & Tellegen, 1985). The dimensions of "positive affect" and "negative affect" fit well within a motivational model. They appear to reflect the general affective tones established by the phasic arousal (elation-depression) and tonic activation (anxiety-relaxation) systems. In addition, they are consistent with evidence that the limbic circuits mediate reward and aversion systems (Berlyne, 1971) and that they are particularly responsive to signals predicting reward and punishment (Gray, 1982).

These primary feeling dimensions appear to become differentiated as response processing develops, providing additional interoceptive feedback. As autonomic mechanisms are engaged, for example, energy-related feelings may become available. Thayer (1989) has recently described dimensions of "energetic arousal" (running from sleepy and tired to vigorous and energetic) and "tense arousal" (running from calm and placid to tense and jittery). As the motivational state develops further and postural sets are recruited, more differentiated interoceptive states are structured within this hedonic or energetic frame. These states may be experienced in terms of "felt action tendencies," such as moving toward, moving away, or moving against (Frijda, Kuipers, & Ter Schure, 1989). Or they may be thought of as prototypical response orientations, such as incorporation, destruction, protection, or exploration (Plutchik, 1980).

The core brain and cognitive-affective interactions. From these primitive roots, more differentiated feeling states may be achieved by an increasing specification of actions or concepts directed toward relevant external objects. The link between felt action tendencies and exteroceptive information could be essential to feelings of intentionality (Brown, 1989). The sense of agency or volition may be a primitive and yet central component of the self.

In addition to arising from response processes, interoceptive states are also influenced by exteroceptive input. Some of these states are elicited by relatively nonspecific features of environmental events. For example, Berlyne (1971) has discussed how the psychophysical (e.g., intensity, rate) and collative (e.g., novelty, unexpectedness) properties of stimulation elicit immediate activity in reward and aversion systems, resulting in rapid fluctuations in hedonic tone. Similarly, Zajonc (1980) has provided evidence that feelings of preference for one object over another can occur rapidly and are based on the general context of the surround. Other interoceptive sensations, resulting from learned associations between events and outcomes, take on an anticipatory quality. These feelings may be simple, such as the nausea elicited by the smell of aversive foods, or more complex, such as the feelings of fear, hope, relief, and disappointment elicited by expectations of various outcomes (Livesey, 1986; Mowrer, 1960).

Buck (1985) has suggested that an important function of emotion is to inform the cognitive system, through a direct read-out to subjective experience, of the organism's current state. More directly, interoceptive states may form a primitive basis for the process of cognitive evaluation itself. Osgood's research with the semantic differential found that Evaluation (good-bad), Activation (quick-slow), and Potency (strong-weak) factors make up core dimensions of meaning (Osgood, Suci, & Tannenbaum, 1957). These dimensions of general cognitive appraisal may describe the same factor space as the pleasantness (good-bad) and intensity (arousal) dimensions of emotion research. Thus the case for rotation to create the positive affect and negative affect dimensions (Tellegen, 1985) could be made for the general domain of concept formation. At the most primitive, and yet essential, level of semantic appraisal, evaluation may be framed by the interoceptive resonance of elementary feeling states, such as are elicited by tonic activation (negative affect) and phasic arousal (positive affect).

Beyond these most elementary dimensions of concept formation, more complex patterns of cognition shape interoceptive experience and thus form an emotional basis for motivated behavior. Cognitive appraisal and attributional processes contribute to complex feelings such as hopelessness, guilt, and gratitude (Frijda et al., 1989; Weiner, this volume). Although the most elementary dimensions of affective/semantic appraisal are probably universal, more complex feeling states may be specific to each person, reflecting that person's history in appraising events by the feelings they engender. Because the primitive dimensions such as positive affect/phasic arousal are unlikely to be elicited out of context, there may always be a complex mix of cultural and personal concepts, as well as elementary interoceptive states, in the process of cognitive evaluation.

Thus, in anatomical terms, it may be difficult to separate the contribution of the paralimbic interoceptive areas from the extensive neocortical networks with which they are interconnected. Yet through the neocortical convergence upon the paralimbic areas, the interoceptive fields may function as a sensitive "sounding board" (James, 1890), adding important evaluative coloring to subjective experience as they resonate to ongoing processes of perception, response organization, and concept formation.

Although the process of vertical recursion would serve to integrate the paralimbic interoceptive representations with more articulated network representations at higher levels of the hierarchy, the recursive activity to achieve this may be a developmental process. As representations are being formed in sensory and motor areas, they recruit interoceptive activity that, because of its inherent evaluative quality, could aid in selecting among the developing response and sensory options. Important here is the notion that feelings are most strongly related to the early autonomic and axial stages of response programming and the earlier global stages of perception (Brown, 1989; Werner, 1957). As processing develops and differentiates, these activated feelings are in a position to evaluate and then guide subsequent sensory and response processing. Although additional environmental and strategic factors will come into play, a simple mechanism for evaluation would be the selection of those currently activated response and sensory options that generate the greatest positive affect and the least negative affect.

Nauta (1971) suggested that the frontal lobe may interact with the interoceptive areas of the paralimbic cortex in setting up a framework for evaluating behavior. He proposed that in planning a particular course of action, there are affective consequences that accompany the representation of each of the alternative courses of action. Although we view the hedonic and threat mechanisms as primary, representations of the internal energy state may also be important. Thayer (1989) suggests that feelings of energetic arousal and tension allow us to continuously assess current energy resources. If resources are low, as in fatigue or depression, then plans requiring vigorous action appear particularly unattractive. Because autonomic and postural states may be relatively enduring, an evaluative framework once established may apply a prolonged bias to ongoing behavior.

In addition to potentiating certain sensory and motor patterns, the reciprocal connections between paralimbic and neocortical areas may provide a means through which interoceptive states could interact with specific conceptual representations. If the thought is compatible (e.g., of success) then positive affect would be enhanced, and back projections from paralimbic to neocortical regions could facilitate the input, thus establishing a type of resonant, reverberating circuit. Given an ongoing state of high positive affect, appreciative and optimistic trains of thought would be supported. In contrast, the negative affect of anxiety could sensitize the person to threatening or frustrating content. At more specific levels, interoceptive content related to energy states and felt action tendencies would come into play (Dienstbier, 1989; Thayer, 1989). If the current energy state is high, these feelings may support cognitions related to coping and control in the face of threatening appraisals. But if the energy state is low, cognitions related to helplessness or hopelessness could be enhanced. Through vertical recursion, higher-level cognitive processes such as appraisals and attributions may be continually grounded within elementary interoceptive states.

Interoception and the bodily core of the self. As activity develops in response, sensory, and interoceptive fields, reciprocal connections among these regions allow certain distributed representations to coalesce and stabilize. Within these multiple levels of representation, it becomes difficult to consider the "meaning" of an object or concept without reference to the motivational and interoceptive context within which it is structured. Werner and Kaplan (1963) referred to such multifaceted cognitive processing as a "dynamic schematization." Rather than simply being activated, objects and concepts are constructed by a schematizing process that intertwines sensory, affective, postural, and imaginal components. This is a developmental or microgenetic process, proceeding from a primordial, undifferentiated sensory-affective matrix to a more articulated, differentiated conceptual form (Werner & Kaplan, 1963).

The interplay between the more primitive bodily feelings and the more articulated representations of external sensations and actions may be shaped differently by the control modes of tonic activation and phasic arousal. Given its redundancy bias and emphasis on focused, object-oriented attention, tonic activation may in some instances bias attention to the external rather than internal world. In states of anxiety, the body may be perceived in relation to a narrow set of external objects. These objects become charged with negative affect, and even though energy levels may be high, the recruitment of protective postures and defensive tendencies leads the body to be construed in a more reactive than active mode. In other instances of anxiety, the body itself can become the primary focal object. In severe social anxiety, for example, the person may become engulfed in anxious self-consciousness, disengaged from the external context.

In contrast, the expansive style accompanying the elated affect of strong phasic arousal seems to promote a broader integration between feelings and sensory events. Given its facilitation of spatial processing, phasic arousal may engage a strong, body-centered image of the physical and social environment. During elated states, this type of construction, along with core experiences of energy and the facilitation of positive exteroceptive input, may contribute to a sense of expansiveness, efficacy, and power. During depressed states, however, this outgoing spatial construction is impaired, and given the low energetic arousal and limited priming of positive external events, the world may seem to collapse inward on the self.

In psychological theory, a distinction has been made between the "bodily self" and the "conceptual self" (James, 1890). The representations emerging at the paralimbic level may form the framework of the bodily self. However, their influence extends into the conceptual domain as well. The numerous ideas and attributions that a person forms about the self may be too extensive, and too context specific, to be organized within a fixed and stable self-concept. Rather, subsets of ideas about the self may coalesce in different patterns at different times to form a somewhat different conceptual self on each occasion. Although some theorists have emphasized the importance of the external environment in shaping the self-concept (Kihlstrom & Cantor, 1984), we would also emphasize the internal environment. Interoceptive processing conditioned by positive and negative affect, energy, and felt action tendencies may underlie the ongoing configuration of the self. Core representations of positive affect and high energy could support the more favorable and optimistic self-conceptualizations, whereas states of negative affect or low energy may promote less favorable constructions. The self can thus be viewed as a multilevel representation, a vertical integration of abstract conceptual processes and elementary bodily feelings.

Summary

This chapter has explored a hierarchical approach to motivation, based on the idea of a vertical integration among brainstem, limbic, paralimbic, and neocortical systems. When viewed in the traditional manner, this hierarchy has been seen in terms of top-down control, with the neocortical regions exerting higher-level, converging influences over the lower regions. When viewed from an evolutionary perspective, the hierarchy proves to be balanced by a complementary pattern of divergent projections ascending from the lower to the higher levels. These ascending systems respond first to the adaptively significant properties of a stimulus, including its novelty, conspicuousness, and need relatedness. By means of their increasingly specific projection patterns, the elementary motivational mechanisms support a progressive narrowing of activity within the cortex.

Selection begins with activity in ascending brainstem systems, organizing the primordial states of tonic activation and phasic arousal. Although these states are relatively general, they bias information processing in specific ways by modulating both the spatial and temporal span of attention. As limbic circuits are recruited, certain classes of adaptive response and perceptual processes are potentiated, bringing into play postural orientations and global perceptions of the environment. This response and perceptual processing promotes activity within the interoceptive fields of the paralimbic cortices, leading to primitive hedonic and energetic representations. Back-projections from paralimbic to successive neocortical fields allow these affective representations to aid further in narrowing sensory and response options. Multiple levels of representation thus work together in gradually focusing and articulating the representations forming within the hierarchical networks of the neocortex.

The recent evidence on neocortical architecture shows that cortical areas tend to be most closely connected with other regions of the same level of architectonic differentiation. Thus the functional units of the cortex may be not lobes or even hemispheres but the growth rings sharing a specific laminar architecture and dense horizontal interconnections. Functional binding—the integration of the distributed representations of the cortex—may take place across these horizontal lines. Furthermore, the density of horizontal interconnections decreases for the more recently evolved neocortical growth rings, such that the primary and sensory and motor cortices are relatively isolated from all but the adjacent architectonic ring. This suggests that the most important functional binding in the cortex occurs at the more primitive, paralimbic network levels.

To be incorporated within integrated patterns of brain function, the representations formed in the articulated neocortical levels must achieve an interaction or resonance with the paralimbic core, cascading through the multiple network levels through some sort of vertically recursive processing. At the paralimbic core, the representations of the network become fused with visceral and somatic representations such that, in an important sense, cognitive evaluation is based on gut-level reactions. Within this anatomical framework, the cognitive activity of the neocortical networks is embodied, developing within a defining context of elementary motivational mechanisms.

REFERENCES

Alheid, G. F., & Heimer, L. (1988). New perspectives in basal forebrain organization of special relevance for neuropsychiatric disorders: The striatopallidal, amygdaloid, and corticopetal components of substantia innominata. *Neuroscience, 27,* 1–39.

Andreasen, N. J. C., & Powers, P. S. (1975). Creativity and psychosis: An examination of conceptual style. *Archives of General Psychiatry, 32,* 70–73.

Antelman, S., & Chiodo, L. A. (1984). Stress: Its effect on interactions among biogenic amines and role in the induction and treatment of disease. In L. L. Iversen, S. D. Iversen, & S. H. Snyder (Eds.), *Handbook of psychopharmacology* (Vol. 18, pp. 279–341). New York: Plenum.

Barbas, H., & Pandya, D. N. (1989). Architecture and intrinsic connections of the prefrontal cortex in the rhesus monkey. *Journal of Comparative Neurology, 286,* 353–375.

Bear, D. M. (1983). Hemispheric specialization and the neurology of emotion. *Archives of Neurology, 40,* 195–202.

Berlyne, D. E. (1971). Aesthetics and psychobiology. New York: Appleton-Century-Crofts.

Bindra, D. (1978). How adaptive behavior is produced: A perceptual-motivational alternative to response-reinforcement. *Behavioral and Brain Sciences, 1,* 41–91.

Bloom, F. E. (1988). What is the role of general activating systems in cortical function? In P. Rakic and W. Singer (Eds.), *Neurobiology of the neocortex* (pp. 407–421). New York: Wiley.

Bolles, R. C., & Fanselow, M. S. (1980). A perceptual-defensive-recuperative model of fear and pain. *Behavioral and Brain Sciences, 3,* 291–332.

Borod, J. C., Koff, E., & Buck, R. (1986). The neuropsychology of facial expression: Data from normal and brain-damaged adults. In P. D. Blank, R. W. Buck, & R. Rosenthal (Eds.), *Nonverbal communication in the clinical context.* University Park: Pennsylvania State University Press.

Brandt, S., Seidman, L. J., & Kohl, D. (1985). Personality characteristics of epileptic patients: A controlled study of generalized and temporal lobe cases. *Journal of Clinical and Experimental Neuropsychology, 7,* 25–38.

Broadbent, D. E. (1977). The hidden preattentive processes. *American Psychologist, 32,* 109–118.

Brown, J. (1987). The microstructure of action. In E. Perecman (Ed.), *The frontal lobes revisited.* New York: IRBN Press.

Brown, J. W. (1989). The nature of voluntary action. *Brain and Cognition, 10,* 105–120.

Buck, R. (1985). Prime theory: An integrated view of motivation and emotion. *Psychological Review, 92,* 389–413.

Buck, R. (1988). *Human motivation and emotion.* New York: Wiley.

Cechetto, D. F., & Saper, C. B. (1987). Evidence for a viscerotopic sensory representation in the cortex and thalamus in the rat. *Journal of Comparative Neurology, 262,* 27–45.

Coburn, K. L., Ashford, J. W., & Fuster, J. M. (1990). Visual response latencies in temporal lobe structures as a function of stimulus information load. *Behavioral Neuroscience, 104,* 62–73.

Damasio, A. R. (1989). Time-locked multiregional retroactivation: A systems-level proposal for the neural substrates of recall and recognition. *Cognition, 33,* 25–62.

Davidson, R. J. (1984). Affect, cognition and hemispheric specialization. In C. E. Izard, J. Kagan, & R. Zajonc (Eds.), *Emotion, cognition and behavior.* New York: Cambridge University Press.

Davis, M., Hitchcock, J. M., & Rosen, J. B. (1987). Anxiety and the amygdala: Pharmacological and anatomical analysis of the fear-potentiated startle paradigm. In G. Bower (Ed.), *The psychology of learning and motivation* (pp. 263–305). New York: Academic Press.

Denny-Brown, D., Meyer, J. W., & Horenstein, S. (1952). The significance of perceptual rivalry resulting from parietal lesions. *Brain, 75,* 433–471.

Derryberry, D. (1988). Emotional influences on evaluative judgments: Roles of arousal, attention, and spreading activation. *Motivation and Emotion, 12,* 23–55.

Derryberry, D. (1989). Effects of goal-related motivational states on the spatial orienting of attention. *Acta Psychologica, 72,* 199–220.

Derryberry, D. (1990). *Attentional consequences of the incentive value and magnitude of visual targets.* Manuscript submitted for publication.

Deutsch, J. A. (1960). *The structural basis of behavior.* Chicago: University of Chicago Press.

Dienstbier, R. A. (1989). Arousal and physiological toughness: Implications for mental and physical health. *Psychological Review, 96,* 84–100.

Doane, B. K., & Livingston, K. E. (1986). *The limbic system: Functional organization and clinical disorders.* New York: Raven Press.

Easterbrook, J. A. (1959). The effect of emotion on cue utilization and the organization of behaviour. *Psychological Review, 66,* 183–201.

Everitt, B. J., Cador, M., & Robbins, T. W. (1989). Interactions between the amygdala and ventral striatum in stimulus-reward associations: Studies using a second-order schedule of sexual reinforcement. *Neuroscience, 30,* 63–75.

Foote, S. L., Bloom, F. E., & Aston-Jones, G. (1983). Nucleus locus coeruleus: New evidence of anatomical and physiological specificity. *Physiological Review, 63,* 844–914.

Foote, S. L., & Morrison, J. H. (1987). Extrathalamic modulation of cortical function. *Annual Review of Neuroscience, 10,* 67–95.

Frijda, N. H., Kuipers, P., & Ter Schure, E. (1989). Relations among emotion, appraisal, and emotional action readiness. *Journal of Personality and Social Psychology, 57,* 212–228.

Fuster, J. M., & Uyeda, A. A. (1971). Reactivity of limbic neurons of the monkey to appetitive and aversive signals. *Electroencephalography and Clinical Neurophysiology, 30,* 281–293.

Gabriel, M., Sparenborg, S. P., & Stolar, N. (1986). An executive function of the hippocampus: Pathway selection for thalamic neuronal significance code. In R. L. Isaacson & K. H. Pribram (Eds.), *The hippocampus* (Vol. 4, pp. 1–39). New York: Plenum.

Galaburda, A. M. (1984). The anatomy of language: Lessons from comparative anatomy. In A. Smith (Ed.), *Biological perspectives on language.* Cambridge: MIT Press.

Geschwind, N. (1965). Disconnection syndromes in animals and man. *Brain, 88,* 237–294.

Goldberg, G. (1985). Supplementary motor area structure and function: Review and hypotheses. *Behavioral and Brain Sciences, 8,* 567–616.

Goldberg, M. E., & Robinson, D. L. (1977). Visual responses of neurons in monkey inferior parietal lobule: The physiologic substrate of attention and neglect. *Neurology, 27,* 350.

Grant, S. J., Aston-Jones, G., & Redmond, D. E. (1988). Responses of primate locus coeruleus neurons to simple and complex sensory stimuli *Brain Research Bulletin, 21,* 401–410.

Gray, J. A. (1982). *The neuropsychology of anxiety.* London: Oxford.

Groenewegen, H. J. (1988). Organization of the afferent connections of the mediodorsal thalamic nucleus in the rat, related to the mediodorsal-prefrontal topography. *Neuroscience, 24,* 379–431.

Gur, R. E. (1978). Left hemisphere dysfunction and left hemisphere overactivation in schizophrenia. *Journal of Abnormal Psychology, 87,* 226–238.

Higgins, E. T. (1987). Self-discrepancy: A theory relating self and affect. *Psychological Review, 94,* 319–340.

Hull, C. L. (1952). *A behavior system: An introduction to behavior theory concerning the individual organism.* New Haven: Yale University Press.

Isaacson, R. L. (1980). A perspective for the interpretation of limbic system function. *Physiological Psychology, 8,* 183–188.

Isen, A. M., Daubman, K. A., & Gorgoglione, J. M. (1985). The influence of positive affect on cognitive organization. In R. Snow & M. Farr (Eds.), *Aptitude, learning and instruction: Affective and cognative processes.* Hillsdale, NJ: Erlbaum.

Isen, A. M., & Hastorf, A. H. (1982). Some perspectives on cognitive social psychology. In A. H. Hastorf & A. M. Isen (Eds.), *Cognitive social psychology.* New York: Elsevier.

Iwai, E., & Yukie, M. (1987). Amygdalofugal and amygdalopetal connections with modality-specific visual cortical areas in macaques (*Macaca fuscata, M. mulatta,* and *M. fascicularis*). *Journal of Comparative Neurology, 261,* 362–387.

338

Jackson, J. H. (1879). On affections of speech from diseases of the brain. *Brain*, 2, 203–222.

James, W. (1890). *Principles of psychology.* New York: Holt.

Johanson, A. M., Risberg, J., Silfverskiold, P., & Smith, G. (1986). Regional changes of cerebral blood flow during increased anxiety in patients with anxiety neurosis. In U. Hentschel, G. Smith, & J. G. Draguns (Eds.), *The roots of perception.* Amsterdam: North-Holland.

Kihlstrom, J. F., & Cantor, N. (1984). Mental representations of the self. In L. Berkowitz (Ed.), *Advances in experimental social psychology* (Vol. 17). New York: Academic Press.

Kinsbourne, M., & Bemporad, B. (1984). Lateralization of emotion: A model and the evidence. In N. Fox & R. J. Davidson (Eds.), *The psychobiology of affective development.* Hillsdale, NJ: Erlbaum.

Krushel, L. A., & Van der Kooy, D. (1988). Visceral cortex: Integration of the mucosal senses with limbic information in the rat agranular insular cortex. *Journal of Comparative Neurology, 270,* 39–54.

LeDoux, J. E. (1987). Emotion. In F. Plum (Ed.), *Handbook of physiology: Sec. 1. The nervous system: Vol. 5. Higher functions of the brain, Part 1* (pp. 419–459). Bethesda, MD: American Physiological Society.

Lewis, D. A., & Morrison, J. H. (1989). Noradrenergic innervation of monkey prefrontal cortex: A dopamine-b-hydroxylase immunohistochemical study. *Journal of Comparative Neurology, 282,* 317–330.

Livesey, P. J. (1986). *Learning and emotion: A biological synthesis: Vol. 1. Evolutionary processes.* Hillsdale, NJ: Erlbaum.

MacLeod, C., Mathews, A., & Tata, P. (1986). Attentional bias in emotional disorders. *Journal of Abnormal Psychology, 95,* 15–20.

Mandler, G. (1985). *Mind and body: Psychology of emotion and stress.* New York: Norton.

Mantz, J., Milla, C., Glowinski, J., & Thierry, A. M. (1988). Differential effects of ascending neurons containing dopamine and noradrenaline in the control of spontaneous activity and of evoked responses in the rat prefrontal cortex. *Neuroscience, 27,* 517–526.

Mathews, A., & MacLeod, C. (1985). Selective processing of threat cues in anxiety states. *Behavior Research and Therapy, 23,* 563–569.

Mesulam, M. M. (1981). A cortical network for directed attention and unilateral neglect. *Annals of Neurology, 10,* 309–325.

Mesulam, M. M. (1988). Central cholinergic pathways: Neuroanatomy and some behavioral implications. In M. Avoli, T. A. Reader, R. W. Dykes, & P. Gloor (Eds.), *Neurotransmitters and cortical function: From molecules to mind* (pp. 237–260). New York: Plenum.

Mesulam, M. M., & Mufson, E. J. (1982a). Insula of the old world monkey: 1. Architectonics in the insulo-orbito-temporal component of the paralimbic brain. *Journal of Comparative Neurology, 212,* 1–22.

Mesulam, M. M., & Mufson, E. J. (1982b). Insula of the old world monkey: 3. Efferent cortical output and comments on function. *Journal of Comparative Neurology, 212,* 38–52.

Mischel, W., Ebbesen, E., & Zeiss, A. M. (1976). Determinants of selective memory about the self. *Journal of Consulting and Clinical Psychology, 44*, 92–103.

Mogg, K., Mathews, A., & Weinman, J. (1989). Selective processing of threat cues in anxiety states: A replication. *Behavior Research and Therapy, 27*, 317–323.

Moran, M. A., Mufson, E. J., & Mesulam, M. M. (1987). Neural inputs into the temporopolar cortex of the rhesus monkey. *Journal of Comparative Neurology, 256*, 88–103.

Mowrer, O. H. (1960). *Learning theory and behavior*. New York: Wiley.

Nakano, Y., Oomura, Y., Nishino, H., Aou, S., Yamamoto, T., & Nemoto, S. (1984). Neuronal activity in the medial orbitofrontal cortex of the behaving monkey: Modulation by glucose and satiety. *Brain Research Bulletin, 12*, 381–385.

Nauta, W. J. H. (1971). The problem of the frontal lobe: A reinterpretation. *Journal of Psychiatric Research, 8*, 167–187.

Ono, T., Tamura, R., Nishijo, H., Nakamura, K., & Tabuchi, E. (1989). Contribution of amygdalar and lateral hypothalamic neurons to visual information processing of food and nonfood in monkey. *Physiology and Behavior, 45*, 411–421.

Osgood, C. E., Suci, G. J., & Tannenbaum, P. H. (1957). *The measurement of meaning*. Urbana: University of Illinois Press.

Pandya, D. N., & Seltzer, B. (1982). Associations areas of the cerebral cortex. *Trends in Neurosciences, 5*, 386–390.

Pandya, D. N., Seltzer, B., & Barbas, H. (1988). Input-output organization of the primate cerebral cortex. In *Comparative primate biology: Vol. 4. Neurosciences* (pp. 39–80). New York: Liss.

Pandya, D. N., & Yeterian, E. H. (1984). Proposed neural circuitry for spatial memory in the primate brain. *Neuropsychologia, 22*, 109–122.

Pandya, D. N., & Yeterian, E. H. (1985). Architecture and connections of cortical association areas. In A. Peters & E. G. Jones (Eds.), *Cerebral cortex: Vol. 4. Association and auditory cortices* (pp. 3–61). New York: Plenum.

Penfield, W., & Faulk, M. E. (1955). The insula: Further observations on its function. *Brain, 78*, 445–470.

Petrie, A. (1952). *Personality and the frontal lobes*. New York: Blakiston.

Ploog, D. (1981). Neurobiology of primate audio-vocal behavior. *Brain Research Reviews, 3*, 35–61.

Plutchik, R. (1980). *Emotion: A psychoevolutionary synthesis*. New York: Harper and Row.

Postman, L., & Brown, D. R. (1952). The perceptual consequences of success and failure. *Journal of Abnormal and Social Psychology, 47*, 213–227.

Powell, G. E. (1981). A survey of the effects of brain lesions upon personality. In H. J. Eysenck (Ed.), *A model for personality* (pp. 65–87). New York: Springer-Verlag.

Pribram, K. H. (1981). Emotions. In S. K. Filskov & T. J. Boll (Eds.), *Handbook of clinical neuropsychology* (pp. 102–134). New York: Wiley-Interscience.

Pribram, K. H., & McGuinness, D. (1975). Arousal, activation and effort in the control of attention. *Psychological Review, 82*, 116–149.

Ragsdale, C. W., & Graybiel, A. M. (1988). Fibers from the basolateral nucleus of the amygdala selectively innervate striosomes in the caudate nucleus of the cat. *Journal of Comparative Neurology, 269*, 506–522.

Reeves, F. B., & Bergum, B. O. (1972). Perceptual narrowing as a function of peripheral cue relevance. *Perceptual and Motor Skills, 35*, 719–724.

Reiman, E. M., Fusselman, M. J., Fox, P. T., & Raichle, M. E. (1989). Neuroanatomical correlates of anticipatory anxiety. *Science, 243*, 1071–1074.

Richardson, R. T., & DeLong, M. R. (1988). A reappraisal of the functions of the nucleus basalis of Meynert. *Trends in Neurosciences, 11*, 264–267.

Rinn, W. E. (1984). The neuropsychology of facial expression: A review of the neurological and psychological mechanisms for producing facial expressions. *Psychological Bulletin, 95*, 52–77.

Rolls, E. T. (1987). Information representation, processing, and storage in the brain: Analysis at the single neuron level. In J. P. Changeaux & M. Konishi (Eds.), *The neural and molecular bases of learning* (pp. 503–540). New York: Wiley.

Rumelhart, D. E., & McClelland, J. L. (1986). *Parallel distributed processing: Explorations in the microstructure of cognition* (Vol. 1). Cambridge: MIT Press.

Rumelhart, D. E., Smolensky, P., McClelland, J. L., & Hinton, G. E. (1986). Schemata and sequential thought processes in PDP models. In J. L. McClelland & D. E. Rumelhart (Eds.), *Parallel distributed processing: Explorations in the microstructure of cognition: Vol. 2. Psychological and biological models* (pp. 7–57). Cambridge: MIT Press.

Safer, M. A. (1981). Sex and hemisphere differences in access to codes for processing emotional expressions and faces. *Journal of Experimental Psychology: General, 110*, 86–100.

Sanides, F. (1970). Functional architecture of motor and sensory cortices in primates in the light of a new concept of neocortex evolution. In C. R. Noback & W. Montagna (Eds.), *The primate brain: Advances in primatology* (Vol. 1, pp. 137–201). New York: Appleton-Century-Crofts.

Saper, C. B. (1987). Diffuse cortical projection systems: Anatomical organization and role in cortical function. In F. Plum (Ed.), *Handbook of physiology: Sec. 1. The nervous system: Vol. 5. Higher functions of the brain, Part 1* (pp. 169–210). Bethesda, MD: American Physiological Society.

Sarter, M., & Markowitsch, H. J. (1984). Collateral innervation of the medial and lateral prefrontal cortex by amygdaloid, thalamic, and brain-stem neurons. *Journal of Comparative Neurology, 224*, 445–460.

Schachter, S., & Singer, J. E. (1962). Cognitive, social, and physiological determinants of emotional states. *Psychological Review, 69*, 379–399.

Schultz, W., & Romo, R. (1990). Dopamine neurons of the monkey midbrain: Contingencies of responses to stimuli eliciting immediate behavioral reactions. *Journal of Neurophysiology, 63*, 607–624.

Serafetinides, E. A. (1973). Voltage laterality in the EEG of psychiatric patients. *Diseases of the Nervous System, 34*, 190–191.

Shaw, E. D., Mann, J. J., Stokes, P. E., & Manevitz, Z. (1986). Effects of lithium carbonate on associative productivity and idiosyncrasy in bipolar outpatients. *American Journal of Psychiatry, 143,* 1166–1169.

Sillito, A. M., & Murphy, P. C. (1987). The cholinergic modulation of cortical function. In E. G. Jones & A. Peters (Eds.), *Cerebral cortex: Vol. 6. Further aspect of cortical function, including hippocampus* (pp. 161–185). New York: Plenum.

Squire, L. R. (1986). Mechanisms of memory. *Science, 232,* 1612–1619.

Supple, W. F., & Kapp, B. S. (1989). Response characteristics of neurons in the medial component of the medial geniculate nucleus during Pavlovian differential fear conditioning in rabbits. *Behavioral Neuroscience, 103,* 1276–1286.

Tellegen, A. (1985). Structures of mood and personality and their relevance to assessing anxiety, with an emphasis on self-report. In A. H. Tuma & J. D. Maser (Eds.), *Anxiety and the anxiety disorders.* Hillsdale, NJ: Erlbaum.

Thayer, R. E. (1989). *The biopsychology of mood and arousal.* New York: Oxford University Press.

Thorpe, S. J., Rolls, E. T., & Maddison, S. (1983). The orbitofrontal cortex: Neuronal activity in the behaving monkey. *Experimental Brain Research, 49,* 93–115.

Tinbergen, N. (1951). *The study of instinct.* Oxford: Oxford University Press.

Toates, F. M. (1983). Exploration as a motivational and learning system: A cognitive incentive view. In J. Archer & L. I. A. Birke (Eds.), *Exploration in animals and humans* (pp. 55–71). Workingham, Eng.: Van Nostrand Reinhold.

Trulson, M. E., & Preussler, D. W. (1984). Dopamine-containing ventral tegmental area neurons in freely moving cats: Activity during the sleep-waking cycle and effects of stress. *Experimental Neurology, 83,* 367–377.

Tucker, D. M. (1986). Neural control of emotional communication. In P. Blanck, R. Buck, & R. Rosenthal (Eds.), *Nonverbal communication in the clinical context.* University Park: Pennsylvania State University Press.

Tucker, D. M., & Derryberry, D. (in press). Motivated attention: Anxiety and the frontal executive mechanisms. *Journal of Nervous and Mental Disease.*

Tucker, D. M., & Frederick, S. L. (1989). Emotion and brain lateralization. In H. Wagner & T. Manstead (Eds.), *Handbook of psychophysiology: Emotion and social behaviour.* New York: Wiley.

Tucker, D. M., Vannatta, K., & Rothlind, J. (in press). Activation and arousal systems and the adaptive control of cognitive priming. In N. Stein, M. Bennett, & R. Leventhal (Eds.), *Psychological and biological processes in the development of emotion.* Chicago: University of Chicago Press.

Tucker, D. M., & Williamson, P. A. (1984). Asymmetric neural control systems in human self-regulation. *Psychological Review, 91,* 185–215.

Tyler, S. K., & Tucker, D. M. (1982). Anxiety and perceptual structure: Individual differences in neuropsychological function. *Journal of Abnormal Psychology, 91,* 210–220.

Ungerleider, L. G., & Mishkin, M. (1982). Two cortical visual systems. In D. J. Ingle, R. J. W. Mansfield, & M. A. Goodale (Eds.), *The analysis of visual behavior* (pp. 549–586). Cambridge: MIT Press.

Van der Kooy, D., Koda, L. Y., McGinty, J., Gerfen, C. R., & Bloom, F. E. (1984). The organization of projections from the cortex, amygdala, and hypothalamus to the nucleus of the solitary tract in rat. *Journal of Comparative Neurology, 224,* 1–24.

Waterhouse, B. D., Moises, H. C., & Woodward, D. J. (1986). Interaction of serotonin with somatosensory cortical neuronal responses to afferent synaptic inputs and putative neurotransmitters. *Brain Research Bulletin, 17,* 507–518.

Watson, D., & Tellegen, A. (1985). Toward a consensual structure of mood. *Psychological Bulletin, 98,* 219–235.

Watts, F. N., McKenna, F. T., Sharrock, R., & Trezise, L. (1986). Colour-naming of phobic-related words. *British Journal of Psychology, 77,* 97–108.

Weltman, G., Smith, J. E., & Egstrom, G. H. (1971). Perceptual narrowing during simulated pressure-chamber exposure. *Human Factors, 13,* 99–107.

Werner, H. (1957). *The comparative psychology of mental development.* New York: Harper.

Werner, H., & Kaplan, B. (1963). *Symbol formation: An organismic-developmental approach to language and the expression of thought.* New York: Wiley.

Wilson, F. A. W., & Rolls, E. T. (1990). Neuronal responses related to reinforcement in the primate basal forebrain. *Brain Research, 509,* 213–231.

Wise, R. A. (1987). Sensorimotor modulation and the variable action pattern (VAP): Toward a noncircular definition of drive and motivation. *Psychobiology, 15,* 7–20.

Witter, M. P., Groenewegen, H. J., Lopes da Silva, F. H., & Lohman, A. H. M. (1989). Functional organization of the extrinsic and intrinsic circuitry of the parahippocampal region. *Progress in Neurobiology, 33,* 161–253.

Yamamoto, T., Oomura, Y., Nishino, H., Aou, S., Nakano, Y., & Nemoto, S. (1984). Monkey orbitofrontal neuron activity during emotional and feeding behaviors. *Brain Research Bulletin, 12,* 441–443.

Zajonc, R. B. (1980). Feeling and thinking: Preferences need no inferences. *American Psychologist, 35,* 151–175.

Subject Index

348

Author Index